Sovereign Anxiety

This book studies issues of public order in late colonial and early postcolonial India. It identifies various governmental practices, such as curfews, bans and police action, that thrive on extraordinary legislation to maintain public order. The colonial regime often deployed extraordinary legislation to curtail the liberties of individuals and groups by citing potential harm to public order. Through public order, a spectacle of sovereign power and politics of contestation between the citizens and law enforcement emerges.

The book will contribute to existing discussions about sovereignty and legitimacy of state power by providing a representative sample of concrete instances such as inter- and intra-community riots, labour riots, labour strikes and nationalist agitation. It will also enable a comparative approach and illustrate processes leading to the evolution of state formation and citizenship in South Asia.

Javed Iqbal Wani is Assistant Professor at the School of Law, Governance and Citizenship, Dr B. R. Ambedkar University, Delhi. He completed his doctoral degree from the Department of History, Royal Holloway, University of London, UK. His research interests are interdisciplinary and pertain to questions of sovereignty and law, particularly law enforcement, law enactment, public order, political violence, crime prevention, extraordinary legislation, and so on.

Sovereign Anxiety

Public Order and the Politics of Control in India,
1915–1955

Javed Iqbal Wani

CAMBRIDGE
UNIVERSITY PRESS

Shaftesbury Road, Cambridge CB2 8EA, United Kingdom

One Liberty Plaza, 20th Floor, New York, NY 10006, USA

477 Williamstown Road, Port Melbourne, VIC 3207, Australia

314–321, 3rd Floor, Plot 3, Splendor Forum, Jasola District Centre, New Delhi – 110025, India

103 Penang Road, #05–06/07, Visioncrest Commercial, Singapore 238467

Cambridge University Press is part of Cambridge University Press & Assessment, a department of the University of Cambridge.

We share the University's mission to contribute to society through the pursuit of education, learning and research at the highest international levels of excellence.

www.cambridge.org
Information on this title: www.cambridge.org/9781009337939

First published 2023

Printed in India by Avantika Printers Pvt. Ltd.

A catalogue record for this publication is available from the British Library

ISBN 978-1-009-33793-9 Hardback

To Sana Khan

Contents

Acknowledgements

This study emerged out of my fascination with the way states across the globe deploy violence against their citizens and the impunity they enjoy. In India, a violent paradigm of state-led thinking has taken root in the common psyche of the nation. Popular mobilisations often argue that the administrative and legal ideology is still colonial in nature. While activists and academics made such statements, few gave satisfactory answers as to why it was so. My student days at Jawaharlal Nehru University (JNU), New Delhi, offered me the initial chance to go to the villages of Singur and Nandigram in West Bengal, where the left-front government had unleashed violence over the peasantry and was forcing them to agree to part with their lands for a Tata Nano car plant to be constructed there. When the peasants demanded fair compensation or, in many cases, refused the offer, they were brutally attacked by the police. No one was spared. This incident initiated me into a study of state sovereignty and pressed me to map its contours. Soon, I was to write my MPhil dissertation, where Rajarshi Dasgupta, my supervisor, further indulged me in the question of political violence.

The seeds of this book were sown in Rajarshi Dasgupta's class on biopolitics at the Centre for Political Studies at JNU. He introduced me to new theoretical frameworks that pushed the limits of my conventional thinking. After completing my MPhil, I was motivated to dive further into the study of the violence of the state. My personal location as a Kashmiri living in New Delhi questioned the violent frameworks that the Indian state was deploying against its own citizens. It was not that the Indian state was violent only towards the people of the regions of Kashmir and the North East; it was equally violent towards Dalits, students and peasants in the rest of the country. Statements about the colonisation of Kashmir and the North East further confused me. There was no way that I was going to leave it there.

After completing my MPhil, I was ready to go for a PhD. While writing a proposal, I could not ignore the question again and ended up proposing a study of public-order laws in India. The Department of History, Royal Holloway, University of London, recognised my motivation and not only offered me a place but also sponsored my research. To top it all, Markus Daechsel, an equally enthusiastic and humane academic, expressed a willingness to supervise the project. Long discussions with Markus made me realise that I had chosen a meaningful topic, and it might offer some answers to my academic and political curiosity.

This book is developed from my PhD dissertation. Markus Daechsel, Taylor Sherman, Amir Ali, Dilip Menon and Julien Levesque provided immensely helpful comments on various draft chapters. Valerian Rodrigues, Tanweer Fazal and Lawrence Liang offered great insights into approaching the subject. Special thanks to the staff at the British Library London, National Archives Delhi and Uttar Pradesh State Archives, Lucknow, where most of the archival work was carried out. The staff at these institutions was very helpful. Special thanks to the Centre for the Studies of Plural Societies (CSPS), New Delhi, for offering me space to sit and make corrections to the draft chapters.

I am grateful to my parents, Kalsoom Akhter and Abdul Rashid Wani, for understanding the significance of my endeavour and relieving me of my essential family duties. My brother Amir Rashid Wani provided great support in times of my father's sickness, allowing me the freedom to continue my research.

The completion of this book would not have been possible without the companionship of Sana Khan. She patiently listened to my ideas, carefully read many drafts and provided critical inputs while being most encouraging.

Sohini Ghosh and Anwesha Rana from Cambridge University Press handled the editorial process quite smoothly. Their professionalism, editorial patience and support greatly motivated me to complete the project within the stipulated time.

Last but not least, the errors and omissions in the book are entirely mine.

Introduction

Independence from British rule ushered in an era of unprecedented opportunity to construct a new polity in India according to the principles of democratic citizenship and nationalism. However, not all civil servants of the new state were equally enthusiastic about the new political climate. Many of them maintained an underlying distrust of ordinary Indian citizens that would have been more appropriate for colonial times. Ram Kinker Singh, the district magistrate of Etah in the United Provinces (UP), for instance, lamented in official communication in 1949 that since independence, 'the Police does not inspire fear' among the masses.[1] He further deplored that 'ignorant and illiterate people have got erroneous and perverted conceptions of freedom' and believed that they now had 'no respect for authority'.[2] Many police officers in the new nation also did not have a favourable opinion about the general public order and the citizen population in particular. The superintendent of police (SP) of Bahraich, for example, concluded that 'with the advent of freedom the public at large had developed peculiar psychology of confusing liberty with license'.[3] He felt that this resulted from a fundamental distrust between the police and the public that had remained unchanged since the British departed. For this reason, the public did not cooperate with the security forces when dealing with criminals.

These comments came in the wake of a complex discussion between various departments of the bureaucracy responsible for maintaining public order and peace in what was soon to become the state of Uttar Pradesh. These high-ranking bureaucrats sounded uncannily like their erstwhile colleagues of the British Raj, who had stressed many times before that Indians could only be given *good* government because they were unsuited to enjoying *free* government.[4] For the colonisers, Indians could not be trusted with their freedom. Engaging with historical contingencies of the politics of public order in India, the main question that this book investigates is: what are the practices of sovereignty that sustained colonial governmental attitudes in a postcolonial India? To this end, it surveys colonial legality and its evolution. It will reveal the nature of legality, both colonial and postcolonial, and how exceptions or extraordinary measures became an integral part of it.

When it came to policing its subjects and maintaining law and order, gathering evidence was often seen as a cumbersome process by the colonial government that led nowhere. Given the essential gulf between the colonisers and the colonised, between the administration and the public, on which the ideology of colonialism ultimately depended, it was normal to distrust a non-cooperative (and alienated) public. Consequently, the British believed that the criminal justice system and the maintenance of law and order would be impossible without specific extraordinary legislative measures that circumvented and perverted the much-invoked colonial ideal of bringing the 'rule of law' to a subcontinent allegedly plagued by 'oriental despotism'.[5] Such 'extra-legal' legislation remained in place throughout the career of the colonial state. When Ram Kinker Singh and the SP of Bahraich voiced their opinions, they argued in favour of maintaining precisely such an apparatus of extraordinary legislation that would short-circuit the due process of law and justice, even after independence when colonial divisions did not apply.

The career of extraordinary measures has only intensified in contemporary India. Undoubtedly, the nature of the colonial and the postcolonial states differ, but their dependence on extraordinary legislation appear to have a common thread, and that seems to be the necessities of governance closely tied to practices of sovereignty. For example, the highly controversial Armed Forces Special Powers Act (AFSPA) is a remnant of colonial violence and authoritarianism that has revitalised itself in service of repression in the postcolonial context.[6] The incidents of state authoritarianism in the Singur and Nandigram areas in West Bengal (2007) while acquiring land to construct a Tata car plant testify to such continuities. Here, the state unleashed violence through police action in the name of 'public good'. In other instances, the frequent detention of human rights activists such as Binayak Sen and others under the Unlawful Activities Prevention Act, 2004 (UAPA), and the frequent invocation of the Jammu and Kashmir Public Security Act, 1978 (PSA), against protesting youth and political leaders in the state of Jammu and Kashmir in the name of fighting insurgency and protecting state sovereignty are noteworthy. The UAPA was legislated in 1967, not long after independence, to 'reasonably' restrict fundamental freedoms under Article 19(1) of the Indian constitution. The stated purpose of the restrictions was to 'safeguard India's integrity and sovereignty'. Since then, the career of extraordinary legislation in India has been sustained by laws such as the Terrorist and Disruptive Activities (Prevention) Act, 1987, known as TADA, and the Prevention of Terrorism Act, 2002, known as POTA. These two laws were repealed in the face of legal challenges that arose due to the inconsistencies in their operation.[7] As a result, the now dreaded UAPA was drafted. More recently, one cannot ignore the frequent slapping of sedition charges under section 124A of the Indian Penal Code (IPC)[8] and the unleashing of draconian laws such as a re-energised UAPA 2019 against various activists in the context of the caste conflict at Bhima Koregaon[9] and others involved in mobilising opinion against the recent Citizen (Amendment) Act (CAA)–National Register of Citizens (NRC) (2020).[10] To intimidate democratic non-violent protests and their organisers, the 'recovery' by attaching properties of the accused in public order cases by the current Uttar Pradesh government is a new episode in the career of extraordinary laws in postcolonial India where a colonial policy has been revived.

With reference to a wide range of contemporary political issues in India related to various laws that have their origins in colonialism, this book examines the question of whether the promulgation of certain laws and legislative techniques and institutions inherited from the colonial past continued into the postcolonial period and, if yes, then in what form. This book offers insight into various instances where the state invoked extraordinary legislation in colonial and early postcolonial India. It argues that the career of the British colonial state in India highlights that right from the beginning of the colonial administration in India, the functioning of law was not about justice but rather risk management. Here 'risk' refers to the potential threats, both overt and covert, that the colonial order could face to its authority. In addition to mapping the invocation and effects of overarching exceptional laws such as the Defence of India Rules or the Rowlatt Bills, the novelty of the book is its engagement with instances that involve laws such as section 144 of the Code of Criminal Procedure in India (CrPC), laws instituting curfews or the ones allowing police firing to control crowds. These laws might appear ordinary and essential in maintaining public peace and tranquillity but exhibit exceptional tendencies. While grand laws such as the Defence of India Act applied to every corner of British India and were top-down in nature, the invocation of ordinary criminal law provisions such as section 144 CrPC and curfews, and the decision to open fire on protestors, were local. Their invocation was always to maintain what the administration referred to as 'public order and tranquillity'.

Public order policing refers to the policing of protestors, campaigners and other large gatherings that exhibit a potential to incite disturbance or violence in society. Guarding public order involves a combination of physically violent and non-violent (political) tactics and strategies based on the social environment within which such challenges arise. The political tactics of the state – although they might not always resort to physical violence – could have a violent presence nevertheless. A unique aspect of public order policing is that it is highly visible and often risks violent confrontation with large gatherings. Police tend to justify violent action on unmanageable groups or crowds citing non-cooperation of people in some cases and the unavailability of sufficient resources to control the public in others. Such action is also not free from the constant dilemmas of the police as to what response would be more appropriate to particular events or situations. However, evidence across chapters in this book shows that the decision is based on the executive authority of a district magistrate or a designated senior police officer and granted by law. The significant role of such vital administrative figures responsible for making decisions in situations of public disorder is noteworthy. Across chapters, the book will emphasise their role and impact on the maintenance of public order. As the chapters will reveal, the position of administrative figures requires further investigation to understand the challenges and limitations faced by efforts towards realising democratic citizenship in postcolonial India. The object of such 'risk management' through extraordinary laws is the 'public'.

Sovereignty and the Law: Some Theoretical Preliminaries

There has been a great deal of interest in the question of states of exception, especially in the wake of various emergency laws that came into being after the events of 11 September 2001. Most countries have passed such laws and are frequently adjudged draconian by commentators.[11] At the same time, states argue for the necessity of such laws to protect sovereignty and citizens. Others see it as a licence to violate citizens' legitimate rights, denying them fair trials and depriving them of justice. However, in a colonial context, the juridico-political paradox remained that trials were not necessarily fair even though they were conducted as per the established rules. When the aim of the law was power and not justice, the provision of a trial did not make the law fair. Debates about states of exception have intensified since the Italian philosopher Giorgio Agamben published his work on 'homo sacer'.[12] Agamben rejuvenated Carl Schmitt's ideas on the question of sovereignty and argued that the problem of exceptional law lay at the heart of the question of sovereignty and its preservation. Agamben's work came in the wake of some highly potent provocations thrown at philosophers and theorists of state and its citizenship by Michel Foucault in the 1970s and 1980s.[13] Foucault's ideas reached debates in India soon after.[14] His ideas enabled scholars to understand the discourses and the practices of governmentality. Foucault argued that citizens participated in such governmental practices and disciplinary regimes[15] without realising their effect on their political life.[16] Besides, Foucault's work consistently highlighted the presence of the 'other' in the state's effort to manage life – behind normality always lurked the figure of the abnormal. The abnormal, as Foucault highlighted in his various works, is what made the normal possible. For the late colonial and the early postcolonial state in India, specific individuals, groups and populations that constituted a 'problem category' provided these constitutive figures of the abnormal.

The 'normal' rule of law is constituted in reference to something outside itself – a state of exception when normality does not apply. Various texts on sovereignty argue that it is the sovereign's sole right to declare the state of exception. By definition, any legal framework that depends on such a declaration for its existence is extraordinary in nature. Carl Schmitt has highlighted that the issue with liberal constitutionalism is that it contends that all legitimate acts of a state are supposedly based on general legal norms – the rule of law – and aim to meet the general and predictable demands of the law as opposed to the arbitrary authority of persons.[17] Contesting such a framework, Schmitt argued that such general legal norms often lack the force to offer determinate guidance if not subject to circumstantial interpretation and interstitial legislation.[18] Hence the unavoidable need for an authority to make a firm decision and effective interpretation of the law. For Schmitt, the law does not interpret and determine itself; it is processed through a sovereign authority that applies general rules to particular instances.[19] Arguing in a Hobbesian vein, Schmitt contends that authority and not truth makes the law.[20] A sovereign decision will override legal norms, or, in other words, the sovereign will decide what interpretation of the law would apply to whom and in what circumstance(s). Furthermore, since it is impossible to ascertain the very nature of an emergency legally, the law can at best determine who can decide when such a situation has arisen. Therefore, the power to act or make a decision during an 'emergency' also rests on the power to determine what constitutes a state of exception.

Once the question of the authority to decide on the 'state of exception' is resolved, the second issue that arises regards the nature of the political. Here, Schmitt argued that the specific nature of the political rests on the distinction between friend and foe.[21] The friend and foe distinction works at two levels: first, as hostility between two groups willing to kill (or harm) each other as a group, and, in the second instance, when a group sides with the sovereign authority in its declaration of an opposing group as an enemy. Therefore, sovereignty itself rests on playing the political difference between friend and enemy. In a way, this boils down to a simplistic logic of collectivist self-defence. The significant point here is the importance of a sovereign power to decide, interpret general law in particular situations, split communities into friends and foes and, finally, justify the elimination of the enemy based on the sequence of such a configuration or arrangement of sovereign power. To a great extent, the colonial state and the idea of the sovereign in Schmitt's conception are comparable.

A state of emergency can be described as the state machinery separating the population into friends and enemies and then waging a ruthless war in various ways against the latter. Sovereign power depends on the ability to isolate specific social constituencies as social problem categories. The question arises as to how to understand the elimination, control/subjugation, or exclusion of these 'problem categories' or foes. Agamben offered a more contemporary reading and further understanding of the state of exception and also provided the classificatory category of the 'homo sacer' – 'one who can be killed but not sacrificed'.[22] The Schmittian friend and foe distinction in the context of the sovereign practice of exception is essential for our discussion of colonial and postcolonial legality because the state tied emergency legislation to administrative decisions about who or what constituted a problem category and fell outside the law for the colonial state, or to whom the law applied in exceptional ways, often calling for the exercise of state violence. Contra Foucault, who argued that the historical emergence of bio-power marked the threshold of modernity, Agamben brings the nexus between sovereignty and bio-political life to the fore.[23] Inspired by such inputs from political theory and philosophy, this book examines public order through the law and the invocation of emergency in late colonial and early postcolonial India. Theoretical inputs in this book do not intend to hijack the potency of historical narrative but enhance its meaning by enabling a conversation between theory and history.

The foundational role of a state of exception usually operates at a theoretical level, silently in the background, so to speak, while the workings of the law as empirically observed belong to the internal universe of standard legality. Exceptional laws are not meant to be utilised in day-to-day governance or be invoked on a day-to-day basis. For this reason, the declaration of an emergency still comes as a shock and is linked to moments of historical importance. In India, for instance, the suspension of the Indian constitution and the declaration of emergency by the Indira Gandhi government in the 1970s is one primary and often referred to example in recent history.[24] The Indian constitution was suspended according to Article 356 of the constitution and approved by the Parliament and courts. Here, the key to suspending the postcolonial constitution was included and available in the constitution itself.

Anti-colonial mass mobilisations consistently challenged colonial claims to sovereignty and directly questioned the British right to rule India. Such contestations exposed the vulnerability of colonial sovereignty and the hesitant foundations of the conflicting politics in which it operated. In these moments, the colonial administration would adopt a manoeuvre that sought to hide issues of sovereignty behind notions of legality as far as it could reduce anti-colonial politics to ordinary legal battles, which would enable it again to decide on the nature of right and wrong and, therefore, to win small sovereign victories. Chapters across the book will show that a politicisation of legality was countered by the legalisation of politics, where the language of the law was deployed to obfuscate colonial repression.

These manoeuvres relied on the fact that legal exceptionalism operated in two modalities. At one level, it affected the everyday politics that unfolded in streets and factories and relied on 'ordinary laws' of emergency such as section 144 CrPC, enabling preventive detentions and curfews. Then, there were significant moments like the First and the Second World Wars where special measures such as the Defence of India Rules and martial law would take over. What this book makes clear at the beginning itself is that between the two World Wars, we notice the emergence of another trend, the gradual conflation of these two modalities, or, in other words, the normalisation of exception. Laws to deal with anarchical and revolutionary crime or the Rowlatt Acts, 1919, are precisely the kind of laws that highlighted the capacity of the sovereign decision and its legal machine to create and interpret laws armed with exceptional powers and insert them into the practices of maintaining everyday law and order. In a colonial situation, the state of exception is no longer simply a matter of the sovereign asserting the powers of life and death. It becomes an altogether new dynamic of governance where human activities and relations are declared criminal to the extent that diverse violent state actions, physical and discursive, become just normal or ordinary.

There is a critical subsidiary theme at play that repeatedly features in this book. Colonial legality was deeply embedded in practices of bureaucracy. The relation between bureaucracy and law is where the latter replenishes the former by consolidating a strict procedure. Such a procedure maintains the order of life because it consistently maintains the order of files. The sheer volume of the records of the Raj available for study today is proof of this. As numerous scholars have discussed, files generate data and, therefore, evidence of social, political, economic and overall administrative transactions.[25] Bureaucratic procedures were based on the argument that their operations were a necessity for the functioning of a rational and just society. On the other hand, such procedures also tightened the state's grip on its subjects gradually and persistently. In the colonial archive, two kinds of public order existed in the functioning of the colonial state in India. The one on paper and in files, and the other that existed on the ground. The two were not necessarily the same. Because of this gap between paper and ground reality, the colonial state needed public order laws such as section 144 CrPC.

The connection between colonial public order and its dependency on emergency measures is a crucial focus of this book. The flirtation with 'emergency' was connected to the rationale of pre-emption – legal action even before a defined crime had been committed. The pre-emptive nature of public order laws highlights their authoritarian character and flexibility to manipulate political situations on the ground into governable outputs. Section 144 CrPC serves as a significant example in this regard. It dealt with the prohibition of a person(s) from certain activities and the use of public space for designated persons and groups. This law was often supplemented by curfews, where public life was suspended in the name of maintaining public order and tranquillity. While the laws mentioned here were promulgated to avoid, most commonly, collective violence or a riot, related administrative tactics such as preventive detention aimed to arrest a person even before the concerned person had committed the alleged offence. An invocation of urgency permitted or enabled the short-circuiting of due process. There were certain persons or groups to whom the normal rule of law did not apply and who could be subjected to severe restrictions without them having to commit any observable offence at all, let alone such an offence having to be proven. The discussion about the 'Criminal Tribes' in the following section will make this point clear.

When the colonial state invoked emergency laws, it aimed to preserve a political order and prevent physical violence since it was the state that had the monopoly over physical violence according to law. But the legal justification was far from straightforward, especially when we move from colonial to postcolonial times. Public order laws could be legitimate only if state sovereignty and popular sovereignty were ultimately imagined as the same and if the interests and ends of the state were projected to be the interests and ends of the subjects or people or citizens. (One could add that even if homogeneity could be achieved, it would not lead to the image of a democratic state in action: the total homogenisation of the public would have assumed its complete docility and subordination under a totalitarian state.) However, such a coming together was always illusory. The very operation of extraordinary law had material implications for the lives of the people too. It led to a compartmentalisation of various publics (based on caste, class, language, ethnicity, religion or region) who were often at loggerheads with each other. The control of the colonial state was not totalising in nature.

Influenced by Edward Said's *Orientalism*, scholars such as Ronald Inden, Homi Bhabha, Bernard Cohn and Nicholas Dirks have shown that the British colonial state actively utilised cultural technologies and classificatory techniques to establish its authority and multifarious efforts to sustain it.[26] Critics of this position, such as David Washbrook and Nicholas Thomas, highlighted the limitation of a purely Saidian framework and its textualist agenda.[27] They argued that it is crucial to recover and emphasise the traces of indigenous people and cultures and their impact on the constitution of colonial knowledge. In short, they argued for recognising the agency of the indigenous in the making of the colonial. Christopher Bayly's historical sociology took this discussion further with an aim to deconstruct the notion of orientalism.

For Bayly, the indigenous was an essential and active part of making colonial knowledge and information processes and not merely an object of European misrepresentation. Bayly argued that British rule in India could not have been established and sustained 'without a degree of understanding of the conquered societies' and was derived considerably 'from indigenous knowledge, albeit torn out of context and distorted by fear and prejudice'.[28] Analysis, for Bayly, 'must reflect the pervasiveness of Indian agency, of the Indian intellectual challenge, and of Indian cultural vitality'.[29] He emphasised the significance of affect in politics while discussing colonial fear and vulnerability. In this light, the necessary heterogeneous nature of the public continued the confrontation between the state and its people even after independence. As the discussion in the opening paragraph points out, the matter of law would remain a question of power rather than justice. Therefore, the law always retained an underbelly, an illegality in its foundation, and it is the provision of emergency in the name of maintaining public order that allowed it to cut loose from the democratic procedure and its obligation to the people. It allowed the state to transform into a sovereign body with limited obligations towards its people, acting primarily out of considerations of self-preservation.

The legal strategies of the colonial government in India were complex and varied and became tied to the co-constitution of a particular kind of knowledge – one based on classification, differentiation, enumeration and creation of hierarchies of culture, power, customs and normative orders. Such an attempt to control by the colonial regime fossilised a normative legal order and dramatically altered the nature of law and justice in the colony and the postcolony.[30] The introduction of this tendency to law and the state did not end with the moment of decolonisation; instead, it continued beyond the 'Age of Empire'. Colonialism and postcoloniality should not be considered specific, disparate historical events but as conceptual categories interwoven historically and interconnected in their logics.[31]

Genealogies of Legal Exceptionalism

The nature of exception evolved during the interwar periods, but its foundational philosophy remained intact. One cannot grasp the evolution without contextualising the formation of colonial legality in India and its interface with the indigenous. Robert Travers has recently examined British conquests in late-eighteenth-century India, where he argues that the empire was reconstructed through contesting ideas such as the 'anomaly' of a trading company acting as an Indian ruler.[32] The basis of such an authority borrowed from the ancient order was perceived as a remnant of the Mughal empire. Traver suggests that the debates about the nature and purpose of empire in India and elsewhere ended in importing and tweaking British political concepts in the aspiration to produce an 'indigenous constitution'. However, such imperial efforts to create new state forms in India were connected to an ideology that wanted to rescue it from 'oriental despotism'. Jon Wilson has also offered an insightful interpretation of the transformation of political thought and practice in colonial India.[33] Tracing the origins of 'modern' ideas such as the state and civil society, Wilson points out that the interaction between the British colonial administration and their colonised Indian subjects was practical. It meant that they were more interested in gaining power and establishing authority than anything else.

In contrast to Travers and Wilson, Mithi Mukherjee, in her work on the British colonial empire in India, has sought to establish 'the discursive history of categories in their alignment with institutions'.[34] Mukherjee constructs an imperial ideological outline where reference to the oppressive and exploitative rationale of resource extraction from the colonies gets relegated to a secondary position under the rubric of 'the colonial'. She asserts that sustained rhetoric of 'good governance' in the Indian subcontinent is stressed in the public domain of parliamentary debates, along with the high ideals of a political imperative, which she designates as 'the imperial'. Mukherjee argues that exploring the possibilities of a supranational imperial vision of justice that confronted the 'colonial' abuse and pilfering of misappropriated indigenous authority within an imperial judicial frame was inclusive of the interests and rights of Indians.

Law began to occupy an essential part in the ideology of British colonialism in India in the final decades of the eighteenth century. Officials of the East India Company deputed themselves to absolving Indians from the 'despotism' of their rulers.[35] For example, Lord Bentick and his moral crusade in India are noteworthy in this regard. He initiated 'modernising projects' which aimed at the westernisation of Indian administration and were influenced by the utilitarian ideas of Jeremy Bentham and James Mill. He started reforming the courts in India and made English rather than Persian the language of the higher courts. Furthermore, he argued for a western-style education for Indians so that they could be incorporated into British bureaucracy. These officials also emphasised the absence of any proper sense of right to property in Indian laws or any universal principles of justice. The Pitt's India Act, 1784, marked the moment of transformation of the Company from a trading company to a governing body. The establishment of institutions and administrative structures was now required to enable and sustain the new order of governance. Security of property, the rule of law and the idea of moral improvement became the broader guiding principles to justify colonial rule in India. Simultaneously, to prevent any abuse of power, a case for embodying universal principles of justice was argued. For this purpose, the first Law Commission for India was established in 1835, an issue I shall return to in the later sections.

From the very beginning of the process of formulating an Indian Penal Code (IPC), British colonial ideology often referred to utilitarian philosophy guided by a liberal constitutionalist framework of some sort.[36] This discourse has been well covered in the existing literature, for instance, in the work of Eric Stokes,[37] Uday Singh Mehta[38] and Karuna Mantena,[39] amongst others. Michael Mann has pointed out an important element of the effect this legal code would have on its subjects.[40] It was based on a scientific approach guided by reason and rationality. Mann argues that a part of the colonised population, at least, had to accept their oppressors' hegemonic claims about universal rationality imported from the 'civilised' west. To be civilised was to be free from specific forms of tyranny. Such a framework denied legitimacy to and actively emptied indigenous forms of reason or rationality. Peter Fitzpatrick, for example, has argued that modern law poses as secular and immune from pre-modern referrals to transcendent power, but, in its claim to universality, it raises the figure of the sovereign to a transcendental level. As a result, the binary of the 'occidental' and the 'savage' is invented where the 'savage' is suppressed within modern law. Modern law emerges as part of the myth-making and surfaces as a constitutive exclusion central to the inoperativeness of the law itself. State power operates to exclude, punish and sometimes exterminate the 'savage' other.[41] A legal system designed to abolish the tyranny of despotism over liberty was part and parcel of the civilising mission in India. From the beginning, this mission was fraught with contradictions between the 'inside' and the 'outside' of law. According to the colonial regime, since Indians were not 'rational' subjects yet, 'normal' legality could not fully apply.

Legal exceptionalism was a constitutive factor in making the colonial legal regime right from the very beginning. Jorg Fisch has argued that though the British emphasised that the Muhammadan law was problematic due to its 'inhuman' and 'inconsistent' procedure, the English law imported to India was much harsher and punitive.[42] Fisch argues that to establish effective control through the rule of law, the British abolished the previous local 'extra-legal' and 'illegal' practices that were outside the control of central power. At the same time, legislation was introduced to check excessive leniency in the existing practices. As a result, criminal law became a terrain for establishing law and order, a struggle to introduce a centralised bureaucratic British rule based on a clearly defined legality. A paradox ensued. The stricter the British colonial desire to abide by the law was, the more severe the law was made. 'Legal' substitutes for extra-legal and illegal practices were provided. Fisch argues that 'the undeniable tendency of the legislation to introduce more severity' is proof 'of the mild character of the Islamic law'.[43] If anything, it predated the compilation of a body of substantive law in India. By the early 1830s, the company administration had already embarked on a concerted effort to use law in ways that were opposed to the legal principles of the enlightenment era: No assumption of innocence until proven guilty, no notion of individual moral responsibility regardless of race, caste or creed and no due process of law based on the presentation of evidence. Instead, law operated as a pre-emptive and extraordinary force.

The 'discovery' of Thugee by the British colonial administration in the 1820s, for example, initiated the development of a regime of legal suppression that was constructed not around the 'rule of law' but a notion of legal exceptionalism, which served as the prototype for similar forms of legislation later. For example, the colonial Frontier Crimes Regulation

(FCR) was first promulgated in 1872. FCR unleashed what Benjamin Hopkins calls 'Frontier governmentality' and excluded the frontier's inhabitants from the colonial sphere, especially the judiciary, and relegated them to a colonially sanctioned 'tradition'.[44] The timing of the anti-Thugee campaign is highly significant: legal exceptionalism in the context of public order legislation predated institutionalised attempts to create a universal rule of law for India through the series of Law Commissions beginning in 1835. In short, legal exceptionalism was an essential ingredient of how the colonial regime used the law right from the beginning. It was neither a later addition nor something that only applied in exceptional circumstances. A brief reference to colonial efforts to deal with Thugs will make this point clearer. The name 'Thug' was given to gangs of 'professional assassins' or robbers whom the British perceived as a major public order problem in the early nineteenth century.[45] With support from Governor-General Lord William Bentick, the anti-Thugee campaign led by William Sleeman, first as the founding superintendent (1835) and then commissioner of the Thugee Department (1839), resulted in the imprisonment, execution or expulsion of thousands of men from British India. Though many amongst the British administrators had conceded by the early 1830s that the threat had been successfully repressed, the extraordinary efforts in ideological and institutional innovation nevertheless continued. With its trademark modus operandi and legal back-up, a dedicated police department was set up to deal with the Thugee 'challenge'.[46] Detective methodologies to understand 'crime' began to be applied, followed by profiling and intelligence-gathering.

The 'legal procedure' involved in convicting the Thugs is significant to understanding the broader argument here. Radhika Singha, among various others, has emphasised the significance of a law called 'Act XXX'.[47] According to this Act, all that the administration needed was an 'approver' to testify that the accused was a Thug.[48] The law did not identify any specific activity as criminal; instead, it specified the members of Thug groups, particular social groups, as hereditary criminals. The punitive and corrective measures of the colonial administration did not spare even the wives and children of the suspected Thugs. Thugee was not something one had to do to be guilty; one simply was a Thug regardless of whether one committed any robberies and murders or not. This construction gained traction in the British colonial legal imagination at precisely the same time, as Radhika Singha notes, 'when a penal code upholding precision and exactness was on the agenda'.[49] Special courts were established for the trial of the Thugs, which lay beyond the Company's jurisdiction at that point in time. The punishment for the 'crime' was life imprisonment. Most of the discourse about Thugs was based on the confessions extracted from arrested Thugs. Shahid Amin has rightly observed that the 'confessions' that dominated and drove all accounts of Thugee were not confessions but 'approver testimonies'.[50] An accused would escape severe punishment if they could help identify another 'Thug', thereby having a vested interest in keeping the myth of Thugee as a criminal phenomenon alive.[51] Therefore, the outcome of the trial was known in advance. Despite Thugee being declared extinct by the 1870s, the methodology and legal practice and imagination it had created survived. Similar methods but with a different target constituency were enshrined in the law in the infamous Criminal Tribes Act of 1871.[52] The chapters in the book will show that the ambit of 'problem categories' and 'risk groups' kept widening in the early twentieth century with the rise in anti-colonial politics.

Situating the Subject: The Consolidation of a New Colonial Legal Subjectivity

Scholars of South Asian Studies have delved into various aspects of the law in India and its functioning. Earlier research dealt with a broad range of issues from personal and religious law(s) to surveillance, the suppression of the vernacular press, civil and criminal procedure, racism embedded in the legal code and the association of legality and colonial liberalism.[53] Many more scholars have touched upon dimensions of law while discussing labour issues or communal conflicts.[54]

The repression of Thugs in a wholesale manner exposed the overt repressive tactic of the colonial administration. Michel Foucault warned us against understanding repression as something purely negative and alerted us to its productive capacity. The administrative persecution of Thugs facilitated the creation of a moral 'non-criminal' other, which helped to maximise the productive aims of colonial government. It delineated the space in which 'normal' legality in its universalist and utilitarian sense could be constituted. Creating extra-legal subjects like the Thugs produced the general parameters of conduct for the legal subjects of colonialism. Indians were reconfigured for a new state of legal incarceration. Such incarceration was aided and achieved through new modes of conducting life, as each Law Commission report proposed. The seven Law Commission reports in colonial India instituted between 1835 to 1860, one by one, founded a new quotidian legal and social order characterised by a revaluation of life in the colony.

The persecution of Thugs created the space for a discourse on the pressing need to deal with the 'criminal other'. It was essential because, otherwise, the moral superiority of the 'non-criminal' would not hold. This resulting binary thus operated on two levels. At one level, it criminalised a population amongst the Indians and, at the second level, established a moral and racial superiority for the 'white'/European/ English. The racist anomalies in the relationship between the colonial state's law and its citizens are central to understanding the 'rule of colonial difference'. Elizabeth Kolsky's intervention provides an instructive insight into non-official white violence in early colonial India.[55] She has shown that white Britons could act with a significant measure of immunity from civil and criminal persecution. It was made possible by an incongruity between criminal law on the books and illegal activity in reality and maintained what Kolsky refers to as 'a place of lawlessness at the centre of law's empire'.[56] Therefore, it was no fundamental contradiction to keep whites out of the legal penalties applicable to Indians, as Kolsky revealed in her study of the nature of 'white violence in colonial India'.[57] After all, the racial differentiation of law made the second split among the subjects of the colonial government possible. In a Schmittian sense, it also divided the Indian population as 'friends' and 'foes' for colonial governance. Therefore, specific measures were put in place to deal with such problem categories whilst on the second track of the colonial use of the law, so to speak, an ideology of universal justice – 'the rule of law' – could be promulgated.

In 1835, the utilitarian philosopher and politician Thomas Babington Macaulay took charge of the Law Commission to draft a penal code for India that represented the other side of colonial legality – the imposition of universalist values and due process. On 10 July 1833, he made an argument before the British Parliament about the future role of British governance in India to give 'good government' to Indians because they did not qualify for 'free government'.[58] The hallmark of such a good government was the 'rule by law'. Macaulay was then serving as the secretary of the Board of Control under Lord Grey. With the passing of the Charter Act, 1833, Macaulay was appointed by the British Parliament as the first law member of the Governor-General's Council. He arrived in India in 1834 and became the chairman of the First Law Commission in 1835, and was assigned the responsibility of drafting a new legal code for India. Foregrounding how

English law set out to level the 'uneven' field of Indian legal system(s), the set of seven law reports eventually published by the Law Commission over the following decades provide us with a bird's eye view of what most preoccupied the British lawmakers in their engagement with colonial society in India.

The commission's seven reports (1835–1870) – even though they were about aspects of civil law – highlight some of the general priorities that would also influence the design of penal law. The usual divisions of public and private fail to consider that the domain of modern law began with a focus on the private in the first instance. For example, in the context of debates around legal pluralism, Michael Anderson has alerted us that the distinction between the 'modern' and 'traditional' spheres or the distinction between the 'indigenous' and the 'alien' presupposes a dichotomy that does not exist. He emphasises that contestation between state and community forms of authority existed before colonialism and further argues that this discord concerns more the political structure than cultural hiatus.[59] The penal law codified by the British interfered in the personal lives of communities by converting distinct communities into a universal 'public' which now had to be processed through the law or a legal framework. Dwelling on the relationship between the British colonial state and society in India, D.A. Washbrook has noted that the 'condition of law may be seen to crystallise the condition of society'.[60] He emphasises that the value of law rests in its social function and argues that the struggle around law is articulated as 'general statements of principle rather than particular statements of private and discreet interests'. Despite all colonial efforts, various Law Commission reports appear more as a collage of facts and highlight that the idea of revaluation was inherent to the theme of profit-making but took place through the mode of 'governance', through 'legitimate' means. These reports outline the process of law-making and its philosophy, consequently leading to the understanding of the 'legitimate' and, by extension, the criminal. Additionally, there was an emphasis on the conduct of conduct, in a Foucauldian vein, a power to act on the actions of the colonised subjects. The rules of everyday social conduct were altered, with a new set of rules instituted by each Law Commission report.[61]

The Turn in Colonial Politics after the Events of 1857

The Great Rebellion of 1857 opened up a political chasm between the coloniser and the colonised. The violent uprising saw many Europeans killed in India, making the colonial administration even more suspicious and hostile towards its Indian subjects. The events of 1857 destabilised the colonial pretence that it had successfully tamed Indians and served as a wake-up call for its 'civilising mission'.

Christopher Bayly's work on the evolution of British intelligence-gathering has offered an account of the intricate networks of Indian spies, runners, and political secretaries, all working to secure information about the colonised subjects of the empire.[62] Mapping such informant's social and intellectual origins, Bayly pointed out that the misinformation was often misinterpreted. The British failed to understand the complex systems of communication in India. For Bayly, the British misunderstood the context of information-gathering, which contributed significantly to their failure to anticipate the anti-colonial mobilisation of 1857. Bayly's thesis has gained popularity with time and continues to serve as a foundational reference for many new works on the anxious and vulnerable nature of the colonial state.[63]

The events of 1857 are essential in terms of legal theory because it was also a moment when the colonised subjects rose in arms against the colonial state intending to decide the sovereign, at least as far as mutineers or rebels were concerned.[64] The events of 1857 highlighted that British sovereignty in India was not yet established completely. Scholars have pointed out in numerous studies that sovereignty in India had a peculiar journey in the eighteenth and nineteenth centuries. The Mughal Emperor, who could be called a grand sovereign in the seventeenth century, was not a sovereign in the strict sense.[65] For example, Farhat Hasan brought to our attention that the relationship of the Mughal government with the Indian subjects was more of revenue collection rather than a total system of direct and uniform government. Therefore, the local administrators internally fractured any aim of the Mughal empire to homogenise and centralise their polity.[66] Sovereignty in India in the nineteenth century until 1857 at least operated autonomously yet overlapped at different levels. On the first level, Bahadur Shah Zafar was the Mughal sovereign, followed by the regional rajas, princes and *nizam*s. On the second level, the East India Company, with powers to control and regulate Fort William and Fort George in Madras and Bengal Presidencies, respectively, acted as the sovereign in its territories given the jurisdiction granted by royal charters along with the *diwani* granted by the Mughals. Also, the Company was an acting sovereign administrating on behalf of its superior and ultimate sovereign, the British Crown.

The events of 1857 gave the colonial administration the chance to overhaul political realities according to its ideological expectations. The British colonial authorities responded to the rebellion with spectacular violence – like mass executions and deportations – motivated in part by vengeance but also to make an exemplary spectacle of its sovereign might.[67] The Mutiny granted the British a reason to tighten their grip on the Indian masses by painting them as inherently rebellious and untrustworthy. It also provided them with a reason to emphasise the 'barbaric nature' of the colonised subjects. The events of 1857 brought a particular administrative urgency: any dissent against the British rule must be crushed to avoid future uprisings. It marked a change in British attitude towards the colonised subjects. It was a moment when the entire population was under suspicion of being the 'enemy' in Schmitt's sense, not just some exotic and largely imaginary public enemy like the Thugs. Over the following years, the suppression of any political opposition and the promulgation of extraordinary laws became central to this operation. In terms of a policy of 'risk management', there is a continuity between the East India Company and the British colonial government.

Almost three years after the events of 1857, the IPC was enacted in 1860. The content of the seven Law Commission reports illustrates that 'law-making' in colonial India was a well-thought-through exercise.[68] Noticeably, crime and punishment did not figure overtly in the law-making process until the seventh report of the Law Commission, at a moment when other aspects of the law had already been largely clarified.

Historically, the primary concern of the British magistrates was projected as one that bridged discrepancies of punishment and the dispute resolution process inherent in the Islamic justice system. The late Mughal model of government did not operate in a monolithic and linear fashion. Instead, it allowed a different permutation of administration adopted locally at times. During the creation of a new penal code for India, the Mughal justice administration system based on the principles of Sharia was gradually replaced by British colonial law. It was argued that the Mughal law as an administrative system was unscientific in nature, guided by the partial attitudes of *qazi*s and their disproportionate punishments.

The seventh report of the Law Commission, published on 11 June 1870, stated as its purpose the revision of the criminal procedure code.[69] In a dispatch of 21 December 1868, the local Government of India observed that there scarcely existed a code of criminal procedure at the moment.[70]

It further recorded that three subsequent Acts had already amended the original code enacted in 1861. A fourth short amendment was suggested under the instruction of Sir Stafford Northcote. It added that there had been many judicial decisions on the construction of the code, and the decisions were often unknown or occasionally conflicting.[71] Such a contradictory narrative complicated the system of administration and the procedure itself.

The British laid the foundation of a new legal subjectivity by devising a legal code for India. The Law Commissions had worked for almost three decades to accomplish this project. The law reports outline the displacement of indigenous modes of conduct by a new English one. Public order could only be maintained once the need for it had been created. It opened up space for colonial authorities to control and manipulate the conduct of the people. Redesigning the social through the legal allowed the colonisers to set up the rules of the colonial form of governance and facilitated the immediate and efficient unleashing of colonial control of various populations.

The formation of the new legal code was influenced by the utilitarian philosophy of Bentham and emphasised the axiom of 'the rule of law'. However, the colonial law-making process faced complicated issues. Various laws operating across different provinces were resulting in an administrative hazard for the administration. This issue was resolved by the Indian Councils Acts of 1861 (and 1892), which changed colonial 'administration' to a form of colonial 'government'. In displacing the earlier practices of the 'Mughal judicial system', new English laws required new jurists. The English magistrates were already meting out decisions to various disputes in the light of the 'new' laws. Institutions were introduced or even transferred from Britain because 'public justice' was supposed to be introduced in contradistinction to 'personal injury', one of the most problematic elements of 'Mohammedan law' for the British in India. The new courts of law would dramatically impact the Indian masses because dispute resolution was now proposed to be more 'just' and 'impartial'. However, there were still issues unresolved. One such issue was racial justice. Elizabeth Kolsky, among various other historians, has pointed out that in the 1890s, when the issue of 'white violence' was at its peak, the British administration was caught in its trap because the champions of 'the rule of law' had to deal with disputes 'uniformly', without favouring Europeans over Indians.

The consolidation of laws in 1893 resulted in the birth of a universal subject in colonial India irrespective of race. Such equality before the law was deeply resented by the majority of the European settlers in India. In the spirit of resolving the 'racial' contradiction in the recently introduced English law, a universal legal code was eventually adopted by emphasising the 'norms of justice' and the responsibility of 'western civilisation'. Even though bitterly opposed by the European settlers in India, the universality of colonial law had to transcend race, at least in letter, to establish maximum control and authority.

The entire exercise of establishing the ultimate authority of the British Crown in India and the formation of the IPC in the 1860s can be read as the initiation of a modern social contract in India. However, it was not until 1893 that the IPC was consolidated and it became one universal overarching body of law. As Kolsky's work has highlighted, it was one of the sovereign's problems of whether to govern by 'the rule of law' or 'rule *by* law'. While the idea of 'the rule of law' simply meant that no one was above the law of the land, the arbitrariness of power was kept in check by a set of written rules. However, 'rule by law' meant that written rules were applied yet did not presuppose equality before law. The consolidation of the IPC in 1893 did claim to transition from a 'rule *by* law' to 'the rule of law', but it did not alter the governance attitude which had already presupposed at the beginning of the nineteenth century that since Indians could not have a 'free' government, they should be provided with a 'good' government.

The British articulated sovereignty in an Indian idiom but felt obliged to justify their rule in a European idiom too. Ranajit Guha's 'Dominance without Hegemony' thesis captures this oscillation of the expression of the colonial state's sovereignty between the Indian and the European idioms.[72] Guha argues that in colonial India, political coercion outweighed persuasive cultural hegemony in civil society, which carried over to the post-independence period. The elite had interests distinctly different from those of the subaltern groups. He further argues that such a split in the state's politics meant that the Indian bourgeoisie, unlike the European bourgeoisie, failed to establish a cultural hegemony in a Gramscian sense over the Indian subalterns. The inability of the colonial state to assimilate civil society into political society led the state to exercise dominance without hegemonic consent. In contrast, Taylor Sherman, for example, has creatively challenged the persistent conceptions of the nature of the colonial and postcolonial state in India. For her, the state in twentieth-century India was replete with tensions. She contests the framework that portrays the state as having the ambition and ability to dominate the population at will and argues that, instead, it was self-limiting and vulnerable most of the time.[73] However, the chapters in this book will complicate such an understanding and show that after the provincial election of 1937, the Congress party was quite hegemonic when it came to the wider nationalist consensus. However, it still had to resort to domination vis-à-vis the working classes and religious interests that digressed from its vision. Further investigation on such themes is required to understand better the complexity of the nature and character of the late colonial state.

Continuing the discussion on the expression of colonial sovereignty in an Indian and European idiom, scholars have drawn our attention to the subtle aims of the 'civilising mission' of the colonial state. The most powerful tool of the civilising mission was the coloniser's claim that the purpose of the colonial enterprise was to improve the locals and aimed at bringing the fruits of progress and modernity to them. Michael Mann has argued that 'the point where the colonisers are about to give up their role as civilisers, the colonised ask to continue as objects of civilising mission'.[74] Therefore, it was inherent in the logic of colonialism that people who were different were inferior. To govern them, they needed to be made similar. Such an understanding drove a seemingly sympathetic attitude of philanthropic enlightenment and the self-inflicted 'duty' of the 'white man'. But this was only one part of the story. The same 'civilisers' who were uncomfortable with 'irrational' Mughal and customary laws did not necessarily follow the spirit and procedure of the so-called rational laws they had introduced. The complete absence of evidence collection and due legal process in the case of Thugee demonstrates the 'irrationality' of the ostentatiously 'rational' administration in India. While the Law Commissions were busy drafting a universalist penal code for India, the suppression of the criminal cult of Thugs remained the main obsession of the British colonial administration.

Colonial law increasingly became preoccupied with risk management rather than justice. In ordinary times, social demographics that were seen as potential problems for the colonial administration were placed outside the operation of the law. Establishing a clear dividing line between the normal and the extraordinary could not only make dealing with such problem categories easier whilst simultaneously maintaining the pretence of a polity built on enlightenment ideals, but it also set norms of conduct for all those who were not perceived as problem categories themselves.

However, the game of ruling through sovereign distinctions of this kind was not successful. As the first two chapters of the book will discuss, the formation of mass anti-colonial resistance in the twentieth century made the boundary between normal and exceptional uses of law very permeable indeed. At least potentially, the entirety of the Indian population could become a problem category – or 'enemy' in Schmitt's sense. The legal exception, in other words, would increasingly become 'normalised' and begin to penetrate how public order legislation would be used in an everyday context.

The Ghadar movement in the second decade of the twentieth century, the Congress mass campaigns and the growth of the labour movement resource mobilisation in India during both the First and Second World Wars were all instances where extraordinary laws became part of the everyday toolkit of the colonial state. What is more, the logic of extraordinary but normalised law did not disappear with the transfer of power to a newly independent India. The new provincial governments, for example, in UP, re-enacted colonial methodology by pursuing a similar sovereign decisionism. One could argue that there was no significant difference between colonial and postcolonial times when it came to the application of extraordinary legislation in India.

There remains a need to delve further into many other practices of legal governance, especially the maintenance of law and order in India. Although a relatively narrow set of specific public order laws are frequently mentioned in traditional political history sources for the colonial period, specific studies that engage and offer elaborate discussion on such laws, how they were evoked and used, and how their use affected late colonial and earlier postcolonial politics in India need further attention. Other than Nasser Hussain's work on 'jurisprudence of emergency', Radhika Singha's work on 'despotism of law', Kim Wagner's work on 'Thugs' and the 'Amritsar Massacre', and the recent provocative study of 'the insecurity state' in colonial Punjab by Mark Condos engage with the problematic of invoking a 'state of exception' and the creation of exceptional legal categories by the colonial administrative regime in India.[75]

A more direct engagement with extraordinary laws like 'Act XXX' to deal with Thugs is evident in the work of Radhika Singha.[76] She has pointed out that before drafting a penal code, the British created legislation in the early nineteenth century that actively repressed communities by declaring them as 'hereditary' criminals. In contrast, Wagner's discussion on the Amritsar Massacre of 1919 continues to argue a familiar framework that proposes that violent actions of the colonial state were 'acts of fear'.[77] Mark Condos extends a similar thesis and offers insight into the 'dark underside' of ideologies that sustained British colonial rule in India and proposes a similar argument that colonial overlords were fearful and felt vulnerable as rulers. Such administrative anxieties informed the basis of colonial violence, which was often concentrated in the hands of the executive. Termed as 'insecurity' by Condos, these factors contribute to the discussion and disagreement on the nature of colonial state-building and imperial sovereignty, law and policing. He proposes that the 'insecurity' has become a postcolonial legacy of the empire.[78] While Radhika Singha's work is more direct in identifying and highlighting the dark underbelly of colonial legal discourse, Wagner and Condos, despite making their case in great detail, limit their analysis to a popular thesis that rests primarily on 'fear', 'unease' and 'insecurity' of the colonial state. It is only partially true, as the discussion in the book will reveal, that there were moments, like the Jallianwala Bagh instance, when colonial rage overtook other administrative sensibilities. Various scholars have also investigated other elements of colonial administrative framework – for instance, the control of 'banditry'[79] and 'goondas'[80] – but the engagement with the complexity of public-order challenges in colonial and postcolonial India needs further investigation.

This book is an important intervention in the growing field of such historical studies and offers a critical perspective on the use of extraordinary public order legislation in India over the first half of the twentieth century covering the period from 1914 to 1955. In so doing, it bridges the conventional divide, now vigorously challenged by recent scholarship, between the colonial and postcolonial periods. It contributes to such scholarship and continues to challenge the conventional notions of decolonisation as a singular change that happened with the transfer of power in 1947.[81] This study begins in the early 1910s, when members of the Ghadar Party and the outbreak of the First World War posed a severe threat to the British Raj. This decade is also significant because, with the passing of the Government of India Act, 1919, the seeds for the protracted decolonisation of India were sown.[82] But most significantly, this decade witnessed the explicit invocation of a state of exception in the form of the Defence of India Act and subsequently the Rowlatt Bills in peacetime. This period also saw significant anti-colonial mass mobilisation in the form of the anti-Rowlatt Bills agitation and the Non-Cooperation and

Khilafat movements. Much work has been done on the scope of these major mass mobilisations in the early twentieth century and various nationalist parties and leaders' roles in it. However, what is still lacking is the analyses of law, its interface with nationalist politics and its impact on how such mobilisations unfolded. The book also investigates some of the major controversies of the 1930s, focusing on events and instances that occurred after the passing of the Government of India Act, 1935. These events and instances demonstrate the scope of legal governmentality once decolonisation had already begun and provincial politics enabled shared sovereignty for the provincial governments.

Some questions need further probing in the broader context of the implication of public order and extraordinary laws. What change in attitude occurred when laws and institutions born out of distinctly colonial modes of governance were used in a postcolonial situation? To what extent did the legal techniques and tactics of invoking states of exception extend beyond colonialism and even the process of decolonisation? When independence finally came, few had a clear idea of what precisely it would mean.[83] In such a scenario, what would happen to the institution of the colonial state that had made such intimate contact with people's lives at both a private and a public level? The colonial state had altered the lives of its subjects with the ushering in of a written penal code that redefined limits and transgressions in life. The revaluation of social and political interaction laid the foundation of a staged 'social contract'.

Studies discussing anti-colonial mobilisations, labour strikes and communal confrontations have pointed out that maintaining public order was one of the most important preoccupations of governance in India. Generally, most studies tend to regard the years from 1947 to 1950 as part of the transfer-of-power period.[84] This study agrees with the scholarship that has argued that the transfer of power, although initially minimal and aimed at preserving rather than dissolving the Raj, started way back with the first Government of India Act, 1919,[85] followed by the rearrangement of power with Indians in the context of the Government of India Act, 1935.[86] However, the issue of limited decolonisation did not result in moving away from colonial attitudes but began redrafting them to suit the nationalist rhetoric of Indian politics.

Scholars such as John Darwin, Mrinalini Sinha and Kama Maclean have highlighted the significance of the interwar years in India's nationalist politics. John Darwin has argued that the decline of British colonialism did not begin during the First World War.[87] For him, it is important to note that during the interwar period, British imperial policy did not offer any firm commitment to the independence of colonies. It continued to actively repress its defiant subjects with vigorous displays of power. Mrinalini Sinha extends the investigation of interwar period politics by discussing *Mother India*, a 1927 publication by the American journalist Katherine Mayo. Sinha argues that Mayo noted that the root cause of social ills in India, particularly concerning the status of women, was an irredeemable Hindu culture that made India unfit for political self-government. Contra Mayo, Sinha argues that the root of social ills in India attributed to the social backwardness of Hinduism was the result of the colonial state's reluctance to implement meaningful social reforms. Such a discourse enabled the reconfiguration of political and social spheres in India and the shaping of a collective identity of women.[88] Kama Maclean enriches this discussion and rightly points out the significance of the interwar period in shaping the political discourse in India by highlighting the interconnected evolution of violent and non-violent strains in the anti-colonial movement.[89] She further notes that it was during the interwar period in India that nationalism gained momentum and saw the development of the left, increased participation of women in nationalist agitation, amplification of caste assertion and communal escalation. It put pressure on the Congress to become a more disciplined organisation, enabling interaction with diverse political groups opposing colonial rule in India.[90] Increasingly, studies have stressed the undeniable significance of the interwar period and argued for considering debates and discussions that intensified the relationship between the colonial state and its subjects.

The question of decolonisation is also closely tied to the question of sovereignty and counter-sovereignty in late colonial India. Movements such as Swadeshi, Ghadar, Non-Cooperation, Khilafat, Quit India and ultimately the entire framework on which nationalist leaders would contest colonial policies pivoted on the question of who the legitimate sovereign was. It is here that a study of public order laws like section 144 CrPC, preventive detention, curfews, cases of police firing on crowds and the creation of other new extraordinary laws offers a unique analytical angle on this contest over sovereignty and the contingent process of decolonisation.

The colonial state began to devolve power to the provinces after the First World War by bringing in the Government of India Act, 1919, followed by the Government of India Act, 1935. It was a deliberate strategy to forestall the development of an all-India political opposition whilst also offering real opportunities for self-governance to Indian political parties and organisations. In consequence, any study of administrative strategy over this period has to by necessity include a regional focus. The process of long decolonisation highlighted the practices of the Congress government at the provincial level both before and after 1947. Second, the invocation or imposition of public order legislation is at the centre of attention in this book – for instance, the use of the infamous section 144 CrPc, which allowed preventive detention, the imposition of curfews and other forms of pre-emptive legal action, was always local in nature. It was the district magistrate who would invoke such legislation, also involving police and other parts of the local administration, and the purview of such laws was always confined to certain specified localities. Observing the working of public order legislation in colonial and postcolonial India necessitates a local focus, which again is most easily maintained by selecting certain provinces as the subject of examination. UP serves as an excellent example of a Congress provincial government that battled labour, communal and sectarian politics. This is also related to questions of source availability. Material from the National Archives in New Delhi and the British Library in London provided a top-down perspective and needed to be supplemented by provincial material to understand the operation and effect of extraordinary legislation at a local level.

While the colonial government of the nineteenth century proposed an understanding of legal exceptionalism that rested on the criminalisation of clearly pre-defined and limited groups of people, the late colonial state extended this criminalisation to any anti-state or anti-colonial activities and, by implication, potentially to the entire Indian population itself. This sense of general suspicion never left Indian governance even after the achievement of independence. There was no root-and-branch reform of the relation between the state and its people or a wholesale cleansing of laws from the colonial presumptions of generalised illegality. Racism, repression and a sense of domination survived.

The book focuses on events in the United Provinces of Agra and Oudh, or Uttar Pradesh, as the unit came to be known soon after independence. It allows us to investigate the fluctuations of power and authority and law and justice in a regional sense, thus offering a reflection on the possibilities of how public order legislation in colonial and postcolonial India worked. To enrich its analytical thrust on legal exceptions and its subjects, this study borrows spectacular historical insights from events such as the Ghadar movement and the Jallianwala Bagh massacre that occurred in Punjab. The selection of UP as a site of study allowed a provincial focus because it enabled a direct comparison of provincial administrative practice led by the Congress before and after 1947. Govind Ballabh Pant, a prominent Congress leader, was the premier or chief minister of UP both before and after the transfer of power took place. Furthermore, such a provincial selection complemented the study of the process of decolonisation, another major theme that the book engages with. Though the book studies public order in UP in the first half of the twentieth century, the conclusions have much to offer to a wider discussion on the nature of public order management in India. This is not to say that the politics of UP can be used to understand the history of extraordinary laws in states such as the Northeast of India or Kashmir. Nor is it a sum total of developments in all of India. By bringing to light the quotidian manifestations of exception, the politics of UP can be productively seen in contrast to the geographies of exception, such as the frontiers.

A few other issues regarding archival practice need to be mentioned right from the start. The book depends mostly on government documents, including governors' fortnightly reports, police reports, confidential letters, and so on, which are part of the legislative, political and judicial files, and media reports from newspapers such as *The Leader*, *Amrita Bazar Patrika*, *The Pioneer*, *Hindustan Times*, *Dainik Vishwamitra*, *Jawala*, *Sanmarg*, and so on, to track and study various instances that involved the invocation of extraordinary legislation. While the legislative, judicial and political files of the Home Department (both colonial and postcolonial) present us with the official version of a story, the newspaper reports mostly offer a different version of it. Thus, such a cross-referencing facilitated the possibility of a nuanced understanding of events. The tone of both the colonial and the postcolonial archive is often patronising, with the emphasis being on the naivety of public protests and the obligation as well as the ability of the government to look at the larger picture. However, following certain political mobilisations, instances or events such as the Kanpur strikes or the Madh-e-Sahaba controversy and tracking them in detail could help us invert such a position and enable us to understand both the immediate position as well as the larger picture. There is more at stake than mere factual accuracy. Any use of the colonial archive needs to recognise how paperwork itself had agency, a life of its own that imposed a certain logic on how the law was used at the everyday level.[91]

Chapter Summary

The book examines the character of extraordinary legislation in colonial and postcolonial India and is divided into five chapters. Chapter 1 is a broad survey that revisits the nature of legality in the early days of the twentieth century. The events of 1857 had led to suspicion of various sections of the indigenous population, followed by strict regulation of the vernacular press, and are important in this regard. The large-scale invocation of problem categories arose once again with the Ghadar movement when the entire indigenous population was suspected and branded as potentially disloyal. It highlights the violent nature of colonial law that thrived on creating a problem category that envisaged anti-colonial politics as a revolutionary crime. With the creation of the Rowlatt Bills and the criminalisation of anti-colonial politics, there emerged a liminal outside of the rule of law, that is, an exception, to exclude and define who fell under or outside its purview. By the end of the 1910s, the entire indigenous population became potential suspects and led to the production of a binary of the loyal and the disloyal subject. It asserted that those who were loyal had nothing to fear, and it was only the disloyal who was discomforted with the creation of the Rowlatt Bills. It once again produced a governmental distinction of its thriving on the element of 'problem category' to define the entire population in colonial India.

From Chapter 2 onwards, the book focuses on the politics of extraordinary legislation in UP. Chapter 2 discusses how emergency legislation cannot only be assigned to an emergency or crisis, but also has an everyday aspect to it. This chapter studies the use of a specific piece of preventive legislation, section 144 CrPC, which was invoked to deal with 'unlawful' assemblies and riotous mobs, and was promulgated to prohibit access to various public spaces. Two important instances from UP will be discussed in the chapter. One instance is from Kanpur (the Kanpur labour strikes), and the second one is from Lucknow (the Madh-e-Sahaba controversy). The former discusses labour riots and the latter communal or sectarian clashes between the Shias and the Sunnis. Both the instances are from the 1930s and are pivotal moments in the late colonial history of UP, especially when it comes to understanding the functioning of public order laws. The chapter will show that there was a continuing and widespread use of colonial tactics of law-and-order control by the provincial Congress ministry in UP even after the passing of the Government of India Act, 1935, and at a time when anti-colonial mobilisation was at its peak. The thrust of the chapter will be to raise important questions about the history of public order legislation, such as its recognised legitimacy amongst the provincial government led by the otherwise nationalist Congress party even after the initiation of limited decolonisation. It will investigate administrative responses to public order issues by a government in which Indian nationalists held at least a position of power and responsibility. It points out why decolonisation as a process must start with the recalibration of laws rather than anything else. The provincial governments and leaders of the Congress party succumbed to colonial tactics when it came to handling public order crises and the use of extraordinary legislation.

Chapter 3 brings together observations from the previous chapter and closely examines the transition from the colonial to the nationalist government. Instead of repeating the oft-told story of the Partition of India, the chapter chooses to reveal larger political shifts through the seemingly marginal but important story of a common man named Peter Budge. Budge was one politically unimportant elderly man who had a devastating experience of decolonisation. He got arrested at a time of heightened communal tension in the months before Partition. Budge then suffered a year of illegal detention without trial solely because he had an unusual or unexpected or different name, spending the dawn of freedom, forgotten, in jail. His story highlights the gaps in bureaucratic procedure in such cases as opposed to the claims often made by the colonial government. The case led to great embarrassment for the provincial Congress ministry in the newly independent India and resulted in a judicial enquiry. Away from the spectacular violence of the colonial state, for example, in the Jallianwala Bagh massacre of April 1919, Peter's story reveals the routine violence of colonial legality mediated by bureaucratic paperwork maintained by low-level officials in police and the judiciary.

Chapters 3, 4 and 5 will show that after the transfer of power, the moment of breaking free from the Raj, there continued the characteristics of the 'social contract' that the colonial state had imposed on the people of India. This book argues that decolonisation marked the entry into a second farcical social contract where the old absolute division between the state and its people was largely carried over. The postcolonial Indian state, as the chapters will show, failed to formulate new rules and standards for maintaining public order and conducting politics.

Chapter 4 discusses the promulgation of law with extraordinary provisions that argued to maintain law and order by identifying 'bad characters' in the province. As noted in the introduction to the book, the colonial government in India had a career of violence and suppression. Such violence was often perpetrated through 'law' by classifying certain sections of Indian society as 'criminals', for instance, 'Thugs' and 'criminal tribes'. In the late colonial period, 'goondas' and 'bad characters' populated such criminal nomenclature. The desire to discipline the masses through the activation of laws did not cease after independence and remained one of the central obsessions of the postcolonial state too. 'Preventive laws' were helpful to the UP Congress ministry to take action against the political 'others'. Three important administrative policies of the UP government that were initiated within the first six months of India attaining its independence are discussed in the chapter to make sense of the newly found independence in India. These discussions are regarding issuing of guns to villages and the formation of Village Defence Societies (VDS) to fight dacoits in UP in January 1948, followed by the passing of the Rakshak Dal Act, 1948, in April 1948, and, finally, the passing of the UP Prevention of Crime (Special Powers) Bill, 1948, by the end of the year. The official discussions revealed various vulnerabilities of the postcolonial state and highlighted how the provincial government and the law-and-order bureaucracy perceived its citizens. The chapter will argue that, on the one hand, the administration in UP distrusted the population and consistently occupied itself with identifying problem categories. Therefore, it tried to sustain a distinction between the governing and the governed. On the other hand, its new policies increasingly blurred the assumed boundaries between the state and society.

Chapter 5 focuses on the institutions of *mukhiyagiri* (village headman) and *chowkidari* (village watchman). It is a more comprehensive study of local policing institutions and administrative practices in UP. *Mukhiyas* and *chowkidars* were important for the colonial state to govern the countryside. The chapter discusses an administrative tradition inherited from the colonial government and highlights the continuity of an older order in the UP administration when it came to governing the village. It will show that the post-1947 UP government could not avoid the seductions of the colonial art of governance and resorted to rebranding old institutions in the face of 'changed times', where the Congress had to actively function as an independent government rather than just a mass mobilising front opposing colonial power.

Colonial categories went on to facilitate postcolonial manoeuvres to maintain law and order. Other than a straightforward handover of political sovereignty, there was barely any effective decolonisation of political understanding. Rather than establishing democracy by legitimising a new juridico-political order, the early postcolonial state in India opted for the 'reasons of the state' logic. As a result, there was a continuity in the imagination between the colonial and postcolonial Indian state as to what was meant by public order and how it could be maintained. While the colonial state, it has been argued, was faced with vulnerability and fear,[92] the postcolonial state, the book argues, was increasingly consumed by sovereign anxiety that underlined its politics and attitude towards its citizens, at least in UP.[93] The source of this sovereign anxiety was the colonial experience. Thus, the active pursuit of 'public order' appeared as its time-tested remedy. The extension of a colonial public order mentality into postcolonial India reveals that it was not an ad hoc colonial arrangement but a liminal space that facilitated control and authority within modern law. Like in psychology, where anxiety at moderate levels might be perceived as beneficial and fostering learning, problem-solving and productivity but overwhelming if too high, sovereign anxiety too manifests itself in various forms through political symptoms. Endless information-gathering and surveillance point to its vulnerability; repeatedly undertaking grand projects to maintain public order highlights the sovereign's lack of focus on defined objectives such as welfare and governance. Reinventing problem categories in postcolonial India reveals its distracted side where sustaining an eternal crisis of public order becomes almost mandatory. In a postcolonial order, both the state and its citizens struggled to make a new sense of each other. The new context arrived with a promise of law that rhetorically empowered citizens and limited government. It was a promise to confer dignity and rights on all sections of the indigenous population who during the colonial experience could claim neither dignity nor rights in law.

Notes

1. See Uttar Pradesh State Archives (UPSA), Secret letter no. 205/ST, dated 10 June 1949, from District Magistrate, Etah, Ram Kinker Singh, to the Secretary to Government (Police-C), Lucknow, part of File No. 464/1948, Department (Police) B.

2. Ibid.

3. See UPSA, copy of confidential letter D.O. No. G/37 dated 20 July 1949, from the Superintendent of Police Bahraich to the District Magistrate Bahraich, part of File No. 464/1948 Department (Police) B.

4. See the oft-quoted minute by the Hon'ble T.B. Macaulay, dated 2 February 1835. Macaulay's 'Minute on Education', 2 February 1835, published in Henry Sharp, *Selections from the Educational Records, Bureau of Education India, I* (Calcutta, 1920), pp. 107–116; also see G.M. Young, *Speeches by Lord Macaulay with His Minute on Indian Education* (Oxford and London: Oxford University Press, 1935), p. 125.

5. See Radhika Singha, *A Despotism of Law: Crime and Justice in Early Colonial India* (Delhi: Oxford University Press, 1998).

6. See A.G. Noorani, 'Armed Forces (Special Powers) Act: Urgency of Review', *Economic and Political Weekly* 44, no. 34 (22–28 August 2009): 8–11; Gautam Navlakha, 'On Ending the War against Our Own People', *Economic and Political Weekly* 46, no. 8 (19–25 February 2011): 24–28; Anand Teltumbde, 'Criminalising People's Protests', *Economic and Political Weekly* 48, no. 14 (6 April 2013): 10–11; Mustafa Haji, 'Armed Forces Special Powers Act: A Call for Repeal', *Counter Terrorist Trends and Analyses* 4, no. 7 (July 2012): 12–15; Adfar Rashid Shah, 'Fall out of Continued Use of the AFSPA', *Economic and Political Weekly* 46, no. 9 (26 February–4 March 2011): 5.

7. Ujjwal Kumar Singh, 'Repeal of POTA: What about Other Draconian Acts?' *Economic and Political Weekly* 39, no. 33 (13–20 August 2004): 3677–3680; G. Hargopal and B. Jagannatham, 'Terrorism and Human Rights: Indian Experience with Repressive Laws', *Economic and Political Weekly* 44, no. 28 (11–17 July 2009): 76–85; Sumanta Banerjee, 'From Parliamentary to Paramilitary Democracy', *Economic and Political Weekly* 47, no. 1 (7 January 2012): 16–19.

8. Anushka Singh, *Sedition in Liberal Democracies* (New Delhi: Oxford University Press, 2018).

9. Mayur Suresh, 'The Slow Erosion of Fundamental Rights: How Romila Thapar v. Union of India Highlights What Is Wrong with the UAPA', *Indian Law Review* 3, no. 2 (2019): 212–223.

10. Bharat Bhushan, 'Citizens, Infiltrators, and Others: The Nature of Protests against the Citizenship Amendment Act', *South Atlantic Quarterly* 120, no. 1 (2021): 201–208; Fathima Nizaruddin, 'Resisting the Configurations of a Hindu Nation', *HAU: Journal of Ethnographic Theory* 10, no. 3 (2020): 726–733.

11. See Ujjwal Kumar Singh, *The State, Democracy and Anti-Terror Laws in India* (New Delhi: SAGE Publications India, 2007). Countries like the USA have passed the Patriot Act; UK has similar laws like the Terrorism Act 2000, Anti-Terrorism, Crime and Security Act, 2001, and the Prevention

of Terrorism Act, 2005; Australia has the Australian Anti-Terror Act, 2005; Canada has the Canadian Anti-Terrorism Act, 2001, the Bill C-51, the Anti-Terrorism Act, 2015; India has the Terrorist and Disruptive Activities (Prevention) Act (1985–1995), Prevention of Terrorist Activities Act (2002–2004) and the Unlawful Activities Prevention Act. Many other European and non-European countries have also passed similar laws recently. Such laws were amended across countries resulting in an even stricter version of them.

12. Giorgio Agamben, *Homo Sacer: Sovereign Power and Bare Life* (Stanford, CA: Stanford University Press, 1998).

13. Edward Said's book *Orientalism* is considered to be one of the first Foucauldian analyses by many scholars.

14. The entire Subaltern Studies project (which runs into volumes) had a strong Foucauldian impression on it.

15. Michel Foucault, *Society Must Be Defended, Lectures at the College de France 1975–76*, trans. David Macey (New York: Picador, 2003), p. 310.

16. Giorgio Agamben, *State of Exception*, trans. Kevin Attell (Chicago: The University of Chicago Press, 2005), p. 104.

17. Carl Schmitt, *Political Theology*, trans. George Schwab (Chicago: The University of Chicago Press, 2010), pp. 18–26.

18. Ibid., pp. 29–35.

19. Ibid.

20. Ibid., pp. 33–34.

21. Ibid., p. 26.

22. Agamben, *Homo Sacer*, pp. 6–7.

23. Ibid. Also see Michel Foucault, *History of Sexuality: An Introduction*, vol. 1 (Westminster: Knopf Doubleday Publishing Group, 2012).

24. See A.G. Frank, 'Emergence of Permanent Emergency in India', *Economic and Political Weekly* 12, no. 11 (March 1977): 463–475; Emma Tarlo, *Unsettling Memories: Narratives of India's 'Emergency'* (Delhi: Permanent Black, 2003).

25. See Ben Kafka, *The Demon of Writing: Powers and Failures of Paperwork* (Cambridge, MA: Zone Books, 2012); Matthew S. Hull, *Government of Paper: The Materiality of Bureaucracy in Urban Pakistan* (Berkeley, CA: University of California Press, 2012); Cornelia Vismann and G. Winthrop-Young, *Files: Law and Media Technology* (Meridian: Crossing Aesthetics and Stanford University Press, 2008).

26. Ronald B. Inden, *Imagining India* (Indiana: Indiana University Press, 2001); Homi Bhabha, *The Location of Culture* (London: Routledge, 2004); Bernard S. Cohn, *Colonialism and Its Forms of Knowledge: The British in India* (Princeton, NJ: Princeton University Press, 1996); Nicholas B. Dirks, *Castes of Mind: Colonialism and the Making of Modern India* (Princeton, NJ: Princeton

University Press, 2002); also see Bernard S. Cohn and Nicholas B. Dirks, 'Beyond the Fringe: The Nation State, Colonialism, and the Technologies of Power', *Journal of Historical Sociology* 1, no. 2 (1998): 224–229.

27. Rosalind O'Hanlon and David Washbrook, 'After Orientalism: Culture, Criticism, and Politics in the Third World', *Comparative Studies in Society and History* 34, no. 1 (June 2009): 141–167; Nicholas Thomas, *Colonialism's Culture* (Princeton, NJ: Princeton University Press, 1994); also see Nicholas Thomas, *Entangled Objects: Exchange, Material Culture and Colonialism in the Pacific* (Cambridge, MA; London: Harvard University Press, 1991).

28. C.A. Bayly, *Empire and Information: Intelligence Gathering and Social Communication in India, 1780–1870* (Cambridge: Cambridge University Press, 1996), p. 7.

29. Ibid., p. 314.

30. Achille Mbembe, *On the Postcolony* (Berkeley, CA; Los Angeles: University of California Press, 2001); Jean Comaroff and John L. Comaroff, eds., *Law and Disorder in the Postcolony* (Chicago: The University of Chicago Press, 2006).

31. Yasmin Khan, *The Great Partition: The Making of Indian and Pakistan* (New Delhi: Penguin Books Limited, 2013); Urvashi Butalia, *The Other Side of Silence: Voices from the Partition of India* (Durham, NC: Duke University Press, 2000); Gyanendra Pandey, *Remembering Partition* (Cambridge; New York: Cambridge University Press, 2001); Haimanti Roy, *The Partition of India* (Oxford: Oxford University Press, 2018); Neeti Nair, *Changing Homelands: Hindu Politics and the Partition of India* (Cambridge, MA; London: Harvard University Press, 2011); Ian Talbot and Gurharpal Singh, *The Partition of India* (Cambridge: Cambridge University Press, 2009); Joya Chatterji, *The Spoils of Partition: Bengal and India, 1947–1967* (Cambridge: Cambridge University Press, 2011).

32. Robert Travers, *Ideology and Empire in Eighteenth-Century India: The British in Bengal* (Cambridge: Cambridge University Press, 2007).

33. Jon E. Wilson, *The Domination of Strangers: Modern Governance in Eastern India, 1780–1835* (Basingstoke; New York: Palgrave Macmillan, 2008).

34. Mithi Mukherjee, *India in the Shadows of Empire: A Legal and Political History, 1774–1950* (New Delhi: Oxford University Press, 2011).

35. Thomas Metcalf, *Ideologies of the Raj, 1800–1899*, vols. 3 and 4 (Cambridge: Cambridge University Press, 1998).

36. See Eric Stokes, *The English Utilitarians and India* (Delhi: Oxford University Press, 1989), p. 350.

37. Ibid.

38. Uday Singh Mehta, *Liberalism and Empire: A Study in Nineteenth Century British Liberal Thought* (Chicago; London: The University of Chicago Press, 1999), p. 245.

39. Karuna Mantena, *Alibis of Empire: Henry Maine and the Ends of Liberal Imperialism* (Princeton, NJ; Oxford: Princeton University Press, 2010).

40. Michael Mann, '"Torchbearers upon the Path of Progress": Britain's Ideology of a "Moral and Material Progress" in India', in *Colonialism as Civilizing Mission: Cultural Ideology in British India*, ed. Harald Fischer-Tine and Michael Mann, pp. 1–28 (London: Anthem Press, 2004).

41. Peter Fitzpatrick, *The Mythology of Modern Law* (London; New York: Routledge, 1992), p. 235; Peter Fitzpatrick, *Modernism and the Grounds of Law* (Cambridge: Cambridge University Press, 2001), p. 261.

42. Jorg Fisch, *Cheap Lives and Dear Limbs: The British Transformation of the Bengal Criminal Law 1769–1817* (Wiesbaden: Franz Steiner Verlag, 1983).

43. Ibid., p. 125.

44. Benjamin D. Hopkins, 'The Frontier Crimes Regulation and Frontier Governmentality', *Journal of Asian Studies* 74, no. 2 (2015): 369–389.

45. It is important to mention that according to the earlier recorders of cases of Thugee, this specific tribe consisted of both Hindus and Muslims with as many as seven tribes of Muslims involved in this occupation. It was claimed that they joined travellers and during the journey gained the trust of fellow travellers, and at an appropriate moment, strangled them with a noose or a handkerchief. After robbing them, these Thugs would bury the bodies of their victims. The terms 'Thug' and 'Thugee' became popular after Philip Meadows Taylor's novel *Confessions of a Thug* was first published in 1939.

46. We must not forget that in this particular decade, Britain itself was in the initial phase of setting up a police force back home.

47. Singha, *A Despotism of Law*, p. 342. Also see Kim Wagner and Nitin Sinha on peripatetic groups.

48. The British administration scuttled its own claims of evidence collection through scientific methods and resorted to accepting a convenient and often cooked-up story as a method of collecting facts in order to nab Thugs.

49. Singha, *A Despotism of Law*, p. 342.

50. Shahid Amin, 'Approver's Testimony, Judicial Discourse: The Case of Chauri Chaura', in *Subaltern Studies V: Writings on South Asian History and Society*, ed. Ranajit Guha and Gayatri Chakravarty Spivak, pp. 166–202 (Delhi: Oxford University Press, 1987), p. 306.

51. Shahid Amin further argues that a confession proper seeks to dilute the guilt of the confession subject, while the approver's testimony, to be fully credible in the eyes of the law, must implicate its speaker as fully as possible in the illegality being described.

52. The 'criminal tribes' were defined as communities who were 'addicted' to committing non-bailable offences such as theft and so on. A campaign to

systematically register them was conducted by the colonial government. These communities, in addition to the Thus, were referred to as 'habitually criminal', which led to the imposition of restrictions on their movement. Also, adult male members of such groups were required to report weekly to their local police station.

53. Stokes, *The English Utilitarians*; Mantena, *Alibis of Empire*; Mukherjee, *India in the Shadows of Empire*; Elizabeth Kolsky, *Colonial Justice in British India: White Violence and the Rule of Law* (New Delhi: Cambridge University Press, 2010).

54. Prashant Kidambi, *The Making of an Indian Metropolis: Colonial Governance and Public Culture in Bombay, 1890–1920* (London: Routledge, 2016); Rajnarayan Chandavarkar, *Imperial Power and Popular Politics: Class, Resistance and the State in India, c. 1850–1950* (Cambridge: Cambridge University Press, 1998); Rajnarayan Chandavarkar, *The Origins of Industrial Capitalism in India: Business Strategies and the Working Classes in Bombay, 1900–1940* (Cambridge: Cambridge University Press, 1994); Chitra Joshi, *Lost Worlds: Indian Labour and Its Forgotten Histories* (London: Anthem Press, 2005); Nandini Gooptu, *The Politics of Urban Poor in Early Twentieth-Century India* (Cambridge: Cambridge University Press, 2001); Subho Basu, ed., *Does Class Matter? Colonial Capital and Workers' Resistance in Bengal, 1890–1937* (New Delhi: Oxford University Press, 2004); Dipesh Chakrabarty, *Rethinking Working-Class History: Bengal 1890–1940* (Princeton, NJ: Princeton University Press, 2000).

55. Kolsky, *Colonial Justice in British India*, p. 252. Also see Martin J. Weiner, *An Empire on Trial: Race Murder, and Justice under British Rule, 1870–1935* (Cambridge: Cambridge University Press, 2009).

56. Kolsky, *Colonial Justice in British India*, p. 35.

57. Ibid., p. 266.

58. Macaulay, 'Minute on Education'.

59. Michael R. Anderson, 'Classifications and Coercions: Themes in South Asian Legal Studies in the 1980s', *South Asia Research* 10, no. 2 (November 1990): 158–177.

60. D.A. Washbrook, 'Law, State and Agrarian Society in Colonial India', *Modern Asian Studies* 15, no. 3 (July 1981): 649–721.

61. For details of the seven Law Commission reports published during 1935–1960, see India Office Records/V/26/100/11.

62. Bayly, *Empire and Information*.

63. Kim Wagner, *Amritsar 1919: An Empire of Fear and the Making of a Massacre* (New Haven, CT: Yale University Press, 2019); Mark Condos, *The Insecurity State: Punjab and the Making of Colonial Power in British India* (Cambridge: Cambridge University Press, 2017).

64. F.W. Buckler, 'The Political Theory of the Indian Mutiny', *Transactions of the Royal Historical Society* 5 (1922): 71–100.

65. Because many other regional sovereigns like the princes and the *nizam*s would owe their ultimate allegiance (in terms of belief) to the Turkish Caliphate, strictly in the religious sense.

66. Farhat Hasan, *State and Locality in Mughal India: Power Relations in Western India, c. 1572–1730* (Cambridge: Cambridge University Press, 2004), p. 144.

67. Kim Wagner, *The Skull of Alam Bheg: The Life and Death of a Rebel of 1857* (London: C. Hurst and Co. Publishers Ltd., 2017).

68. See India Office Records /V/26/100/11.

69. The members of this Law Commission were Sir John Romilly, Sir Edward Ryan, Robert Lowe, John Macpherson Macleod, William Milbourne James and Sir Robert Lush.

70. Enclosed in the Duke of Argyll's letter of 23 April 1869.

71. See India Office Records /V/26/100/11.

72. Ranajit Guha, *Dominance without Hegemony: History and Power in Colonial India*, Convergences (Cambridge, MA: Harvard University Press, 1997).

73. Taylor C. Sherman, *State Violence and Punishment in India, 1919–1956* (Abingdon: Routledge, 2010); also see Taylor C. Sherman, *Muslim Belonging in Secular India: Negotiating Citizenship in Postcolonial Hyderabad* (Cambridge: Cambridge University Press, 2015).

74. Harald Fischer-Tine and Michael Mann, *Colonialism as Civilizing Mission: Cultural Ideology in British India* (London; Anthem Press, 2004), p. 4.

75. See Nasser Hussain, *The Jurisprudence of Emergency: Colonialism and the Rule of Law* (Ann Arbor, MI: University of Michigan Press, 2009).

76. Singha, *A Despotism of Law*, p. 342.

77. Wagner, *Amritsar 1919*.

78. Condos, *The Insecurity State*.

79. Markus Daechsel, 'Zālim Ḍākū and the Mystery of the Rubber Sea Monster: Urdu Detective Fiction in 1930s Punjab and the Experience of Colonial Modernity', *Journal of the Royal Asiatic Society* 13, no. 1 (2003): 21–43.

80. See Suranjan Das, 'The "Goondas": Towards a Reconstruction of the Calcutta Underworld through Police Records', *Economic and Political Weekly* 29, no. 44 (1994): 2877–2883; Lancelot Graham, 'British India', *Journal of Comparative Legislation and International Law* 16, no. 3 (1934): 131–141; Radhika Singha, 'Punished by Surveillance: Policing "Dangerousness" in Colonial India, 1872–1918', *Modern Asian Studies* 49, no. 2 (September 2014): 241–269; Radhika Singha, 'Goonda', in *Key Concepts in Modern Indian Studies*, ed. Gita Dharampal-Frick, Monika Kirloskar-Steinbach, Rachel Dwyer and Jahnvi Phalkey, p. 95 (New York: New York University

Press, 2015); Debraj Bhattacharya, 'Kolkata "Underworld" in the Early 20th Century', *Economic and Political Weekly* 39, no. 38 (2004): 4276–4282.

81. See Taylor Sherman, William Gould and Sarah Ansari, eds., *From Subjects to Citizens: Society and the Everyday State in India and Pakistan, 1947–1970* (Delhi; New York; Cambridge: Cambridge University Press, 2014); also see Vazira Fazila-Yacoobali Zamindar, *The Long Partition and the Making of Modern South Asia: Refugees, Boundaries, Histories* (New York: Columbia University Press, 2007); Khan, *The Great Partition*.

82. See Stephen Legg, 'Dyarchy: Democracy, Autocracy, and the Scalar Sovereignty of Interwar India', *Comparative Studies of South Asia, Africa and the Middle East* 36, no. 1 (2016): 44–65.

83. See William Gould, *Bureaucracy, Community and Influence in India: Society and the State, 1930s–1960s*, Routledge Studies in South Asian History (London: Routledge, Taylor & Francis, 2010).

84. See Sherman, Gould and Ansari, *From Subjects to Citizens*; also see Zamindar, *The Long Partition and the Making of Modern South Asia*; Khan, *The Great Partition*.

85. See Legg, 'Democracy, Autocracy, and the Scalar Sovereignty of Interwar India'.

86. For literature on decolonization see D. Chakrabarty, R. Majumdar and A. Sartori, *From the Colonial to the Postcolonial: India and Pakistan in Transition* (New Delhi: Oxford University Press, 2007), p. 3; Srirupa Roy, *Beyond Belief: India and the Politics of Postcolonial Nationalism* (Durham, NC: Duke University Press, 2007), p. 27; Meera Ashar, 'Decolonising What? Categories, Concepts and the Enduring "Not Yet"', *Cultural Dynamics* 27, no. 2 (1 July 2015): 255, 262–263; Jayanta Sengupta, *At the Margins: Discourses of Development, Democracy, and Regionalism in Orissa* (New Delhi: Oxford University Press, 2015), p. 9; Partha Chatterjee, *The Politics of the Governed: Reflections on Popular Politics in Most of the World* (New York: Columbia University Press, 2004), pp. 7, 12, 29, 34, 36. (However, Ted Svensson, *Production of Postcolonial India and Pakistan* [London, Routledge, 2013], and Harshan Kumarasingham, *A Political Legacy of the British Empire: Power and the Westminster System in Post-Colonial India and Sri Lanka* [I.B. Tauris, 2013], have argued that the postcolonial state was quite dissimilar to the late colonial one, since it was a rupture rather than continuity and had starkly different South Asian characteristics to it.)

87. John Darwin, 'Imperialism in Decline? Tendencies in British Imperial Policy between Wars', *Historical Journal* 23, no. 3 (1980): 657–679.

88. Mrinalini Sinha, *Specters of Mother India: The Global Restructuring of an Empire* (Durham, NC; London: Duke University Press, 2006), pp. 23–65.

89. Kama Maclean, *A Revolutionary History of Interwar India: Violence, Image, Voice and Text* (London: Hurst & Company, 2015), pp. 1–23.

90. Ibid.

91. Ann Laura Stoler, Along the Archival Grain: Epistemic Anxieties and Colonial Common Sense (Princeton, NJ: Princeton University Press, 2009); Matthew Hull, *Government of Paper: The Materiality of Bureaucracy in Urban Pakistan* (Berkeley, CA: University of California Press, 2012); Emma Tarlo, 'Paper Truths: The Emergency and Slum Clearance through Forgotten Files', in *The Everyday State and Society in Modern India*, ed. C. Fuller and V. Benei, pp. 68–90 (Delhi: Social Science Press, 2000); Nayanika Mathur, *Paper Tiger: Law, Bureaucracy, and the Developmental State in Himalayan India* (Cambridge: Cambridge University Press, 2016).

92. Bayly, *Empire and Information*; Wagner, *Amritsar 1919*; Condos, *The Insecurity State*.

93. Harold Fischer-Tine, ed., *Anxieties, Fear and Panic in Colonial Settings: Empires on the Verge of a Nervous Breakdown* (New York: Palgrave Macmillan, 2016); Uday Singh Mehta, *Anxiety of Freedom: Imagination and Individuality: Imagination and Individuality in Locke's Political Thought* (Ithaca; London: Cornell University Press, 1992); Derek Malone, *Faith, Fallibility and the Virtue of Anxiety: An Essay in religion and Political Liberalism* (New York: Palgrave Macmillan, 2012); Gilles Delueze and Felix Guattari, *A Thousand Plateaus: Schizophrenia and Capitalism* (Minneapolis: University of Minnesota Press, 1987); Franz Neuman and Herbert Marcuse, *The Democratic and the Authoritarian State: Essays in Political and Legal Theory* (Glencoe, IL: Free Press, 1957); Achille Mbembe, 'Provisional Notes on the Postcolony', *Africa: Journal of the International African Institute* 62, no. 1 (1992): 3–37; Franz Fanon, *The Wretched of the Earth* (New York: Grove Press, 2004); Franz Fanon, *Black Skin, White Masks*, Get Political (New York: Grove Press, 2008); Frantz Fanon, *Decolonizing Madness: The Psychiatric Writings of Frantz Fanon*, ed. Nigel Gibson (London: Palgrave Macmillan, 2014); Riley Quinn, *An Analysis of Franz Fanon's The Wretched of the Earth* (London: Macat Library, 2017).

1

Invoking Exception and Defining Enemies

Extraordinary Legislation and the Colonial War on Terror in Early-Twentieth-Century India

The administration of public order in colonial India used the law by way of a twin strategy. On the one hand, it emphasised an ideological notion of 'the rule of law' whilst, on the other hand, it created a catalogue of exceptions through the delineation of certain problem categories to which the rule of law did not apply in the usual way. Ever since the formation of the first Law Commission in 1835, the colonial administrators in India argued for the necessity of a new legal code that would deliver impartial justice, even though it took until 1893 for this promise to be truly realised, eventually leading to the removal of racial exemptions to the rule of law.[1] At the same time, the operation of colonial law always remained dependent on a basic premise of exclusion. It started with creating problem categories like the Thugs and other criminal tribes in the nineteenth century. However, it later extended – as the nationalist movement was gathering force – to include, at least potentially, an entire disloyal indigenous population. The initial marking of such problem categories for the colonial state depended on a moral distinction between criminality and non-criminality. The later extension of legal exceptionalism to potentially the entire population introduced a new language of governance predicated on notions of war and emergency and a categorical separation between friends and foes in Carl Schmitt's sense. The central question that the chapter aims to investigate is the nature of the tactics that the colonial state would resort to to maintain what it termed public order. Also, can a state of exception be unleashed without a necessity? The chapter will highlight that when the authority of the colonial state was challenged, it resorted to three different tactics. It could declare an emergency, granting special powers to civil authorities; call in the military to aid the civil administration; and declare a state of martial law. The underlying logic of order was often based not on any principle of 'the rule of law' at all, but on risk-management calculations that depended once again on the demarcation of certain classes of people as problem categories. The exceptional laws designed to deal with such people involved a short-circuiting of standard procedures of law.

The authorities often argued, for instance, that the police administration was unable to collect and produce evidence against such persons, hindering the conduct of regular legal procedures. Such exceptionalism soon applied not only to certain categories of 'criminals and offenders' who could be identified in advance of any crime taking place but potentially to the entire colonised population, now perceived as the 'enemy'. One could argue that colonial governance was conducted through an 'institutionalised exception' in the nineteenth century, whereas the twentieth century saw the foundations of a 'normalised exception'. The chapter will focus on three critical political moments in the early twentieth century to show such an evolution in colonial governance. First, the Ghadar movement and the passing of the Defence of India Act, 1915, during the First World War; second, the passing of the Revolutionary Crimes Act, 1919; and finally, the Jallianwala Bagh massacre, followed by the imposition of martial law in Punjab. These events are generally studied as distinct from each other. The chapter will show a continuity in the discourse on extraordinary laws and stress that all these events require attention as part of a larger colonial discourse on extraordinary provisions of law.

Ghadar (1913–1919) and the Defence of India Act: Public Grievances, Revolutionary Diaspora and Anti-colonial Insurgency

By the beginning of the twentieth century, the colonial government in India had already witnessed significant mass resistance, not the least the activities of the Bengal revolutionaries and the Swadeshi movement. The next decade brought the First World War and the outbreak of rebellion in colonial Punjab. Unrest in colonial Punjab, like in the rest of India, had mainly been limited to conflicts and contestations amongst various classes or religious communities.[2] However, it gained a rather unusual momentum in the 1910s when the colonial government directly became the target of political and revolutionary activities during the Ghadar movement.[3] Ghadar remains one of the most significant anti-colonial revolutionary movements against the British in India. The post-Ghadar account of General O'Dwyer, the then Lieutenant-Governor of Punjab, puts the story in perspective. He understood Ghadar as a significant and dangerous threat to the British Empire.[4]

Scholars have highlighted the scope of Ghadar in numerous studies. Some have considered it a prominent case study where anti-colonial mobilisation against the British rule in India and Burma took place abroad, mainly on the west coast of North America. However, early radicalism was predominantly a north Indian phenomenon. Southeast Asia served as a major route for Ghadar attempts to infiltrate propaganda and arms into India to spark revolts and subsequently an armed insurrection against British rule.[5] Others have noted that the Ghadar movement was a convergence of many strains of thought and agitation. A movement operated by Lala Har Dayal – later on by many others, for example, Ram Chandra after 1914 – mobilised and organised Punjabi and Sikh migrant workers in North America to return to India and reproduce a rebellion along the lines of 1857.[6] Various studies have outlined the range of organisational skills of the Ghadarites in Canada and the patterns of Sikh mobilisation against British rule in India.[7] Others have elaborated on the ideological dimensions of the Ghadar Party, detailed the collaborative efforts of US, Canadian and British officials to deport the Indian radical and Ghadar Party leader Har Dayal under the anti-anarchist law in 1914 and focused on the anti-imperial character of the Ghadar movement.[8]

Studies have emphasised the mobilisation of the sepoys working for the British Raj as a critical element of Ghadar. Such studies of the soldiers of the British Empire – both Sikh and Muslim sepoys – highlight the utility of religious mobilisation to invoke rage amongst regiments of Indian soldiers in the British Army. In addition to the references made to Sikh and Muslim honour and pride at being the followers of great Gurus and Prophet Muhammad, the economic condition of the sepoy was equally relevant for his mobilisation for mutiny.[9] All such studies demonstrate the significant role Ghadar had in the anti-colonial mobilisation in India and abroad. This section utilises existing scholarship on Ghadar and further enables it by focusing on the invocation of extraordinary laws at different levels – unleashing a state of exception – activated to curtail the momentum of Ghadar. The difference of this study lies in its focus on the colonial state of exception invoked by the British administration at a crucial time when anti-colonial Ghadar mobilisation coincided with the First World War. Out of fear of rebellion, the British administration instituted extraordinary measures that did not rely on the standard rule of law.

The influence of Ghadar not only mobilised the masses in a new active and aggressive manner but also had an overt revolutionary character. Due to the economic downturn in India, many Indians, the majority of them Punjabis, sought to emigrate to North America. Noticing a massive influx of Indian immigrants, the Canadian government decided to bring in a set of laws to check the influx of South Asians. Such discrimination led to growing protests and a rise in anti-colonial sentiments, especially among the Punjabi community. It led the community to organise into new political groups. Many who had moved to the United States encountered similar problems there too.[10] Initially, they voiced grievances through a minor political organisation called the Hindustani Workers of the Pacific Coast. This organisation later became the Pacific Coast Hindustan Association and finally, in 1913, the Ghadar Party was formed under the leadership of Har Dayal and others. The Urdu word *ghadar* translates into revolt or rebellion, and the ultimate aim of this organisation was to overthrow British rule in India. A weekly paper, *Ghadar*, was started to disseminate the views of the Ghadar Party. The aggressive posture of the Ghadar Party was already spelt out with absolute clarity in its first issue from San Francisco on 1 November 1913. It carried a caption on the masthead – *Angrezi Raj ka Dushman* – which translates as 'the enemy of the British rule'. It made a foundational distinction between the colonial government and the people of India and then declared war against this newly declared existential 'enemy'. The message could not have been more explicit as the timing of the movement coincided with the outbreak of the First World War.

Men and resources from India were immediately mobilised for the British war effort. In addition to the regiments of soldiers from India deployed overseas, many ordinary Indians were mobilised as labourers to build trenches, roads and bridges and serve as porters. When Indians, mostly Sikhs and Muslims from Punjab and Gurkhas, were sent to fight in France, they experienced different racial politics – once forbidden to confront Europeans, now deployed abroad to kill 'White men'. The emergence of Ghadar and the possibility of a civil and military mutiny at the time of war was an alarming prospect. The British colonial government in India reacted by immediately creating a new law called the Defence of India Act, which came into being on 18 March 1915.[11] This Act aimed to provide for special measures to secure public safety and the defence of British India. It also offered new and speedier procedures for bringing certain offences to trial, mainly revolutionary activities.

The Defence of India Act, 1915, was a criminal law amendment that extended to entire British India. It stated that 'it shall be in force during the continuance of the present war and for a period of six months thereafter'.[12] Nevertheless, it would continue to operate beyond these temporal limits for all cases registered during its enforcement period. Also, '[l]egal proceedings pending under this Act at the time of the expiration thereof may be completed and carried into execution as if this Act has not expired'.[13] Once invoked, the law had the power to make its own rules. Invoked during the First World War, it had the power to bring almost anything under its authority. The law empowered civil and military authorities to act against any person(s), group(s) and property posing any 'threat' to British authority. It also dealt with securing harbours, trains, tracks and roads for this purpose.[14] Besides the powers to arrest and seize property, the Governor-General in Council now had the manufacture, preparation or extraction of any article or thing at his disposal. He could demand any goods of utility in the war, including the whole or any part of the output of any factory, workshop, mine or other industrial concern. The Indian industry was required by this law to 'facilitate' the war efforts of the British colonial authority in every possible way.

The Defence of India Ordinance III of 1915 was considered inadequate for the war situation and, therefore, was repealed, and the ordinance had to be modified.[15] The colonial authorities considered it insufficient to deal with the foreign threats since the revolutionaries were also actively supported and engaged by other anti-British European powers. The modified rules made under section 2 of the Defence of India Act, 1915, stipulated that any contravention thereof or any other order issued under the authority of any such rule shall be punishable by imprisonment for a term that could extend to seven years, or a fine, or both. It further stated that if the intention of the person contravening any such rule or order was to assist the King's enemies or to wage war against the King, the offence shall be punishable with death, transportation for life or imprisonment for a term that could extend to 10 years and the possible addition of a fine.[16]

Little difference remained between actual transgressions and mere suspicion under this law. For instance, section 3 of this Act stated:

> Where in the opinion of the Local Government, there are reasonable grounds for believing that any person has acted or is acting or is about to act in a manner prejudicial to the public safety, or the defence of British India, the Local Government may, by order in writing, direct such person to relocate, extern or discipline themselves and abstain from such acts.[17]

Section 6 of this law stated that any officer could direct person(s) by the general or special order of the local government to get photographed, give fingerprints, furnish the designated officer with specimens of their handwriting and signature and mark presence at the directions of the designated officer for any of the preceding purposes. Failure to comply or attempts to evade would be punishable with imprisonment, which could extend to six months or with a fine of up to 1,000 rupees or both.[18] As this was a wartime law, it enabled military authorities to make arrangements for securing public safety. However, there was an element of authoritarian compensation involved too. The law provided that the chief presidency magistrate in a presidency-town and the district magistrate elsewhere could award compensation that he thought to be reasonable to an affected person, and such awards were final.[19] The military authority held the right to access lands or buildings and temporarily suspend the right of way through such property. Refusal to comply would amount to contravention of the law. Surveillance and control of the sea, channels and rivers, placing tighter border controls that allowed frisking of baggage, post, publication, and so on, was also part of it.[20] This law activated the dormant absolutist tendencies of the colonial state.

Justice under such a law was quick and avoided the regular process. For example, section 4 of this Act specified that local governments would appoint commissioners for trials. These commissioners could be appointed for a whole province or a part of it or just for the trial of the accused persons. As per the Act, three commissioners, of whom at least two had to be persons who had served as sessions judges or additional sessions judges for a minimum of three years, could hold such trials. Others who qualified under section 2 of the Indian High Courts Act, 1861, to serve as commissioners at the trials were advocates of a High Court, advocates of a Chief Court or pleaders of 10 years' standing.[21] Suspicious of German–Hindu conspiracy and the migration of Indians to foreign countries, the colonial government had a precursor to the Defence of India Act. During the outbreak of the First World War, the Ingress Ordinance was passed in September 1914. It enabled the colonial government to detain, screen or restrict people entering or returning to India.

Meanwhile, a stridently anti-colonial tone emerged amongst Indian radicals spearheaded by the Ghadar Party. Publications with self-explanatory titles like *Ghadar-di-Gunj* (Echo of Mutiny, referring to 1857), *Ilan-i-Jang* (Declaration of War), *Naya Zamana* (The New Era) and a leaflet titled 'The Balance Sheet of British Rule in India', were considered the most controversial publications at the time. *Ghadar-di-Gunj* consisted of poems or songs and was among the first books that the Yugantar Ashram undertook to publish. In 1914, it published the first edition of 10,000 copies in Gurmukhi, followed by a later edition in Urdu. This publication exacerbated colonial anxiety to a great extent. For example, the judgment of the Lahore Conspiracy case conducted as per the Defence of India Rules described the writings of the *Ghadar-di-Gunj* as one proclaiming:

> ... The British as a nation, all white men as a race and the English Government in particular, are all maligned in a spirit born of a depraved nature. Facts are not only distorted but most maliciously perverted to appeal to the lowest passions of Indian subjects. In the most open, defiant and unmasked manner mutiny is preached. All sense of decency has given place to foulest abuse of the worst possible vulgarity. The entire pamphlet is meant to incite the masses against the British Government.... Sikhs are excited by the references to the doings of their Guru; Muhammadans are similarly excited by reference to the Balkan War, for which England is blamed. Political convicts and Hardayal are praised to the skies.[22]

Such publications openly challenged overt and covert modes of colonial self-assurance about its racial superiority and efforts to civilise the Orient. Though in a directly pejorative tone, the reciprocal classification of the colonial order questioned its aims and inverted its meanings and efforts.

Similarly, the *Ilan-i-Jang* described India as a downtrodden land trampled on by foreigners who exported and drained its produce. It further claimed that Indian soldiers were kept in the front during the war while Europeans were allowed to serve in the less dangerous rear.[23] The pamphlet explicitly urged Muslims to kill the 'pork-eaters'. It incited them against England fighting Turkey (the land of the Caliphate) while also stating the imposition of a new Khedive in Egypt. It exhorted Hindus and Muslims to make common cause and to establish a republic in India.

Naya Zamana, a pamphlet allegedly written by Har Dayal, explained the role of Congress leaders in the cycle of British oppression and attacked famous Indian leaders such as Gopal Krishna Gokhale, Pherozeshah Mehta and Dadabhai Naoroji. The argument was that these men were members of the Imperial Legislative Council headed by the British. It noted the Congress as an official assembly and its members 'flatterers' and 'timid men'. The pamphlet accused Congress members of parroting sentences they had learnt over the years and begging the British government for their rights. According to the pamphlet, such a politics could not prevent famines, reduce taxes, spread industry, administrate real justice, feed the population and control plagues. These publications were a concerted attack on Indian participation in the British colonial bureaucracy by exposing them as collaborators to the colonial project.

These pamphlets invoked a peculiar sense of history and religious pride, which often glossed over the hostility that historically existed between groups such as the Muslims and the Sikhs. The resentment against British rule was meant to unite these communities. Though Sikhs dominated the Ghadar movement, Muslims also participated in large numbers. Ghadar, as we understand it now, was a larger pan-Indian plot to inspire mutiny against British colonial rule in India during the First World War. The mutiny plot had many participants ranging from the Ghadar Party operating from San Francisco to many Indian revolutionaries working underground against the British Rule within India, the Berlin Committee comprising of Indians in Germany and the crucial support of the German Foreign Office through the German consulate in San Francisco.[24] It was why the colonial archive recorded the mutiny as the German–Hindu mutiny in some places. Hence, it was a transnational movement and involved various 'enemies' of the British Empire, both internal and external.

Ghadar attempted to appeal to and mobilise the masses and highlighted the oppressive administrative practices of the colonial government. At the dawn of the First World War, Ghadar incited soldiers to turn their guns on the British. It was a rather anxious situation for the British. The Central Investigation Department (CID), the successor to the Thuggee department, first founded in the 1830s, came in handy when it successfully infiltrated a spy named Kirpal Singh into the main group planning to launch a wider mutiny all over British India starting from Lahore on 21 February 1914.[25]

The police foiled this plan by arresting some key members, but the most 'notorious' Bengali revolutionary, Rash Behari Bose, escaped.

A special tribunal under the Defence of India Act passed in March 1915 later heard the Punjab mutiny event that occurred in 1914 and is popularly known as the Lahore Conspiracy case.[26] With 63 of the persons accused in the dock and 18 still absconding, the trial began on 26 April 1915. One of the absconders, Nidhan Singh, was arrested later and put on trial in the same case. Others were tried in supplementary cases. The final list of persons tried in the first instance numbered 82 because many absconders were arrested during the trial. The total number of approvers was 10. Only one of the accused, Umrao Singh, became an approver during the trial in the first case.[27]

The men on trial were accused of conspiring and waging war against the Crown, inside and outside India. They were accused of seducing troops to mutiny and committing dacoities. Two of them were charged with murder, abetting murder or attempting murder. Some were further accused under the Explosives Act. In this case, the number of accused was high, and due to the fears of a possible armed attempt to rescue them, the trial took place in Central Jail Lahore with no access to the general public. English newspapers of the province strongly opposed the official reporting of the proceedings and the lack of direct access to the trials. The main trial lasted from 26 April 1915 to 13 September 1915. The magnitude of the trial was enormous, as the record comprised 704 pages of printed matter containing abstracts of the statements of 404 prosecution witnesses, the statements of the accused, and abstracts of the statements of 228 defence witnesses. Later, the same tribunal tried a supplementary case. This trial began on 29 October 1915 and ended on 30 March 1916. One hundred and two accused were named in the plaint, of which 11 were absconders. Two of them were arrested after the trial had begun and sentenced to death by the tribunal in cases taken up during a postponement of the main one. In the Lahore Conspiracy case and later supplementary cases up to 1919, there were 154 persons tried in total. Twenty-four were acquitted, 19 hanged, 55 transported for life and 56 awarded lesser sentences of rigorous imprisonment.[28] There were other cases related to Ghadar, but the Lahore Conspiracy case demonstrates the scope of such trials under the Defence of India Act.

A similar case, popularly known as the Delhi Conspiracy case, further sheds light on the nature and scope of the invocation of Defence of India Rules.[29] While hearing the Delhi Conspiracy case, Sir Donald Campbell Johnstone on 10 February 1915 stated the amended[30] charges against the 11 accused persons:

> That you between 27th day of March, 1913, and 31st March, 1914, both at Delhi and Lahore and other places in British India, did agree with one another, and other persons unknown, to commit the offence of murder under section 302, Indian Penal Code, and that you were thereby parties to a criminal conspiracy to commit the offence of murder, to wit the murder of Ram Padarath, was committed at Lahore on 17th May, 1913, and that you thereby committed offences punishable under sections 302/102-B and 302/109 of the Indian Penal Code within my cognisance.[31]

The case to which the current case was an appeal lasted from 21 May 1914 to 1 September, and on 5 October, court orders acquitted five of the accused persons[32] and convicted the other six[33] under section 302/102-B, IPC. The court sentenced three to death[34] and three to transportation for life.[35] Simultaneously, the court tried two of the accused on a charge under sections 4, 5 and 6 of Act VI of 1908 (Explosive Substances Act)[36] in connection with a bomb cap allegedly found in their possession on 16 February 1914 and found them guilty and sentenced them to transportation for 20 years under section 4 of the Act. Though the finding of the bomb cap came from a different case, it was sufficient to frame them under the extraordinary law.[37] The court created a convenient narrative by linking evidence. It concluded that 'reasonable ground' existed for believing that the accused had joined hands in a conspiracy to wage war against the British Crown and procured arms in Europe for the conspiracy. It added that the accused collected money in Calcutta (now known as Kolkata) for the objective and persuaded other persons to join their conspiracy in Bombay (now known as Mumbai). They published writings advocating their objective in Agra and transmitted from Delhi to Kabul the money collected at Calcutta. To prove the complicity of the accused, the investigating agencies used a letter containing the account of the conspiracy as evidence.[38]

The details of the Lahore and Delhi Conspiracy cases demonstrate not only the scope of the use of the Defence of India Act to curtail anti-colonial activities but also the narrative and level of threat the colonial government perceived. Throughout the trial, crimes such as murder or abetting murder – that could have been tried under ordinary criminal law – took a prominent place. The broader Ghadar movement, along with the

Lahore and Delhi Conspiracies, made the colonial government paranoid. As the preceding description proves, the geographical scope of the anti-colonial mobilisation traversed provinces and involved frontier territories. Sovereign anxiety armed with special provisions, it appears, exaggerated plots to the extent where they appeared as grand conspiracies. It allowed the colonial administration to exhibit its surveillance capacities, consistent attention to detail, and force to control all things within its limits.

The main trigger for the Ghadar panic came from overseas in the shape of the deportation of Indians from Canada and the United States. The iconic case of the ship *Komagata Maru* requires some contextualisation in the ongoing discussion. It was chartered by a Sikh, Gurdit Singh, carrying many Indians, mostly Punjabi Sikhs and some Muslims, and others, from Manila, Hong Kong, Shanghai, Moji and Yokohoma. All of them attempting to emigrate to Canada were denied entry. When the ship arrived at Vancouver on 24 May 1914, the emigrants were told that no one could alight except for former residents and some students. An appeal against this order was made in the case of one passenger, Mansa Singh, and taken up at Victoria as a test case to decide the fate of all the passengers.[39]

Meanwhile, Indians in Canada held many mass meetings discussing the situation. On 17 July 1914, orders were passed in the case of Mansa Singh, and his appeal was rejected. Orders of deportation were then served on all the passengers, but they acted defiantly, locked up the captain and his officers, and refused to allow the ship to leave. On 19 July, the immigration authorities attempted to board the ship to regain control but were prevented from boarding it by the people on board.[40] Later, the immigrants agreed to carry out the orders of the authorities to depart[41] if they were provided with sufficient supplies for their voyage.[42] Supplies were sent on board,[43] and the ship left with orders to proceed directly to Hong Kong.[44] This ship was later dealt with under the Ingress into India Ordinance.

The passengers on the ship were aggrieved after the contestation and confrontation with Canadian authorities in Vancouver. It was evident to the colonial authorities that such a distressed crowd of 300 failed emigrants (with Ghadar in the background) could constitute a serious challenge to public tranquillity if permitted to land in Calcutta and left to find their way to Punjab unassisted. Their arrival could easily trigger a renewed agitation over Indian migration to other colonies. Therefore, it was decided to make use of the Ingress into India Ordinance and organise the immediate return of the passengers to Punjab under strict government control, with a special train arranged at government expense. In the wake of the First World War, owing to fears that war conditions might provoke 'enemies within' to plot armed insurrection against the British government with support from outside, the government promulgated the Ingress into India Ordinance, 1914, and the Defence of India (Criminal Law Amendment) Act IV of 1915. The Ingress Ordinance authorised the government to seclude 'foreigners' from the local population and restrict Indians arriving from foreign countries to certain areas. Furthermore, it directed restraining the influx of Indian revolutionaries, mostly Ghadarites, from abroad. Under this measure, thousands of Sikhs returning to Punjab from abroad were now under surveillance and scrutiny.[45]

The then Lieutenant-Governor of Punjab, Sir Michael O'Dwyer, noted that such extraordinary laws were the primary 'safeguards' available to the colonial administration against the 'returning Ghadar conspirators'.[46] He referred to the scenario for British officials in India as 'living over a mine full of explosives'.[47] Ghadarites had appealed to Punjabis and Sikhs living in North America to return to India to participate in an organised mass revolt against British rule. The prospect of the arrival of thousands of Ghadarites back into India was a major concern for the British officials. The circulation of Indian migrants and the revolutionary anti-colonial political mobilisation across the Pacific, even before the First World War, served as a pretext for the British colonial state to strengthen its exceptional character and expand it in the name of 'national security'.[48] By 1917, the United States and the British Indian states had enacted laws aimed precisely at the mobility and activism of Indians. Gurdit Singh and some of his immediate followers were to be detained at Ludhiana pending enquiries into the circumstances of the voyage of the *Komagata Maru*.

Four Sikh police officers and one British police officer from Punjab were deputed to deal with the passengers of the ship. A district magistrate was sent to Calcutta to represent the Punjab government with full powers under Ordinance V of 1914 to deal with these passengers. The ship arrived at the mouth of the Hugli on the evening of 26 September with 321 passengers on board and was detained at Kalpi, almost 6 miles below Diamond Harbour. On 27 and 28 September, the ship and its passengers were searched for arms. On 29 September, the ship was brought up the river to Budge Budge, where a special train to Punjab was waiting for them. The passengers refused to disembark from the ship and stated that they would only land at Howrah. They declined to travel by special train. What is important here is that the passengers of the *Komagata Maru* were neither under arrest nor convicts or accused, or even foreigners. Therefore, the grounds of their transportation on a special train to Punjab were flimsy. However, the Ingress Ordinance made them available – as potentially dangerous immigrants – for scrutiny and surveillance to the colonial state. Altercations between the police and some of the passengers led to a violent confrontation and later firing.[49] A riot followed, leading to the death of a European officer of the Calcutta Police, a head constable and a constable of the Punjab police, a shopkeeper, a Bengali spectator and an officer of the Eastern Bengal State Railway. Three of the officials were wounded, including three sergeants of the Calcutta Police, one Indian officer and four men of the Punjab police. A cordon was placed around Calcutta to capture the passengers who escaped from the ship following the riot. By 11 October, 201 of the rioters were captured. Of the 321 passengers on the *Komagata Maru*, 62 had left quietly for Punjab, and 18 had been killed or had died of wounds; 1 drowned, 9 were in the hospital and 202 interned in jail under the Ingress Ordinance.[50] The colonial government's response to the arrival of the passengers of the *Komagata Maru* at Calcutta highlights the flimsy reasons guided by paranoia that the government invoked to deal with the already disgruntled emigrants. As a result, the passengers of the *Komagata Maru* would now fit the colonial classification of Indian immigrants (all potentially Ghadarites) returning from North America as dangerous, seditious and therefore mutinous. The following section will discuss how even after the end of the First World War, the late colonial government in India continued to promulgate another set of extraordinary laws to deal with what it called 'revolutionary crime'. Initially, the focus of restrictions was on potential Ghadrites, who were planning a mutiny and had recently returned from North America. Soon, it extended to the rest of the population too who began to be perceived as potentially conspiring against the colonial government in India by possibly providing support to the Ghadrites. A civilian version of the Defence of India Act was enacted in the form of the Rowlatt Bills.

There Is No 'Outside' of War: 'Revolutionary Crimes Act', 1919, and the Normalising of Exception in Colonial India

With immaculate structures of intelligence-gathering in place and the swift use of extraordinary laws like the Defence of India Act and the Ingress into India Ordinance, the colonial government successfully dealt with the Ghadarites. However, an explosive movement like Ghadar was bound to influence the broader nationalist movement in India, which was gathering pace against British colonialism. The spillover effect of Ghadar required containment in every possible way. The emergency triggered by Ghadar would exceed the time frame of emergency legislation limited to the First World War and the conclusion of the Delhi and Lahore Conspiracy trials. Though the Defence of India Act was supposed to continue for only six months after the declaration of peace, the colonial administration had plans for a longer term. A committee was already working on a report that assessed the situation of revolutionary crimes in India. As a result, the Revolutionary Crimes Act, 1919, replaced the Defence of India Rules, 1915. The following section analyses the politics around the promulgation of the Revolutionary Crimes Act, 1919, and will show that it enabled the normalisation of a state of exception and extraordinary laws in late colonial India.

Following the events of Ghadar, in the name of dealing with 'anarchical and revolutionary crime', the colonial government in India started the process of passing the Anarchical and Revolutionary Crimes Act, popularly known as the Rowlatt Acts. It owed its name to Justice Sidney Arthur Taylor Rowlatt. He was the president of a sedition committee already set up in December 1917 by the British colonial government to examine and analyse political terrorism in India. The colonial government decided to appoint the commission to draft laws based on its recommendations. The committee consisted of five members. Justice Rowlatt, who was a prominent judge of the King's Bench Division, was its president. It had two British and two Indian members. The British members were the Chief Justice of Bombay and a member of the Board of Revenue in the United Provinces. The two Indian members were a judge of the Madras High Court and an additional member of the Bengal Legislative Council. The committee presented their recommendations, later approved by the Governor-General in Council and finally assented to by the Secretary of State for India.[51]

The committee's findings gave birth to the infamous Rowlatt Acts, which replaced the Defence of India Act. The report identified dangerous conspiracies in Bengal, which also engendered murders and robberies sustained by persistent propaganda conducted by young men belonging to the educated middle classes in India. Chitpavan Brahmins stirring

Maratha nationalism was another source of disturbance in the Bombay Presidency. Insurgency in Punjab by emigrants who returned from America was mentioned as an additional source of disturbance against colonial rule.[52] While the Defence of India Act, 1915, was a wartime law and therefore 'emergency' in nature, the Rowlatt Acts were proposed to be permanent and meant as a reincarnation of the Defence of India Act for 'normal' times. The colonial administration exhibited the desire to deal with everyday crime under emergency laws. The Rowlatt Bills were met with great opposition during the debates in the Imperial Council and other official forums. To aid deliberations and dispel public suspicion, Oxford University Press brought out a booklet explaining the details of the Act. The contents of this booklet are vital because they neatly laid out the administrative position of the colonial government.

By explaining the context of the situation in question, the booklet foregrounded that 'India is swept by a storm of political feeling … which is difficult to account for'.[53] The Ghadar movement created minor conspiracy cases and resulted in entire regiments revolting randomly against the British in numerous places. Protests all over India erupted, with activists and nationalist leaders voicing their fears that the Act would be used to silence political dissent against the colonial government. Humphrey Milford, who published the booklet, asserted that most people opposing the Rowlatt Acts had never read it. He wrote:

> A little while ago, in Nasik, a political agitator who had spoken vehemently against the bill admitted in conversation with a Government officer that he has never read it. This was indeed a case of blind leading the blind. Are thoughtful Indians going to be content with such second-hand ignorance (we cannot call it knowledge)? Or will they read or judge for themselves?[54]

Milford warned readers that they would encounter words like 'anarchical and revolutionary crime' later in the booklet. He proceeded to define what the Act was directed against precisely. Most of such 'crimes' were directly connected to the aim of overthrowing the government. While challenging the prevalent claims against the Rowlatt Acts, Milford elaborated that neither (*a*) orderly rational criticism of the government and the peaceable expression of political opinion nor (*b*) criminal offences not committed from political, anti-government motives were included under the definition of 'anarchical and revolutionary crime'. The booklet contended that the rise in revolutionary terrorism in Bengal a decade earlier could not impact the colonial government in any substantial way. However, it did render unsafe the life and property of innocent and peace-loving citizens.

Activities that fell under the purview of the Rowlatt Acts were divided into two classes: (*a*) murders – by members of revolutionary gangs – of officials and police officers who in some way or the other had made themselves obnoxious to them and (*b*) dacoities, that is, organised and violent robberies, carried out with the object of securing funds for the furtherance of revolutionary schemes and often accompanied by murder or attempts to murder. The Rowlatt Acts were a law devised for all of India and would give vast powers to the local government to deal with almost any oppositional situation.

Milford's analysis, quite similar to the colonial government's statements, was not shy of pointing out that the ordinary laws could not deal with such a situation due to the difficulty of procuring evidence, the intimidation of witnesses, and delays in standard legal procedure. The effect of these obstacles, according to Milford, was that anarchical crime made swift headway against the authorities because a greater proportion of the 'criminals' were difficult to book and prosecute. Many of those tried had to be released, though guilty, because of the lack of proper legal evidence. Furthermore, it emphasised that the assumption that the government failed in its duty of protecting law and order and safeguarding the life and possessions of its people was not owing to any lack of zeal on its part, but simply due to the 'defective state of law' when it came to 'anarchical and revolutionary crime'.

It claimed that the Ghadar movement and the Lahore and Delhi Conspiracy cases had provided British authorities with alarming facts and evidence that 'seditious' societies in India were in league with German agents to overthrow British power. It reminded the readers that the colonial government had promptly adopted strong measures and claimed certain special powers, incorporated in the Defence of India Act of March 1915. The rules under this Act, even though more stringent than the new Rowlatt Acts, Milford's booklet asserted, were accepted by the country in general without any protest, given that the invocation of these rules supplemented war efforts. The Defence of India Act gave the authorities facilities for the prompt arrest and internment of persons known to be dangerous and arranged for their speedy trials by special tribunals. As a result, the government used the Defence of India Act to deal with revolutionary activities in Punjab and Bengal. Milford's booklet argued:

[T]he effect of these wise measures for the defence of the country against both its internal and its foreign enemies was immediate and startling. Anarchy in Bengal and elsewhere was practically stamped out, a dangerous plot for the importation of German arms and a general revolt in India was detected and thwarted, and, in a word India during the wars was enabled to enjoy the blessings, the order and the commercial well-being of peace, without any interference in the rights and liberties of her law-abiding subjects.[55]

Such laws were based on a Schmittian 'friend' and 'foe' distinction. Any activity, be it the conspiracies to overthrow the colonial government or collaboration with Germans, would invite action under this law. The rest, who had the interest of the colonial government in mind and a love for peace, would come under the 'friend' category and had nothing to worry about.

As discussed earlier, the Defence of India Act was a war measure and was to remain in force for only six months after the termination of the war. The colonial government felt that on its removal, the government might have to face a new outburst of opposition activity resembling the 'terrorism' in Bengal from the years before the war. The colonial government was not convinced that ordinary laws or the Code of Criminal Procedure (CrPC) could deal with such acts, persons or groups. Various pro-government sections increasingly perceived ordinary laws as utterly inadequate to deal with the danger faced by the British colonial government in India. The powers granted to the authorities under the Rowlatt Acts, as discussed earlier, highlight its exceptional character. The Rowlatt Acts gave vast powers to the government under special and carefully defined conditions for dealing with 'anarchical and revolutionary movements'. The remit of this could be exceedingly wide – not only offences against the state, such as waging war, conspiring to overthrow the government, and so on, but also more common offences against persons and property, such as rioting with deadly weapons, murder, robbery, dacoity, damaging roads and bridges, house-breaking, criminal intimidation and various offences connected with the use of explosives and arms, provided that such offences now connected with 'anarchical and revolutionary movements'.[56] Given the context of a raging anti-colonial mobilisation, all acts of resistance could potentially come under the Act.

Once the Act came into existence, it was to remain in force for three years from the date of the termination of the war and extended to the whole of British India. The pamphlet warned people from rushing to hasty conclusions and urged them to read the first section of each of the three main parts of the Act, where it was 'clearly and expressly' stipulated that the special powers offered by the Act to local governments should not come into force in any part of the country unless the Viceroy in Council (that is after due deliberation with his British and Indian advisers) would decide that 'anarchical or revolutionary movements' were being promoted in that part. The situation was severe enough to warrant the application of some or all of the special provisions of the Act to that region of the country. Once again, it was stressed that the Act did not apply to 'ordinary criminal offences' but only to those included in a 'special schedule'. However, how common offences could get interpreted as offences in the 'special schedule' remained a significant source of ambiguity.

One cannot overlook Milford's observation and approach when he noted:

> Indeed it is possible, and even, we hope, probably, that no part of India may ever be subjected to it. It is a measure to be used in an emergency only and against a particularly dangerous class of criminals; just as a wealthy man who saw a robber entering his room, might seize up a stick with which to defend his property and life. He might even, if he were wise, keep such a weapon handy in case of need. And if he did so, would his family and his friends have a right to consider themselves insulted and mistrusted? Obviously, the only people who would ever need to fear it would be his enemies.[57]

Such an assurance comes with a warning – a notice to correct oneself and fall in line with the current order. Otherwise, anybody could fall into the category of a seditious criminal. Milford's booklet took great pains to explain '[w]hat the Act is not'. In the nationalist discourse, the Act was a measure that gave special and tyrannical powers to the police and robbed Indians of free speech and imposed restrictions on the expression of political opinion. Contrary to such nationalist apprehensions, Milford took pains to explain and assure that the government would not arrest people without reason, and only a speech, publication or newspaper article that incited the people to outrage and rebellion would most probably come under the schedule. He also added that there was nothing new in the prohibition of such speeches or writings. They had been criminal offences for the last four years already. Many sections of this law were already available to the authorities as part of the CrPC. However, as an emergency measure, the Act had acquired the power to strike terror in the minds of nationalist and revolutionary persons and groups in colonial India. At the same time, there were high expectations that the war would bring reforms to the colonial state, which it did in the form of the Montagu–Chelmsford reforms later. The Rowlatt Acts were an extraordinary law conferring special powers on the government in 'exceptional cases'. Milford was confident of the safeguards the Rowlatt Acts contained and therefore argued that the Acts could 'harm neither the purse, nor the liberty, nor the dignity, of any good citizen of India'.[58] The image of a good, obedient, disciplined, non-revolutionary citizen was clearly stated in these laws. Whoever would decide otherwise had to be ready for the 'consequences'.

The Rowlatt Acts, being a civilian version of the Defence of India Act, made possible the swift transition of exceptional laws – until now primarily a sovereign prerogative – into extraordinary laws, which would still be exceptional but, in contrast to the Defence of India Act, now available to the civilian government. The nature of the laws suitable for operating exclusively to deal with the challenges of war was modified to suit the purposes of civilian administration. Even though the Rowlatt Acts were repealed three years later, in 1922, they paved the way for the rise of a forceful surveillance state. They succeeded in further enabling the dark side of extraordinary colonial laws to be used thereafter. Such laws normalised the capacity of the colonial state to use the 'maxim' of exception permanently. The message was that the late colonial state in India could not only do everything but anything to protect its authority. The following section takes the discussion forward by discussing 'martial laws', a scenario where the civilian administration failed to maintain law and order and requested military assistance. Consequently, if the situation got further out of control, the military could take over complete control of the administration from the civilian administrative machinery. Such laws, again, were exceptional and enlighten us about the various layers in which exception was invoked in colonial India.

Legality and Moral Legitimacy: Satyagraha, Martial Law and the Massacre at Jallianwala Bagh

The Rowlatt Acts finally got passed despite the unanimous opposition of all non-official members of the Imperial Council.[59] Vast sections of the Indian population and their political leadership became agitated about the government's indifference to their opposition to the Rowlatt Acts. As part of the collective response, Mohan Das Karamchand Gandhi started a *satyagraha* (literally, insistence on truth) on 23 March 1919 to oppose the Rowlatt Acts. An all-India *hartal* (strike) day on 6 April 1919 was declared to be observed with 24 hours of fasting and suspension of business. On 1 March 1919, Gandhi, in a statement to the press, opposed the Rowlatt Acts. His statement is of great relevance to the broader argument of the chapter in particular and the book in general. The report of the Rowlatt Committee, while taking stock of revolutionary crimes in India, had opined that secret violence was confined to 'isolated and very small parts of India' and 'to a microscopic body of the people'.

Gandhi responded that although the existence of such men was indeed a danger to society, the Rowlatt Bills would affect the whole of India and its people. For Gandhi, the design of the Bills laid bare a colonial conspiracy of arming the government with powers out of all proportion to its stated aims. In other words, Gandhi – himself a lawyer – is pointing out the capabilities of such extraordinary laws. He was aware of the sweeping powers this law would grant the government. It would make the distinction between ordinary and extraordinary disappear or make it so porous that ordinary crimes could get interpreted as a part of the revolutionary conspiracy. For Gandhi, the Rowlatt Bills were a greater danger than revolutionary crime itself. He argued that millions of Indians were by nature the 'gentlest people on the earth'. He further considered the Bills to be 'the unmistakable symptom of the deep-seated disease in the governing body'.[60] While pleading with the government to use 'ordinary laws' to deal with revolutionary crime, he exhorted that a potent 'remedy' like the Rowlatt Bills should only be prescribed once all the milder ones had been tried. His use of the metaphor of the body to signify the body politic is noteworthy here. Without contesting the colonial concerns of revolutionary crime, Gandhi seemed concerned at the possibility of terming any opposition to the colonial state as 'revolutionary' and inviting action under the Rowlatt Bills. It could endanger his advocacy of non-violent protests and peaceful demonstrations. British administrators indeed were not likely to listen to his spiritual and moral advice; instead, they were the makers of an empire that had violence at its heart and legality in its head. The anti-Rowlatt Acts political mobilisation resorted to *satyagraha*. The *satyagraha* vow against the Rowlatt Acts was as follows:

> Being conscientiously of the opinion that the Bills known as the Indian Criminal Law (Amendment) Bill No. 1 of 1919 and the Criminal Law (Emergency Powers) Bill No. 2 of 1919 are unjust, subversive of the

principle of liberty and justice and destructive of the elementary rights of individuals, on which the safety of the community as a whole and the State itself is based, we solemnly affirm that in the event of these Bills becoming law and until they are withdrawn, we shall refuse civilly to obey those laws and such other laws as a committee to be hereafter appointed may think fit and we further affirm that in this struggle we will faithfully follow the truth and refrain from violence to life, person or property.[61]

Despite nationwide opposition, the Rowlatt Bills were passed into law on 18 March 1919. It was carried by the 35 government votes and opposed by 20 out of 25 non-official Indians. In total, 187 amendments were proposed by the Indian members, and the official bloc defeated every one of them.[62] Leaders such as Jinnah, Aiyangar, Mazharul Haque, Khaparde, Sunder Singh and Zulfiqar Ali, who all along strongly opposed the Bill, were absent as a mark of protest on the last day of voting.[63] Meanwhile, Gandhi was welcomed in Madras on 18 March and 20 March 1919 by a huge mass meeting following his call for *satyagraha*. Gandhi opposed the Rowlatt Bills but described the character of the western form of government peculiarly in his speech of 20 March, which one Mr Desai read because Gandhi was not feeling well. Gandhi's message stated:

> By demonstrating to the party of violence the infallible power of *satyagraha* and by giving them ample scope for their inexhaustible energy we hope to wean that party from the suicidal method of violence.[64]

Gandhi's message rejected Sir William's contention that the movement had great potential for 'evil' and retorted that it had only a potential for good. The appeal constituted an attempt to revolutionise politics and restore moral force to its original importance. After all, the government did not believe in a principled avoidance of violence or physical force. It, in a way, operated on a Weberian logic where only the state had the monopoly over the use of physical force. Gandhi emphasised that the ultimate principle of western modes of governance represented by the colonial government of India was succinctly expressed by President Woodrow Wilson in his speech delivered to the Versailles Peace Conference at the time of introducing the League of Nations Covenant, where he said:

> Armed force is in the background in this programme, but it is in the background, and if the moral force of the world will not suffice, physical force of the world shall.[65]

Gandhi denounced physical force and affirmed the supremacy of moral force, which, according to him, India possessed and the west did not. Though Gandhi had already announced *satyagraha*, the first real confrontation occurred on 23 March 1919 when Gandhi gave a call for an 'All India *Hartal* to be observed on 6 April 1919 against the Rowlatt Acts.[66] Gandhi issued four significant instructions for the observance of this *hartal*, which included *satyagraha*, 24-hour fasting, suspension of all work other than those necessary in the public interest and, finally, public meetings all over India would pass resolutions for the withdrawal of these Bills. All instructions aimed at a moral, non-violent mobilisation of the anti-colonial sentiment.

Another message from Gandhi read to a mass meeting in Madras on 30 March 1919 draws our attention to the framework of his understanding of *satyagraha* and its relation to law and order. The message read:

> A *satyagrahi* is nothing if not instinctively law-abiding, it is his law-abiding nature which exacts from him implicit obedience of the highest law, i.e., the voice of conscience, which over-rides all other laws. His civil disobedience even of certain law is only seeming disobedience. Every law gives the subject an option either to obey the primary sanction or the secondary; and I venture to suggest that the *satyagrahi* by inviting the secondary sanction obeys the law. He does not act like the ordinary offender who not only commits a breach of the laws of the land, whether good or bad, but wishes to avoid the consequences of that breach.[67]

Gandhi's statement and positive expectation of justice from the law are interesting from a critical legal perspective. In his famous essay 'Force of Law', Jacques Derrida has worked out a logic of operations of the law.[68] Derrida argued that since modern law is neither foundational nor anti-foundational, it is a law not because it is just but because it has force. It has the quality of enforcing itself. Initially, Gandhi's calls for *satyagraha* were opposed by some prominent sections like the left-wing of the Congress and the leaders of the Home Rule movement. It was a time when Gandhi had not yet become a national leader. It was only after the events of 1919 that Gandhi began to dominate the national scene completely. Some of it is attributable to how events unfolded. Gandhi's political approach distinguished him from many others. The element of obedience and discipline in Gandhi's exhortations is noticeable. It appears that Gandhi was quite aware of the scope of exceptional laws yet moralised conduct by referring to the conscience. He appealed to the masses to accept the consequences of the law rather than avoiding them.

Satyagraha committees were formed in every part of India. The *satyagrahi*s of Delhi made arrangements to observe Sunday, 30 March 1919, as a day of self-humiliation and prayer among the citizens of Delhi under the guidance of Swami Shradhananda, popularly known as Mahatma Munshi Ram of the Haridwar Gurukul School. It was also a protest meeting against the government's passing of the Rowlatt Bills.[69] On 30 March, as proposed by the Delhi *satyagrahi*s, no shops were opened, and the few that did speedily closed at the organisers' requests. After accomplishing a shutdown of bazaars and transport, some workers proceeded to the railway station to persuade the shopkeepers to comply with the call for *hartal*. The shopkeepers refused to close their shops and argued that their contracts bound them to keep them open. It resulted in a minor altercation, after which the police took two of the demonstrators into custody. Delhi was already observing *hartal*, and the news of the arrest led to more people rushing to the spot to request the police to release the arrested. The police rejected their request and caned the crowd. As a result, a clash ensued.

When the police were unable to control the growing size of the protestors, intimation was sent to the administration seeking its support to handle the situation. An additional district magistrate arrived at the spot with a small military force and two machine guns by noon. He ordered the crowd to disperse, which the protestors defied. Following this, the machine gun was fired first in the air and then on the crowd, killing a few and wounding more. The crowd withdrew to the Queen's Garden, Clock Tower and the Chandni Chowk area. It then tried to enter the garden of the municipality to form a procession but the military guarding the building fired on them, killing a few protestors and wounding many more. It was an extreme response from the authorities. The number of dead was around eight. Mahatma Munshi Ram arrived on the spot and pacified the crowd by explaining to them what had happened. By the afternoon, the number of protestors had reached around ten thousand. The district magistrate and commissioner were expecting more violence from the crowd and told Mahatma Munshi to at once call off the gathering as it posed a danger to public peace. Mahatma Munshi explained that the gathering would only observe peaceful protest and took responsibility for peace and order if any untoward incident happened after that. After Mahatma Munshi Ram pleaded with the crowd to follow the principle of *satyagraha* and protest non-violently, the crowd agreed to observe a peaceful protest. Despite experiencing military firing and deaths, this meeting concluded with a peaceful passing of a resolution protesting the Rowlatt Bills. The meeting terminated and later the crowd dispersed by 6 p.m.[70]

Though 30 March 1919 had passed off without further protests after the military firing, the following day there was tension when people demanded the dead bodies of those killed in the firing from the police and refused to open their shops in protest. After much pleading and soliciting, the Chief Commissioner, Mr Barron, ordered the release of the dead bodies. Delhi mourned on 31 March, and both Hindus and Muslims performed the last rites for their dead, with thousands participating in the funerals.[71] Later in the evening, on 31 March, a citizens' conference was held where a private and independent enquiry commission was appointed to record evidence and report on the incident. It consisted of Rai Saheb Piyare Lal, Hazi-ul-Mulk, Hakim Ajmal Khan, Rai Bahadur Sultan Singh and others. A committee of 16 members was also appointed to help them secure evidence for the preparation of this report. In a press statement, Gandhi, who was visiting Madras, condemned the firing on Delhi protestors.[72] He said that 'local authorities in Delhi have made use of a blacksmith hammer to crush a fly'.[73] The Delhi Satyagraha Sabha decided that the city had already suffered in the *hartal* of 30 March and should be spared participation in the *hartal* planned for 6 April 1919. However, on 6 April, Delhi observed a total shutdown like the rest of India. People defied government orders by organising mass gatherings and distributing prohibited *satyagraha* newspapers. Following the success of the 6 April *hartal*, Gandhi issued a message that said:

> We are now in a position to expect to be arrested at any moment. It is, therefore, necessary to bear in mind that if anyone is arrested, he should, without causing any difficulty, allow himself to be arrested, and if summoned to appear before a Court, he should do so.[74]

A more significant part of this message directed people not to offer any defence or engage any pleaders if they got arrested. If they were fined as an alternative to imprisonment, people should opt for imprisonment.[75] On a characteristic note, Gandhi also wanted the *satyagrahi*s to follow prison rules if arrested because he stated that the current campaign did not aim to reform prisons. His emphasis is an attempt to demonstrate that the truth of the illegitimacy of colonial law could be highlighted by following the law. His advice was to first violate the 'untruthful' law in the service of upholding truth – *satyagraha* – through a peaceful protest in the first place and yet follow the rules once a prisoner in jail. Gandhi appears to be quite aware that anti-colonial protests could succeed by challenging colonial law through simple, straightforward and precise issues. The political move to hold an all-India *hartal* based on *satyagraha* protests against colonial repression exposed the myth of the forceful colonial laws. It enabled the emergence of a unique counter-tactic in the form of *satyagraha* to challenge the nature of colonial legality.

The most prominent of these all-India *hartal*s was the one at Lahore in Punjab. On 2 April, the superintendent of police issued a notice requiring the convenors of processions and meetings to apply for a licence not later than 10 a.m. the previous day. The government passed orders against two famous leaders, Dr Satyapal, a medical practitioner, and Dr Saif-ud-Din Kitchlew, bar-at-law, prohibiting them from addressing any public meetings.[76] On the *satyagraha* day, that is, 6 April, a meeting was scheduled at Bradlaugh Hall, which generated a difference of opinion among the local leaders after the administration put official pressure on them to abandon the event. On 2 April, after deliberations at a meeting, two options were proposed. Ratan Chand moved for the cancellation of the Bradlaugh Hall meeting. At the same time, Dev Raj Sawhney urged that the meeting should go ahead as planned, given that the protest against the Rowlatt Acts was far more important than any other consideration. Proposals were put to the vote, and the latter proposal to go ahead with the meeting was adopted 18 to 2. As per the plan, on 6 April, all businesses were suspended in Lahore and shops were closed without exception. The leaders of the *hartal* in Lahore managed to keep the situation largely peaceful despite the intensity of the agitation and slogans against the Rowlatt Acts.

The participation of Hindus, Muslims and Sikhs in large numbers was a salient feature of the protest. The Bradlaugh Hall meeting was supposed to take place at 5 p.m. but began earlier as the hall was packed. Three overflowing meetings were also held simultaneously in the adjoining grounds outside the hall. Pandit Rambhuj Dutt addressed the meeting in the hall, and a resolution entreating the King-Emperor to disallow the Rowlatt Bills was passed. It recorded the Bills as constituting a direct insult to millions of his law-abiding and loyal subjects in India. Three more resolutions were passed. They voiced disapproval of the repressive orders against Dr Satyapal, Dr Kitchlew and others, strong disapproval of the recent firing on unarmed civilians by the Delhi authorities and, finally, a resolution requested the president of the meeting to forward the resolutions passed to the Secretary of State for India, the Viceroy and the Lieutenant-Governor of Punjab.

Mahatma Gandhi was travelling from Bombay to reach Delhi on 9 April but was arrested at an earlier station, Palwal, and sent back to Bombay. He was ordered not to enter Punjab or Delhi but restrict himself to Bombay. News of Gandhi's arrest spread like wildfire and caused great resentment amongst the people in Lahore, Amritsar and Delhi.[77] Allegedly, Gandhi was arrested on instructions from the Punjab government. A peculiar autocratic character of the colonial administration started to emerge barely a month after the Rowlatt Acts were passed, which confirmed the concerns voiced during the Rowlatt agitations in March 1919 and raised questions about whether a non-violent approach to colonial repression was a feasible one.

The government in Punjab intended to break the momentum of *satyagraha* in the province. The Deputy Commissioner, Amritsar, called two popular leaders of Punjab, Dr Satyapal and Dr Kitchlew, to his house and arrested them. News of their arrest spread quickly, and all the shops shut down by noon. By 12.30 in the afternoon, a large procession marched towards the residence of the Deputy Commissioner, intending to make a representation for the release of their leaders. The crowd was fired upon and forced back.

Meanwhile, another massive crowd marched to the business area of the city. They burnt the National Bank, the Chartered Bank, the Alliance Bank, the Town Hall, the Mission Church and the depot of the Punjab Religious Book Society. They also attacked and killed European officials (Mr Stewart and Mr Scott) of the National Bank and (Mr G.M. Thomson) of the Alliance Bank.[78] The telegraph office was also attacked and was rescued by soldiers from a Pathan regiment sent to the spot. Dr Easdon, a lady doctor working at the Municipal Zenana Hospital, was also attacked. She had to hide in a closet for hours after being rescued by her Indian friends. Sergeant Rowland, a cantonment electrician, was killed near Rego Bridge while walking towards the fort. Robinson, an ex-Northumberlander Fusilier serving as a railway guard, was beaten to death with *lathi*s in the goods yard. Another woman, Nurse Sherwood, was also injured. The situation in Amritsar was now out of hand. Europeans were terrified and running for their lives, and any of them unfortunate enough to be spotted by the protestors was dealt with immediately. Most pertinently, in the newspaper reports, the Europeans attacked or killed had their names mentioned. In contrast, Indians who were killed by the police or the military remained nameless and found mention simply as the 'riotous mob' in subsequent government reports.

When the riot occurred, the garrison in Amritsar consisted of one company of Somerset Light Infantry under the charge of Captain Massey, half a company of Garrison Artillery and the 12th Ammunition Column. Since extraordinary laws like the Rowlatt Bills were now at the disposal of the colonial administration and revolutionary crime a stated enemy, additional forces were mustered to control the situation. On its way to Peshawar, a company of the 9th Gurkhas was stopped and armed under the command of Captain Crompton, who used them for patrolling streets and roads. Another company of the 6th Sussex Regiment from Lahore and the 24th Baluchis under the command of Major Donald were deployed, in addition to additional troops from Jullundur, including the 25th Londons.[79] On 11 April, the next day, the entire city was surrounded by British and Indian troops. Finally, late in the evening, Brigadier-General Dyer reached Amritsar. By 13 April 1919, Amritsar was already under an undeclared martial law.[80] On 15 April 1919 – as similar protests spread to other parts of Punjab – the Punjab government declared martial law following a communiqué issued by the Home Department of the Government of India a day before. It was known as the Martial Law Ordinance or Ordinance No. 1 of 1919 and came into operation on the night between 15 and 16 April 1919. This ordinance provided for the takeover of local 'law and order' administration by military authorities. The promulgation of such a law proves that the civil administration in Punjab had failed. The anti-colonial protestors ruled the streets, even though for only a short period.

The fear of Ghadar was still haunting the colonial administration. Offences were to be tried by commissions appointed by the local government comprised of persons who had served as session judges and additional sessions judges for not less than three years or as judges of the High Courts. These commissions had all the powers of a General Court Martial under the Indian Army Act, 1911. The finding and sentence of such a commission were not to be subject to confirmation by any authority. In short, it was an imposition of military authority over the region of Punjab in response to the riots of 10 April 1919.

As stated earlier, martial law was declared in the entire Punjab province on 15 April 1919, but Amritsar had already come under total military control since 13 April.[81] The military was requested to support the efforts of the local administration in Amritsar in maintaining law and order from 11 April onwards. Furthermore, 13 April coincided with the religious festival of Baisakhi. The civil administration did not feel confident about remaining in charge of law and order in Amritsar in the wake of growing crowds that had come to observe the Baisakhi festival. The administration, already fearful and suspicious of its local population, ultimately handed over the charge to military officials. The arrival of the military in Amritsar signalled the imminent possibility of formal invocation of martial law. The panic-stricken officials, both civil and military, were ready to deal with anti-colonial protestors.

There is a distinction between calling the military in aid of civil administration and the complete takeover of civilian administration by the military under martial law. Since 11 April 1919, Amritsar was under partial military control. The administration punished the city of Amritsar by depriving it of electricity and water. Evening blackouts were intended to stop people from gathering or moving during the night. Trains stopped third-class bookings for Amritsar from the neighbouring towns so that protests did not get outside support. General Dyer – himself in command of the 45th Brigade at Jullundur – also brought more reinforcements to Amritsar. Before he arrived in Amritsar, he had already sent 100 British and 200 Indian soldiers to Amritsar at the request of the local administration. On 12 April, he made a round of the city with a posse of 120 British soldiers, 320 Indian soldiers and 2 armoured cars.[82] A plane was also hovering in the air. It was a tactic of intimidating the people of Amritsar and sending a clear message to the leaders that the administration was now in the hands of the military and that no one should dare to think of it as a civil administration. The colonial display of military might became a war-like situation – a war to be fought in the streets and roads of a city where the civil administration had failed. It was a moment of uncertainty for the British colonial government, which feared the outcome of the political momentum. The arrival of the military unmasked the facade of colonial peace and order. It was a moment where the naked claws of sovereign power were on display. Its ability to withdraw civil administration appeared in full sight and exhibited its capacity to unleash physical force. The magnitude of confrontation had escalated to a level higher than in typical situations of crowd control involving the police. It was now an absolute Schmittian distinction between friend and foe, and the defiant population in Amritsar was now as if declared the enemy.

While staging his military takeover of Amritsar on 12 April 1919, General Dyer experienced some confrontation with the crowds in the streets. He made a proclamation warning people against damaging any property and against acts of violence and collecting in groups numbering more than four in the streets and other public areas. The proclamatory warning of Dyer was somewhat similar to section 144 of the CrPC – available to the civilian administration – which could ban public space for public gatherings. The following day, Dyer marched through the streets with troops and issued another proclamation under the Seditious Meetings Act, warning the people against assembling and holding meetings, which were declared liable to be dispersed by the force of arms. The same fateful day, 13 April, General Dyer got the news that a huge crowd had collected at Jallianwala Bagh to hold a meeting. He immediately marched towards the spot with 25 British rifles, 40 Gurkhas, 25 Indian rifles and 2 armoured cars with machine guns. He arrived at the spot at 5 p.m.

The Bagh was also a spot for a Baisakhi *mela*, and for this reason, many people had come there unaware of proclamations and orders. The proclamation of law and its interpretation by subjects could be two quite different matters. The crowd in the Bagh had come to celebrate Baisakhi. However, it could equally be interpreted as a 'mob' that had assembled for seditious purposes challenging the administrative authority of the military general at the helm of affairs. Also, the quick and effective overnight transmission of any official communication prohibiting public gatherings remains questionable. According to some estimates, the number of people in the Bagh ranged between sixteen thousand and twenty thousand. After reaching the spot, General Dyer, so enraged by what he perceived as the people's defiance, ordered firing immediately. It continued for 10 to 15 minutes. People ran in all directions and mainly towards the few narrow exits. Dyer kept directing fire towards the areas where the crowd was the thickest. Firing continued until the ammunition ran out. Altogether 1,650 rounds were fired. The Bagh was full of dead bodies, and the number ran into hundreds at least. British official figures put the number of dead identified at 379,[83] while the number of dead claimed by the Congress was over a thousand.[84]

Whatever the number of dead might be, it was enough to consider it a massacre. Dyer did not warn the crowd because the enemy need not be warned but attacked ruthlessly and crushed. Later, he submitted to the Hunter Commission that he could have dispersed the crowd without warning, but then they would have assembled again, making a mockery of his orders. It would have resulted in making a fool of himself. Therefore, 'his duty was to fire and fire well'. Most shockingly, General Dyer left the wounded on the spot without any medical assistance. It was nothing short of not caring for the injured and dead of the enemy on the battlefield. Amritsar remained under the protection of the 'dutiful' General Dyer for almost a month. A significant characteristic of the application of state machinery is that a civilian administration aims to 'maintain law and order'. In contrast, the military administration aimed at crushing even the slight hint of opposition to the colonial government.

Even though martial law was proclaimed on 15 April 1919, Dyer understood – as his statements at the Hunter Commission point out – that martial law came into being *ipso facto* from the moment he took command on 11 April 1919, that is, the moment the civilian administration failed to maintain peace and sought military assistance to establish order. As a military general, Dyer had no doubts about his authority and control over Amritsar. Civilian subjects were now military subjects, and any disobedience or disturbance would face only a martial response. Dyer held a *durbar* on 14 April and forced people to open shops even when the city was still disturbed, and people were searching for the dead bodies of their family and relatives. The humiliation of Indians on the streets followed. Flogging for minor offences or defiance in the streets, making people crawl on the streets and ordering them to 'salaam', or salute, every European they came across were some of the initial steps General Dyer took after the massacre at Jallianwala Bagh.[85] The day following the massacre, a meeting of residents, municipal commissioners, magistrates and merchants was held at the *kotwali* (police station) at around 2 p.m. The commissioner, Mr Kitchin, while making a threatening speech, only exposed his helplessness. He stated:

> Do you people want peace or war? We are prepared in every way. The Government is all powerful. Sarkar has conquered Germany and is capable of doing everything. The General will give orders today. The city is in his possession. I can do nothing. You will have to obey orders.[86]

Dyer and other British officials – all extremely angry – reached the Kotwali around 5 p.m. Dyer's speech, or rather threat, to the meeting is noteworthy here. He asserted:

> You people know well that I am a Sepoy and soldier. Do you want war or peace? If you wish for war the Government is prepared for it, and if you want peace, then obey my orders and open all your shops; else, I will shoot. For me the battlefield of France or Amritsar is the same. I am a military man and I will go straight. Neither shall I move to the right, nor to the left. Speak up, if you want war.[87]

He also offered the attendees to turn collaborators. According to the deposition to the Congress Inquiry Committee, he further said:

> You must inform me of the budmashes. I will shoot them.[88]

Mr Miles Irving, the Deputy Commissioner, took Dyer's speech as a cue and followed it by making a straightforward statement:

> You have committed a bad act in killing the English. The revenge will be taken upon you and your children.[89]

These threatening speeches created a difficult binary between an abstract 'law-abiding citizen' and a 'wicked' *badmash* that needed punishment.

As soon as the news of Amritsar spread, the mood in Lahore turned tense too. The city was already observing protests since 10 April 1919, but now it had become more violent. Like the military takeover of Amritsar, in Lahore too military men belonging to the 43rd Brigade headquarters arrived on 11 April and posted pickets all over the city. On 12 April, the military under Colonel Frank Johnson was ordered to go into Lahore city with 800 men. He entered the city through the Delhi Gate, supported by four planes overhead.[90] He entered the city at 9.30 in the morning and left at 1.30 in the afternoon, leaving three detachments inside the city. He ordered that no detachment should move about unless it consisted of at least 200 men. The scale of military presence was grand. Amritsar and Lahore became a spectacle of sovereign violence, and the costs of rebelling against the colonial state were made clear.

On 13 and 14 April, the *hartal* continued in Lahore and paralysed the life of the city. On 15 April at 11 a.m., Colonel Frank Johnson issued his first proclamation informing the people of Lahore that marital law was now officially declared. Lahore remained under martial law until the end of May.[91] Under martial law, orders were passed to lift the *hartal* and resume business immediately. The military authorities began this campaign in Anarkali Bazaar. The Badshahi mosque was closed to the public for six weeks. Minor arrests and flogging of people followed in Amritsar. As these disturbances were underway in India, the Secretary of State for India presented a draft for a new constitution for India – which came to be known as the Government of India Act, 1919 – to the British Parliament in London. There were expectations in India that there would be colonial reforms in India at the end of the First World War. It was expected because of India's support to the colonial government during the war. The opposition to the Rowlatt Acts and the extreme colonial repression in response to that put some pressure on the British Parliament.

Owing to the pressure of the anti-colonial mobilisation in India in the wake of the upcoming Government of India Act, 1919, to be passed later in December 1919, a Disorders Enquiry Committee, also known as the Hunter Committee,[92] was appointed on 14 October 1919 to enquire into the incident at Jallianwala Bagh. It began on 29 October and sat for 46 days, 8 in Delhi, 29 in Lahore, 6 in Ahmedabad and 3 in Bombay. The Congress was outraged and boycotted it and instead set up a parallel non-official committee of enquiry.[93] The Hunter Committee prepared a report of its findings. The three Indian members, called the 'minority', dissented from the European majority on some broader issues and produced a separate report, but published in the same volume as the combined report. The difference between them lay in the approach as well as the conclusions. The European members held that elements of rebellion were persistent throughout the disturbances. The Indian members conceded that certain acts might amount to waging war in a legal sense but could not be described as an open rebellion. The European members stressed the magnitude of the movement and maintained that it might have 'developed into a revolution' with which the Indian members disagreed. Both European and Indian members reacted unfavourably to Dyer's handling of the Jallianwala meeting, and the difference between their reports is one of degree rather than substance. However, the iron-fist response by the colonial administration to civilian protestors through a military takeover confirms the extent of mobilisation by Ghadarites and the fear of a potential mutiny it had generated in the colonial administration.

The committee criticised General Dyer in two respects: First, he started firing without giving the assembly a chance to disperse. Second, he continued firing for a substantial time after the gathering had started to disperse. Dyer himself never suggested any emergency circumstances for the use of firing without warning but expressed that he had made up his mind to shoot.[94] Following the murder of Europeans in Amritsar during the *hartal* of 10 April, the European community was supportive of the general policy and martial law imposed by the then Lieutenant-Governor of Punjab, Michael O'Dwyer.[95] The element of racism surfaced again.[96] The *hartal* of 6 April 1919 was the highest point of the anti-Rowlatt mobilisation. However, the events unfolded in manners unexpected involving colonial violence of unimagined proportions.[97] What is significant here is that General Dyer was greatly criticised both in India and abroad.

However, one newspaper in London ran a campaign to generate a reward fund for General Dyer, who was stripped of his pension by the British government. The newspaper succeeded in generating a grant of 26,000 pounds. It hailed him as the 'saviour of Punjab' who had served the British Empire and had guarded and avenged the honour of English women in Punjab during the disturbances.[98] Despite the criticism, sections within the colonial administration supported Dyer and saw him as a dutiful military general who had crushed the opponents of the British Empire.[99] A quick reference to Hannah Arendt's 'banality of evil' could be helpful here. Dyer, like Adolf Eichmann, one of Hitler's generals, who played a major role in conducting the genocide of Jews in Germany during Nazi rule, was just following and giving orders. He was a loyal soldier of the British Empire. Dyer is another example of bureaucratic rationality combined with military rationality that could justify sovereign commands and following orders to one's best capability, pure and simple.

Jallianwala Bagh has indeed become a central focus of scholars studying the violence of imperial Britain. While some have called Dyer 'the Butcher of Amritsar', others have also joined the chorus in condemning his actions in Amritsar. Taylor Sherman has noted that General Dyer justified his actions in Jallianwala Bagh on the grounds of 'necessity' and fired to produce a 'sufficient moral effect' on entire Punjab.[100] The then Lieutenant-Governor of Punjab Michael O'Dwyer and the Hunter Committee condemned Dyer for his actions, criticised his strategy and questioned his judgement. Sherman notes that the then Secretary of State reiterated his commitment to the 'minimum use of force necessary' and held Dyer responsible for complete violation of the principle of the use of minimum force.[101] However, most works pay less attention to military atrocities in Lahore and other towns of Punjab province.[102] Most of the criticism of Dyer emphasised his lapse in following procedure by not warning the crowd. Even the Viceroy who shielded Dyer from criticism had to concede that Dyer did not act with sufficient humanity against the congregated crowd.

Consequently, Dyer was removed from command and forced to resign. Despite highlighting the criticism of Dyer, scholars tend to focus more on the violation of rules prescribed for crowd control rather than offering us an analysis of the 'necessity' for his action – that Dyer stated in the first place – as a symptom of sovereign violence. As if the procedure-following colonial administration was utterly humane in other instances and this was an aberration from the usual pattern of upholding the rule of law by all officials always. Such an analysis misses the point by putting the onus on Dyer alone and understands it as a 'single officer' using his 'discretion'. By singling out the sole deviation from procedure by Dyer, most scholars unintentionally humanise colonial 'rule of law'. Before the chapter attempts to discuss the concept of martial law, Kim Wagner's argument about the Amritsar massacre highlights a trend. He argues that the Hunter Commission report rejecting Dyer's rationale in 1920 conceded that the use of violence might even be counterproductive. He argues that 'colonial violence ultimately undermined colonial rule by alienating the native population and turning its victims into martyrs of nationalist movements'.[103] Sites of colonial violence became central to anti-colonial narratives and remained so until its last moments, in both India and elsewhere. He further argues that 'colonial violence was self-defeating' and 'that the reliance on spectacles of violence was anything but triumphant and ultimately proved to be the undoing of the empire'.[104] He sees a continuity in such spectacles of colonial violence, for example, in earlier cases of repression during the 1857 mutiny, soon followed by the Kukka rebellion in the 1870s. In the aftermath of Ghadar, the events of the 1919 mobilisation are yet another episode in a colonial cycle of violence where colonial anxiety was expressed in the form of sovereign rage.

The much-evaded question in this entire episode, of the martial law, requires further investigation. Nasser Hussain facilitated our understanding in this regard and noted that the central point of the entire exercise of the Hunter Commission was highlighting Dyer's 'bad judgement' and his flawed logic for justifying his actions rather than finding fault with the invocation of martial law – replacing the civilian administration – in an already volatile political situation. The Hunter Commission did recognise Dyer's sense of duty but concluded that it was 'misconceived'. The questioning of Dyer by members of the commission points out that even firing on the crowd was acceptable, but continuous firing was wrong.[105] Hussain extended his discussion of the event by dissecting the nature of 'martial law'. He extrapolated the deeper relationship between law and violence that martial law demonstrates by reading the Amritsar massacre through a reading of Walter Benjamin. According to him, emergency covers the general jurisprudential doubt that exists on a continuum from military aid to the civil power to the more intensified manifestation of martial law.[106] Hussain further pointed out that martial law occupies a profoundly ambiguous place in jurisprudential writing because it is considered both a properly legal question and a marker of law's absence. According to Hussain, on the one hand, there is recognition of the inevitability of martial law in certain situations where it represents the force of the state at its purest, the necessary condition if both law and the state are to survive. On the other hand, an insistence on rules that determine the moment of emergency is noteworthy – an insistence that the law shall appear at its vanishing point to determine the rules of its failure. He notes:

> Martial law, like other responses to emergency, simply rested not on an authorisation of ordinary law but on the legal maxim *Salus populi suprema est lex* (safety of the people is the supreme law).... [Here it becomes] the manifestation of both the highest law and no law at all. But while martial law is based on necessity, there are rules that can govern the perception of what constitutes necessity, and these rules are historically variable. It becomes possible, thus, to approach martial law as a changing cognitive question.[107]

Taking a cue from Albert Venn Dicey, a British jurist and constitutionalist, Hussain points out that understanding the ideological and jurisprudential significance of martial law requires it to be read within the general prerogative of the Crown or the sovereign to resort to violence to check a challenge to its authority, be it in connection with the form of response to domestic riots or rebellions.[108] In short, martial law emerges as a sovereign decree for swift and efficient control of a situation bypassing lengthy civil law and administration procedures that rely on producing evidence.

Exception highlights law's ability (martial or civilian) not to do everything but anything. Even though it can intervene at every level, it does not. The primary function of the myth of disturbance to law and order was the conferring of identity to the population involved, such as 'unruly' crowd, rebellious mob, mutinous subjects and insurgents. Martial law was an exception in contrast to the CrPC that applied in the everyday. In this light, the CrPC is the interiority of law, its usual, whereas martial law, an exception, is its exterior. However, for Dyer, this was routine. In the Amritsar massacre, martial law became the interiority of General Dyer's consciousness as a military general, reflected in the materiality of external circumstances. Therefore, martial law was not a standard law to be understood as per the usual 'rule of law' maxim. It served as an outside to the civilian administration but, once invoked, controlled the inside in the process. Even though it enveloped the everyday conduct of the population, it remained dissociated from all interiorities. In other words, it is a darkness that has no limits. It was an expression of the sovereign's dissatisfaction with the conduct of its subjects.

After the Punjab disturbances, Gandhi had to temporarily withdraw his *satyagraha* as he concluded that the masses did not understand the discipline and patience required in such political situations. The anti-Rowlatt *satyagraha* could not achieve its declared end, that is, the repeal of the Rowlatt Acts. It could not enforce non-violent political mobilisation on the masses, especially in Punjab. Nevertheless, it turned Gandhi into a national leader and *satyagraha* as a more acceptable, creative and moral political weapon known and available to millions of colonised Indians. With the arrival of the Government of India Act, 1919, both the Congress and the Muslim League were unhappy with the new constitution, as it did not meet their demands. As per the new constitution, some seats were set aside for the nominated members of the legislative bodies for the first time. Each body was about to have a majority of elected members. In the central assembly, a vast scope for the elected members was given 'to argue', 'make noise' and 'create a fuss' – but they would have no control over the government. The Governor-General or the Viceroy and his executive council reserved all powers of the government. Assembly votes did not bind the government, nor could the government be dismissed by a vote. In the provinces, it was a half-step toward establishing a 'responsible' government. It proposed a set-up in which the cabinets would include ministers who were elected and therefore were responsible to the councils and executive councillors who would, as before, be appointed by the Governor and therefore were accountable only to him. Under this arrangement, some portfolios would be transferred to ministers while others would be 'reserved' and be under the executive councillors. The system at the provincial level was termed 'diarchy'.

Conclusion

In the first two decades of the twentieth century, management of public order in India was marked by the invocation and promulgation of three different kinds of extraordinary laws – a combination of the Ingress into India Ordinance and the Defence of India Rules, the Rowlatt Bills and the use of martial law. While the Defence of India Rules – a proper wartime measure – might seem a logical legislative course of action to safeguard law and order in exceptional circumstances, there was no such easy justification at play when the Rowlatt Bills were passed. The continuity of the Defence of India Rules in the name of the Rowlatt Bills for the next three years – before being repealed in 1922 – raised important issues in the study of colonial legality. The colonial state, which claimed to rule for justice and by law, often violated the premises of its administrative ideology. It invoked the Defence of India Act to mobilise resources for military purposes and maintain order and prevent the outbreak of an armed mass rebellion. The self-declaration of the Ghadar Party as 'angrezi raj ka dushman' and the charge of sedition used in subsequent trials of the Lahore and Delhi Conspiracy cases highlight a political environment in which Carl Schmitt's distinction between friend and foe had become generalised and upended the normal operations of legality. The call to arms against the sovereignty of the King legally necessitated treating the revolutionaries as the 'enemy' of the colonial state. However, the enemy was not specific. The entire population was considered a potential hotbed of 'revolutionaries'. By examining the operation of extraordinary laws in late colonial India at the beginning of the twentieth century, from the Ghadar Movement and the promulgation of the Defence of India Rules during the First World War to the infamous Rowlatt Acts and the subsequent events associated with the anti-colonial mass mobilisation that invited the use of martial law, the discussion across various sections in this chapter shows the administration of public order in colonial India through the use of law by way of a twin strategy.

On the one hand, it emphasised an ideological notion of 'the rule of law' applicable to obedient subjects, whilst on the other hand, it sustained itself by creating a catalogue of exceptions that rested on the delineation of certain problem categories or its enemies to which extraordinary laws could be applied. It was best demonstrated in the Ingress into India Ordinance and in the Defence of India Act and its subsequent extension as the Rowlatt Acts. Also, the reference to 'anarchical violence' alluded to the uncertain nature of the insurgent tactics as opposed to the organised politics of the then-emerging Congress Party founded on ideas of liberalism and constitutionalism within the colonial dispensation. The use of the Defence of India Rules and the further extension of pre-emptive legislation in the name of the Rowlatt Bills prove that colonial authority normalised exception by the successive implementation of extraordinary laws. The reason for the extension of these extraordinary laws was to maintain order, prevent civil war and contain revolutionary violence. In an era of anti-colonial mass nationalism, the scope of such laws was not very difficult to decipher. One of the significant impacts of the passing of the Rowlatt Bills was that it explicitly exposed the violent character of the colonial government in India. Furthermore, Jallianwala Bagh served as a symptom of the possibility or the potential of repeating such a cycle of colonial violence. It established that peaceful mass gatherings were not always safe from colonial repression.

The invocation of exceptional laws in late colonial India demonstrates the governmental 'crisis' of the colonial administration. The Defence of India Rules and the subsequent Rowlatt Bills, as well as the invocation of martial law in Punjab, highlight the fact that the colonial government was quite aware of the 'exceptional' tactics at its disposal within the 'fair and just' laws framework it often boasted about. Such extraordinary laws facilitated the normalisation of colonial violence at a quotidian level. The period 1913–1920 emerges as the proper establishment of the colonial state as the 'enemy' of the Indian masses. A contestation for sovereignty on both sides hence ensued.

On the one hand, the demand for *swaraj* from colonial rule emerged at a mass level. On the other hand, the attempts to preserve the colonial order from insurgency intensified. The utilisation of extraordinary laws by the colonial state highlights its strategy to rule by fear rather than law and exposes its fragility and fear of uprisings. Sovereign anxiety guided by motives of self-preservation overpowered colonial legal rationality.

Thus, in different forms, the state of exception became the frequent resort of the colonial state.

By undertaking an extensive codification exercise in the latter half of the nineteenth century, the colonial state in India had created a myth of its commitment to the rule of law in India. Close attention to its administrative practices reveals that it operated as a dissimulate state in its own right. It posed as the flagbearer of modernity and the rule of law in India but unleashed exceptional violence in volatile situations that challenged its authority. The colonial state posed as the one upholding justice, fairness, impartiality and the rule of law and yet often repressed its subject population by invoking exceptional laws such as the Defence of India Rules and the Rowlatt Bills. With time, it kept on expanding the domain of exception. The frequent use of exception exposed a monolithic character of colonial sovereignty in times of crisis. As demonstrated through various events in this chapter, the colonial government declared war on its subjects and immediately transitioned its activities from the maintenance of law and order to a repressive machine utterly external to the usual everyday government. Undoubtedly, opposing the government was not waging a 'war'. It was an everyday protest against a colonial regime. The colonial administration used its sovereign power to draw its limits on what kind of protest stood outside the law and what could be allowed and tolerated. It was a limit negotiated by extraordinary laws where any relationship of responsibility of the colonial state towards its subject population could be denied or severed.

Notes

1. See Elizabeth Kolsky, *Colonial Justice in British India: White Violence and the Rule of Law* (Cambridge: Cambridge University Press, 2009).
2. For a broader discussion see, N.G. Barrier, 'The Punjab Government and the Communal Politics', *Journal of Asian Studies* 27, no. 3 (1968): 523–539; N.G. Barrier, *The Punjab Alienation Land Bill of 1900* (Durham, NC: Duke University Program in Comparative Studies of Southern Asia, 1966); also see R.G. Fox, 'Urban Class and Communal Consciousness in Colonial Punjab: The Genesis of India's Intermediate Regime', *Modern Asian Studies* 18, no. 3 (1984): 459–489.
3. For complete proceedings of the case and information about incidents regarding the Lahore Conspiracy case and others, please see Malwinder Singh Waraich and Harinder Singh, ed., *Ghadr Movement Original*

Documents Vol.-I, Lahore Conspiracy Cases I and II (Chandigarh: Unistar Books Pvt. Ltd, 2008), p. 514.

4.   Michael O'Dwyer, *India as I Knew It: 1885–1925* (New Delhi: Mittal Publications, 2004), p. 197.

5.   Nicholas Tarling, *The Cambridge History of South East Asia*, vol. 2, *The Nineteenth and Twentieth Centuries* (Cambridge: Cambridge University Press, 1992), p. 315.

6.   Kama Mclean and J. Daniel Elam, eds., *Revolutionary Lives in South Asia: Acts and Afterlives of Colonial Political Action* (Oxon: Routledge, 2015), pp. 3–4.

7.   Hugh J.M. Johnston, *The Voyage of the Komagata Maru: The Sikh Challenge to Canada's Colour Bar* (Vancouver: University of British Columbia Press, 2014), pp. 15–24.

8.   Seema Sohi, *Echoes of Mutiny: Race, Surveillance and Anti-colonialism in North America* (Oxford: Oxford University Press, 2014), p. 259.

9.   Gajendra Singh, 'The Anatomy of Dissent in the Military of Colonial India During the First and Second World Wars', Edinburgh Papers in South Asian Studies, no. 20 (2006), p. 45.

10. For more discussion, see Hew Strachan, *The First World War*, vol. 1, *To Arms* (Oxford: Oxford University Press, 2001).

11. *The Defence of India, Act V of 1915 (As Amended by Act II of 1916) With Rules and Notification Thereon* by Pt. Bhagat Ram, B.A. L.L.B., Pleader, Amritsar (Printed at the Union Steam Press, Lahore, 1917). p. 35.

12. See ibid., p. 1.

13. Ibid.

14. Ibid., pp. 2–3.

15. Ibid., p. 4.

16. Ibid., pp. 4–5.

17. Ibid., pp. 4–5.

18. Ibid., pp. 6–7.

19. Ibid., p. 8.

20. Ibid., pp. 9–25.

21. Ibid., p. 26.

22. See the judgment for Lahore Conspiracy case in 'Special Tribunal', quoted in F.C. Isemonger and J. Slattery, *Account of the Ghadr Conspiracy: 1913–1915* (Lahore, Punjab: Printed by the Superintendent, Government Printing, 1919), p. 25 (File IOR/V/27/262/9, British Library: Asian and African Studies, London).

23. For a broader discussion, see Gajendra Singh, *Testimonies of Indian Soldiers and the Two World Wars: Between Self and Sepoy* (London: Bloomsbury Publications, 2014), p. 224.

24. For a broader discussion on the scope of the Ghadar mutiny, see O'Dwyer, *India as I Knew It*, pp. 190–210; Tarling, *The Cambridge History*, vol. 2, p. 315; Mclean and Elam, *Revolutionary Lives*, pp. 3–4; Johnston, *The Voyage of the Komagata Maru*; Sohi, *Echoes of Mutiny*, p. 259; Singh, 'The Anatomy of Dissent', p. 45.

25. See Part II, specifically 'Kirpal Singh Spy's Evidence', in *Ghadr Movement Original Documents*, vol. I, *Lahore Conspiracy Cases I and II*, ed. Malwinder Singh Waraich and Harinder Singh (Chandigarh: Unistar Star Publications Pvt. Ltd., 2008), p. 38.

26. The commissioners were Major Irvine and Mr. Ellis, sessions judges, and Rai Bahadur Pandit Sheo Narain, a leading lawyer of the Chief Court.

27. See Appendix C, 'Summary of the Criminal Cases Arising out of the Ghadr Movement', in *An Account of the Ghadr Conspiracy 1913–1915*, compiled by F.C. Isemonger and J. Slattery, Indian Police, Punjab, Lahore: Printed by the Superintendent, Government Printing, Punjab, 1919, p. xii.

28. See Appendix T, ibid., p. xlviii.

29. Appeals Nos. 851 to 854 and Nos. 905 and 921 to 924 of 1914 and Revision No. 2069 of 1914, against the order of H.M. Harrison, Esquire, Additional Sessions Judge, Delhi, dated 5 October 1914.

30. The original case was heard by sessions judge on 11 July 1914, in Trial No. 6, and further the charges against the accused were added or amended during the course of the trial.

31. A special bench comprising Sir Donald Campbell Johnstone, Kt., Judge and Justice Rattigan heard the case. Six prisoners named Balmokand, Abad Bihari, Amir Chand, Hanwant Sahai, Balraj and Basant Kumar Biswas filed appeals in their names against an order of 5 October 1914 by H.M. Harrison, Additional Sessions Judge, Delhi.

32. Namely Chota Lal (called Ram Lal in the rest of this judgment) alias Ram Lal, Charan Das, Mannu Lal, Raghobar Sharma and Khushi Ram.

33. Namely Basant Kumar Biswas, Abad Bihari, Amir Chand, Balmokand, Balraj and Hanwant Sahai.

34. Namely Abad Bihari, Amir Chand and Balmokand.

35. Namely Basant Kumar Biswas, Balraj and Hanwant Sahai.

36. Namely Abad Bihari and Amir Chand.

37. See 'Complete Judgement of the Punjab Chief Court, Lahore in the Delhi Conspiracy Case', dated 10 February 1915, together with the abstract of the findings of the judges, 1915, Lahore, printed by S.S. Deane, Manager, at the Punjab Steam Press, p. 3.

38. Ibid., p. 5.

39. 'Komagata Appeal, Thrown out by Canadian Court, Court's Ground of Rejection', *Amrita Bazar Patrika*, Thursday, 9 July 1914, p. 5.

40. '"Komagata Maru" Hindus and Police', *Amrita Bazar Patrika*, Tuesday, 21 July 1914, p. 5.

41. '"Kamagata" Hindus, Cost of This Venture, the Komagata Passengers, Will Return to Hong Kong', *Amrita Bazar Patrika*, Friday, 10 July 1914, p. 5. This news item puts the venture costs of the *Komagata Maru* at £14,000.

42. '"Komagata" Hindus, Government Refuses to Defray Expenses, the Government Proposes to Make an Example of the Present Case', *Amrita Bazar Patrika*, Monday, 13 July 1914, p. 5.

43. *An Account of the Ghadr Conspiracy 1913–1915*, pp. 37–39.

44. '"Komagata" Case, Deportation Difficulty Settled', *Amrita Bazar Patrika*, Friday, 24 July 1914, p. 5.

45. Kalpana Kannabiran and Ranbir Singh, *Challenging the Rule(s) of Law: Colonialism, Criminology and Human Rights in India*, Penal Strategies and Political Resistance in Colonial and Independent India (New Delhi: Sage Publication, 2008), p. 235

46. O'Dwyer, *India as I Knew It*, p. 197.

47. Ibid.

48. For an elaboration of colonial concerns regarding immigrants in North America, see Sohi, *Echoes of Mutiny*, p. 259.

49. 'Komagata's Return, Fatal Array at Budge Budge, Sudden Attack on Police Officers, Deplorable Loss of Life', *Amrita Bazar Patrika*, Friday, 2 October 1914, p. 5.

50. *An Account of the Ghadr Conspiracy 1913–1915*, pp. 55–56.

51. Humphrey Milford, *The 'Rowlatt Act', Its Origin, Scope and Object* (Elphinstone Circle, Bombay; Esplanade, Madras: Oxford University Press, 1919), pp. 7–8.

52. *Report of Committee Appointed to Investigate Revolutionary Conspiracies in India* (London, 1918), Cd. 9190, p. 75. Other members of this committee were Sir Bail Scott, Chief Justice of Bombay, C.V. Kumaraswami Shastri, Madras High Court judge, Sir Verney Lovett, member of the UP Board of Revenue, and P.C. Mitter, additional member of the Bengal Legislative Council.

53. Milford, *The 'Rowlatt Act'*, p. 32.

54. Humphrey Milford made such an assertion on the first page of this booklet.

55. Milford, *The 'Rowlatt Act'*, p. 8.

56. Ibid., p. 8.

57. See the Rowlatt Bills and also Milford, *The 'Rowlatt Act'*, p. 9.

58. See Milford, *The 'Rowlatt Act'*, pp. 13–14.

59. 'The Imperial Council, Rowlatt Bill Passed, Madras Member Resigns', *The Madras Mail*, Wednesday Evening, 19 March 1919, p. 5.

60. See D.G. Tendulkar, *Mahatma: Life of Karamchand Gandhi*, vol. 1 (Bombay: The Times of India Press, 1951), p. 251.

61. See the message sent by Gandhi to the Madras meeting in *The Bombay Chronicle*, 22 March 1919 and 4 April 1919.

62. Details of some of the amendments can be seen in 'The Imperial Council, The Rowlatt Bill, Plethora of Amendments', *The Madras Mail*, Monday Evening, 17 March 17, 1919, p. 6.

63. For a discussion regarding the character of the Rowlatt Bills and the positions on Indian members, see 'The Rowlatt Bill, A Foregone Conclusion, Position of Indian Members', *The Tribune*, Saturday, 22 March 1919, p. 2.

64. See the message sent by Gandhi to the Madras meeting in *The Bombay Chronicle*, 22 March 1919 and 4 April 1919.

65. Broader context for Woodrow Wilson's quote can be seen in W. Wilson, A. Shaw, and United States President (1913–1921: Wilson), *The Messages and Papers of Woodrow Wilson: With Editorial Notes*, vol. 2 (New York: Review of Reviews Corporation, 1924), p. 634.

66. Harendra Nath Mitra, ed., *Punjab Unrest, Before and After* (Calcutta: N.N. Mitter, Annual Register Office, Sibpur, April 1920), pp. 433 approx.

67. See the message sent by Gandhi to the Madras meeting, *The Bombay Chronicle*, 4 April 1919.

68. Jacques Derrida and G. Anidjar, *Acts of Religion*, particularly Chapter 5 titled 'Force of Law: "The Mystical Foundation of Authority"', 189–228 (London and New York: Routledge: 2002).

69. 'The Black Act Day, Day of Humiliation and Prayer, A Twenty-four Hours Fast, Mr. Gandhi's Recommendations, Effective Public Demonstration', *The Independent*, Wednesday, 26 March 1919, p. 1.

70. For a complete reporting on the Delhi firing see, 'Satyagraha Day, Exciting Times in Delhi, Soldiers Fire on Protestors', *The Madras Mail*, Tuesday Evening, 1 April 1919, p. 5; 'Satyagraha Day, Delhi Riots, Further Details', *The Madras Mail*, Wednesday Evening, 2 April 1919, p. 5; 'Sequel to Satyagraha, Rioting at Delhi', *Times of India*, Tuesday, 1 April 1919, p. 7; 'Rioting at Delhi', *Times of India*, 2 April 1919, p. 9, also on the same page 'The Delhi Tragedy, Facts and Comments'; 'Situation in Delhi', *Times of India*, Friday, 4 April 1919; 'Situation in Delhi, Official Report', *Times of India*, Saturday, 5 April 1919; 'Satyagraha Demonstration, A Day of National Mourning, Observance All Over Country', *Amrita Bazar Patrika*, Wednesday, 2 April 1919, p. 4; 'The Delhi Tragedy, Official Report', *Amrita Bazar Patrika*, Sunday, 6 April 1919, p. 4; 'The Delhi Tragedy', *The Independent*, Wednesday, 2 April 1919, p. 7.

71. See 'The Delhi Tragedy, Impressive Funeral Processions, Alleged Use of Ball Cartridges', *The Independent*, Thursday, 3 April 1919, p. 1.

72. See 'The Delhi Tragedy, Mr. Gandhi's Congratulations, Hindu Muslim Union', *The Independent*, Saturday, 6 April 1919, p. 7.

73. See 'Delhi Tragedy, Mahatma Gandhi's Message, Blacksmith's Hammer to Crush a Fly, Appeal for Self Restraint', *Amrita Bazar Patrika*, Sunday, 6 April 1919, p. 4.

74. 'Opening of Satyagraha Campaign, Laws Regarding Prohibited Literature and Newspapers, Registration to be Civilly Disobeyed', *The Independent*, Wednesday, 9 April 1919, p. 6.

75. 'The Anarchic Measures, to be Fought with Satyagraha, Campaign Enunciated in Bombay, "Refuse Civilly to Obey"', *The Independent*, Saturday, 1 March 1919, p. 1.

76. These leaders were already actively organising public meetings and protests, against the Rowlatt Bills in Punjab. One of the earlier grand mobilisations by them can be noticed in 'Rowlatt Bills, Punjab's Protest', *The Tribune*, Tuesday, 11 March 1919, p. 2.

77. 'Mahatma Gandhi's Arrest, Scenes on the Train and on the Station, By an Eye Witness', *The Independent*, Saturday, 12 April 1919, p. 7.

78. 'Amritsar Disturbances, 3 Europeans Reported Killed, "C&M Gazette's Version", "Excitement Caused by Local Leaders Arrest"', *The Independent*, Sunday, 13 April 1919, p. 7.

79. Most of the official details can be seen in April 1919 issues of *Civil and Military Gazette* (*C&M Gazette*). Only *C&M Gazette* was allowed to cover the disturbances in Punjab. The rest of the press could only use official information from the *C&M Gazette*.

80. 'Prussianism in Punjab, Publication of Accounts of Disturbances Prohibited', *The Independent*, Tuesday, 15 April 1919, p. 1.

81. 'Martial Law in Lahore and Amritsar', *The Independent*, Thursday, 17 April 1919, p. 7.

82. Details of military campaign in Punjab were published as an official version of events in the *C&M Gazette*, whereas other publications were prohibited to publish details of the events unless sourced and produced from the *C&M Gazette* itself.

83. Nigel Collett, *The Butcher of Amritsar, General Reginald Dyer* (London: Hambledon Continuum, 2006), pp. 266, 337.

84. Brian Lapping, *End of Empire* (London: Palladin, 1985), p. 38.

85. Taylor Sherman, *State Violence and Punishment in India* (London: Routledge, 2010), p. 246.

86. The Congress Inquiry Committee to investigate Punjab disturbances and Jallianwala Bagh excesses. Chapter V, 'The Martial Law', in *Report of the Commissioners Appointed by the Punjab Sub-Committee of the Indian National Congres*, vol. 1 (Lahore: K. Satnam, 1920), p. 59.

87. Ibid.

88. Ibid.

89. Ibid.

90. The colonial military campaign against the Punjab disturbances of April 1919 also saw the bombing of civilians by planes. For example, see 'Fresh Shooting at Amritsar, Crowds Bombed at Gujranwala', *The Independent*, Friday, 17 April 1919, p. 1.

91. For more details, see P.S. Sivaswami Iyer, *Martial Law Administration in the Panjab: As Described by the Official Witness* (Madras: The Madras Liberal League, 1919).

92. See 'Report of the Disorders Inquiry Committee 1919–20, Government of India, 1920', published in *Punjab Disturbances 1919–20*, vol. 2 (New Delhi: Seep Publications, 1976), p. 275.

93. An Urdu compilation of the Congress Committee report is by Lala Pandi Das, *Panjab Mein Pehla Marshal Law, Congress Committee ki Report* (Urdu) (Lahore: Fiction House, 1996), p. 452.

94. V.N. Datta, *Jallianwala Bagh* (Published by V.K. Arora, Kurukshetra University Books and Stationery shop, Kurukshetra, for Lyall Book Depot, Ludhiana, 1969), pp. 118–119.

95. Michael O'Dwyer, *The Punjab Disturbances of April 1919: Criticism of the Hunter Committee Report* (London: Indo-British Association, 1919).

96. An interesting take on such issues can be noticed in Alfred Nundy, *Political Problems and Hunter Committee Disclosures* (Calcutta: S.K. Roy, 1920).

97. For Gandhi and Rowlatt *satyagraha* see Chapter 5, 'The Rowlatt Satyagraha', in Judith Brown, *Gandhi's Rise to Power, Indian Politics 1915–1922* (London and New York: Cambridge University Press, 1972), pp. 160–189.

98. See Collett, *The Butcher of Amritsar*.

99. Alfred Draper, *Amritsar, Massacre that Ended the Raj* (London: Cassell, 1981); Hari Singh, *Gandhi Rowlatt Satyagrah and British Imperialism: Emergence of Mass Movement in Punjab and Delhi* (Delhi: Indian Bibliographies Bureau, 1990); R. Kumar, ed., *Essays on Gandhian Politics: The Rowlatt Satyagraha of 1919* (London: Oxford University Press, 1971); Kamlesh Mohan, 'The Jallianwala Bagh Tragedy: A Catalyst of Indian Consciousness', in *Jallian Wala Bagh Massacre*, ed. V.N. Datta and S. Settar, pp. 52–79 (Delhi: Pragati Publications, Indian Council of Historical Research, Delhi, 2000).

100. Sherman, *State Violence and Punishment in India*, p. 33.

101. Ibid., p. 34.

102. For details see Chapter V, 'The Martial Law', in *Report of the Commissioners Appointed by the Punjab Sub-Committee of the Indian National Congress*, vol. 1 (Lahore: K. Satnam, 1920).

103. Kim Wagner, "'Calculated to Strike Terror": The Amritsar Massacre and the Spectacle of Colonial Violence', *Past and Present* 233, no. 1 (November 2016): 223–225.

104. Ibid.

105. Nasser Hussain, *Jurisprudence of Emergency: Colonialism and the Rule of Law* (Ann Arbor, MI: University of Michigan Press, 2003), p. 101

106. Ibid.

107. Ibid., p. 103.

108. Ibid., p. 104.

2

Controlling 'Mobs' and Maintaining Public Order in the United Provinces, 1930–1940

The first three decades of the twentieth century saw the emergence of a vigorous anti-colonial mobilisation. In addition to grand events such as the First World War, the Ghadar movement, the promulgation of the Defence of India Rules followed by the Rowlatt Acts, the initiation of *satyagraha* politics and the Jallianwala Bagh massacre, many other mobilisations such as the Khilafat and the Non-Cooperation movements also followed. With the Jallianwala Bagh massacre involving military brutality in Amritsar and Lahore, the colonial state of exception had reached its apogee. It had managed to secure its power through spectacular violence but lost authority in the face of resistance.

It is essential to make a quick distinction between power and authority here. In a legal sense, a stable political regime wields power and authority; where power refers to its punitive capacity without necessarily fostering political acceptance amongst the constituency, authority, on the other hand, generates regard for power despite its ability to punish. The first chapter revealed that the colonial state succeeded in replenishing its power through the exhibition of military might but lost substantial authority over its subjects. With the arrival of the Government of India Act, 1919, and the politically cosmetic changes it introduced, a challenge to colonial public order began to be mounted through everyday defiance of colonial law in the form of *satyagraha* as a tactic introduced by Gandhi. Hereon, the colonial state frequently invoked section 144 of the Code of Criminal Procedure

(CrPC) to deal with what it called 'unlawful assemblies'. Unlawful assemblies were one of the major everyday challenges of the colonial government. The purpose of this chapter is to map the normalisation of colonial exception through seemingly ordinary laws like section 144 CrPC and curfews, which served as an important colonial tool to criminalise quotidian anti-colonial politics. Both the provisions aimed to prohibit mass gathering, ban public places for public access and individuals from addressing the public and came under the set of laws that dealt with 'public peace and tranquillity', that is, public order.

A decade and a half after the Jallianwala Bagh massacre, the colonial state continued to invoke public-order laws to criminalise politics on the ground. The difference is that many of the contestations would now also involve inter-community, intra-community and workers' issues. In addition to anti-colonial politics, indigenous rights and claims within the colonial paradigm became central. These contestations emerged in the light of the Government of India Act, 1935.

Public-order laws like section 144 and curfews continued as an unchallenged part of administrative tactics even after passing the Government of India Act, 1935, and the subsequent provincial elections in 1937. The Act of 1935 was important because it granted more powers to Indians and, for the first time, allowed them to form majority governments at the provincial level since the inception of British colonial rule in India. The Congress emerged as a victor in the provincial elections of 1937. Rather than opposing the colonial government, it now had to govern the provinces.

The thrust of the chapter is to raise important questions about the history of public-order legislation and its continuity after the initiation of decolonisation. The key question it investigates is: What is the emergent nature of the colonial public order in the face of the first significant attempt at decolonisation after the passing of the Government of India Act, 1935? Did it alter its exceptional character once a nationalist organisation such as the Congress party was at the helm of provincial affairs? It will reveal a continued and widespread use of colonial tactics of law-and-order control by the provincial Congress ministry in the United Provinces (UP). The chapter will examine administrative responses to issues of public order by a government in which Indian nationalists held at least a position of power and responsibility. Decolonisation here refers to those moments when the coloniser was willing to allow limited decision-making participation to the colonised in their everyday government. The chapter will discuss two critical instances from UP to examine the questions raised earlier. One instance is from Kanpur (November 1936) and the second is from Lucknow (June 1937). The former discusses labour riots and the latter investigates communal/sectarian clashes between the Shias and the Sunnis. Both instances are pivotal in the late colonial history of UP, especially when understanding the functioning of public-order laws. These instances enable an understanding of the Congress's attitude towards its political others, such as the socialists and the Muslim League, and its governance techniques under the guardianship of the provincial premier, Govind Ballabh Pant (G.B. Pant), who would serve as the long-time chief minister of the same province after 1947. Therefore, it will allow us to make broader observations about the decolonisation of legal regimes in India in the long run.

Both the labour and the Shia–Sunni conflict continued until 1947 and beyond; the period under review here represents the height of the tension and the governmental crisis in UP. The majority Congress government in the province, despite being autonomous, resorted to time-tested colonial tactics to contain civil disturbances or riots. The cities of Kanpur and Lucknow remained a significant 'law and order' concern for the UP government because they were the main urban centres of UP in addition to Benares and Allahabad and hosted industry and the corresponding influx of migrant population from across the province and beyond. The chapter will highlight that the Congress as a government did not move away from the colonial understanding of alienation between state and society. Both the instances erupted in an urban set-up; however, they would mobilise and draw support from outside the city and the province. The Kanpur and Lucknow instances fit within a wider scholarly debate about the relationship between urban growth and the nature of late colonial politics. Scholars such as Rajnarayan Chandavarkar,[1] Nandini Gooptu,[2] Prashant Kidambi,[3] Subho Basu[4] and Chitra Joshi,[5] to name a few, have in the past elaborated on issues concerning rural-to-urban migration, the survival of migrant workers through the sustenance of rural networks while working or struggling for jobs in the city, the emergence of a class of 'troublemakers' from amongst the informal non-regularised workers, contingent workers' mobilisations within the factory and outside or communal confrontations between communities because of the direction of politics at a broader (national) level.

Nevertheless, this chapter approaches these instances by investigating public-order laws and the legal regime. The urban–rural interaction offers insight into the self-perception of diverse publics, such as religious communities and labour, and their relation to the colonial state. The influx of migrants to such towns and cities in the context of an increasingly intensifying nationalist movement involved contestations and confrontations about the future(s) of these publics. Here, mass protests and riots served as a potent tool to assert political demands and thus invited administrative action under the various public-order laws. However, before discussing the two instances, it is crucial to understand the political context in which they emerged.

Responsibility without Power: Congress and the Government of India Act, 1935

The Government of India Act, 1919, followed by the Government of India Act, 1935, were two significant constitutional moments of the colonial state in India. One Act followed by another aimed at widening the ambit of the colonial model of democracy in India. However, the 1935 Act faced vociferous resistance and rejection from the Congress. Much of it had to do with ideological shifts within the Congress party and an assertion from its political others, such as the communists and the Muslim League. It had no choice but to engage with the 1935 Act.

By 1934, the Civil Disobedience movement had fizzled out, and Gandhi had temporarily withdrawn from political events. Disagreements among various groups within the Congress emerged mainly on the issues of council entry and office acceptance. Notably, disagreements had erupted earlier when Gandhi withdrew from the Non-Cooperation movement. In May 1934, the left wing of the Congress formed the Congress Socialist Party within the Congress. It was an elusive arrangement of radical nationalism influenced by Marxian scientific socialism. The year 1935 was a watershed moment in the colonial history of India. The Government of India Act passed in August 1935 would come into force only after the provincial elections held in February 1937. With the passing of the 1935 Act, the colonial state introduced controlled and limited decolonisation by broadening the membership of the provincial assemblies to include more Indian representatives. It also enabled them to form majorities and to form provincial governments. Federalism was a core project of the original Act but was never introduced. This Act increased the franchise from seven million to thirty-five million, thus widening the ambit of the colonial democracy. The Congress opposed the Act because it argued for 'real power' at the central-government level. The colonial state was unwilling to consider this demand.

The Act of 1935 should be noted as an important moment in the career of the colonial state in India because it achieved two goals simultaneously. It offered increased yet limited participation to Indians in provincial decision-making and succeeded in distracting the Indian national movement from demands of immediate dominion status. In this regard, the Lucknow Congress of 1936 was significant in some ways. With Gandhi's approval, senior Congress leaders such as Rajendra Prasad and Vallabh Bhai Patel accepted that contesting elections and subsequently accepting office under the 1935 Act was a better option than a confrontation with the colonial state. Next year, in August, the All-India Congress Committee (AICC) meeting was held in Bombay, where it decided to contest the elections. The meeting resolved to defer the decision to accept office until the conclusion of the elections. In *Empire, Politics and the Creation of the 1935 India Act*, Andrew Muldoon has observed that 'the vision many in British governing circles had of the Indian Act raises important questions about how the Raj worked'.[6] Other scholars have noted that the supporters of the 1935 Act within the British Parliament believed that the plans for federation and provincial autonomy in India would effectively counter the growing nationalist movement by potentially creating a split in the All-India National Congress and would, therefore, succeed in distracting Indians from a united nationalist movement.

Furthermore, according to the 1935 Act, the British central government retained the right to suspend the provincial governments, and the provincial governors retained significant reserve powers. Even though Indians believed that they deserved dominion status and powers to run responsible governments on their own like Australia and Canada at that time, the British Parliament disagreed with such claims. Moreover, Britain granted dominion status to Egypt and ignored India despite its enormous contribution (both economic and manpower) to Britain's war efforts. Many in India felt agitated with the British government over this issue.

The years 1936–1937 intensified contestation and political articulation amongst all sections of Indian society. The Congress, which was undergoing a reconstitution of its provincial committees, had signalled to reject the new Act. Meanwhile, Jawaharlal Nehru and Vallabh Bhai Patel were canvassing for support to secure the post of the Congress president. In the wake of the new Act, Congress leaders reacted to the new political reality, that is, the possibility of provincial elections in ways that furthered their aims. Due to the lack of a clear position of the Congress on the new Act and the upcoming elections, a columnist in *The Leader* in December 1936 raised questions regarding its dilemma as follows:

> In December, the National *Congress* will decide its attitude towards the new constitution. Will it enter India's new Parliament? If it does, will it enter to bring the legislative machine to a deadlock, wrecking and obstructing? Or will it accept office if in a majority, and work for the constitution?[7]

The column highlights political uncertainty in the light of the Congress's ambiguous position. It also informed that the Muslim League and other organisations would accept the new Act positively, leaving the Congress party no choice but to engage with it eventually. Recovery for the Congress was possible only through the new constitution that the 1935 Act had brought. The columnist continued in a resilient tone, 'But – whatever happens – the new constitution is going to be worked despite Indian discontent with it.'[8] A political message to the Congress party is evident in the tone of the columnist. It was a veiled invitation to the Congress to shun political ambiguity and take control of the electoral contest.

Other political organisations also highlighted the Congress's dilemma and did not hold back from challenging its indecisiveness on the new constitution and the upcoming elections. Increasing pressure and sharp political attacks from the Muslim League, National Liberal Association, National Agriculturalists and the communists forced the Congress to take a clear stand on the new constitution, which it had tried to postpone until after the elections.[9] There was also an intense mobilisation of trade unions and the peasantry. Congress leaders like M.N. Roy appealed to 'radicals' to understand the predicament and find a pragmatic and country-specific solution to 'socialism'.[10] Meanwhile, Mohammad Ali Jinnah of the Muslim League made it clear that the League would positively contest the upcoming provincial elections with an open mind.[11] Chimanlal Setalvad and Cowasji Jehangir of the Indian Liberal Association and Liberal Federation also urged the masses to make the new constitution work by extracting the greatest good possible out of it. Opinions in support of the possibilities created by the new constitution began to appear in the newspapers. For example, in a letter to the editor published in *The Leader*, A.A. Zakaullah, a Muslim League supporter, stated:

> The advantages of the new constitution are so self-evident and obvious for the Indian states and the disadvantages of the refusal to federate so patent that it is difficult to understand why the states should not have been able to make up their minds in this regard long, long ago and should still be hesitating.[12]

As the nominations concluded and Nehru was re-elected as the president of the Indian National Congress, the Congress clarified its policy, raising two objections to the 1935 Act.[13] The first objection was that the constitution was an imposition from the outside, and the second and a greater objection was the understanding that it did not give genuine self-government to Indians. In the end, the matter required a pragmatic approach, and the Congress issued a statement. It stated:

> If the new constitution can be utilised in any measure to take us nearer to that supreme goal, there would be no point in refusing to put it to such a use simply because it has been imposed by an outside authority.[14]

The Congress party explained that even though the party's manifesto started with the presumption that the new legislatures could not yield substantial benefits, many reforms promised in the manifesto could be achieved very much within the competence of the new legislatures. It further emphasised that the upcoming legislatures could expand the development of administrative measures essential to the freedom of Indians and help with the work to be done on the ground – outside the assembly and the councils – among the masses. The two instances to be discussed in the following sections will show that the provincial Congress government, once formed, would work against the freedoms on the ground by invoking various colonial prohibitions and repressing the political others.

The build-up to the 1937 elections underlined the upcoming political conflicts once the provincial government was formed. Pertinently, an important line of Nehru's campaign for his re-election as Congress president and canvassing support for the possible candidates was his openly socialist rhetoric arguing for the abolition of the *zamindari* system under Nehru's leadership. The right wing of the Congress was unhappy with this departure because *zamindars* were a vital constituent of the UP Congress. To attract the peasantry towards the Congress in UP, Nehru took a strong position against the *zamindari* system. By December 1936, when the Indian Congress's *Agrarian Committee Report* came out, it proposed 'drastic curtailment of the zamindars' rights, writing off the arrears of rent and the wiping out of debts and alteration of the law of inheritance'.[15] The committee also urged the imposition of death duties on *zamindari* property above a certain level and suggested that the rent be a charge on surplus produce after deducting the cost of production and maintenance expenses of peasants. Broadly, the report aimed to appeal to a broader mass of people by acknowledging their problems and taking a very comprehensive view of the various defects of the agrarian system. During this period, many letters to the editor of *The Leader* warned that the drastic curtailment of *zamindari* rights could have adverse effects. The recommendations of the Congress report were more an attempt to emphasise the movement's commitment to the cause of the peasantry and the working classes rather than practical policy suggestions.

Meanwhile, mill and factory workers were already growing closer to communist organisations – another matter of concern for the Congress. Many *zamindars* who felt threatened by the socialist posture of the Congress moved towards the National Agriculturist Party of the *nawab* of Chhatari, which represented the interests of the landlord class. Muhammad Ahmad Said Khan Chhatari, known as the *nawab* of Chhatari, was a Muslim *zamindar*. He enjoyed great proximity to the colonial state. He held critical administrative portfolios such as minister of the cabinet in UP from May 1923 to January 1926, minister of agriculture in UP in 1931 and the acting governor of UP from April 1933 to November 1933.

To deliver on these socialist promises, the Congress would have to participate in the upcoming elections with full strength and win government power at the provincial level. On 6 December 1936, the UP Congress Committee elected its new office bearers, and it was evident from its composition that the left wing of the party was now dominant in the UP Congress Committee. Acharya Narendra Deo became the new president of the UP Congress, replacing Rafi Ahmed Kidwai. Jawaharlal Nehru, Rafi Ahmed Kidwai, Babu Purshottam Das Tandon and G.B. Pant became the vice presidents. Pandit Keshodev Malviya, Sampurnanand, Pandit Mohanlal Gautam and Damodar Swaroop Seth became the secretaries.[16] Numerous members of the committee were elected too. When the Congress finally entered the electoral arena, it stated that its sole purpose of playing along with the new constitution was to 'wreck' it.

It announced a *hartal* on 1 April 1937, the first day of the working of the 1935 Act after the conclusion of the provincial elections.

There was further anxiety and contestation within the Congress party about candidature for the elections. At times, there was more than one popular Congress leader in a constituency, and local candidates were nervous about making space for a party stalwart from elsewhere.[17] The preparations for the upcoming provincial elections were mired in many such controversies for the Congress. Nominations for the new provincial government had to be completed by 20 December 1936, and elections to the new provincial assembly and councils in UP under the new constitution (Government of India Act, 1935) had to be concluded by the end of the following February. After the finalisation of nominations and declaration of candidates, elections took place amidst great enthusiasm. For the UP assembly of 228 seats, the Congress won 133, the Muslim League 26, the National Agriculturists 22, and independents 47. For the UP legislative council of 60 seats, the Congress won 8, the Muslim League none, the National Agriculturists 4, independents 40 and Europeans 8. The significant outcome of the election was that the Congress emerged as the strongest party in UP. The Muslim League won less than half of the seats reserved for Muslims, only 26 out of 64. UP saw the emergence of the Congress as the dominant party in the legislature. Initially, it declined to form the government, and the then governor Harry Graham Haig invited the *nawab* of Chhatari to form the minority government in April 1937. However, the Congress revised its decision and asserted its claim to office in July 1937. The governor accepted the claim, and the Congress formed the provincial government under the leadership of G.B. Pant soon thereafter.

The election process and the results offered new potential to the Congress in UP. On the one hand, the Congress party humiliated the Muslim League by securing a majority of the reserved Muslim seats and emerged as the dominant political voice in UP. On the other hand, even after Nehru declared socialist policies in the election manifesto, the Congress failed to secure a broad and formidable backing amongst the smallholders of UP because peasants were not usually enfranchised unless they owned some land. It was evident in the substantial success of the National Agriculturists. Also, there started to appear a general discontent amongst socialists and Muslims over whether they should be a part of the Congress's nationalist movement or not. The Government of India Act, 1935, delegated powers to provincial governments, granting a considerable measure of autonomy from the central government of India. Provincial governments now had substantial financial and law-enforcement powers. In a way, autonomous provincial governments led by the Congress would now pursue the ends of the colonial government.

Given the political context in which the provincial government in UP was formed, the two instances discussed in the following sections will highlight that police repression and the use of extraordinary laws such as section 144 CrPC or curfews were perfectly acceptable to both the British administration and the provincial Congress government if it did not deal with imminent politics but focused on known problem categories. The previous chapter showed that the colonial administration adopted a similar strategy in the nineteenth and the early twentieth centuries.

Antonio Gramsci has argued that the ruling class can manipulate the value system and mores of society so that their view becomes the world view.[18] Terry Eagleton has also proposed that Gramsci's use of the word 'hegemony' refers to a governing power that wins consent to its rule from those it subjugates.[19] Ranajit Guha sees hegemony to be a kind of persuasion. According to Guha's subaltern thesis, the Indian case experienced dominance without hegemony. In colonial India, political coercion outweighed persuasive cultural hegemony in civil society, which carried over to the post-independence period. The postcolonial elite had distinctly different interests than the subaltern groups in the new nation. Guha argues that such a split in the state's politics meant that the Indian bourgeoisie, unlike the European bourgeoisie, failed to establish Gramscian cultural hegemony over Indian subalterns. The inability of the colonial state and the independent nation to assimilate civil society into political society led the state to exercise dominance without hegemonic consent.[20] The two instances to be discussed in this chapter will highlight that the Congress ministries, even before independence, had internalised the colonial administrative strategy of dominance. The colonial state had to often resort to dominance because it partially failed to establish hegemony in the face of a persistent anti-colonial mobilisation. The provincial governments could not persuade the subjects to remain peaceful now that they had their ministry. As the instances will show, the first administrative reflex of the UP Congress ministry was to resort to the time-tested formula of the colonial state, that is, dependence on extraordinary laws and the creation of new problem categories.

The Congress, the Mazdur Sabha and Labour Militancy in Kanpur, 1936–1938

The late colonial administration tended to criminalise the agitating worker or the 'urban poor'. Socialists within the Congress increasingly mounted pro-peasant and pro-worker rhetoric. Such an approach destabilised the Congress's hold over the mass organisation, leading to open disenchantment with the Congress Socialist Party. The Congress Socialist Party was an organisation floated in May 1934 within the larger Congress and aimed to highlight the concerns of the peasants and the workers. The possible reason for the emergence of a socialist organisation can be deduced from what Shahid Amin and Gyan Pandey noted about the nature of peasant mobilisation in UP (then Oudh/Awadh) in the early twentieth century and have amply demonstrated its militant character. Shahid Amin has highlighted how the local peasant commodity production often depended on the timing of the harvest, the timing of the need for money and the dates when rents would fall due.[21]

Misalignment between any of these factors would lead to peasant distress at the hands of moneylenders and *zamindar*s. Gyan Pandey has demonstrated how peasant mobilisation against the Oudh Rent Bill during 1920–1922 created a peasant political consciousness which was at times inspired by the figure of Gandhi and at other times motivated by very local factors.[22] What remains most notable in Gyan Pandey's analysis is the emergence of the Kisan Sabha as the most potent organisation wielding substantial influence on the UP peasantry. It was also during the period of peasant unrest in rural UP that Jawaharlal Nehru 'discovered' the 'peasant'. Pandey has noted that despite the 'localism' and 'isolationism' of the peasant movement in Awadh, 'it needed an ally among other anti-imperialist forces in the country. But the chief candidate for this role, the party of the growing urban and rural petty bourgeoisie, had turned its back on the peasant movement long before that time'.[23] When the Kisan Sabha signalled that it was ready to learn organised politics from the Congress, the Congress ignored, if not declined, the Kisan Sabha's offer of the association because the Congress as an organisation pledged to the Gandhian idea of non-violence.

On the other hand, the Kisan Sabha had revolt as its guiding principle, which did not rule out violence, if required. The Congress did not want to alienate the political interest of the peasantry and the working class in joining the anti-colonial efforts. At the same time, it did not want to steer away from its commitment to the principle of Gandhian non-violence. Hence, the Congress Socialist Party could deal with the drawbacks of following the principle of non-violence, which the militant working classes and the peasantry often ignored.

In the provincial elections in 1937, the socialists within the Congress became dominant in the legislative assembly and, as pointed out earlier, they remained in control of much of the provincial Congress organisation.[24] While the socialists within the Congress were active in organising labour and the peasant movement and mobilised workers, the other section came to dominate the new UP government and, like the colonial state, began to see strikes and protests as a disorder. The use of section 144 CrPC by the UP provincial government led by the Congress to control and prohibit strikes raises uncomfortable questions about the positive attitude of the Congress, which had earlier campaigned to safeguard the freedoms of the people, towards the colonial legal system and the purpose of the provincial government. The Kanpur labour strikes are embedded in the challenges of governing industrial towns where casual workers further contribute to the number of the urban poor.

Kanpur emerged on the urban map of north India after the arrival of British forces in 1778 and the rise of the commercial activity of the East India Company under the protective presence of the army. It was one of the important centres during the 1857 uprisings. After the uprisings, the town was restructured with an expanded cantonment, a new civil line and district offices. It became one of the important manufacturing centres in the province, mainly serving military demands and supplying cotton twist and yarn to local weavers in north India. In the 1860s, the arrival of the railways opened the town to trade with its hinterland and became a distribution point for cotton yarn, textiles, piece goods, grain, sugar, oil, oilseeds and animal hides. In addition to British merchants who owned most mills and factories, indigenous bankers later became small-scale industrial entrepreneurs in the first quarter of the twentieth century. As a result, rural labourers, mostly peasants, gradually began to migrate to Kanpur.

With time, the growth in trade resulted in an increasing demand for a workforce, and Kanpur became one of the main sites of workers' agitation in UP. During 1930–1937, the total number of mill workers in the city increased by 31.2 per cent.[25] The 1930s was a decade of 'political change and urbanisation, steady development of industrial activity and changes of social lives of Indian workers and peasants'.[26] Migrant labourers often resided in slums or *basti*s that were neighbourhoods of the city largely organised around caste and religious community, a situation that was reinforced as a wider array of peasant communities made their way to the city.[27] The new and urban set-up threw numerous challenges to the migrant peasant labourer. A major repercussion of the changing demography and occupational relations in the towns was that it had a significant impact on urban politics. Employed as a casual worker, the peasant labourer had inadequate workplace patronage relations. Also, with no permanent and dignified place to stay, the peasant labourers aggravated concerns about maintaining or enforcing social control over them. To deal with this challenge, 'a range of measures was introduced to discipline them, to regulate their living and working habits, and to control their cultural expressions, public conduct and political behaviour'.[28] Nandini Gooptu has argued that 'material deprivation' of the 'urban poor' went hand in hand with more 'overt forms of discipline and social subordination'.[29] The following sections will show that the colonial tactics of labour discipline and its social subordination continued after the Congress had formed the provincial government in UP.

In the 1930s, workers in Kanpur city had a powerful political presence and could threaten the industrial life of the entire province. Labour unrest shaped a significant part of late colonial politics in UP. During periods of intensified political disturbances, a range of special coercive regulations was introduced. These coercive instruments were often used to deal with the 'menace' of tumult associated with crowds of onlookers, supporters and participants at demonstrations. Pickets and processions were also sought to be governed and regulated by an elaborate set of rules, supplemented by an armed police force frequently resorting to baton charges or firing. Nandini Gooptu has argued that 'the aim of such intervention in collective activities was to impose restrictions and discipline on the "turbulent" and "lawless element"'.[30] By the end of 1936, elections to choose new party office bearers in the UP Congress were to take place, followed by the provincial elections soon after. Pertinently, this was also a major year for strikes. In the interwar years, deprivation and dispossession of the poor worsened in the towns of UP. The urban poor were further marginalised due to the decisive shifts in local town-improvement measures and taxation policies, which 'impinged more directly and extensively on the economic activities and housing and settlement patterns of [the] poor'. The 'urban poor' faced a housing crisis because of the new local policies. As a result, 'urban living became more conflictual and unstable, and all experienced greater vulnerability and insecurity'.[31] This sharpened class differences in Kanpur, resulting in bitter opposition and often hostility among the 'urban poor' not only against urban authorities but also against the propertied classes. Moreover, the urban poor became aware of the unrepresentative nature of their existence, and their exclusion from power and rights, in the political system.[32]

Henceforth, the 'urban poor', of which the industrial labour was a substantial number, became militant. Force and coercion involving police action often began to be employed by the local administration, which contributed significantly to the extensive political unrest and violence in urban north India in the interwar period. As a result, the image of the poor as 'lawless, disorderly, violent and criminal' was amplified and 'provided justification for their control and discipline through policing'.[33] It is in such a context that the Kanpur case study begins.

Workers' Strikes at the Cooper Allen Factory

In November 1936, workers of the Cooper Allen leather factory in Kanpur went on a strike over a supposed cut in salaries and recognition of the Mazdur Sabha as the union for factories in Kanpur. On 5 December, more than 3,000 workers who were supposed to resume work failed to turn up at the factory despite 15 of their representatives having had a two-hour meeting with M.L. Carnegie, the company's managing director. It was reported that the management would agree to the demands of the representatives provided the workers returned to work at eight the next morning. The workers did not show up, and the management put out a notice stating that no further negotiations would take place until the workers returned. A notice at the factory gates also appeared, announcing the management's refusal to dismiss 150 strike-breakers who were hired as workers to clear hides. It would cause difficulty in the return of the dismissed workers. It further maintained that no cut in the wages had taken place.[34] However, the striking workers resorted to picketing to keep others away from attending the factory. Meetings were held at the Parade Grounds, Kanpur, the main venue of labour meetings during the strike.[35] By 8 December, the situation did not improve, and the picketing continued, and the city administration imposed section 144 CrPC in the vicinity of the factory. The unwillingness of the factory management to take back the earlier sacked 150 workers was the main point of contention and was seen by the workers as victimisation and penalisation of the striking workers.[36] At this moment, factional infighting emerged within the Congress regarding labour issues and the upcoming provincial elections. At a meeting of the Kanpur Municipal Board on 12 December, with B.P. Shrivastava as the chairman, a resolution was passed sympathising with workers and requesting the board to allow 10,000 rupees for the immediate relief of the striking workers who were now out of work for three weeks.[37] A committee led by B.P. Shrivastava was also appointed to bring about a settlement of the issue.[38] Meanwhile, the company's legal adviser, Rai Bahadur Vikramjit, served a notice to some of the striking workers. It demanded that these workers vacate their quarters in the Allengunj settlement area.

Under a police escort, European employees of the factory visited the Allengunj settlement to persuade the workers to return to work. This effort was unfruitful. The management also tried to employ hundreds of strike-breakers but had to drop them because they did not have the required skills. In the meetings, the workers condemned the interference by the police in an industrial dispute.[39] In the light of a lack of settlement and the ongoing electoral process in the province, the district magistrate extended an existing order under section 144 CrPC to the whole of Kanpur for a period of two months. According to newspaper reports, the order specifically noted that in processions, strikers displayed red flags and 'slogans advocating revolution were shouted to the disturbance of ordinary trade and terror of peaceful citizens'.[40] Given the ongoing elections for the Congress president and the upcoming legislative assembly and legislative council elections, political parties were, in general, busy with election affairs and paid little or no attention to the situation in Kanpur. Also, the invocation of section 144 CrPC for two months was part of a calculated tactic of the Kanpur administration in the light of the upcoming elections that were to conclude by the end of February 1937.

Several 'important persons' connected with the strike were arrested for violating section 144 CrPC when factory workers organised a huge procession moving through the main streets of Kanpur. Sympathising with the cause of striking workers, a *hartal* was observed on 20 December by both the Hindu and Muslim shopkeepers of Kanpur. According to one report,

> Fierce attacks against the attitude of the proprietors of the Cooper Allen Factory as well as the police were made in a public meeting held at Shraddhanand Park on December 20th. Various leaders from the Congress party attended the public meeting.[41]

For the first time, the Congress's active involvement in the workers' campaign can be noticed. The timing and purpose of this intervention are apparent here. Nothing substantial resulted from the numerous workers' protest meetings as UP was busy with the new provincial government elections.

When the elections concluded in February 1937, the results reshaped the political forces in UP. The significant outcome was that the Congress emerged as the strongest party in UP. Once the newly formed Congress government started functioning with G.B. Pant as the prime minister (or the premier), the issue of factory strikes once again preoccupied matters of governance in Kanpur. The strikes, to which little attention was paid during the elections, now resurfaced, creating a difficult situation for the newly formed Congress government. Letters to the editor questioned the strategy of the Congress party to attain *swaraj* (self-government) under the new constitution and sought clarifications about its plans to 'wreck the constitution', as the Congress declared before and during the elections.

Meanwhile, workers were getting restless over the growing virtual *mistri raj* (rule of foremen and supervisors) in the Kanpur mills, who would serve as low-level supervisors often supporting the factory management rather than ordinary workers and did not bother much about regulations.[42] The growing impatience of the workers with the lackadaisical attitude of factory managements towards their key concerns resulted in several other mills in Kanpur joining the strike. Soon, all major factories and mills in Kanpur went on strike with a common cause – demanding recognition for the Mazdur Sabha as the legitimate representative of the workers in Kanpur factories. By the end of July, the representatives of the Sabha offered to mediate between the strikers and the mill management but were declined. Two representatives of the workers, Harihar Nath Shastri (a Congressman) and Sant Singh Yusuf (a communist), met the district magistrate in this connection, and the district magistrate promised to explore avenues to arrange a meeting between the management and the Mazdur Sabha representatives. Harihar Nath Shastri, who was the representative of the

Mazdur Sabha, had recently been nominated to the UP legislative council. A worker's meeting in Kanpur organised to congratulate Harihar Nath Shastri on his nomination resolved to request the government – now under the Congress's control – 'to lift the ban under section 144 CrPC in order to enable the workers to organise'.[43] The incorporation of the Mazdur Sabha representative into the UP legislative council by the Congress highlights the subtle yet important link that the Congress had with the agitation and, as a result, would be able to maintain a successful control of the situation hereafter.

Provincial Congress Government and Labour Mobilisation in UP

Meanwhile, the colonial government had published a report on the labour situation in India titled 'Industrial Disputes in India, 1926–36'. It published statistics that suggested that the number of disputes and the loss of working days had dropped since 1928. One newspaper editorial discussed its publication and mentioned that the improvement could be attributed to the appointment of the Royal Commission of Labour in India.[44] The commission, the editorial observed, had had considerable influence over 'moderate labour leaders' towards 'constructive activity and cooperation'. It credited the commission with persuading most labour leaders to realise that strikes did not yield prosperity for the workers, and it was peace in industry and cooperation with the management that could improve working conditions. It argued that managements must listen to the legitimate grievances of the workers, or else extremist leaders of the workers would thrive. It also criticised labour leaders for frequently resorting to strikes and emphasised that strikes worsened workers' plight. The editorial maintained that workers were easily misled and must carefully choose their leaders, saving themselves 'misery and suffering', and expressed hope that the employers would 'adopt a more progressive attitude towards labour so that extremist leaders may not be able to acquire influence'.[45] The content of the editorial is quite straightforward in the context of the Kanpur strikes.

With Harihar Nath Shastri being nominated to the UP legislative council now, the situation began to change. Neither the assurances of a sympathetic response by the UP premier nor the appeals of labour leaders could calm the workers' unrest. Instead, labour politics in Kanpur re-energised itself with the formation of a 60-member committee to run the strike and to demand the withdrawal of section 144 CrPC from various localities of Kanpur. It gave considerable anxiety to the colonial administration and the provincial government. Yusuf, the secretary of the Mazdur Sabha, wrote a letter to the premier of UP requesting him to constitute an enquiry committee to investigate the details of the wage-cut issue.[46] Noticing an increase in labour unrest and more factories joining the strike, the local administration arrested Yusuf on the evening of 3 August 1937 to prevent the labour unrest from spreading. The district authorities became more vigilant and began drafting more police from outside the district to cope with the 'emergency'. These developments required immediate attention from the provincial government. It was reported that the UP minister for Industries, K.N. Katju, was expected to mediate between the mill owners and the workers. The mill magnates also held a meeting in the face of the crisis and organised their interests by forming an association called 'The Northern Mill-owners Association' with representatives from the concerned factories.[47] The governor's situation report had noted that the Mazdur Sabha was anxious to bring about a general strike. Therefore, the district magistrate had to issue new orders under section 144 to prevent the assemblage of persons at street corners and the mill gates.[48] On 5 August, Katju finally arrived in Kanpur to bring a settlement to the strikes. Labour leaders Harihar Nath Shastri, Suraj Prasad Avasthi and Rajaram Shastri met the minister to convey their terms for an agreement. The recognition of the Mazdur Sabha by the mill owners, the appointment of a committee to examine the issue of wage cuts and assurance that striking workers would not be victimised for trade union activities were the workers' key demands. Various mill representatives such as Sir Tracy Gavin Jones, Lala Padmapat Singhania, H.A. Wilkinson, C.W. Tosh, R. Menzies and T.I. Smith also met the minister. They expressed their inability to recognise the Mazdur Sabha, stating that it was neither sufficiently representative nor influential enough to impose its decision on labourers. The Congress minister failed to resolve the dispute and returned to Lucknow.

The Congress leader Balakrishna Sharma, who accompanied the minister on this trip, deplored the attitude of the mill owners for not recognising the Mazdur Sabha and expressed that 'if the situation was allowed to develop, a first-class labour crisis was anticipated in Cawnpore (Kanpur)'.[49] A resolution to the strike appeared further away when 4,000 workers from the Kanpur textile mills downed their tools and joined the strike. These workers held their meeting at the Muslim High School grounds because the area fell outside the designated zone of prohibition under section 144 CrPC. A resolution passed at this meeting criticised the policy of the UP government and expressed resentment at the arrest of their 'comrade' Yusuf.[50] For the first time, the workers had begun to blame the UP government for their problems. The onus of the entire crisis began to shift from the factory management to the Congress ministry of UP.

By 6 August, almost twenty thousand workers from seven mills in the city had joined the strike. On one occasion, superintendent of police (SP) G.A. Pearce, Assistant Superintendent D.P. Kohli and Joint Magistrate W.G. Raw were confronted by the workers and pelted with stones near the Elgin Mills, where prohibitory orders under section 144 CrPC were in force.[51] The police resorted to a *lathi* (baton) charge, and later armed police were drafted in too. A similar situation occurred at other mills. Six thousand striking workers of Juggilal Kamlapat Mills attacked the factory and damaged buildings and equipment. The police responded with firing, wounding a worker with a pistol shot. Around 40 workers were arrested at the Juggilal Kamlapat Mills. The situation had become grim, and the workers' movement was at the peak of its militancy. While the district magistrate eagerly took stock of the situation, the premier G.B. Pant was in touch with authorities and Congressmen in Kanpur. He sent Acharya Narendra Deo, president of the UP Provincial Congress Committee, to Kanpur to intervene and survey possible solutions.[52] As more workers from other factories joined the strike, it was reported that around four thousand workers of the New Victoria Cotton Mills had gone back to work. Local Congress leaders had a meeting with the managing committee of the Employers' Association of Northern India with proposals forwarded by the Mazdur Sabha. After the meeting, the Employers' Association passed the following resolution:

> Provided all mills in Cawnpore [Kanpur] resume normal work by Monday morning, Aug 9, the *Mazdur Sabha* will be recognised by the Employers' Association of Northern India. It, however, has to be understood that recognition will only be accorded provided no further strikes take place without reasonable and due notice of such intention being given to the association.[53]

The minister for industries, who had earlier failed to resolve the crisis, returned to Lucknow. He made a somewhat ambiguous speech addressing the workers' situation in Kanpur. On the one hand, he recognised the workers' hardship and yet criticised them for going on a strike. On the other hand, he praised the mill owners of Kanpur and recognised their services to the growth of industry in UP. The mill owners, according to Katju, were 'generous and sensible persons' and could not have tyrannised workers.[54] Katju's statement reflects the Congress's motivation in the post-1937 elections scenario, where it cleverly sought support from the urban liberal bourgeoisie without overtly undermining the protest of the working classes.

The number of workers joining the strikes kept increasing. According to one newspaper report, between twenty-five and thirty thousand workers were on strike in the city of Kanpur. Meanwhile, the workers' defiance of prohibition orders continued, and police *lathi* charges on protest demonstrations did not stop. When the labour unrest in Kanpur did not show any signs of abating, the provincial government issued a communiqué stating that it would appoint a committee of enquiry to investigate and report the relations between employers and workers and the condition of workers in Kanpur as well. It also appealed to strikers to maintain calm to facilitate the enquiry. The communiqué added that it was the duty of the government to 'maintain order and tranquillity' and hoped that the district magistrate would act in 'a spirit of impartiality' to ensure that the police acted with restraint while discharging their duties.[55] The government communiqué is a perfect example of a calculated and forceful governmental decision. It assured investigation into the condition of workers and yet asserted the necessity of public order and tranquillity. It also recognised that the use of force was inevitable and that it was the duty of the governmental apparatus to actively respond to threats to public order.

The strikes gained the sympathy of various sections of the Congress party in UP and made the Congress socialists anxious about the situation. The executive committee of the all-India Congress Socialist Party in Patna passed a resolution criticising the UP government. It criticised the promulgation of section 144 CrPC, *lathi* charges and police firing on protesting workers and the imprisonment of their leaders.[56] It demanded that the UP government withdrew all 'repressive orders' and released imprisoned workers. Most pertinently, it reminded the UP Congress of its election manifesto where it had emphasised 'the rights of workers, a living wage, and freedom of speech, association and strike'.[57] The Congress Socialist Party in Allahabad and Benares passed similar resolutions too.[58]

Given the criticism from various sections within and outside the Congress, G.B. Pant, the premier, had to head to Kanpur to resolve the crisis personally. Upon his intervention, the Employers' Association accepted the 18 demands of the Mazdur Sabha with some modifications. The premier congratulated the mill owners and labour leaders on this development and gave 'chief credit' to the district collector and magistrate, L. Owen, who, based on the communiqué of the labour welfare officer of Kanpur, had promulgated banning orders under section 144 CrPC. According to the premier, the magistrate had worked consistently for the 'cause of industrial peace' and showed 'uncommon tact, patience, and ability in dealing with an extremely difficult situation'.[59] The SP, G.A. Pearce, was also appreciated for his role in handling the crisis.

This settlement did not materialise, and the strike took a complicated turn when the workers rejected the settlement reached between the Employers' Association and the Mazdur Sabha. Their continuing strike violated the fundamental principle of the settlement that they should resume work. The workers objected to the settlement on the basis that the Mazdur Sabha did not consult the recently formed strike committee. They demanded an immediate increase in wages irrespective of the findings of the enquiry committee promised by the government. A new group called the 'blue shirts' emerged from amongst the workers who, in an unexpected twist, discredited the settlement and called on the workers to hold on to their earlier position. Members of both the Mazdur Sabha and the Congress made frantic efforts to resolve the crisis and exhorted the workers to resume work.[60] Confusion and misunderstanding were partly to blame for this chaos. One of the issues that came to light was that, as per the agreement, when workers turned up for work at some factories, the work did not start until the afternoon due to the insufficient steam required to run the equipment. The workers perceived this as evidence of the dilly-dallying attitude of the factory management. Newspapers later reported that due to the huge numbers of workers present on the day of the announcement of the agreement, accurate information could not reach all workers simultaneously due to the unavailability of a loudspeaker. According to newspaper estimates, nearly four thousand workers in Kanpur continued to be out of work by 10 August 1937.[61] Editorials appeared exhorting the government to reform the executive of the Mazdur Sabha to ensure the confidence of the workers in it.[62] This only points out that the communist elements within the workers' ranks were dissatisfied with the Congress elements at the helm of the Mazdur Sabha and did not leave any opportunity to frustrate and humiliate the provincial Congress and its members among the Kanpur workers.

In the face of the continuing strike, the Employers' Association expressed that they felt cheated in the entire process of recognising the Mazdur Sabha. They reiterated that the Employers' Association would have recognised the Mazdur Sabha earlier had it been satisfied that the Sabha members possessed the 'powers and experience necessary for the efficient handling and administration of such a body'.[63] The disagreements within the various sections of Kanpur workers put the status and ability of the Mazdur Sabha in question. Another possibility was that disgruntled non-Congress socialist elements, primarily communists, perceived the settlement as a Congress triumph and expansion of its labour base.

The Congress's Justification for the Use of Force on Agitating Workers

The Congress had earlier opposed the new constitution and, while campaigning for the provincial elections, had argued that the 1935 Act did not give maximum freedom to India. Yet, at the same time, when it came to power, it actively curtailed workers' rights and freedom to organise and protest. The attitude of the Congress provincial government is reflected in the statements of Jawaharlal Nehru, the then national president of the Congress party and a member of the UP Provincial Congress Committee. When Nehru was asked to explain if the police firing on protesting workers in Kanpur was consistent with the Congress's policy of non-violence, he replied:

> Open violence should only be met by force. Open violence, if it is allowed, will dislocate the whole business, trade, and normal life of a city, and so it should be suppressed by any Government. Whether it is violence by Labourites, or a communal riot, which is only looting innocent people, it must be met by effective measures.[64]

Nehru further stated that a Congress minister would instruct the police not to take peremptory action and to judge each case on its merits before resorting to violence. However, he also conceded that he considered violence as 'vulgar' and differentiated non-violence as a creed propagated by Gandhi from non-violence as a policy. He added, 'Idealist utopia where there was no war, no violence, no strife, did not exist. All the same, violence seldom solved a problem.'[65] Nehru's statement sheds light on the policy of the Congress as a pragmatic government. It would maintain that it was influenced by Gandhi but was not significantly different from the earlier colonial policy that suppressed labour unrest or protest. Labour unrest in Kanpur mills provides a window into the politics of public-order laws and demonstrates that different issues influenced politics locally. It also indicates that provincial governments and political organisations, specifically the UP Congress, the spearhead of the nationalist and anti-colonial mobilisation, repressed political others responsible for 'public disorder' and would invite extraordinary measures as a standard remedy to deal with them. In such strikes, a small party of policemen often felt easily overwhelmed by a crowd numbering in thousands.[66] The police responded with *lathi* charge and firing. It was understood that any situation that endangered the lives of policemen justified police violence.

Moreover, the Employers' Association in Kanpur had already accused the Mazdur Sabha of 'communist tendencies' and of raising a 'Red Worker's Army' for the next fight.[67] Chitra Joshi has done an elaborate discussion on the militant spirit of Kanpur workers in 1937 in this regard.[68] The premier of UP finally discussed with the Employers' Association and the workers to find a common path of establishing the enquiry committee. Eventually, Babu Rajendra Prasad was appointed as the chairman of this committee.[69] The enquiry committee had to work in a tense environment because there were fresh reports of workers' assault on *mistris* and clerks in some factories.[70] The Congress was facing general criticism regarding police firing on workers during the strikes. Nehru's statements in favour of police action did not go unnoticed. For instance, in a letter to the editor, a Congress sympathiser from Benares wrote:

> The Congress Ministries, in Provinces where they are in power, profess that theirs is a 'civilized Government'. It is right that this be so. Only one is a little surprised to hear certain Congress Ministers say that *lathi* charges are not a taboo even now and it was shocking to read the statement of the Congress president justifying the recent firing and lathi charge on the Kanpur strikers. Firing and lathi charges on a crowd which is unarmed are acts which no civilised Government can allow, much less perpetrate. The best way of dispersing such crowds is the use of tear bombs. May I hope that Congress Ministers will introduce this avowedly more civilized method of coping with similar situations in future and save their supporters from being disappointed in them?[71]

While addressing a meeting of the University Law Society in Allahabad, Jawaharlal Nehru indicated that he was aware of the need to get rid of old laws. However, his reference to 'old laws' was rather confusing. He often referred to old laws as traditional customary laws. While talking about Hindu laws, Nehru said that if law students 'wanted to have good laws then the laws should be such as would suit the conditions prevailing and should be changed when the conditions changed'.[72] Little did he deal with the need to decolonise Indian law, now that Congress was in power in most provinces. He further stated that 'behind every law there was some power – it was public opinion, and if public opinion went against law it would become impossible for the law to have any force. The present laws have proved to be useless, considering the conditions of the world and of India'.[73] Nehru lectured the law students regarding changed times and the then changing international situation arguing for India to enter the modern world. However, he did not speak about discarding the repressive laws that originated in a colonial context.

Towards the end of September 1937, Nehru had had enough of the recurring strikes in Kanpur mills. He wrote a special article in the daily *Pratap*, contextualising his perception of the labour action.[74] In this article, Nehru emphasised that though Kanpur labour faced great problems, it had to bear in mind that out of the fifty million people living in UP, the workers in Kanpur numbered only fifty thousand. He added that the majority of the population was peasants, and unless the issue of poverty was addressed, restlessness in the country would remain. He further argued that if the condition of the 'peasant' did not improve, the condition of the 'labour' who came from among the peasants could not be bettered. Nehru pointed out that it was on account of the unemployment of the peasants that the mill owners could take advantage and recruit workmen from the cultivators. Hence, strikes failed despite the strength of labour organisations.

Nehru's article was both an offer of conciliation, an attempt to bond with the working class, and advocacy for the Congress's policy of abolishing the *zamindari* system. However, Nehru's statement also tried to draw up an 'order of things' in UP. He attempted to attract general support by highlighting his awareness of issues beyond the labour question. The latter would resolve eventually, but only after the peasant question had been dealt with. In the end, for Nehru, the emancipation of labourers was connected to achieving the freedom of India. The main difficulty, according to Nehru, was that 'as soon as [the labourers] realised that they had obtained strength they began to think they could do anything they liked and forgo they had to contend with bigger forces'.[75] Noticeably, when Nehru himself arrived in Kanpur towards the end of September, his tone had changed from a warning to a threat. He emphasised that a strike should only be an action of last resort. In a letter addressed to the striking workers in Kanpur, he argued:

> Our work and our organisation can only proceed if we are non-violent and peaceful. There are people who believe that they can terrify and browbeat others and force them to concede their demands by threats or by violence. Such people are living in a fools' paradise and are completely deluded. If violence is resorted to, is it impossible that the Government should not interfere, and the army or the police should not be called. The workers should remember that the Government is very powerful, and that it must put down violence by violence, and that the workers in no time will be subdued, and this will have a very bad effect on the workers' organisation as a whole. It will become weak and the attention of the public will be diverted from the reasonable demands of the workers to the quarrels.[76]

There is a change of tone in Nehru's remarks, but a possible outline of a course of action that the Congress government could take to deal with the ongoing strikes in Kanpur is also noticeable.

Mohandas Gandhi also expressed his views on the law-and-order situation in the October issue of *Harijan*. He wrote, 'civil liberty is not criminal liberty', and when law and order were under popular control, 'ministers of that department cannot hold their portfolios if they act against the popular will'.[77] Emphasising that assemblies were not sufficiently representative of the whole people, suffrage was wide enough to make them representative. Gandhi added:

> [I]n provinces where the Congress ruled it has been assumed by some persons that individuals can say what they like. But so far as I know the Congress mind, it will not tolerate any such license.[78]

Most importantly, Gandhi explained that the extraordinary provisions in the CrPC, the Indian Penal Code (IPC) and other special legislations that the British had enacted for their safety and which can be easily identified should be ruled out from the operation of the Congress ministers who must be guided by the working committee's interpretation regarding law and order. He suggested that 'such powers must be exercised by the ministers against those, who in the name of civil liberty preach lawlessness in the popular sense of the term'.[79] He concluded that 'non-violence is a new weapon still in the process of evolution. Its vast possibilities are yet unexplored'.[80] While Nehru made threats, Gandhi made a 'moral' appeal. But he ignored that during the Non-Cooperation movement, he had himself instructed Indians to disobey certain laws that curtailed the liberty of Indians.

In a secret letter (personal) dated 23 December 1938, the governor wrote that he visited Kanpur to attend the jubilee dinners of the India Chamber of Commerce, where the district magistrate appeared delighted with the effects of his orders under section 144 because it practically stopped 'undesirable' speeches and demonstrations organised by the communists. The governor further noted that the magistrate was not interested in prosecuting individuals for their speeches. However, the condition in Kanpur was not 'satisfactory' yet, and orders under section 144 continued to result in 'resentment' against these orders.[81] The administration saw the strikes as undisciplined labour and invoked Section 144 as an effective tool to control them.

Soon, major newspapers such as *The Leader*, amongst others, became critical of the striking workers and distinguished between the unorganised, spontaneous and violent actions of 1937 and the organised and peaceful strikes of 1938. Terms like 'violent', 'aggressive', 'defiant', 'unruly' and 'threatening' were used in the daily news reports and official accounts to describe the striking workers. Contemporary newspapers like *The Aaj*, *The Pioneer* and *The Leader* were full of such accounts. Most importantly, the police were always reported to have 'fired in self-defence'.[82] Also, any police violence was seen as justified because the workers had supposedly violated section 144. We observe a ménage à trois between Congress politicians, the administration and the press when it came to legitimising violence on workers. Public order and peace were the terms that could neutralise the workers' claims of police atrocities.

The provincial government appointed the Cawnpore Labour Enquiry Committee, which recommended methods of improving the living conditions of workers and published data that described labour conditions across cotton mills in Kanpur. The findings of the committee highlighted the uncooperative attitude of the employers in supplying information. It also reported the employers' hostility to the only organised trade union in Kanpur – the Mazdur Sabha.[83] The wages at Kanpur mills were much lower than in other centres of industry in India, and such low wages were found unjustified by the report when compared to the level of profitability in those mills. The committee suggested some increments in the workers' wages.[84]

The relationship between the labour organisation and the Congress remained chequered during this period. After the death of Ganesh Shankar Vidyarthi in 1930, the leadership of the Mazdur Sabha passed to Harihar Nath Shastri. Harihar Nath Shastri, as a Congressman, was devoted to building a Congress labour movement in Kanpur and the rest of the country. As noted in the earlier sections, there was a short period of close coordination between the Sabha and the Kanpur City Congress Committee. Such coordinated action gave strength both to the Congress as an organisation and to the trade union movement. However, it also ran the risk of Congress factions getting involved in the affairs of the Mazdur Sabha. They were acceptable if they benefitted the Congress's interest by serving as its instrument. During the Kanpur strikes, local communists entered the Mazdur Sabha and worked in coordination with the Congress for a while. The Sabha gained prominence and strength during the strikes with Harihar Nath Shastri as its president and Sant Singh Yusuf, a communist, as the general secretary. As the strikes extended from late 1936 to late 1937, the communists soon acquired representation of 17 or 18 members on the 40-member council of the Sabha, though the Congress still had a clear majority. Internal factionalism in the Congress weakened its hold over the Mazdur Sabha, and it was in the 1938 Sabha elections that communists acquired complete control with the support of Balakrishna Sharma and his supporters who were opposed to Harihar Nath Shastri. As a result, Sant Singh Yusuf became the new president of the Sabha in 1938. Here, a Congress leader, whose primary interest did not lie in the labour movement and had little interest in controlling the affairs of the Sabha – which was already getting out of hand – allied with the communists for the sole purpose of defeating a factional opponent in the Congress party.

Also, when the enquiry report was released, the Employers' Association rejected it the following month.[85] As a result, workers in all Kanpur mills went on strike simultaneously, with the total number of workers participating being up to forty thousand approximately. The Mazdur Sabha, which was stronger than ever, extended its full support to the strike.[86] The consolidation of the workers' movement in Kanpur under the communist-dominated Mazdur Sabha declined after 1938. It was partly because of the 'People's War' politics of the communists. Later, during the Second World

War, the communist support to the British war efforts led to a thinning of the ranks of the Mazdur Sabha to a significant level. The working class in Kanpur and the public in general perceived it as a betrayal of the struggle against the British and the fight for complete *swaraj*. Moreover, during the war period, the promulgation of the Defence of India Rules restricted political activity and made political organisation difficult.[87] Any political organisation creating 'unrest' or 'disorder' would now amount to sedition.

The Congress's initial rhetoric of securing freedoms for Indians and later justification and necessity for the use of violence by the state points to the complex nature of the contexts in which such measures got legitimised with time. Three initial observations can be made from the Kanpur instance. First, there was competitive political diversity amongst Congress nationalists and others in late colonial India. Second, the Congress party saw itself as the only legitimate voice of the nationalist movement and became intolerant of its political others. And third, the Congress provincial government in UP did not shy away from sustaining its power by using violence and manipulating the crisis to its advantage. Like the colonial state, the Congress too felt vulnerable and suffered political anxiety in the face of increasing opposition to its hegemonic discourse. It faced complex political challenges while leading the provincial government, which punctured its claims to moral politics, that is, *satyagraha*, that opposed colonial violence. As a result, it failed to offer a new administrative vocabulary and found instant refuge in the juridical/law, which was forcefully colonial in nature.

The chapter will now discuss the second instance of sectarian conflict in the city of Lucknow and show another face of public-order management by the UP provincial government led by the Congress under the leadership of G.B. Pant.

Reciting 'Public Disorder': Madh-e-Sahaba and the Politics of Manipulating Chaos in Lucknow, 1937–1940

Muslims constituted a significant number of the population in UP. Shias and Sunnis, the two main sects, were at loggerheads over a historical debate and disagreement in Islam. This disagreement shaped a controversy that was a cocktail of religion, politics and nationalism and produced an unusual challenge for the administration in the city of Lucknow. The controversy was known as the Madh-e-Sahaba controversy or the Tabarra agitation of 1937. The UP government struggled to control communal/ sectarian conflicts between the Shia and the Sunni Muslims of Lucknow.

As a result, the UP Congress government and the local administration in Lucknow invoked prohibitory laws such as section 144 CrPC and curfews to maintain 'public order and tranquillity'. Challenges to public order were not always a direct binary contestation between the police and the 'mob'. On various occasions, a chaotic social order was sustained or even encouraged to manipulate the political situation in favour of various political interests. This section discusses one such instance of sectarian violence in Lucknow, where a historical religious debate between the Shias and the Sunnis overtook contemporary political alignments. The Congress was at the helm of affairs after the provincial elections of 1937 and had to deal with the issue at hand. A calculated response by the Congress and delayed management of the crisis turned it into an everyday public-order issue in the city of Lucknow. This section will discuss the conflict in detail and will show that the provincial Congress government actively intervened in Muslim politics in Lucknow. While it instituted curfews and other prohibitory orders to control the conflict, it carved a space for itself to intervene in the life of the community directly. The chapter will argue that large-scale political mobilisations did threaten provincial governments but also offered opportunities to rearrange political calculus to their benefit. The discussion will be divided into three parts. The first part will contextualise the significance of Lucknow and outline the origins of the conflict in the colonial era. The second part will highlight the factors that led to the recurrence of the conflict in various instances without any signs of its resolution. The third section will highlight that the political contestations between the Congress and the Muslim League interfered with the issue and sustained the crisis. The administrative response by the provincial Congress government in this instance was lackadaisical and was more intent on capitalising on the crisis.

The Significance of Lucknow and the Origin of Conflict in the Colonial Era

The Madh-e-Sahaba controversy was a very prominent case of sectarian conflict amongst the Muslims of Lucknow and a core administrative concern of the Congress ministry of UP in the 1930s. Scholars such as Francis Robinson, Mushirul Hasan, Farzana Sheikh and many others have demonstrated how developments in the wider Islamic world influenced the political ideologies of north Indian Muslims in the 1920s and the 1930s.[88] However, the conflict in Lucknow had much older roots. It was connected to the ancient religious debate between the Shias and the Sunnis over the identity of the 'legitimate' caliph/*imam* after the death of Prophet Muhammad. The Shias and Sunnis have different views on this issue. While the Sunnis believe in the notion of *khilafat* (a purely worldly political leader who succeeded the Prophet in his political and military capacity), the Shias believe in *imamat* (a religious as well as a political and military leader who also inherited parts of the Prophet's spiritual charisma through direct family descent). Central to this distinction was the role and status of the Prophet's son-in-law and nephew, Ali.[89] The Sunnis consider all the four immediate successors to the Prophet, including Ali, in high regard and as rightful. The Shias, in contrast, hold that the first three successors of the Prophet and Ali's rivals were usurpers and guilty of acts of tyranny and oppression against the Prophet's kin. The month of Muharram in the Islamic calendar represents a period of mourning for the sons of Ali – Hassan and Hussain – who were massacred by the caliphate's army in a civil war between the two parties. In India, violent sectarian confrontations between the two groups occurred especially during the month of Muharram.

Francis Robinson has noted that where the Shias live in South Asian towns and cities, arguably no community has been more visible or audible.[90] Visible because of their grand processions at Muharram, and audible, certainly at Muharram, but also throughout the year in their *majlis*, where they gather across localities to recount the events of Karbala, often transmitting them by loudspeaker to the *mohalla*.[91] Scholarship on Muslim politics in India during colonial rule has implied that both Shias and Sunnis overlooked their religious and sectarian differences during the late colonial period and worked on a common platform for the broader Muslim interest. Many have agreed that such a perspective is especially true for the formative moments of Muslim separatist politics, for example, the period from the Muslim deputation to Lord Minto in 1906 to the end of the Khilafat movement in 1924.[92] Towards the end of the nineteenth century and later, Shia public figures had to abrogate their Shia identity and project themselves as representatives of the broader Muslim community due to the nature of the political climate. Justin Jones has argued that many Shias later departed strongly from such a position, even in Muslim cities like Lucknow, which was seen as a significant centre of the major ideologies and edifices of Muslim separatism in late colonial India.[93] Jones has demonstrated the discourse of community formation that emphasised the differences and separateness of the Shias from the Sunnis that eventually led to the systematisation of their political differences.[94]

A brief description of the significance of the city of Lucknow is necessary here before any further discussion about the issue at hand. Historically, Lucknow was the seat of the Mughal government of the Suba of Awadh from the late sixteenth century. Asaf-ud-Daulah, the Shia *nawab* of Awadh, founded Lucknow as his capital city in 1775 after the decline of the Mughals. Under the *nawabi* court patronage, Lucknow became one of the most flourishing towns of north India in the late eighteenth and early nineteenth centuries. With its majestic *nawabi* buildings and artisan industries, it also became famous as a literary, commercial and cultural centre. Artisanship comprised *chikan, kamdani, zardozi* (embroidered lace, silver and gold thread work), silver ornaments, calcio printing, bleaching, dyeing, shoe-making and ivory work. The events of 1857 brought about the demise of the *nawabi* culture and polity of Lucknow. As a result, the Muslim courtly classes, which depended on *nawabi* patronage, became the most notable casualty after 1857. Their decline led to the emergence of Hindu and Jain bankers and merchants who gained social prominence in the town as moneylenders to the indigent *wasiqdar*s or royal pensioners and as financiers of artisan industries and trade. Kanpur emerged as the chief trading location in UP due to the railways, but Lucknow also had a railway junction with large workshops connected to it. Lucknow retained its significance as a centre of the grain trade in Awadh. However, many of its artisan industries received a severe setback due to the loss of royal and courtly patronage. Muslims constituted much of the city's population. Most importantly, Lucknow housed the provincial legislative council and was maintained as an administrative centre by the British.[95]

One of the most significant social factors contributing to the Shia–Sunni conflict throughout the 1930s was the massive shift in population and demography in Lucknow. Before the 1920s, colonial Lucknow had been slow to modernise and remained largely stagnant in economic and population growth. However, Lucknow's rapid development thereafter into a major provincial centre of industry and trade saw the city's population spiral after 1921 from 217,000 to 387,000 in just 20 years. This sudden increase stemmed partly from a broader trend of urbanisation in interwar north India and owed to the establishment of Lucknow as the political capital of UP. After the Government of India Act, 1919, it became the seat of the provincial governor and the UP legislative council. As a result, Lucknow attracted an ever-increasing number of politicos, officials and investors, quickly transforming the city's size, composition and character.[96] It also gave rise to new contestations.

The sectarian clashes between Shia and Sunni Muslims of Lucknow went back to at least 1905. Ashutosh Varshney has noted that in 1905, quite a while after the end of Shia princely rule in Lucknow, the Sunnis began to insist on holding processions involving the public recital of verses in praise of all the four caliphs, also known as the *Madh-e-Sahaba*.[97] The Shias responded with Tabarra processions of their own, which involved public curses on the first three caliphs and praises to Ali and his family. It led to severe violence and conflict between the two communities between 1905 and 1909. A British committee headed by Arthur Pigott determined that the *Madh-e-Sahaba* was a recent Sunni invention and prohibited its public recitations.[98] Varshney has pointed out that Sunni rituals were considered an innovation because such public expressions of Sunni dominance had simply been inconceivable under Shia princes earlier. In the subsequent decades of mass politics, the issue resurfaced in the year 1935, adding to the administrative difficulties of the Lucknow administration.

Factors That Led to the Recurrence of the Conflict in Various Instances

In 1936, arrests were made during confrontations between the two sects that occurred when Sunnis began to recite *Madh-e-Sahaba* verses every Friday for almost three months.[99] The controversy did not end, and the city of Lucknow witnessed a series of riots owing to clashes between Shias and Sunnis in June 1937. During this period, the newly elected provincial government of G.B. Pant was already facing a strained relationship with the British colonial government over the issue of seeking the release of political prisoners of the famous Kakori case and other nationalists who were lodged in Andaman jails, and the mounting political pressure due to the workers' strikes in Kanpur. The governor's situation report regarded the Madh-e-Sahaba controversy as the 'most important event of this kind'.[100] The provincial government could not continue mass arrests due to the sectarian clashes because the number of prisoners awaiting trial in UP prisons was already rather large owing to the Kanpur labour crisis, communal riots at Allahabad and Benares, and now the frequent Madh-e-Sahaba riots in Lucknow. As a result, in June 1937, curfew orders and orders under section 144 CrPC were promulgated to control the situation. The provincial government quickly resorted to instituting prohibitory measures at the very first instance of confrontation. The premier of UP, G.B. Pant, and his minister of education quickly visited the affected quarters of Lucknow city and appealed to Muslims, both Shia and Sunni, to bring about a 'better atmosphere'.[101] Sheikh Iqbal Ali, who was the chairman of the Education Committee, Lucknow District Board, appealed to Muslims to maintain 'peace and harmony' and congratulated the Deputy Commissioner, Mr H.J. Frampton, and Mr Charles, the city magistrate, for the tactful handling of the Shia–Sunni riot. He was convinced that they both deserved the gratitude of the Muslim community too. Sheikh Iqbal Ali confidently expressed that for the first time in Lucknow, a riot had been brought under control within such a short time.[102] However, efforts at a compromise between the two communities were not fruitful even after the formation of a joint conciliation board. The board appeared to have failed in its purpose because both sides refused to express regret for their share in the origin of the riots. Meanwhile, sectarian newspapers such as the Sunni *al-Najm*, *Haram*, *Asad*, *Naqqara*, and so on, and Shia newspapers represented by publications such as *Sarfaraz*, *Zulfiqar*, *al-Wai'z*, *Hukumaran*, and so on, continued to advocate the causes of their respective communities throughout this conflict.[103] The self-congratulatory observations of the provincial government and the local administration in Lucknow overlooked the simmering communal posturing of these publications that continued the discussions around the discord.

In a meeting of its provincial unit under the leadership of Ali Zaheer, the Muslim League on 6 June 1937 discussed the question at length and passed a resolution. However, it failed to reach any clear decision. The meeting authorised Ali Zaheer and Ahsanul Rahman to invite the annual session of the All-India Muslim League in Lucknow for consultation of the general opinion.[104] The language of the Muslim League resolutions was rather clever. It tried to deal with the situation in its way but put much of the emphasis on the failure of the Congress government. The expression of political rivalry between the Congress and the Muslim League cannot be overlooked here. It regretted the riots and the loss of life and property of Muslims, and opined that such 'lawlessness' did not benefit any party and therefore was a 'menace' to the growth of nationalistic ideas in the country. A second resolution was also passed, which was lengthy and a tricky one. It expressed the apprehension of the Shias that the Madh-e-Sahaba agitation was started to put pressure on the colonial government to alter its previous decision to classify the Sunni procession ritual as an 'illicit' innovation.[105] It was held that the Sunnis aimed to coerce the Shias to surrender their 'legitimate and old established rights'. It was further held that acts of violence, along with the *fatwa*s and organised processions denouncing the Shias as *qafir*s (disbelievers) and their *azdari* ((lamentation, mourning for the Imam) as an act of sacrilege, brought rupture between the two communities/sects. It deplored the attitude of some Sunni leaders who persisted in carrying out 'nefarious propaganda' and refused to join the Shias on the conciliation board. It also stressed that peace and order were essential at that political juncture. The meeting resolved that the UP government should not be influenced by predesigned propaganda and threats by a section of the Sunnis, bearing in mind that the Shias were a minority within a minority and deserved a just resolution of the dispute.

The third resolution of the 'Central Standing Committee' of the Muslim League Conference observed that the Shias of Lucknow had shown great restraint and forbearance in the face of continuous and organised provocation and sympathised with the relatives of those who had lost lives or were injured during the riots.[106] The Shias in the Muslim League tried to convey their position to the government as a request and a covert threat. Through these resolutions, they claimed to take responsibility as dutiful 'citizens' for maintaining law and order by identifying the origin of the dispute.

The Majlis-e Ahrar, a Sunni organisation that was politically closer to the Congress and opposed to Jinnah's ideas, also organised a meeting of its working committee on 23 June 1937.[107] Presided over by Muhammad Ahmad Quazim, member of the legislative assembly (MLA), the meeting passed resolutions requesting the government to expedite the publication of the report of the Madh-e-Sahaba enquiry committee. The resolutions argued that the delay was causing anxiety in the minds of both sects and expressed apprehension that it might create 'fresh intrigues'.[108] Furthermore, the meeting deplored the recent sectarian riots and requested the colonial government to release political prisoners.[109] The nationalist and sectarian interests are intertwined here. Justin Jones has pointed out that Madh-e-Sahaba and Tabarra processions were used as a garb for political battles.[110] In both the meetings discussed here, nationalist, political and sectarian politics are intertwined. The demand for the release of political prisoners was common to the resolutions passed in both meetings.

Muslim leaders such as Wazir Hasan and Sayyid Haider Mehdi, affiliated with the Congress party, emphasised that the conflict was not sectarian but aimed at the government's restrictions on their religion. Soon the Congress party had to face the wrath of the Shia Tabarra agitators when along with the first three caliphs to be cursed, the names of Mohandas Gandhi and Jawaharlal Nehru were also added to the list. Jones has observed that there were social and class rivalries involved in this issue. The Madh-e-Sahaba front constituted mainly of Ahrars, from the urban, middle-class and artisan backgrounds who were considered by the British as lacking moderation and frequently criticised as 'degenerates', whereas, on the Tabarra front, noble, aristocratic Shia families close to the municipal government were in evidence. Therefore, the sectarian controversy was an attempt by poor Muslims who were mostly Sunnis to seize political control and initiative in the urban space of Lucknow.[111] A contrast between both the groups, the language of their resolutions and the framework of their demands is notable here. On the one hand, Shias used the tactics of pressurising the Congress government, invoked the need for urgent peace and order and regretted riots. On the other hand, Sunnis could not hide their anxiety and haste and demanded that the enquiry report be published at the earliest.

The conflict remained irresolvable in 1937, and only a temporary calm was restored. Scholars have pointed out that as early as 1932–1933, 'Muharram was becoming ever more schismatic, increasingly marked by the separation of Shi'a and Sunni *majlis* assemblies and processions, and the conflation of mourning and *munazara*'.[112] A wider range of new associations such as the Darbar-i-Hussaini, the Idara-i-Yadgar-i-Husaini and the prolifically active Ajnum-i-Nasr-ul-'Aza emerged within a few years and continued to invigorate *ta'ziyadari*[113] and emphasised the specifically Shia understanding of Muharram as an occasion of lamentation.[114] As a result, Muharram increasingly became a month that Shias and Sunnis began to experience separately from each other in an atmosphere appropriate to emphasise their differences. While earlier, some Sunni figures had argued that 'taking of *ta'ziya* had to be accompanied by the recitation of praises for the Caliphs', the agitating Majlis-e-Ahrar went a step further. They believed that Shia 'innovations', particularly *ta'ziyadari*, should cease entirely among Sunnis.

The UP government failed to resolve this intra-religious conflict in Lucknow in 1938 too. The problem for the district administration had increased further because of its inability to intervene in the dispute in a direct way. Moreover, given that the Muslim community of UP was involved in this dispute, the Congress was cautious not to let them slip into the hands of the Muslim League. The scale of the meetings becomes clearer from a confidential letter from the Government of United Provinces to R.M. Maxwell, who was the secretary to the Government of India, Home Department.[115] According to the letter, on 31 December 1937, about fifteen hundred Sunnis attended an Ahrar meeting at Tila mosque, Lucknow.[116] The meeting criticised the delay in publishing the Madh-e-Sahaba Committee enquiry report and threatened to launch civil disobedience if the government did not publish the report by 7 January 1938. The letter notes that the threat was later withdrawn partly on the advice of Maulana Habibur Rahman, who argued that such conduct could embarrass the Congress government, and partly because they could not organise it properly in the wake of a parallel agitation that was going on in Lahore in connection with the Shahidganj mosque issue.[117]

Another confidential letter from the UP government to Maxwell further points out that in the meantime, attempts were being made to bring about a compromise under the guidance of Maulana Abul Kalam Azad.[118] However, these attempts failed in the face of new challenges. The Congress had made it a regular observance to celebrate 'Independence Day' on 26 January of every year. The occasion was usually celebrated by taking out *prabhat pheris*,[119] followed by many flag-hoisting ceremonies and meetings later in the day. An 'Independence Day' pledge was taken at such meetings. But in January 1938, the celebrations of such an 'Independence Day' led by the Congress interfered with a Madh-e-Sahaba procession, which attempted to take over the park where the Congress 'Independence Day' meeting was being held. A clash ensued. The local police managed to intervene in time and averted a serious clash. However, considerable excitement prevailed in the city, and the police had to patrol the streets. This clash highlights the strained relationship between the Sunnis and the Congress party.

A confidential letter from the Government of UP to the Government of India emphasised that the Madh-e-Sahaba controversy continued to be a matter of contention and had by now assumed a more political complexion.[120] As a result, the UP government started contemplating publishing the report of the Madh-e-Sahaba Committee along with the UP government's resolution to the conflict.[121] But owing to the resignation of the UP cabinet in connection with the demand for the release of political prisoners, the publication of the report had to be postponed until after Muharram.[122] The ministers who tendered their resignations reached a settlement on 25 February 1938.[123] Finally, the report of the enquiry of the Madh-e-Sahaba Committee was published on 28 March 1938.

The governor of UP, H.G. Haig, in a secret letter to the viceroy and governor-general of India, Lord Linlithgow, expressed that, contrary to many apprehensions, the report was received 'very quietly'. It further reported that the Ahrars, who initiated the trouble on the Sunni side, 'seem definitely unwilling at the present stage to embark on any direct action'.[124] Moreover, the Shias expressed their satisfaction with the conclusions of the Madh-e-Sahaba report, which stipulated that 'while the Sunnis have the right to recite the *Madh-e-Sahaba* under suitable conditions and at suitable times, they must not do so to annoyance or danger of the public, or in manner provocative to Shias'.[125] However, the governor's letter immediately doubted whether in practice Sunnis could be allowed to make any public recital of the *Madh-e-Sahaba* in Lucknow and that this matter, therefore, would remain a matter of executive decision and hence might prove to be a complex problem.[126] The Allsop Committee that led the inquiry stated in its report that though the Madh-e-Sahaba recitations were allowable 'in theory', they should be disallowed in practice because of their provocative nature.

Riots between Shias and Sunnis again took place on the occasion of Chehlum when Sunnis allegedly attacked a Shia procession returning from the Karbala burial ground, resulting in the clashes. According to the governor's report, 'Sunnis most evidently were the aggressors'.[127] The police were able to control the situation quite late. By that time, 11 persons were already dead in various assaults, and about a hundred were injured. The atmosphere in the city was so volatile that the authorities had to summon the military. The government was also considering a temporary addition to the Lucknow police force, though, owing to political apprehensions, they were not prepared to make the Muslim inhabitants pay for it. The provincial Congress government, despite invoking extreme measures like bringing in the military to control the situation, refrained from punitive policing due to political calculations. It was hesitant to make the inhabitants pay for maintaining order in Lucknow. Both Sunni and Shia leaders were arrested for containing the situation.

While the Shia leaders deposited the required security in courts to secure their release from detention, Sunni leaders such as Maulana Abdul Shakoor and Zafar-ul-Mulk chose to go to jail.[128] The Sunnis in Lucknow were displeased with the committee report's findings and, on numerous occasions, threatened civil disobedience if the recitation of the Madh-e-Sahaba was not permitted. Shias and Sunnis continued to clash on numerous occasions regarding the reciting of the *Madh-e-Sahaba* and carrying out Muharram *ta'ziya* processions in Lucknow. By mid-May 1938, the Sunnis had given up their 'civil disobedience' and, as a result, 150 persons who were arrested during the Chehlum riots were released. Meanwhile, prominent Muslim leaders such as Maulana Zafar Ali Khan, Shaukat Ali and the Raja of Pirpur, who were touring on behalf of the Muslim League, delivered 'intensely provocative speeches' against the Congress government, particularly at Bara Banki and Allahabad.[129] In a political scenario where the Muslim League had faced political defeat at the hands of the Congress in the recently held elections, it upped its ante to reclaim its ground.

Political Contestation between the Congress and the Muslim League

The involvement of the Congress in the Shia–Sunni dispute further complicated the issue because the two Muslim ministers in the new Congress ministry of 1937 were both Sunni. The Congress was more inclined to support Sunni claims for *Madh-e-Sahaba* recitation. It obliged the Congress ministry to offer 'theoretical support to the Sunni side'.[130] However, the Congress also had the support of Shias in Lucknow city, where, unlike elsewhere in the province, most Sunnis supported the League. The All-India Shia Conference had a substantial support base in Lucknow. Syed Ali Zaheer, a prominent Shia leader, was a Congress member elected to the provincial legislative assembly from Lucknow. Also, Chaudhary Khaliquzzaman, a prominent League member, was elected to the legislative assembly from the city with substantial Sunni support.

Given the political circumstances, it is not difficult to decipher that the Congress was interested in winning Sunni support in the city of Lucknow and sought to use the controversy for this end. Some leaders of the Jamiat-e-Ulema convinced G.B. Pant that it was possible to ally if the ministry allowed Sunnis to take out a procession during *barawafat* (12th day of the Islamic month of Rabial-awwal, claimed to be the day of Prophet Muhammad's birth) and recite the *Madh-e-Sahaba*. Pant was inclined to allow Sunnis to recite the *Madh-e-Sahaba* to work political calculations in favour of the Congress, but Rafi Ahmed Kidwai, a Sunni Muslim and Congress leader, was opposed to the idea. In such circumstances, positive political signals from the Congress ministry in UP emboldened Sunni claims.[131] The ongoing provincial politics further complicated the sectarian issue between the Congress and the Muslim League.

On 30 May 1938, after clashes between the two groups, section 144 CrPC was promulgated in Lucknow for a month. It was reported that Sunnis were reciting the *Madh-e-Sahaba* by holding *milad*s (celebratory gatherings to commemorate Prophet Muhammad's birth anniversary), and the Shias in adjacent places were holding *majlis* reciting the *tabarra*. On a couple of occasions, the local deputy SP, Sardar Sunder Singh, handled the situation quickly and averted serious clashes.[132] The authorities assumed that now that the more aggressive party, the Sunnis, had given up the civil disobedience, the situation might improve. However, by the first week of June, the crisis once again flared up. Surprisingly, Shias, who had taken modest positions until then, were allegedly responsible for the conflict. Apprehensive that Sunnis would obtain some concession from the government, they passed a series of resolutions and threatened to recite the *tabarra* if Sunnis were shown any consideration and allowed any opportunity to recite the *Madh-e-Sahaba*. As a result, the began organising religious meetings where recitations of the *Madh-e-Sahaba* would take place. As a result, clashes erupted, and the district magistrate again promulgated section 144 CrPC.[133] On 2 June, in the face of severe tension between the two communities, Lucknow authorities decided to enforce another curfew order for a fortnight. It would impose restrictions during the night between 7.30 p.m. and 5.30 a.m.

The peculiar feature of these section 144 CrPC orders was their applicability to only Muslims. The situation did not improve as both sides frequently organized *milad* (Sunnis) and *majlis* (Shia) in a tit-for-tat spirit. According to some newspaper reports, the situation had exacerbated to such an extent that the majority of the members of both communities were now unwilling to listen to any reason and behaved in a manner having no other desire except to 'fly at each other's throat'.[134] The deputy SP, Sardar Bahadur Sundar Singh, and the officiating city magistrate, Mr Kacker, were kept awake at night because of the situation. In this highly charged atmosphere, special police arrangements were made in connection with the *alam* (a symbolic representation of the martyrs of Karbala) to be taken on the occasion of 'Nauchandi Jumerat', that is, the first Thursday in the lunar calendar of every Islamic month.[135] Nauchandi Jumerat, which is considered pious and usually involves only prayers, were used to make a political statement by taking out a procession.

Four Sunnis, including Maulana Abdul Qayum, were arrested on 3 June for holding a *milad* at Masjid Bisatyan. As the *milad* was commencing, the police asked the organisers to finish soon to avert trouble, owing to the nearness of a Shia mosque.[136] Since such processions would now aim at only confrontations, they created a frequent law-and-order problem for the city administration. An emergency meeting of the Lucknow Municipal Board was held to consider a resolution expressing anxiety over the frequent imposition of curfew orders and requesting the authorities to withdraw those orders because they were creating difficulties for the general population of Lucknow. This resolution also requested the authorities to call a representative meeting of Shias and Sunnis to settle the dispute. The resolution was passed by nine votes to five. It deplored the strained relations between Shias and Sunnis and appealed to them to resolve their differences. The most important aspect of this resolution was the argument that the frequent curfew orders caused hardship to innocents rather than the actual 'culprits' of violence and therefore appealed to authorities to adopt measures by which only 'culprits' would be punished.[137] It is an important break from the resolutions adopted by the Shia and Sunni organisations. This resolution expanded the scope of the conflict by drawing attention to its impact on the non-participating parts of the city and society. In a different register, it appealed to the members of both sects to exit the cycle of violence and recognise themselves as 'responsible' for their actions. It also created a moral binary between the 'innocent' and the 'culprit' and provided everyone with a moral opportunity to reclaim oneself as a responsible community member. Embedded in this proposition of 'culpability' was a moral discourse of 'criminality', which opened the possibility for a discourse that rested on a presumption that everyone had a duty to discipline oneself and had a clear choice not to participate in sectarian violence. It directly ran counter to the pre-emptive logic of emergency orders that imposed bans and other restrictions on all members of an identified problem category regardless of their actions – in this case, Muslims.

None of the three resolutions had any effect on the conflicting parties. On 7 June 1937, almost a hundred persons were detained for violating the curfew order but were allowed to go the next morning. From 8 June the curfew order was reduced by one hour and instead of 7.30 p.m. would start at 8.30 p.m.[138] According to a newspaper report, various conciliatory meetings requested the authorities to withdraw curfew orders, which greatly harmed trade in the city. Most importantly, the newspaper reported that picture houses were hit hard by the curfew orders, and two were on the verge of closing.[139] Finally, the curfew order under section 144 CrPC promulgated by the district magistrate for a fortnight ended on 15 June.

The governor lauded the UP premier, Pandit G.B. Pant, for his 'reasonable attitude' towards the protests and clashes. Pant regretted that 'even if [ordinary] people were not encouraging the agitation, they must suffer this inconvenience because they did not discourage it'.[140] It is an important statement by a Congress stalwart. Here, Pant, in a way, recognised that curfews and section 144 hit the everyday business of a city and, thus, conflicts must be resolved by the active participation of the communities themselves before they escalate to such levels. Else, they must be prepared to bear the brunt of state measures. He completely ignored the fact that Congress leaders and the Muslim League were active parties to the conflict. He also deliberately overlooked the fact that multiple efforts in the process failed to yield results, and it was party politics that had overtaken the entire matter. Thus, his statement is a careful political manoeuvring of Muslim politics in the city and the province.

The controversy did not cease to exist, nor did the clashes stop. Lucknow remained a hotbed of political and religious conflict between Shias and Sunnis. In 1939, after the Madh-e-Sahaba report was published, a government communiqué allowed Sunnis to carry out *Madh-e-Sahaba* recitation and processions. It would grant permission only on the condition that the authorities would decide the route and time of the processions. Shias were also to be allowed to carry out a *tabarra* procession under the same conditions. It is a clear example of an active interference by the provincial government in overtaking community decisions in everyday life. However, this did not please the Shias, who saw it as a betrayal by the Congress ministry.

Justin Jones has argued that these agitations by Shias as well as Sunnis 'can be interpreted as having taken style and idioms of popular politics as it matured during the interwar period, commonly characterized as the era of ascendant mass-nationalism'.[141] Both agitations were craftily mobilised and over the period were peaceful resistance or just organised disobedience, which were primarily Congress tactics. Here, the Congress's tactics of sabotaging colonial law and order were adopted by the masses of different political hues. The majority of the 'leading protagonists of both the agitations were attached to the Indian National Congress' in one way or another – for example, the nationalist Majlis-i-Ahrar and the followers of Husain Ahmad Madani on the Sunni side andfigures such as Sayyid Wazir Hasan and Sayyid Ali Zaheer, who directed the Shia Political Conference, among the Shia politicians.[142] Conflicts in the machinations of party politics during the Congress ministry of 1937 were also a significant dimension of these otherwise sectarian clashes.

It was the provincial Congress government that conceded to the demands initially and reignited the controversy earlier suppressed, if not settled, by the colonial administration. Two sets of observations can be deployed here. First, that prominent Muslims, like the two Muslim members of the UP Congress Committee, other than just Husain Ahmed Madani, were sympathetic to the Sunni cause. Second, that the Congress attempted to expand its fragile support among the UP Muslims in the face of a not-to-be-ignored growing popular support for the All-India Muslim League in the province. Therefore, it appears that the Congress was, in a way, willing to grant a concession to the demand of the Sunni majority. Administratively, the Congress, as noted in the description of the clashes and subsequent mobilisations in the sections earlier, exploited the dispute to benefit from the divisions among the Muslim vote-bank when the League was attempting to establish its ideological platform with the advent of provincial politics.[143] The Congress administration, to a great extent, handled Shia–Sunni relations with a manipulative skill quite similar to their British predecessors who had attempted earlier to find cracks in Muslim unity during the issue of Muslim university, jihadist and pan-Islamic agitations, as already discussed by other scholars.[144] Therefore, the Madh-e-Sahaba or the Tabarra agitations were a garb under which not religious or sectarian but political battles were fought.

The 'unprecedented volume of British, Congress, Muslim League and other political activity and the accompanying increase in journalistic output that accompanied Lucknow's new status as provincial capital gave wider resonance to municipal events'.[145] In August 1939, the Punjabi Khaksar leader Allama Mashriqi and many of his followers visited Lucknow and offered help to the UP Congress ministry to resolve the crisis. Members of both sects appreciated Mashriqi's intervention and agreed to stop the recitations for the time being.[146] However, this only shifted the source of the problem. The Khaksars were non-sectarian, but they were also a trained paramilitary organisation subscribing to an idiosyncratic version of fascism.[147] They kept arriving in Lucknow, which fuelled increasing administrative fears of more disorder.

The Sunni and Shia agitations of the 1930s were different from earlier events. The Madh-e-Sahaba conflict or the Tabarra agitation differed in their 'public impact, advanced organization and heavy public participation'.[148] These prolonged agitations were mass mobilisations, with an implied language of government petitioning and highly resonant of the political contestations that characterised north India since the early twentieth century. These agitations were no more restricted to episodic limits of Muharram and just sporadic local clashes between Shias and Sunnis. Muslim sectarian politics borrowed slogans of collective piety and used them as tools of agitation. The agitation did not remain an isolated Lucknow event but expanded in scope to other towns of UP and other provinces. During the agitations, numerous 'outsiders' from outside Lucknow, as well as the province, arrived to participate in these grand religio-political spectacles. The Majlis-i-Ahrar recruited most of its volunteers from neighbouring *qasba*s (small towns or large villages) and towns such as Kakori, Malihabad, Barabanki, and so on, and Punjab more widely. Even after the arrest of its substantial population, the Shia agitation was sustained by an influx of activists from Rampur, Agra, Fayzabad, Barabanki and Allahabad.[149] This only shows that Muslim sectarianism in Lucknow was merely a tool to settle political scores and reconfigure power relations in the changed political landscape after the provincial elections of 1937. Before the provincial elections of 1937, the Madh-e-Sahaba or the Tabarra agitations offered a convenient opportunity for inciting anti-government protests. The colonial administration then often responded by suppressing public processions in the name of maintaining peace and public order. As a result, it often meant 'direct government involvement in the regulation of religious rituals and festivities'. The colonial administration's intervention thus transmuted matters of religious procedure into political and legal disputes.[150] The matter was hardly any different under the provincial Congress government in UP because it also relied on the language of law to respond to the issue; the only difference was that the political stakes for the Congress were different.

When processions of both Sunnis and Shias, duly authorised and announced by government communiqué, were about to occur, a massive riot ensued, resulting in the district authorities banning the recital of both the *Madh-e-Sahaba* and the *tabarra* for an indefinite time. One of the biggest problems for the district administration was that now both Sunnis and Shias from outside Lucknow and even outside UP began to arrive in Lucknow to join the *Madh-e-Sahaba* and *tabarra* recitations. Scholars have rightly pointed out that despite G.B. Pant's criticism of past British practice of prohibition orders and police action, the Congress ministry in UP stuck firmly to the 'tried and tested' mechanisms for dealing with religious quarrels that the Raj had devised.[151] On the one hand, 'customs' continued to be the guiding principle for mediating public rituals. On the other hand, whenever the situation got out of control, standard containment strategies were resorted to in the usual order starting with appeals for restraint, negotiating with community leaders, *lathi* charges, the promulgation of section 144, curfews and firing by police and troops.

Banning public space and police action were the tried and tested measures of the British colonial government before 1935 and would be equally vigorously deployed by the new Congress ministry in UP. In Lucknow, the controversy resulted in the ban on processions of both Shias and Sunnis in the end. However, during the action, the administrative tactic of using section 144 and bringing in troops served as a handy tool to control the immediate situation and as a political manoeuvre to incarcerate society at large. It sent a message to the larger community of Lucknow that unrest could paralyse life not of a particular community but of the whole town. These were also the moments when the institutional character of the Congress in the government would become visible as it also resorted to banning access to public space and interfered with religious practices. It thus tried to flip the conflict in its favour and served only to fulfil its political desires. It highlights that whether it was the British Raj before 1935 or partial *swaraj* after 1937, the weapons to deal with unlawful assembly, section 144 and curfews, would never become obsolete. It would only intensify now that the Congress was in power, and opposition to this 'partial' *swaraj* was unacceptable.

Conclusion

In the light of the Kanpur labour strikes and the Madh-e-Sahaba controversy in Lucknow, the Congress ministry sought to control two kinds of problem categories: Labour under the increasing control of communists in the Kanpur instance, and the Muslim community in Lucknow under the influence of sectarianism in the other. In both these instances, the UP Congress first attempted to intervene through political manipulation, but when this failed, it resorted to repressive mechanisms similar to the tactics of the pre-1935 colonial government. Once the Congress began to lead the provincial government, its politics fluctuated due to class and community issues. Its dominance was consistently challenged by the diversity of political hues that existed in the province.

Certain paradigms of law discussed by legal theorists could enable us to understand the nature of the legal regime in the case studies discussed earlier. Legal theorists have argued that the four paradigms of law are important to understand any process of making and enforcing the law.[152] In the two instances discussed earlier, the attitude of the UP Congress ministry towards cases of public order enforced these legal paradigms in UP.[153] It fulfilled the 'reference paradigm' because it conducted a government according to the IPC drafted by the British colonialists in 1860; therefore, the Congress ministry in UP stuck to its meta-references to natural law or the availability of a self-sufficient legal code. It is ironic how the Congress first wanted to wreck the 1935 Government of India Act but not the overtly repressive IPC drafted in a colonial context. The frequent invocation of section 144, *lathi* charges, curfews and occasional police firing derived from the 'salvation paradigm' of law because the justification for the police violence progressed from the fact that a situation of disorder necessitated state violence in achieving the ideal of justice as law's end, that is, violence calls for violence. Public-order laws also enforced the 'universality paradigm' of legal theory by imposing a legal culture on people who were not direct stakeholders in the conflicts in Kanpur and Lucknow. Finally, it enforced the 'consensus paradigm' by rejecting a social consensus that criticised police violence and section 144. The consensus in support of section 144 CrPC was generated by multiple interventions from Nehru, Muslim and socialist leaders within the Congress, the statement of the governor and the publication of official reports mediated by mass media through continuous reports, letters to the editor, and editorials.

Instances like the ones discussed in this chapter, I would like to argue, show a blurring of the line between the legal potential of public-order laws and their actual political utilisation. These instances not only emphasise but also expose the limits and the power of public-order laws.

Protests in both Kanpur and Lucknow highlight the logic of 'maintaining public peace and tranquillity' for the provincial Congress government in UP. Situations of anti-government mass mobilisations or other kinds of public action such as riots safeguarded the self-sufficiency of these laws. The Congress ministry's use of public-order laws and the justification it provided point towards a biopolitical thinking, where the use of public-order laws in various circumstances would aim to establish a normalised understanding of how populations ought to behave or are expected to behave once such laws were promulgated. The Kanpur and Lucknow protests discussed earlier offer a clear illustration of several watermarks in the career of laws like section 144, curfew, and so on, containing emergency provisions in the late colonial period. It is evident that these laws were being invoked regarding specific cases of disorder but furthered other aims, such as replenishing the ambit of coercion entailed by foregone administrative reforms. As a practice of colonial state power, public-order laws, such as section 144 CrPC and curfews, blurred the boundaries between the colonial norm and the context of the post-1937 elections. The brutality of the dominance of the colonial government, and later the Congress ministry, was achieved in the name of apolitical rationality, which thrived on criminalising mass politics and the political other. It was a far cry from the Congress's politics in the legislature.

Notes

1. See R.S. Chandravarkar, *The Origins of Industrial Capitalism in India: Business Strategies and the Working Classes in Bombay, 1900–1940* (Cambridge: Cambridge University Press, 1994).

2. See Nandini Gooptu, *The Politics of the Urban Poor in Early Twentieth Century India* (Cambridge: Cambridge University Press, 2001)

3. See Prashant Kidambi, *Making of an Indian Metropolis: The Colonial Governance and Public Culture in Bombay, 1890–1920* (Hampshire; Burlington, VT: Ashgate, 2007).

4. See Subho Basu, 'The Paradox of Peasant Worker: Re-conceptualizing Worker's Politics in Bengal 1890–1939', *Modern Asian Studies* 42, no. 1 (2008): 47–74.

5. See Chitra Joshi, *Lost Worlds: Indian Labour and Its Histories* (London: Anthem Press, 2003).

6. Andrew Muldoon, *Empire, Politics and the Creation of the 1935 India Act* (Farnham: Ashgate, 2009), p. 3.

7. See Edward Thompson, 'What Will Congress Do in December?' *The Leader*, Tuesday, 1 December 1936, p. 10.
8. Ibid.
9. See 'Office Acceptance Issue, Decision Postponed till the Election', *Amrita Bazar Patrika*, Friday, 11 December 1936, p. 10.
10. See 'Do Not Raise Remote Issues, Mr. M.N. Roy's Appeal to Radicals', *The Leader*, Sunday, 20 December 1936, p. 7. Also see 'Mr. M.N. Roy's Plan, Independence before Socialism for India, to Cooperate with Congress', *Amrita Bazar Patrika*, Wednesday, 2 December 1936, p. 9.
11. See 'Muslim League's Aim, Mr. Jinnah Explains, We Stand by the Interests of the Country', *Amrita Bazar Patrika*, Wednesday, 16 December 1936.
12. See Letter to Editor, by A.A. Zakaullah, *The Leader*, 2 December 1936, p. 7.
13. See 'President-Elect at Faizpur, Unique Procession, Enthusiastic Reception to Pandit Jawaharlal', *Amrita Bazar Patrika*, Thursday, 24 December 1936, p. 7.
14. See 'Congress Policy', *The Leader*, Sunday, 20 December 1936, p. 5.
15. See 'Indian Congress Committee's Report', *The Leader*, 5 December 1936, p. 19.
16. See 'UP Congress Committee, New Office-Bearers and Members', *The Leader*, Thursday, 10 December 1936, p. 13.
17. See 'Split among Pilibhit Congress Workers, Is Mr. Pant a Candidate?' *The Leader*, Saturday, 19 December 1936, p. 15.
18. Quentin Hoare and Geoffrey Nowell Smith, eds., *Selections from the Prison Notebooks of Antonio Gramsci* (London: Lawrence & Wishart, 1971), pp. 7–11.
19. Terry Eagleton, *Ideology: An Introduction* (London: Verso, 1991).
20. Ranajit Guha, *Dominance without Hegemony: History and Power in Colonial India*, Convergences (Cambridge, Mass.: Harvard University Press, 1997).
21. Shahid Amin, *Sugarcane and Sugar in Gorakhpur: An Inquiry into Peasant Production for Capitalist Enterprise in Colonial India* (Delhi, Oxford University Press, 1984).
22. Gyan Pandey 'Peasant Revolt and Indian Nationalism: The Peasant Movement in Awadh, 1919–22', in *Subaltern Studies I: Writings on South Asian History and Society*, ed. Ranajit Guha, pp. 143–197 (Delhi: Oxford University Press, 1982).
23. Ibid., pp. 189, 191.
24. See Gooptu, *The Politics of the Urban Poor*, pp. 400–401.
25. Joshi, *Lost Worlds*, p. 359.
26. William Gould, *Religion and Conflict in Modern South Asia* (New Delhi: Cambridge University Press, 2012), p. 117.
27. See William Gould, 'Defining Spheres of Community, Society, Religious Mobilisation and Anti-colonialism', in *Religion and Conflict in Modern South Asia* (New Delhi: Cambridge University Press, 2012), p. 119.

28. Gooptu, *The Politics of the Urban Poor*, p. 65.
29. Ibid.
30. Ibid., p. 128.
31. Ibid., p. 109.
32. Ibid.
33. Ibid., p. 110.
34. See 'Cawnpore Leather Factory, Strike Situation Worsens', *The Leader*, Tuesday, 8 December 1936, p. 18.
35. See 'Cooper Allen Strike', *The Leader*, Wednesday, 9 December 1936, p. 14.
36. See 'Cooper Allen Strike', *The Leader*, Saturday, 12 December 1936, p. 17.
37. See 'Cawnpore Leather Factory Strike, Municipal Board Votes Rs.10,000 for Relief', *The Leader*, Monday, 14 December 1936, p. 4.
38. See 'Labour Strike in Cawnpore, Expression of Sympathy by Municipal Board', *Amrita Bazar Patrika*, Monday, 14 December 1936, p. 10.
39. See 'Cooper Allen Strike', *The Leader*, Saturday, 16 December 1936, p. 14.
40. See 'The Cawnpore Strike', *The Leader*, Tuesday, 22 December 1936, p. 2.
41. See 'Ban on Processions in the City', *The Leader*, Friday, 25 December 1936, p. 14.
42. See Joshi, *Lost Worlds*, p. 148.
43. See 'Cawnpore Labour Trouble, Miur Mill Strike, Reported Assault by Mill Hands', *The Leader*, Wednesday, 4 August 1937, p. 11.
44. See editorial titled 'Workers and Employers', *The Leader*, Sunday, 1 August 1937, p. 8.
45. Ibid.
46. See 'Strike in Swadeshi Cotton Mills, Statement by Mazdur Sabha Secretary', *The Leader*, 4 August 1937, p. 11.
47. See 'Labour Situation in Cawnpore, Millowners Organise', *The Leader*, 6 August 1937, p. 14.
48. Governors Fortnightly Report, United Provinces, 5 August 1937, L/P/J/5, India Office Records, London, The British Library.
49. See 'Cawnpore Labour Crisis, No Settlement, Millowners Reject Mazdoor Sabha Terms', *The Leader*, 7 August 1937, p. 10.
50. See 'Cawnpore Labour Trouble, No Sign of Abatement, Textile Mills Workers Down Tools, Govt. Policy Criticised', *The Leader*, Saturday, 7 August 1937, p. 17.
51. See 'Police Fire on Strikers, Defiant Attitude of Workers, Police Party Stoned, Strike Spreads at Cawnpore: 20,000 Down Tools', *The Leader*, Sunday, 8 August 1937, p. 9.
52. Ibid.
53. See 'Employers' Resolution', *The Leader*, Sunday, 8 August 1937, p. 9.

54. See editorial titled 'Congress Minister Condemns Strike', *The Leader*, Monday, 9 August 1937, p. 8.

55. See 'Cawnpore Mill Strike, 10,000 More Workers Join, "Lathi" Charges in Rowdy Crowds, Govt. Issue Communique, Decision to Appoint Committee of Enquiry', *The Leader*, Monday, 9 August 1937, p. 10.

56. See 'Firing in Cawnpore, U.P. Congress Ministry Criticised, Socialist Resolution in Patna', *The Leader*, Tuesday, 10 August 1937.

57. See ibid.

58. See 'Socialists Resolution at Allahabad', *The Leader*, Wednesday, 11 August 1937, p. 10; see 'Benares Socialists Condemn "Lathi" Charge', *The Leader*, Saturday, 14 August 1937, p. 10.

59. See 'Labour Welfare Officer's Communique', *The Leader*, 13 August 1937, p. 9.

60. See 'Cawnpore Strike Continues, Picketing Becomes More Aggressive, One of the Signatories to Agreement Assaulted, Armed Guards Patrolling Affected Areas', *The Leader*, Thursday, 12 August 1937, p. 9.

61. See the entire page 11 of *The Leader*, Thursday, 12 August 1937, especially 'Mazdoor Sabha Repudiated, Mammoth Meeting of Strikers'.

62. See an editorial in *The Leader* titled 'The Cawnpore Strike and After', Saturday, 14 August 1937, p. 8.

63. See 'Cawnpore Strike, Supported by Congress Members, Forced to Recognise Mazdoor Sabha, Statement by Employers' Association', *The Leader*, Saturday, 14 August 1937, p. 9.

64. See 'Violence Must Be Suppressed, Congress President on Firing on Cawnpore Workers, Questions to be Discussed by Working Committee, Attitude, towards Coronation in India and Federation, Mr. Jawaharlal Nehru Interviewed', *The Leader*, Saturday, 14 August 1937, p. 13.

65. See ibid.

66. See 'Cawnpore Police Firing, Commissioner's Statement', *The Leader*, Sunday, 15 August 1937, p. 13.

67. See 'Labour Strike and After', *The Leader*, Sunday, 29 August 1937, p. 14.

68. See the chapter 'Lal Kanpur' in Joshi, *Lost Worlds*, p. 359.

69. See 'Cawnpore Labour Problem, Inquiry to Be Made, Premier Meets Members at Lucknow, Dr. Rajendra Prasad to be Chairman', *The Leader*, Thursday, 2 September 1937, p. 12.

70. See 'Cawnpore Labour Trouble Again, Stay-in Strike in Swadeshi Cotton Mill', *The Leader*, Saturday, 4 September1937, p. 16.

71. See a letter to editor by Brij Mohan Das, Gola Gali, Benares City, 25 August, titled 'Congress Ministers and Firing on Unarmed Crowd', published in *The Leader*, Saturday, 4 September 1937.

72. See 'Secret of Good Laws, Revolutionary Tendencies in Society, Sino-Japanese Struggle and Russia, Mr. Nehru's Reading of International Situation', *The Leader*, Saturday, 4 September 1937, p. 11.

73. See ibid.

74. This special article in Pratap was also discussed in *The Leader*, Saturday, 25 September 1937, p. 5, 'Cawnpore Labour Crisis, Mr. Nehru Rebukes Labourers, Deprecates Strikes for Minor Grievances, Advice to Call of Strike'.

75. Ibid.

76. See 'Organize Yourselves, When Strike Should Be Resorted to, Congress President's Appeal to Workers, Analysis of Situation', *The Leader*, Monday, 27 September 1937, p. 5.

77. This summary of this article published in *Harijan* was reported in *The Leader*, Monday, 25 October 1937, p. 16, as 'Law and Order, "Civil liberty Is Not Criminal Liberty", Mahatma Gandhi's Views'.

78. Ibid.

79. Ibid.

80. Ibid.

81. See Governors Fortnightly Report, United Provinces, 6 January 1939; Governors Fortnightly Report, United Provinces, 20/22 January 1939, L/P/J/5, India Office Records, London, The British Library.

82. See Joshi, *Lost Worlds*, pp. 217–218.

83. See Chapter 5 'Supply of Unskilled Labour' in Amiya Kumar Bagchi, *Private Investment in India 1900–1939* (London and New York: Cambridge University Press, 1972), especially pp. 142–143.

84. *Report of the Cawnpore Textiles Labour Inquiry Committee Appointed by the Government of the United Provinces* (Allahabad: Superintendent, Printing and Stationery, United Provinces, 1938), p. 40.

85. See Vislakshi Menon, *From Movement to Government: The Congress in the United Provinces, 1937–42*, SAGE Series in Modern Indian History (Delhi; Thousand Oaks; London: SAGE Publications, 2003), p. 117.

86. Joshi, *Lost Worlds*, p. 213.

87. Ibid, p. 236.

88. Francis Robinson, 'Strategies of Authority in Muslim South Asia in the Nineteenth and Twentieth Centuries', *Modern Asian Studies* 47, no. 1 (2013): 1–21; Francis Robinson, 'Municipal Government and Muslim Separatism in the United Provinces, 1883 to 1916', *Modern Asian Studies* 7, no. 3 (1973): 389–441; Mushirul Hasan, 'Traditional Rotes and Contested Meanings: Sectarian Strife in Colonial Lucknow', *Rivista degli studi orientali* 69, Fasc. 1/2 (1995): 151–171; Katherine Prior, 'Making History: The State's Intervention in Urban Religious Disputes in the North-Western

Provinces in the Eary Nineteenth Century', *Modern Asian Studies* 27, no.1 (1993): 179–203; Justin Jones, 'The Local Experiences of Reformist Islam in a "Muslim" Town in Colonial India: The Case of Amroha', *Modern Asian Studies* 43, no. 4 (2009): 871–908; Rebecca M. Brown, 'Abject to Object: Colonialism Preserved through the Imagery of Muharram', *RES: Anthropology and Aesthetics*, no. 43 (Spring 2003): 203–217; Farzana Shaikh, 'Muslims and Political Representation in Colonial India: The Making of Pakistan', *Modern Asian Studies* 20, no. 3 (1986): 539–557; Farzana Shaikh, 'From Islamisation to Shariatisation: Cultural Transnationalism in Pakistan', *Third World Quarterly* 29, no. 3 (2008): 593–609.

89. See William Gould, *Hindu Nationalism and Language of Politics in Late Colonial India* (Cambridge; New York: Cambridge University Press, 2004), p. 213.

90. See Francis Robinson, Introduction, 'The Shi'a in South Asia', to *The Shi'a in Modern South Asia: Religion, History and Politics*, ed. Justin Jones and Ali Usman Qasmi (Cambridge: Cambridge University Press, 2015), p. 1.

91. Ibid.

92. Justin Jones, *Shi'a Islam in Colonial India: Religion, Community and Sectarianism* (Cambridge: Cambridge University Press, 2012), pp. 151–152.

93. Ibid., p. 153.

94. See Jones, *Shi'a Islam in Colonial India*.

95. D.A. Thomas, 'Lucknow and Kanpur, 1880–1920: Stagnation and Development under the Raj', *South Asia* 5, no. 2 (New Series) (1982): 68–80; H.R. Nevill, *Lucknow: A Gazeteer, Vol. XXXVII of the District Gazeteers of the United Provinces of Agra and Oudh* (Allahabad: Printed by F. Luker, Government Press, Allahabad, 1904), pp. 39–45, 50–53; V.T. Oldenburg, *The Making of Colonial Lucknow, 1856–1877* (Princeton, NJ: Princeton, 1984), pp. 3–26, 145–151.

96. Jones, *Shi'a Islam in Colonial India*, p. 203.

97. See Ashutosh Varshney, *Ethnic Conflict and Civic Life* (New Haven, CT: Yale University Press, 2008), especially a section on 'Shia-Sunni Violence of 1935–42' in Chapter 7.

98. Jones, *Shi'a Islam in Colonial India*, p. 189; Gould, *Hindu Nationalism*, p. 214.

99. Gould, *Hindu Nationalism*, p. 214.

100. Governor's Situation report dated 4 June 1937 for the United Provinces, L/P/J/5, India Office Records, London, The British Library.

101. Ibid.

102. See 'Lucknow Shia-Sunni Riot, Appreciation of Dy. Commissioner's Services', *The Leader*, Sunday, 6 June 1937, p. 11.

103. Jones, *Shi'a Islam in Colonial India*, p. 194.

104. See 'Lucknow Shia-Sunni Dispute, Compromise Efforts Fail?' *The Leader*, Tuesday, 8 June 1937, p. 2.

105. See 'Shia–Sunni Riots and After, Shia Political Conference Resolutions', *The Leader*, Friday, 18 June 1937, p. 5.

106. Ibid.

107. See 'Madhe Sahaba Enquiry, Early Publication of Report Urged', *The Leader*, Friday, 18 June 1937, p. 14, Also see Ali Usman Qasmi and Megan Eaton Robb, introduction to *Muslims against the Muslim League: Critiques of the Idea of Pakistan*, ed. Ali Usman Qasmi and Megan Eaton Robb, pp. 1–34 (Cambridge: Cambridge University Press, 2017); For a broader discussion on UP politics, also see Venkat Dhulipala, 'Nationalists, Communalists and the 1937 Provincial Elections', in *Creating a New Medina: State Power, Islam, and the Quest for Pakistan in Late Colonial North India*, pp. 25–48 (Cambridge: Cambridge University Press, 2015).

108. Ibid.

109. See 'Madhe Sahaba Enquiry, Early Publication of Report Urged', *The Leader*, Friday, 18 June 1937, p. 14.

110. Jones, *Shia Islam in Colonial India*, pp. 201–202.

111. Ibid.

112. Ibid., pp. 190–191.

113. The act of taking out a mourning procession by Shias during Muharram.

114. Jones, *Shi'a Islam in Colonial India*, p. 190.

115. Confidential Letter D.O.N. F.12/2-C.X. dated 8 January 1938, from the Government of United Provinces, Lucknow, to R.M. Maxwell, the Secretary to the Government of India, Home Department, New Delhi, part of the Governor's situation report dated 10 January 1938, pp. 2–3 of the letter and pp. 278–279 of the IOR/L/PJ/5/265.

116. Ibid.

117. Ibid.

118. Confidential Letter No. f.1/1-C.X. dated 19 January 1938, from the Government of United Provinces, Lucknow, to R.M. Maxwell, the Secretary to the Government of India, Home Department, New Delhi, part of the Governor's situation report dated 22 January 1938, p. 3 of the report and p. 267 of the File L/PJ/5/265.

119. Early morning processions.

120. Confidential letter D.O. No. F.1/2-C.X. dated 7/9 February 1938, from the Government of United Provinces, Lucknow, to R.M. Maxwell, the Secretary to the Government of India, Home Department, New Delhi, part of the Governor's situation report dated 9 February 1938, p. 3 of the letter and p. 250 of the File IOR/L/PJ/5/265.

121. Ibid.

122. Confidential letter D.O. No. F.2/1-C.X. dated 18/21 February 1938, from the Government of United Provinces, Lucknow, to R.M. Maxwell, the Secretary to the Government of India, Home Department, New Delhi, part of the Governor's situation report dated 22 February 1938, pp. 4–5 of the letter and pp. 221–222 of the File IOR/L/PJ/5/265.

123. For more discussion, see Visalakshi Menon, *From Movement to Government: The Congress in the United Provinces 1937–42* (New Delhi; Thousand Oaks, CA; London: SAGE Publications, 2003), pp. 82–85.

124. Secret Letter No. U.P. 64, dated 8 April 1938, from H.G. Haig, Governor of UP, to the Viceroy and Governor General of India, Lord Linlithgow, p. 3 of the letter and p. 124 of the File IOR/L/PJ/5/265, part of the Governor's situation report dated 8 April 1938.

125. Ibid.

126. Ibid.

127. Secret Letter No. U.P. 72, dated 23 April 1938, from H.G. Haig, Governor of UP, to the Viceroy and Governor General of India, Lord Linlithgow, p. 9 of the letter and p. 108 of the File IOR/L/PJ/5/265, part of the Governor's situation report 23 April 1938.

128. Secret Letter No. U.P.-78 dated 13 May 1938, from H.G. Haig, Governor of UP, to the Viceroy and Governor General of India, Lord Linlithgow, pp. 1–2 of the letter and pp. 58–59 of the File IOR/L/PJ/5/265, part of the Governor's situation report for 13 May 1938.

129. Confidential Letter D.O. No. F.5/2-C.X. dated 2/4 June 1938, from Panna Lall, Chief Secretary to Government, UP, to J.A. Thorne, Secretary to the Government of India, Home Department, Simla, part of the Governor's situation report dated 27 May 1938, pp. 2–3 of the report and pp. 50–51 of the File IOR/ L/PJ/5/265.

130. See Gould, *Hindu Nationalism*, p. 214.

131. See Asghar Ali Engineer, *Communal Riots in Post-independence India* (Hyderabad: Sangam Books, 1991), p. 153.

132. 'Sec. 144 Promulgated in Lucknow, Strained Feelings between Shias and Sunnis', *The Leader*, Thursday, 2 June 1938, p. 13.

133. Confidential Letter D.O. No. F.5/2-C.X. dated 2/4 June 1938 from Panna Lall, Chief Secretary to UP Government, to J.A. Thorne, Secretary to the Government of India, Home Department, Simla, p. 2 of the letter and p. 17 of the File IOR/L/PJ/5/265, part of the Governor's situation report dated 17 June 1938.

134. Ibid.

135. See 'Curfew Order at Lucknow, Assembly of More Than 5 Prohibited, Continued Shia-Sunni Tension', *The Leader*, Sunday, 5 June 1938, p. 11.

136. See 'Madhe Sahaba, Four Muslims Arrested', *The Leader,* Monday, 6 June 1938, p. 12.

137. See 'Shia–Sunni Differences, Govt. Requested to Withdraw Curfew Order, Resolution Passed by Lucknow Municipal Board', *The Leader,* Wednesday, 8 June 1938, p. 11.

138. See 'Curfew Order at Lucknow, 100 Arrests for Violation', *The Leader,* Friday, 10 June 1938, p. 17.

139. See 'Curfew Order Lifted, Situation Much Improved, Sequel to Shia–Sunni Tension in Lucknow', *The Leader,* Saturday, 18 June 1938, p. 15.

140. Secret Letter No. U.P.-90 dated 17 June 1938, from M.G. Hallet, the Governor of United Provinces, to Lord Linlithgow, Viceroy and Governor General of India, p. 9 of the letter and p. 12 of the File IOR/L/PJ/5/265, part of the Governor's situation report dated 17 June 1938.

141. Jones, *Shi'a Islam in Colonial India,* p. 200

142. Ibid.

143. Ibid., pp. 200–201.

144. Ibid., p. 201.

145. Ibid., p. 204.

146. See Naseem Yousuf, *Pakistan's Freedom and Allama Mashriqi: Statements, Letters, Chronology of Khaksar Tehrik (Movement) Period: Mashriqis Birth to 1947* (Liverpool; New York: AMZ Publications, 2004), p. 65.

147. For a broader discussion See Markus Daechsel, *The Politics of Self-Expression: The Urdu Middle-class Milieu in Mid-twentieth Century in India and Pakistan* (London and New York: Routledge, Taylor and Francis), pp. 18–93.

148. Jones, *Shi'a Islam in Colonial India,* p. 197.

149. Ibid.

150. Ibid., p. 200.

151. Ian Copland et al., *A History of State and Religion in India* (London: Routledge, Taylor & Francis, 2013), especially the Chapter 'Rule of Law', p. 226.

152. See the preface to Thanos Zartaloudis, *Giorgio Agamben: Power, Law and the Uses of Criticism* (Oxon, New York: Routledge, 2010), p. 327.

153. Thanos Zartaloudis has discussed how in contemporary times, the four classic paradigms of legal theory have lost their meaning. I have tried to use these paradigms analytically in a different manner to look at the operation of public-order laws in the post-1935 Congress ministry in UP.

3

Bureaucratic Encounters and the Question of Justice in India

A Kafkaesque Tale of Official Discretion, Errors and Oversights

Late colonial juridical practice in India was prone to bureaucratic errors and shared with the police a basic disinterest in the liberty of ordinary persons. This chapter tells the politically marginal but highly revealing story of a series of errors during the arrest and subsequent detention of an elderly man called Peter Budge – an innocent bystander in a situation of heightened communal tensions – that led to a momentary scandal in the United Provinces (UP) administration in the year 1947–1948. Budge's case disappeared between the cracks of bad record-keeping, leading to his lengthy and unlawful detention. The chapter raises questions about the complementary relationship between law and violence and about the fictitious nature of public-order laws. In contrast to a growing segment of historical literature that has discussed the spectacular violence of the colonial state by studying the revolt of 1857, the Ghadar movement, the Jallianwala Bagh massacre, and so on,[1] this chapter looks at the 'other' acts of violence of the state and argues that the everyday reality of public-order enforcement is key to understanding the nature and operations of the late colonial state (and the postcolonial state). While doing this, it will delineate the gap between procedure and substance in bureaucratic practice.

Contrary to some claims that bureaucracy has taken a backseat,[2] we notice that the discussions about bureaucracy have not withered in India. Bureaucracy remains the most common point of interaction between the citizens and the state. Max Weber's assertion on the nature of ideal types of bureaucracy remains the key interlocuter in discussions of coherence and purpose of bureaucracy.[3] Studies of bureaucracy are increasingly focusing on the nature of the everyday state and have stressed the significance of studying everyday bureaucratic practice to comprehend state authority and its legitimation.[4] Such studies have mostly studied either the ordinary citizen's narrative of the state[5] or the ones produced by the state.[6] Across the literature, two poles of investigative framework exist. At one extreme, the works of Franz Kafka dominate the discourse that emphasises the facade of rationality and reveals the monstrosity of bureaucracy[7] and, on the other, Hannah Arendt leads the discussions that stress its role in depoliticising processes.[8] Bureaucracy remains an important topic of study because it comprises the most common interaction between citizens and the state, involving diverse components such as the judiciary and the police.

In India, the historical connection between various bureaucratic institutions and British colonialism must not be ignored. The colonial administration introduced a particular discipline of rules dealing with the registration and identification of its subjects.[9] Eric Stokes has lucidly enumerated the arrival and entrenchment of utilitarian thought when it came to creating modern institutions for India.[10] The creation of a legal code for India was based on a Benthamian philosophy and approached law and its effects by deploying the *felicific calculus*.[11] This enabled the colonial state to wield power and control over its subjects as well as facilitated a disciplinary arrangement based on the interaction between various departments such as the police, the executive and the judiciary. Money, both in the form of fee (official) and bribe (unofficial), was involved in such bureaucratic interactions.[12] Colonial bureaucracy sustained the interaction between the subject and the state through an elaborate system that prescribed the use of various kinds of application forms. Each form was meant for a specific purpose and had to be supported by different kinds of documents that required different types of credentials.[13]

Paperwork constituted the core of colonial governance. Matthew Hull, for example, has pointed out that the foundations of the East India Company were based on a Hobbesian framework of 'body politik', with a clear chain of command and hierarchy.[14] The movement of paper through various channels ensured the conduct of colonial business of the Company. This was later reflected in the late colonial government too, when the Crown took over the business of government in India and, notably, continued even after independence. Ben Kafka, whose work is an exercise in the 'psychohistory' of paperwork, has argued that bureaucracy is as much a myth as material reality. Both the materiality of bureaucracy and its conceptual-fantastical fashioning should be grasped together.[15] Like most myths, bureaucratic ones, he further argues, are about managing structural contradictions in how we are governed and how we govern ourselves.[16] For him, the structural contradictions of the liberal-democratic project were responsible for the amount of paperwork that was required not only to govern but also to be governed in the modern world.[17] Bureaucratic rationality has always demanded that 'governing paperwork' creates a sense of certainty to infuse legal order with legitimacy. Such a legal order is based on a system of vouching. Matthew Hull argues that the 'government of paper' established a bureaucratic system where 'vouching was done by artefacts, not people'.[18] All official documents had to be 'vouched' through signatures, stamps and entries made by a different official at each level.

The establishment of the British colonial administration and the drafting of the legal code for India also meant that the alleged despotism or 'discretion' of the traditional rulers would not operate anymore.[19] It was robustly proposed by the colonial administration that facts would now sustain law and legal institutions. However, in the colonial arrangement of vouching through and across paperwork, this chapter will point out, official 'discretion' often mediated the direction paperwork would take. Moments of official discretion, anthropologists have noted, operate as 'alien authority' that constitutes the law of the state.[20] Such an authority comprises the unwritten and unspoken laws of the state that operate between the written law and its application.

Illustrating the horrors of bureaucratic practices in late colonial India, this chapter dwells upon the unfortunate story of the arrest of a commoner named Peter Budge. Peter Budge was an Indian Christian, a middle-aged brown man, an ordinary figure, who dared to venture out on the streets of Lucknow in a time of unrest and communal disturbances preceding the partition of India.[21] Volatile localities with potential for communal clashes in many parts of India were under various prohibitory orders such as the Communal Disturbances Act, the Indian Arms Act, section 144 of the Code of the Criminal Procedure (CrPC), and so on. In such a tense atmosphere, Budge, the protagonist of this story, was stopped by two constables named Muhammad Saghir and Doodh Nath. They stopped him to enquire about his identity and his purpose of roaming on the streets in such a volatile atmosphere. He informed them that he was merely taking a walk. An altercation took place between Budge and the two constables, and as a result, he was detained. According to the first information report (FIR) lodged by the constables, Budge was stated to be a potential lunatic, and his walking stick was confiscated under the Indian Arms Act. This points out that actual circumstantial reality could be irrelevant when individuals are left to the discretion of a policeman.

Budge was taken to the police station and a case was registered against him. Not only was he not taken for a psychiatric examination, since the FIR mentioned him to be a potential lunatic, but his misfortune began with the accidental mis-recording of his name. The error owed to the handwriting in *nastaliq*, where Peter was recorded as 'Peer' and Budge came to be read as 'Bajar'.[22] Furthermore, the name of Peter underwent another error where the initially mis-recorded name 'Peer Bajar' was again mis-recorded as Peer Baksh. His father's name too was recorded with errors. The same person or the physical body had multiple names recorded for him at multiple bureaucratic institutions and their respective records. Such repetitive mis-recording of names made Budge's freedom difficult because no institution had a corresponding name for the physical body present in jail. The police station had recorded the name incorrectly and later the judge – despite asking for the accused to be presented – found him repetitively absent and kept summoning the person/name recorded in the paperwork. In reality, Peter Budge was in jail. When the summons for Peter Budge reached his locality, people denied the knowledge of any person by the name 'Peer Bajar' residing there. Due to repetitive errors in the paperwork of his case, Budge languished in jail for almost a year. His detention exceeded much beyond the time he would have served had he been found guilty of the charges against him.

Budge's case is particularly poignant since he was arrested during a time of heightened communal tensions in June 1947 and was released a year later. Forgotten in jail, he missed the glorious event of India's independence. Recent scholarship has emphasised that there is a need to bridge the gap between the study of 'high' and 'low' politics of South Asia.[23] Some scholars have already discussed 'low' politics by studying issues such as refugee rehabilitation and the recovery of abducted women in the aftermath of partition.[24] Low politics is as significant as high politics when it comes to experiencing state and citizenship in South Asia. This chapter offers an insight into a different aspect, that is, local disturbances and the experience of illegal detention of ordinary citizens during the crisis of public order. As a result, it investigates state functioning at the local level at the expense of the liberty of its citizens when left to the whims and fancies of officials of the police and the judiciary armed with discretionary powers. Recent historiography has also warned against the limitations of scholarship that debates 'whether or not 1947 marked a distinct break in the history of the subcontinent' and has argued that the 'transition was too complex to be encapsulated in the dichotomy change/no change'.[25] This assertion is vital. However, the analysis of continuities and discontinuities could enable new scholarship to probe the impact of certain state practices that continued into the postcolonial order and were sometimes either modified or dropped. It could be instructive to deliberate upon the nature and significance of such adoptions, mutations or omissions and their impact on the experiences of postcolonial citizenship in South Asia.

Undoubtedly, the partition, with the arrival of independence in India, did have a profound impact on the everyday lives of ordinary citizens. Scholars have noted that it not only altered geography but also extended and expanded the state's responsibilities. Furthermore, it provided opportunities for governments to pursue policies distinct from colonial predecessors.[26] However, when it came to issues of public order, as Budge's case will show, the nascent postcolonial state seemed hesitant to grab such opportunities. The powerful underpinnings of public order and tranquillity laws did not alter the state's modus operandi with the advent of independence; it only intensified. In the emergent postcolonial state, although citizens made demands on the state, the state too made demands (of discipline) on its citizens.

In addition to the grand stories of mass displacement, arson, rape and murder, there are other ordinary stories such as that of Peter Budge that problematise the very nature of the state during the formative years of independent India. Although later citizenship was defined using the language of abstract rights, the situation was far more complex when it came to balancing the procedural and substantive sides of the law. Budge's story stands witness to the state practices in a situation of heightened tensions and demonstrates the purpose and scope of the postcolonial state.

This story is also significant in that it is not about a member of a political party, nor is it about a person arrested for protesting the colonial government or the local administration or while participating in a riot.

It is a story of an ordinary person who, in addition to having been in the wrong place at the wrong time, was subjected to bureaucratic manhandling simply because of his name, a name which was not Indian but could be easily confused with other names available. Most significantly, Budge's ordeal highlights the quotidian practices of the local police, jail authorities and the judicial bureaucracy while handling marginal cases of ordinary figures who would appear to be politically insignificant. For example, K.G. Kannabiran has noted the case of a famous communist agitator named A.K. Gopalan.[27] When the Madras government released many prisoners on the day India attained independence, Gopalan was not released. He remained imprisoned under section 124-A IPC for seditious activities against the British Empire. He had to celebrate India's independence within the walls of the prison, where he walked the length of the jail carrying the national flag, which he later hoisted on the roof. For this act, he was produced before the additional district magistrate of Calicut on the accusation that he was agitating against the British Empire even in jail. Notably, the implications of independence had not seeped into the legal bureaucracy yet. While making a statement in front of the additional district magistrate, Gopalan stated:

> There is some incongruity in bringing me to trial at this time when on face of it we have just achieved freedom. I am sorry that things should have come to such a pass.[28]

On the contrary, the government did not see any break from the past. For it, the processes of governance had continued and did not augur a change in the legal or social order. Within the legal bureaucracy, many held the opinion that the old political institutions (colonial) did not die a sudden death giving birth to completely new ones. According to this perspective, the transition of the political regime was more of a process of evolution rather than the destruction of the previous institutions.[29] Gopalan was released on 12 October 1947, only to be rearrested on 17 December the same year. The difference was that this time he was arrested under preventive detention laws. Gopalan's case is just one illustration of the attention the administration paid to political agitators. In contrast, an ordinary figure like Peter Budge did not fit into any ready-made colonial problem category and hence received little attention while 'more important' issues were dealt with. The administration was primarily occupied with efforts to deal with the mayhem unleashed by the violent communal climate in the wake of the partition and its aftermath. Budge's story may be marginal to the spectacular event of India's independence, but it offers a unique window into the complex operations of the legal bureaucracy in India during moments of public-order crisis. In a way, it was symptomatic of what was to follow. Budge's legal case disappeared between the cracks of bad record-keeping and insufficient information sharing between various government departments and led to his lengthy and unlawful detention.

The marginal story of Peter Budge's detention, when it got published in a newspaper, became a moment of embarrassment for the UP government in the newly independent nation.[30] It is difficult to say how Budge's case came to be published in the first place. Yet such reportage does accomplish a wider political work. Anthropologists have argued that newspapers (the media) are often crucial mediators of state acts.[31] They enable the state to revisit, argue, course correct, substantiate and sometimes reiterate its commitment to a fair experience of citizenship. Budge's ordeal highlights the Kafkaesque nature of Indian colonial bureaucracy, which short-circuited the intention of 'the rule of law'. It indicates that the bureaucracy, far from being rule-guided, functioned as per the 'discretion' of the various officials ranging from the lower to the higher levels. Documents or paperwork could sometimes allow passage, but on other occasions could also determine entrapment. One could argue that legal bureaucracy in India turned out to be a form of organised despotism, where individuals became the means to juridical ends mediated through paperwork. Furthermore, Budge's ordeal raises important questions about the complementary relationship between law and violence and about the nature of legal bureaucracy – particularly when it concerned the public-order laws. The everyday reality of public-order enforcement is key to understanding the nature and operations of the late colonial state in India. Ironically, such a design of public-order enforcement set the pace of administrative bureaucracy for independent India too. While discussing Budge's ordeal, this chapter will tease out two primary concerns. First, it will lay bare the complexities and challenges involved in the colonial government of paperwork within the legal bureaucracy and, second, it will highlight that official discretion, both formal and informal, guided the operations of quotidian legal bureaucracy in India. Together, these concerns will expose a fundamental flaw in the nature of law in colonial India and its operation on the ground.

Official Discretion and Administrative Violence: The Political Context and Climate Surrounding Budge's Arrest

Nasser Hussain has argued that the concept of colonial law was premised on emergency. By discussing the examples of the Rowlatt Bills and martial law, Hussain has shown that in times of political crisis, the colonial state would short-circuit due process in the name of administrative emergency.[32] However, the British colonial authorities continued to emphasise on the rule of law and the legal protections available in the Indian Penal Code (IPC). Hussain has argued that it also bestowed the executive and the judiciary with the power of 'discretion' precisely because it was a regime of conquest. This prerogative of discretion was later extended to the local executive too. In the context of law, discretion refers to the power of a public official to make a decision based on his or her opinion within the prescribed guidelines. It 'involves considerations of right and wrong and the weighing of mitigating and aggravating factors' in a legal context.[33] Recently, scholars such as Andrew Lowenstein, Amie Ely, Laurie Levenson, Angela Davis and James Vorenberg have extensively discussed various dimensions of official 'discretion'. While Lowenstein understands discretion as leverage that enables prosecutors (officials) to devise and execute their 'own enforcement strategies',[34] Ely notes it as part of an official responsibility motivated by a quest for justice.[35] In contrast, Levenson recognises discretion as a necessary outcome of legal imprecision.[36] Scholars such as Davis[37] and Vorenberg[38] have separately argued that discretion is dangerous and amounts to tyrannical power. It has come to be seen as a threat to justice, fairness and rule of law.

Hussain points out that all claimants to the discretionary power in colonial India refused to admit that it abrogated the rule of law.[39] Discretion enabled arbitrary acts that aimed to ensure the stability of the colonial regime and must be seen as a 'part of the legal sovereignty of the state itself'.[40] The British colonial regime did aspire to foster political legitimacy, but the reality remained that it was a regime of conquest. Various events in the career of British colonial rule in India point out that the colonial regime repetitively resorted to the discretionary authority of its executive and the force of its military. The colonial state created a structure of administration with a strong executive and judiciary and consistently insisted that its certain acts would remain outside judicial inquiry.[41] In the following sections, Budge's case will highlight that the implication of the provision of discretion is antithetical to the idea of the rule of law and, on the contrary, placed the executive or a policeman as prior to the law. However, what is even more important is that such moments of discretion also highlight the law's limits. It aims to fill the gap that the imprecision of law creates.

Recalling the political context of 1946–1948 is important to understand the location of Budge's case in the larger scheme of things. In 1946, a year after the Second World War had concluded, the Cabinet Mission was sent to India to discuss the modalities of the transfer of power to the Indian people. The two major parties, the Congress and the Muslim League, were both dissatisfied with the proposal of creating groups of religiously demarcated provinces while yet retaining some form of unity at the federal level. While the Muslim League wanted safeguards for Muslims in the Constituent Assembly with the power to veto, the Congress, on the other hand, was not content with the 'communal' framework the Muslim League proposed. Also, the Muslim League had already started an agitation for a separate Muslim state of Pakistan. Such politics gradually exacerbated communal tensions between Hindus and Muslims all over India. In UP too,[42] communalism gained momentum. A particularly alarming point was reached when Meo Muslims were reported to be raiding Jat Hindu villages near Agra, Mathura and Meerut and, in retaliation, Jats attacked villages populated by Muslims.[43] There were reports that weapons, including swords, *lathi*s and guns, were being brought into the province in preparation for communal clashes. A press note from the district magistrate of Lucknow on 21 May 1947 lays bare the administrative anxiety.[44] It mentioned the strong possibility that ex-servicemen who had just returned from serving in the Second World War had brought a large number of firearms into the province from the war zones. The district magistrate's note emphasised that 'the possession of a firearm without a license is an offence under the Indian Arms Act punishable with imprisonment up to three years and with fine'.[45] It was decreed that ex-servicemen in possession of unlicensed arms should produce such arms before 'the nearest stipendiary magistrate or the police station officer within one month' of the notification.[46] All ex-servicemen were encouraged to report such weapons with an assurance that their application for a licence would be considered favourably and they would be exempted from prosecution.

The rise of communal tensions in the months preceding partition resulted in the promulgation of the UP Communal Disturbances Prevention Ordinance, 1947, just five days after the notification for the declaration of unlicensed arms.[47] This ordinance incorporated a government Bill for the suppression of communal disorders in the province. The law granted 'special measures'[48] to the local authorities responsible for the maintenance of law and order to prevent any disturbances. Such special powers included the power to shoot at sight any person violating a curfew and to declare whole towns as 'disturbed areas'.[49] The UP Congress ministry promulgated this ordinance after the passage of the Bill through both the houses of the legislature because the normal process of getting the assent of the governor-general would have entailed considerable delay. The UP government defended the suspension of the due procedure by maintaining that given the high communal tensions in the province, the situation necessitated immediate action and could not afford the delay involved in getting the governor's assent. The bypassing of the governor's assent in the face of an emergency highlights that since the process of transfer of power was now initiated, provincial governments could make such decisions for themselves within a legal framework. The gradual transfer of sovereignty made such autonomy possible.

Under the new law, punishments for certain offences were enhanced,[50] and the powers of the police and the magistrates gained a different impetus. The Communal Disturbances Prevention Ordinance enabled ordinary policemen to use their discretion to decide who would fall in what category of crime. For example, they would now be able to decide whether a person was participating in disorderly activities or had a weapon. Persons could potentially be recorded and arrested as prospective 'miscreants', and ordinary belongings like a walking stick could easily transmute into a weapon. The decision to make such a distinction rested within the 'discretion' of the concerned official. First-class magistrates, on the other hand, were now empowered to award all the heavy sentences, including transportation for life. Earlier, for similar offences, they could award only two years' imprisonment and a limited amount as fine. Furthermore, no appeals could now be made to intermediate courts over the decisions of these magistrates because they would now go directly to only a High Court. This law extended to ordinary non-gazetted employees too. Employees who were to be found guilty of bribery, loot or partiality during communal disturbances were to be dismissed by their appointing authority.

In the light of such laws, the relationship between the police and the judiciary stands at the very heart of the policies of control. While the function of the judicial wing appears to be clear, that is, conducting trials based on evidence, the purpose of the police remains more difficult to define. Unlike the judges, the policemen (or one of the superiors) had a great deal of discretion over whether or not and how to act in a particular situation of public order. But Budge's case will reveal that uncertainty did not wholly lie on only one side of the relationship between the two institutions. As a result, discretion could unleash violence at the hands of the officials. Walter Benjamin has argued that 'all violence as a means is either law-making or law-preserving'.[51] If its claims do not emanate from these predicates, 'it forfeits all validity'.[52] Benjamin has highlighted that 'law sees violence in the hands of the individuals as a danger undermining the legal system'.[53] Still, such violence could not be faulted; instead, illegal ends would be questioned. Benjamin argued that 'a system of legal ends cannot be maintained if natural ends are ... still pursued violently'.[54] According to him, law and its interest in the monopoly of violence over individuals could not be explained by the maxim of preserving legal ends but preserving law itself. Therefore, 'violence, when not in the hands of the law, threatens it not by the ends that it may pursue but by its mere existence outside the law'.[55] As a result, violence can only be justified if it is in accordance with the law.

In moments of a threat to public order, official discretion in the hands of the police or the judiciary becomes all the more threatening, a legal threat, assuming the character of fate, where the identity of the legal subject, such as Peter Budge, would not only be marked but the future unfolding of the events about the case would also depend on it. Through Budge's story, the chapter will show that discretion serves as a law preserving violence that threatens violence. It argues that official discretion becomes violence granted for legal ends, which also has the authority to decide these ends itself within undefined limits. Official discretion, whether of the police, the clerks or even the judges, oscillates between being a decree and a disposition. It is this oscillation that enables the assertion of legal claims for a decree and puts it at the disposal of such ends. Discretion, especially in the name of a threat to public order or administrative crisis, aims to serve as justified means (violence) for just ends (public order and tranquillity). Thus, the police could intervene, for example, for the maintenance of public order, that is, for the security of life, liberty and property.

At the Wrong Place at the Wrong Time: Peter Budge's Initial Entry into the Labyrinth of Legal Bureaucracy

Amidst heightened communal discord building up to the partition of India, curfews and prohibition orders became frequent. With the promulgation of the Communal Disturbances Prevention Ordinance, 1947, and the invocation of the Indian Arms Act supplemented by curfews and orders under section 144 CrPC, life on the street became even more difficult. These disturbances were not motivated against the colonial administration as such. There were violent attacks and counterattacks by religious communities in the wake of the numerous uncertainties that arose with the possibility of the partition of India. In such uncertain times, Peter Budge decided to take a walk on the morning of 2 June 1947, just two months before India achieved independence. While walking, he was confronted by two constables, Muhammad Saghir and Doodh Nath, from the Alambagh Police Station of Lucknow, who were patrolling the Charbagh area at that time.[56] The constables confronted Budge and asked about his motives and presence on the street. Following an argument with the constables, Budge was arrested, and his walking stick was also confiscated. This happened around 11.15 a.m., according to the FIR. Budge was recorded as an Indian Christian, with *sanwla rang* (brown skin colour) and as a resident of Kandhari Bazar, Lucknow.[57] The reason for his arrest mentioned in the FIR stated that 'he was found carrying a bamboo stick in contravention of the orders under section 144 CrPC and refused to give up the stick when asked to do so by the constables'.[58] His refusal to hand over his walking stick led to the recording of the stick as a 'weapon' because it contravened the prohibition orders in place. In this context, the two constables and their act of arresting Budge neatly fit into what is referred to as 'street-level bureaucracy'.[59] According to such an understanding, policemen are typical street-level bureaucrats because of their regular and direct interaction with citizens concerning issues of law and order, and are characterised by the power to exercise discretion over matters they are directly responsible for. In times of public disorder, a prescribed format of social life applied, and it also narrowly defined the legitimate, although vaguely. When public-order laws were activated, there lurked a general atmosphere of distrust. The police approached all individuals or groups and their activities with an assumed suspicion. Paul Ricoeur's discussion on hermeneutics might offer some insight into the modality of such a suspicion.

Ricoeur has emphasised that the true meaning of a text emerges only through interpretation. He defines hermeneutics as 'the theory of the rules that preside over an exegesis – that is, over the interpretation of a particular text or of a group of signs that may be viewed as a text'.[60] He distinguished between two kinds of hermeneutics. The first is the 'hermeneutic of faith' and the second is the 'hermeneutic of suspicion'. The hermeneutic of faith aims to restore meaning (to a text), whereas a hermeneutic of suspicion aims to decode meanings (in a text) that are disguised. What is important to his manoeuvre of interpretation is distantiation.[61] By 'distantiation' Ricoeur meant the distance in time, culture, world view, language, and so on, between the author of the text and its reader. Ranajit Guha has emphasised that when accessing archival material, there exist two intentions. First, the intention of the law and, second, the intention of the historian or scholar.[62] For a historian who wants to reclaim the event, Guha proposed, the mediation of the law poses a challenge. The challenge is a struggle between the two claimants, law and history. However, Guha makes a significant point that the law has arrived in the archive much before the arrival of the historian. In the light of Guha's warning, Ricoeur's distinction between the two hermeneutics is helpful to make sense of the report of the judicial inquiry that took place to ascertain the reasons behind Budge's detention. This exercise of hermeneutics, I contend, could also be applied to a legal 'context'. Such an extension of Ricoeur's hermeneutics from text to context has a pertinent implication. In a time of public disorder, the context enabled the policeman, who otherwise was expected to operate on faith, to suddenly apply suspicion to all people and their movements. Anthropologists have noted that 'suspicion (like doubt) occupies the space between the law and its application'.[63] Hence, legal bureaucratic systems of the modern state 'presuppose organized suspicion, [and] incorporate margins of uncertainty'.[64] Here, it is pertinent to emphasise the borderline character of the legitimate and the illegitimate in such a context. The manoeuvre of translation (of things and persons) bridges the gap between the legitimate and the illegitimate. Such a translation stops midway at deciphering only the context and does not engage in its explanation. The extraordinary character of the public-order laws blurred the distinction between the understanding and the explanation of the context. All immediate contexts were subsumed in the overwhelming context of the administrative crisis here. The policeman, according to the premise of modern law, is supposed to be impartial. Therefore, he has to act based on a distantiation. In Budge's case, suspicion enabled constable Doodh Nath and Muhammad Saghir to interpret Budge's presence on the road as a potential threat to public order and, as a result, the discretion granted by law empowered them to confiscate his walking stick and interpret it as a weapon.

After the argument between Budge and the constables and the eventual confiscation of his walking stick, he was taken to the police station, detained in the *hawalaat* (police lockup) for a day and then sent to the city magistrate's court the next day at 12.25 p.m. The *challan* (charge sheet) stated that he was booked under section 152 CrPC[65] and section 188 IPC.[66] After obtaining a complaint from the district magistrate, Budge was sent to jail the very same day. He would stay incarcerated for almost a year from then, without anyone noticing his detention or his legal case being advanced or dealt with. It was only in a letter dated 15 May 1948 that the deputy commissioner, Lucknow, A.D. Pandit, enclosed a note on Peter Budge informing the deputy secretary to the UP government about the details of the case.[67] Budge's ordeal was published by a prominent newspaper, raising questions about the functioning of law-and-order administration in the province.[68] The premier (chief minister) of UP had to personally intervene after the news was published. He rang the deputy secretary to enquire about the case and ordered him to deal with the ensuing scandal. Since India was an independent country now, the story of such an administrative lapse causing such suffering to a common man embarrassed the provincial government. The news story pointed to a potentially dark legacy that the postcolonial Indian bureaucracy was yet to overcome. This story is significant to understand that everyday legal practices had yet to be decolonised, suggesting that decolonisation was an extended process lasting several decades rather than a mere moment. It highlights the contradictions of a government that was now run mostly by Indians themselves but still following a colonial legal code.

To deal with the Peter Budge fiasco, the UP government finally appointed Justice M.C. Desai, district and sessions judge of Lucknow, to conduct a judicial enquiry into the case. Anthropologists have argued that enquiries often served as opportunities for the state to re-imagine itself or to offer a different meaning of itself.[69] In this light, Justice Desai's enquiry report, as the following sections will explain, in a way mapped different parts of the state (the police, jail authorities and the courts) acting in relation to each other. It asserted that clear regulations were already in place to guide each bureaucratic step, but it was careless officials who were to blame for the mess. It was discovered that sometimes various institutions copied information as such from the paperwork of other institutions and on other occasions did also cover for each other. However, the enquiry report also exposed the gaps that bureaucratic communication suffered. Hence, such enquiries act as the state's reaffirmation of its promise to uphold law and regulations.

It is pertinent to discuss the difference between an investigation and an enquiry here. The former should not be confused with the latter.[70] In the legal bureaucracy, the police are responsible for the investigation of a circumstance, refer to and evaluate a context as either legitimate or illegitimate, and then charge the individual(s) for a particular violation. On the other hand, an enquiry is aimed at ascertaining that an action that is defined as criminal actually took place and must establish the source of the act. Michel Misse refers to an enquiry report as a 'piece composed of technical reports, accounts recorded by a notary public and a legally-oriented report, signed by a police commissioner (in this case an inquiry ordered by the government, and conducted by a Judge) with a degree in Law'.[71] An enquiry is meant to identify facts and isolate heresy. It aims to restore what investigation had failed to achieve, that is, re-examination based on complete facts. It is a double accusation: one on the original accused and the second on the investigating agencies. It was with the purpose of fact-finding that the enquiry was instituted into the illegal detention of Peter Budge. More than the circumstances of Budge's detention, the fact-finding report, as the following sections will reveal, exposed the chaos within the legal order itself. In this chaos, Budge's freedom became unseen, as law and legal facts came to constitute an altogether different way of experiencing citizenship. According to Justice Desai's enquiry report:

> On 21.5.1947, the District Magistrate Lucknow issued an order under section 144 Cr.P.C. prohibiting any person from going about armed with any *lathi* or stick in any street or thoroughfare or assembling together in parties or groups of more than five persons. The order was passed on account of strained communal and party feelings and was to remain in force for two months.[72]

Budge was arrested on the thirteenth day of this order on 2 June 1947 and just two months before India's independence. The scope of the section 144 CrPC order is significant for understanding the case. According to the enquiry report:

> If a person disobeys an order lawfully issued under section 144 Cr.P.C. and if the disobedience causes or tends to cause obstruction etc. to any persons lawfully employed, he is liable to be punished under section 188 I.P.C. An offence under section 188 I.P.C. is non-cognizable and bailable. The police have no power to arrest a person accused of this without warrant. Government have the power of issuing notification under section 10 of the Criminal Law Amendment Act 1932 making an offence under section 188 I.P.C cognizable but no such notification was issued by the government in June 1947.... According to section 195 Cr.P.C no court can take cognizance of an offence under section 188 I.P.C. except on the complaint in writing of the public servant concerned.[73]

The report made it evident that a complex set of regulations applied to the designated official making an arrest or detention. It focused on the misapplication of law and avoided making any comment on the dark side of official 'discretion' at moments of administrative crisis. Notably, discretionary powers allowed the manufacture of legal reality in the process. As opposed to a substantiated accusation, discretionary laws not only 'determine' facts instantaneously but also produce them. The relationship between law and facts must be also examined. The following sections will substantiate that Justice Desai's enquiry report, while examining the circumstances of Budge's detention, exposed the idiosyncrasies and banality that plagued the quotidian functioning of the legal bureaucracy in UP.

The Problem of Language and Legibility: Following the Trails of Paperwork in Peter Budge's Case

During the investigation, Peter Budge's detention case turned out to be the result of improper initial charges under which he was booked and a series of 'clerical errors' while recording his details. As mentioned earlier, he was repeatedly subjected to a conclusively unfortunate spelling blunder. Such errors were primarily owed to Urdu–English transliteration problems. Budge's name was sloppily written in *nastaliq* and was later wrongly romanised. The report in the general diary of the head *moharrir* (clerk) Munis Khan recorded the name of the accused as 'Peer Bajar s/o Tanik Bajar' whereas the real name was 'Peter Budge s/o Tommy Budge'.

Justice Desai's report highlighted that it was this simple carelessness that was responsible for all the confusion that had arisen in the case. Though Munis Khan did not know English, the report opined, he should have taken care when confronted with a strange name and should have recorded it correctly. Therefore, Munis Khan, according to Desai, could not be absolved from the blame for the incorrect entry. Sub-Inspector (SI) Zahir Khan's report, which was treated as the *chalani* report, also recorded the name as 'Peer Bajar'. The SI did not check the facts for himself and copied information as such from the general diary of *moharrir* Munis Khan. Though the SI wrote that the man appears to be 'cracked head and insane' and suggested his medical examination to ascertain whether he should be sent to an asylum, yet, notably, the medical examination was not conducted, and the question of arresting a person with an unsound mind and remanding him in custody still remained.

Police constables Saghir Ahmad Khan and Ram Lakhan took Budge to the district jail on 3 June 1947 with the warrant, and he was admitted to jail. During the enquiry, it was discovered that the papers of this transfer and the warrant for the jail were lost and declared untraceable. A further error occurred when the same man Peter Budge was thrown into jail under the name 'Peer Buj s/o Tomi Buj',[74] adding to the confusion of administrative bureaucracy. The enquiry report observed that the courts did not adopt the actual practice of returning the warrants immediately after examining the period of remand. As a result, the courts in Lucknow district repeatedly failed to return the warrants. In the case of Peter Budge too, the 'City Magistrate signed the warrant remanding the man in jail custody up to 17.6.1947, he did not open any file and did not make any entry about the matter in any register'.[75] Now, as the arrest was illegal in the first place, 'the remand to jail custody was also illegal'.[76] The problem on the part of the city magistrate was that he did not take cognisance of the offence under section 188 IPC and could not do so without a complaint by the district magistrate. Hence, he could not remand Budge for even one day. However, according to the report, he was remanded for 14 days.

The story of clerical errors did not end here. On 4 June 1947, the city magistrate's court *moharrir* sent the *chalani* report of SI Rashid Ahmad together with the connected papers to the district magistrate for sanctioning the prosecution of Budge under section 188 IPC.[77] In such a case, when the police inspector required the district magistrate's sanction for any case, he had to fill out a form and send it to the district magistrate for his signatures. When prosecuting SI Yusuf Ali Khan sent this form along with the *chalani* report to the district magistrate, he wrote the name of the accused as 'Peer Bakhair s/o Tank Bakhair',[78] leading to further alteration in Budge's name in police and court records. Not only this, but the *ahalmad*[79] also took almost 15 days to get the district magistrate's signature on this form. Delays at every level created various challenges in such a case.

On 21 June 1947, when the prosecuting inspector's office sent the report to the city magistrate's court, the city magistrate at first transferred the case to the court of the additional city magistrate. Finally, on 16 July 1947 when the case was registered in the court of the city magistrate, the *ahalmad* opened a file of the case but wrote the name as 'Pir Bakhair'. In the *misilband* (case diary) register no. 1, he wrote down the name as 'Pir Baksh s/o Tank Bahadur'.[80] This kind of careless entries and alterations made it impossible to trace the man later. By this time, the name 'Peter' had been altered to 'Pir' and 'Budge' had been changed to 'Bakhair'. Errors did not even spare Budge's father's name. Budge's parentage was also recorded incorrectly by different authorities. Budge's father's name, 'Tommy Budge', was also recorded incorrectly first as 'Tanik Bakhair' and later as 'Tank Bahadur'. Nobody even noticed that the city magistrate had opened a file, though under a corrupted name. Also, nobody took any notice of the suggestion in the police report that the man should be medically examined to ascertain his mental health. No letter was sent to the jail superintendent for his medical examination either.

Budge was not sent to the court in accordance with the rules when his remand expired on 17 June 1947. In the warrant, the next date fixed for it was 8 August 1947. The report highlighted that this implies that the warrant was not extended, and Budge was detained without any authority up to 8 August 1947.[81] The enquiry report held the assistant jailor Radha Raman Tewari responsible for this unlawful detention.[82] Notably, such practices thrived on fictitious entries and emanated from neither law nor authority and did not consider complete facts of the case. These were acts of official discretion, which were neither questioned nor condemned but seen as integral to the functioning of the legal bureaucracy.

When the city magistrate fixed 8 August 1947 as the next date of appearing before the court, he also ordered summons to be issued against the accused. The carelessness of the judiciary becomes evident here because if an accused was already in jail, there was no need for the summons to be issued. In addition to the *ahalmad*s and *moharrir*s, the magistrates too were not careful and attentive to paperwork. Neither the *ahalmad* nor the magistrate seems to have read the *chalani* report and the copy of the report of the general diary.

During the enquiry, the reader of the court, Oudh Behari, admitted that there was Urdu writing on the complaint. It read as 'mulzimaan muqayyad hain' (the accused is under detention). But Oudh Behari claimed that he read it as 'muqayyad azad hain' (the detainee is free). The enquiry report disagreed with the possibility of reading 'muqayyad' as 'azad'. Adding to the confusion, the prosecuting SI Yusuf Ali Khan stated that these words did not even exist when he sent the form to the district magistrate for his signature. Therefore, the enquiry report owed this error to Oudh Behari's negligence in not going through the papers properly. It can be observed that the issue of legibility, transliteration and the vernacular all made official records confusing. Also, certain bureaucratic habits contravening rules and regulations had become unofficially acceptable practices. Be it the careless handling of papers by the bureaucracy or different authorities, be it the police, jail, or judiciary, all copied each other's information (sometimes incorrectly) without due investigation.

On 8 August 1947, the jail authorities did send the accused to the city magistrate's court on requisition. The court *moharrir*, Mukhtar Ahmad, now understood that the case was against 'Peer Bajar'. We know of the *moharrir*'s false assumption because he sent the requisition note in this name to the jail for the accused's attendance on 8 August 1947. However, when the date arrived, the city magistrate fixed another date for 15 September 1947 because the accused was not produced before the court and was noted as absent by the magistrate. Hence, the magistrate ordered another summons to be issued. The problem once again was that there existed no person of the assumed name. Furthermore, issuing a summons to a man who was already in jail custody was technically wrong. The city magistrate could not note an accused as 'absent' when it was the jail authorities who repeatedly did not produce him. The enquiry report noted the city magistrate's failure to enquire into the cause of the absence of the accused.

Lower-level officials resorted to practices, such as the entry of fictitious dates, that complicated cases further. It was later found that the court *moharrir* had carelessly put down a fictitious date of 23 August 1947 in the warrant and returned it to the jail. Therefore, the enquiry held

Mukhtar Ahmad, the court *moharrir*, responsible for entering fictitious dates. However, Mukhtar Ahmad, in his defence, stated that the city magistrate had given him a standing order 'to fix a date 14 days ahead in every warrant'.[83] This was a highly irregular order, if at all given. When the issue of the fictitious dates was raised, the *moharrir* stated that he never enquired from the reader about the next date in any case. He understood his jurisdiction for this task more as returning the undertrials to jail before 5 p.m. and, therefore, did not always enquire about the next date of their appearance either from the reader of the court or from the file. The enquiry report noted, 'Since an accused would be sent to court by the jail only on requisition, the noting of a date in the warrant was only a formality meant to justify the detention in the jail.'[84] If the *moharrir* had enquired from the reader about the next date fixed in the case, the reader would have noted that the accused was actually in jail. However, the practice prevailing in the court, it was discovered, was to ignore the details. Hence, the court administration itself was unaware of many facts in the case.

Budge's misfortune was also a result of frequent transfer of judges in the court. Justice B.D. Sanwal, who was hearing the case, also got transferred at this stage, and Justice C.B.L. Dube began presiding over the court now. Even on the next date of hearing, 15 September 1947, no one enquired about the 'absence' of Peter (the accused), and the court issued another summons. But this time the city magistrate ordered the summons to be issued for 25 September 1947 and to be given *dasti*[85] to a constable. However, apparently, there existed no summons issued on 15 September 1947. According to the statement of the clerk-constable of Police Station Kaiserbagh, no summons reached the police station at all. The *chalanbahi*[86] of the *ahalmad* also did not contain an entry about the despatch of the summons. It was discovered that despite the effort on the part of the judge it was the then *Ahalmad* Ram Sudhrisht Lal who failed to issue the summons. Once again, a new date of hearing, 3 October 1947, was carelessly endorsed by the court *moharrir*. The court *moharrir* was supposed to maintain a register of the undertrials remanded by the magistrate in jail. But in the lock-up register, head constable Liaqat Ali had falsely recorded that Budge was released on bail on 10 August 1947. However, no correspondence existed for the date, and hence head constable Liaqat Ali had entered a fictitious date in the cause list. It is evident by now that the clerks often recorded information without checking the papers and were used to recording dates and names carelessly and often fictitiously.

Noting the 'absence' of Peter Budge in the court, Justice Dube once again issued a fresh summons for the hearing on 13 October 1947. The magistrate once again failed to enquire about the successive absence of the accused from the hearing. Later, the enquiry report noted:

> When the accused was absent again and again it was his [magistrate's] duty to give personal attention to the matter and to find out why he was absent.[87]

At this time, Justice Dube was also transferred, and Justice M.G. Kaul had taken over as the new city magistrate. When the accused was absent again on 13 October 1947, Justice Kaul at once ordered a bailable warrant to be issued against the accused on 11 November 1947. Most interestingly, the summons issued for 13 October 1947 was issued against 'Pir Bakhair s/o Tank Bakhair'. On the top of the summons was written: 'Pir Baksh *Isai*' in Hindi and 'Pir Baksh' in Urdu. The error of recording an incorrect name that began from the local police station returned to the point of its origin without anyone noticing any familiarity with the case.

In addition to having an unusual name, Budge's fate was complicated by issues of legibility and a careless bureaucratic culture. Throughout, he was treated like a nondescript, a Christian by religion and Indian by race but with an English name. Therefore, he also did not fit into any ready-made category. The Police Station Kaiserbagh returned the summons on 12 October 1947, stating that no trace of 'Pir Bakhair Christian' could be found in Mohalla Qandhari Bazar. The *ahalmad* of the court had failed to endorse the date on which he received the summons back. If he had received the order on or before 13 October 1947, the order of the city magistrate would have been wrong. The next step would be to find out the correct address of the accused instead of an order to issue a warrant. A warrant could only be issued if the accused was evading service of the summons. Magistrate M.G. Kaul too 'failed to go through the file and discover that the man was rotting in jail since 3.6.1947'.[88]

On 11 November 1947, the city magistrate transferred the case to special magistrate Dr S.N. Bose without noting anything about the presence or absence of the accused. The office of the special magistrate too repeated the mistakes and kept issuing summons. The next date of the hearing was 5 January 1948, and the accused was absent once again. By this time, Budge had already spent eight months in detention. The special magistrate once more issued summons for 16 January 1948, but on this occasion, he took the precaution of issuing it through the challaning authority, which meant careful recording of facts that would make any follow-up on the case easier. The special magistrate still did not bother to enquire himself about the 'absence' of the accused. When the summons order was not received back from the police station, the case was adjourned to 26 January 1948 and another summons was issued through the challaning authority. When once again the accused was 'absent', the special magistrate dismissed the complaint on the ground that the accused was untraceable. The case against Budge came to an end on 26 January 1948 without anyone noticing that he was still rotting in jail. He was physically present but absent (misrepresented) in the bureaucratic paper trail. Notably, it was the paperwork that legitimated his presence.

One of the appendices in the enquiry report includes a letter that the jail superintendent wrote to the district magistrate on 7 November 1947 enclosing a total of 93 warrants, including the one for Peter Budge, for fixing new dates. The letter sent to the district magistrate was lost in his office, and nobody had any idea about it either. Warrants were repeatedly sent to the courts for fixing dates but were received back as such. It is at this point that the warrant was received but not indexed. It was later revealed that the judicial assistant did receive the letter in the district magistrate's office together with the warrants on 8 November 1947 because he had forwarded this to the prosecuting inspector. This error owed to the dispatcher who did make an entry in the *rasid bahi* (receipt book) though he wrongly put down the number of the letter as 222 instead of 272. The enquiry report argued that the office of the district magistrate had been careless because no attention was paid to paperwork after it was sent to the prosecuting inspector. Had the letter been indexed, it would have appeared in the register of unanswered references after a month, and the district magistrate would have been able to note that full compliance was not done. The court *moharrir* Mukhtar Ahmad was held responsible for the detention of Budge till 29 October 1947 because he kept on endorsing fictitious dates in the warrant without any authority from the city magistrate. Meanwhile, the jail superintendent should have refused to admit the case of an accused not authorised by the criminal court because he derived his authority only from the warrant of custody. The enquiry report argued that if the warrant authorised detention up to a specific date, the jail superintendent was bound to send the undertrial to the court and must refuse to accept him back unless the date was extended. There is a failure on the part of the jail superintendent too, and a blatant violation of habeas corpus.

The enquiry report concluded that the initial blame lay with the magistrates and court *moharrir*s who were in the habit of doing fictitious work and did not realise their responsibility in such matters. But it was the court too that was inattentive even though the jail superintendent kept sending warrants time and again. According to the enquiry report, 'it was a question of liberty of an individual who had already undergone unlawful detention'.[89] However, one can argue that it was more a question of the banality of legal procedure.

During the enquiry, it was also discovered that the jail superintendent did send Budge to the court on three occasions after January 1948, but on each occasion, he was returned by the court. When repeatedly no notice of the matter was taken, the superintendent wrote a letter on 28 April 1948 to the district magistrate bringing this unlawful detention to his notice. The magistrate received the letter on 6 May 1948 and immediately ordered the jail authorities to present Budge before the court. Budge was presented before the magistrate the very next day and was immediately released under section 249 CrPC.[90] By this time, Budge had spent almost a year in detention. The case that began with the discretion of policemen ended with the discretion of the magistrate because section 249 CrPC pertains to a situation where:

> When the proceedings have been instituted upon complaint, and on any day fixed for the hearing of the case, the complainant is absent, and the offence may be lawfully compounded or is not a cognizable offence, the Magistrate, in his discretion, notwithstanding anything herein before contained, at any time before the charge has been framed, discharge the accused.[91]

Using his granted discretion, the magistrate released him on the ground that there were no papers connected with his detention, and he was never produced before the court.[92] Therefore, his detention was held illegal. The irony remains that the court did not trouble itself to enquire if there was any mistake on its part or whether the system was itself inefficient or careless. Moreover, Budge had himself sent two applications from jail, drawing the city magistrate's attention to his detention without trial. The first application was sent on 13 March 1948, followed by another on 24 April 1948.[93] Even these applications were untraceable in the city magistrate's court, but the *ahalmad* admitted to having received them. More accurately, he was forced to admit it because he had signed the jail *dak book* (postal register); otherwise, even this instance could have been denied.

The entire fiasco highlights that the neglect to deal adequately with the inspection notes of various inspecting officers further contributed to the unlawful detention of Budge. The police, the magistracy and the staff of the jail and the district magistrate's office were all responsible in one way or another for the unlawful detention of Budge. Such uncertainty of law was not only the potential site of everyday injustice in late colonial UP but also a complex and lengthy exercise that laid bare its banality. I would argue that such errors in the justice system should not be seen as only 'accidental' but should be taken as 'constitutive' of the larger legal practices in India. The case of Budge proves that juridical-bureaucratic rationality was often punctured by moments of small decisions that each official made at every step.

Law and Its Lies: Misapplication and Misinterpretation of Laws in Budge's Case

Peter Budge's case demonstrates that legal bureaucracy conducts itself through a complex network of paperwork. The significance of paperwork has been noted by various scholars across disciplines. Akhil Gupta and Veena Das have argued that writing and recording information is one of the central activities of the state and constitutes the core of government technologies.[94] Mathew Hull has also argued that in a government of papers, documents are imbued with privilege and act both as means of diffusing responsibility and of producing collective agency.[95] As a result, files, papers, signatures, stamps and entries in diaries, at various levels, lend legitimacy to the entire process. No doubt language creates law, but it also creates its subjects and their materiality. These subjects could only be identified by a particular name. In the domain of law, a person comprises a body and a definite name. Through Budge's story, the chapter has revealed by now that in legal processes there exists a fundamental split between the name and the body. A wrongly attributed name could result in unfortunate consequences for a person and could create new contexts of exclusion and violence. Such exclusion and violence are enabled by the paperwork that conducts legal bureaucracy.

In the case of Budge, we observe a very neat system of commands, recording of facts and registration of documents at the superficial level. Such conduct mediated by paperwork was supposed to ensure that individual officials did not commit error(s) in the process.

It was proposed to be a system that was designed to defy errors. But Budge's case demonstrates that the entire system of vouching collapsed when incorrect names were registered for the same person. This not only endangered the liberty of the concerned individual but also exposed the fragility of the conduct of papers. The chance of a human error set in motion a series of errors and, in a way, destabilised the government of papers. Here, an error does not merely constitute bureaucratic practice but its design too. Budge's case enables us to understand 'the implications of such a thorough paper mediation of relations among people, things, places and purposes'.[96] It lays bare not merely the absurdity but also the banality of the bureaucratic facade exposing the Kafkaesque nature of the justice system in late colonial India, where official discretion made illegal detention possible.

After the enquiry into Budge's ordeal was over, Justice Desai eventually submitted a 28-page report. The enquiry report was meant to demonstrate that the Congress government in UP was sensitive to the suffering of ordinary citizens. Budge's case makes evident that the state can both be the author of suffering and offer hope for a better future. Hence, the enquiry served as an act of inclusion on the part of the state; it brought the margins of the state to the centre of the discussions. Here, practices of the state emerge as a zone of indistinction, both redemptive and repressive. In the aftermath of independence, the state in a way reconstituted itself through such practices of inclusion and exclusion. However, such moments also exposed the solidity often attributed to the state.

Most importantly, the enquiry report concluded that 'the arrest by the constables without a warrant or order from the magistrate was altogether illegal'. Though there was a provision under section 54 that empowered a police officer to arrest without a warrant, that applied only when a person had been implicated in any cognisable offence.[97] However, such was not the matter in Budge's case. Moreover, this section could not be invoked when the offence of section 188 IPC is non-cognisable.[98] Also, under section 57, a police officer had the right to arrest a person who had committed a non-cognisable offence in the presence of a police officer along with refusing to give his name and residence address when asked. This is only aimed at ascertaining the name and residence of the person in question. This did not apply to Budge's arrest under section 57 because the constables did not even ask Budge his name and residential address. Therefore, the report argued, they could not have relied upon this provision.

Furthermore, when his name and residence were later ascertained at the police station, his detention had to cease. So, we now know that Budge's detention itself was unlawful.

The police case stated that the accused was arrested under section 151 CrPC.[99] This provision could be used for arresting a person for a non-cognisable offence. There was no question of preventing the commission of any offence because mere disobedience of an order under section 144 CrPC is not an offence. It is an offence only if the disobedience causes or is likely to cause obstruction, annoyance or injury, or risk of obstruction, and so on, to any person lawfully employed. The statements of police constable Saghir Ahmad and SI Manzoor Ali did not suggest anything of this nature. As mentioned earlier, Budge was recorded as a potential lunatic in the FIR, and a report for his medical examination was also prepared. However, this medical examination never took place. It is incomprehensible how such a 'half-witted man',[100] when disobeying the order, could have caused any obstruction to the legal order. His resistance and refusal to surrender his stick could have been a cognisable offence, but the police or the court did not bring any such charge against him in the first place. Therefore, the constables had no authority to demand that the stick be surrendered to them. District and sessions judge M.C. Desai concluded that 'the arrest itself was illegal'.[101]

The Banality of Bureaucratic Paperwork: When Officials Admitted Mistakes in Budge's Case but Saw It as an Occupational Hazard

During the enquiry, it was found that the *challan* report sent by the Alambagh Police Station was untraceable now. The prosecuting inspector blamed it on the theft of a box in his office in which he had lost many papers and presumed that Budge's *challan* papers were also lost with it. Furthermore, no warrant of custody addressed to the jail superintendent was issued for Budge, and he was admitted to the district jail in contravention of the Jail Manual (Para 15). Under Para 39 of the police regulations, the enquiry note pointed out, it was the duty of the court *moharrir* to obtain the magistrate's orders for the detention in the lock-up in the first instance and then the subsequent remand as well. The *moharrir* of the city magistrate's court who was responsible during the case had retired by the time of the enquiry and was blamed for his negligence. According to the enquiry note:

[E]ach Court Moharrir maintained an unofficial register of undertrial prisoners in which the details of the case against them, the various dates of remand and the date of bail etc. are mentioned. Therefore, entries regarding his case [Budge] were not made in the register prescribed in Form I of the Oudh Criminal Rules (the Misalband Register) because no actual papers reached the City Magistrate.[102]

As a result, it became impossible for the city magistrate to know about the case. According to the report, the city magistrate Judge Sanwal was subsequently replaced by Judge Dube in September for a month before Judge Kaul finally took over at the beginning of October 1947. Budge's case kept getting delayed because of the repeated transfers of the judges.

In addition to the magistrate in whose court the case was under consideration, there were other mechanisms available to check on the unnecessary detention of undertrials. According to the rules and routine, three levels of bureaucratic checks had to be made. First, a monthly inspection of the district jail by the district magistrate had to take place. Second, periodic inspections by the commissioner and sessions judge or non-official visitors took place[103] and third, a monthly list[104] of undertrials was sent to the district magistrate by the jail, under Para 439 of the Jail Manual.

The first inspection after the detention of Budge was carried out by the additional district magistrate on 15 September 1947, followed by another inspection on 10 January 1948. The additional district magistrate mentioned the name of Budge in the list attached to the inspection conducted on 10 January 1948, and a note was sent to the city magistrate for a report 10 days later. Though the city magistrate responded on 27 February 1948 with regard to other prisoners, he could not report on Budge as he had no documents in his court about his case. During the enquiry, it came to light that he did promise to make enquiries at the *sadr* (locality) lock-up of the *moharrir* but forgot. The magistrate also reported that the monthly lists of undertrials received from September 1947 to the first week of April 1948 were untraceable in his office. His roundabout excuse was that his office could not have received any lists between February and April 1948, as 'the jail staff was heavily worked owing to the R.S.S. and other detenues'[105] following the assassination of Gandhi. Also, the district magistrate stated that the monthly list of undertrials received from the jail was sent by the judicial assistant, in the original, to the courts for circulation. Therefore, owing to the large number of courts involved, the lists sometimes got lost, and reports were never received from courts in time. The lapse in following stipulated regulations was justified by blaming the shortage of staff in the courts, and it was argued that the office of the district magistrate had to deal with a huge volume of correspondence all the time. The district magistrate's office used this moment as an opportunity to remind the government that it was working under duress. The district magistrate's office did file a request for an increase in staff, but no official sanction was granted until this point. An attempt to shift the burden of error from individuals to blame general overwork is evident here.

The note of the district magistrate admitted that the jail inspection notes by various officers did not receive adequate attention from the magistrates largely because there was heavy congestion in the courts. He informed that the average number of undertrials belonging to all courts was around 500.[106] According to him, this led to the inefficiency of the court staff, leading to improper entries in warrants of custody when cases were transferred from one court to another. As a result, the jail authorities or the prosecuting inspector were unable to decipher whether a case was pending and with what office. During the enquiry, even the superintendent of the jail complained about the overwork. He complained that the undertrial clerk too was subjected to overwork and often had to do overtime. The institutions that would appear so ordered and would premise their work ethic as rule-based, in reality, operated under constraints. The facade of the order in the legal bureaucracy was exposed when the upholders of such a systematic order proved to be the most chaotic and lawless of all. Budge's case demonstrates that at the heart of this 'government of paper'[107] is an element of error, neglect and confusion.

The district magistrate pointed towards a 'fault' in the system where magistrates did not record cases in their cause-list in which a charge sheet had not been received, but only remands were being granted. The note admits without any further explanation that remands were granted on paper at the request of the police, and the undertrial was never taken out of jail until the hearing of the case started.[108] This points to an indirect confession by the judicial administration that there existed a practice of violation of due process. Furthermore, Budge's case was in a way pre-decided by the two constables, who, without sufficient information about him, lodged a report against him for 'violating' a curfew and carrying a 'weapon'. Also, clerks both in the police station and in the courts did not pay attention to facts and, due to multiple layers of paperwork, repeatedly registered his details incorrectly. The judicial system was also inattentive to the possible errors that could be committed in the process. It overlooked a general disregard for details and followed a standard habit of issuing warrants and conducting trials without ascertaining the facts of the trial or the accused.

Conclusion

Peter Budge's story reveals the nature of the bureaucracy of paperwork, the repercussion of official discretion on ordinary lives, and the question of justice and procedure in late colonial India. Bureaucracy and its paperwork were administrative strengths of the British colonial government in India. Legal procedure dominated bureaucratic rationality and enabled an environment where the colonial state could master and control the colonised by way of definition, classification and calculation. An administrative apparatus of depoliticised bureaucracy, impartial judiciary, rule-bound norms and dutiful police was argued to improve the lives of the indigenous population. This apparatus sustained itself through an *order of files*, which was proposed by the colonial state to contain facts and, therefore, truth. Legal formality and bureaucratic management of life aimed to reinforce elements of precise control at each level. Though legal procedure specified the rules of conduct, the conduct itself was not always legal. Budge's story and the enquiry report have challenged such a convenient understanding of colonial bureaucracy, exposing the fabricated nature of the paperwork involved.

The colonial experience had already extended the reach of bureaucracies to their widest extent. Such extensions, especially in the first half of the twentieth century, brought to the fore new strengths and vulnerabilities of the state. It opened up not only opportunities for corruption[109] but also distortion of the procedure. Corruption here does not mean merely a monetary or personal gain, but practices that were either quasi-official or crypto-official. Informal rules and fictitious records were commonplace in clerical practice. Such practices were constitutive of the emergent postcolonial state.

Budge's ordeal exhibits that in situations of a challenge to public order, police officials could declare someone's presence a violation of public tranquillity or declare an object a weapon. What is pertinent is the basis on which such action could be taken. Charging a person with a particular extraordinary crime and then proving it were two different sides of the administrative machinery. Ideally, a respite from injustice could be expected by challenging the official prejudice involved. But in this case, official incompetence, both in language and the law, further complicated the process. The career of laws like section 144 CrPC, curfews, and so on, that granted discretionary powers to various officials emerges as a corrupt and potent remnant of colonial legality. Laws like section 144 CrPC and curfews highlight the significance of the performative aspect of state power. Such laws enabled a disciplinary and punitive image of the state. It included exemplary use of force to maintain law and order in the districts to send a disciplinarian message to the population at large. The administrative crisis before, during and after partition was often characterised by spectacular displays of state power by invoking extraordinary legislation.

Spectacular displays of state power underscore the state's claim to legitimacy and to align citizens' vision of public order with that of the state. Detentions and violence due to the promulgation of laws such as section 144 CrPC demonstrated the state's capacity to discipline its citizens with disregard for the consequences of such laws and the supplementary discretionary powers on ordinary citizens. The state and its practices are always written into ordinary lives, but Budge's marginal story enables us to make those practices visible. Budge's ordeal highlights that the spectacular in the law trumped the substantive, and disciplining the population undermined the liberty of ordinary citizens. Hence, public-order laws such as section 144, and so on, hid the vulnerabilities of the postcolonial state in India in its formative years. Budge's story demonstrates that the state and its legal machinery were often internally incoherent, and its officials enjoyed unchecked powers and followed practices contrary to the stated claims. Individual officials like the local policemen, the *ahalmad*s, the *moharrir*s and even the judges acted in ways that circumvented the stated objectives of the state.

Budge's story brings to the surface the violence of legal bureaucracy in India, where individuals could get trapped in a mechanical world of bureaucratic procedures that served little reason other than its perpetuation. As a result, the centrality of justice was often rendered irrelevant in the web of bureaucratic hierarchies and rules. Rules became bureaucratic goals in themselves, undermining the principal intention that instituted them.

In this process, they became ends in themselves. In Budge's case, informal bureaucratic norms and practices were innovated by low-level officials of the police and the judiciary to achieve their formal ends. Within the bureaucracy, these officials remain the main point of contact and interaction between the state and citizens. The late colonial bureaucracy became a self-perpetuating institution that replenished its legitimacy through only rules. Given that colonialism as a context mediated the relationship between the state and its subjects and was consistently challenged, it lacked a substantive thrust. As a result, it had severe implications for the subjects.

It is evident in Budge's case that despite the availability of meticulously laid out rules, colonial law could not sustain the balance between law and justice. This imbalance occured because the context of colonialism led to a decoupling of the procedural and the substantive elements of law. However, the two elements coexisted and maintained the overall framework of the justice system in India. Each procedural misstep in Budge's story brings to light nothing but law's own nature or making and highlights that official discretion was constitutive of the idea of justice. Right from the moment of Budge's detention to the orders for his release and the subsequent enquiry by Justice Desai, a complex and strained polarity towards procedure is dominant and notable. The enquiry report, thus, is an exercise to salvage law by blaming procedural distortions. Such an enquiry facilitates covering up the gap between the procedural and the substantive in colonial law. Budge's story is prodigiously instructive of this dilemma and exposes a fundamental problem in the nature of colonial legality. The question of justice exhausts itself as the story of Budge's illegal detention unravels. Law ends up in failure, both at the procedural and the substantive levels. The enquiry report could not note the indeterminacy of law and the salutary production of injustice in the entire process. As a result, the injustice suffered by Budge got assimilated into the narrative of law by the rehabilitation of procedure through the enquiry report.

Notes

1. Taylor C. Sherman, *State Violence and Punishment in India*, Royal Asiatic Society Series (Abingdon: Routledge, 2010); Mark Condos, *The Insecurity State: Punjab and the Making of Colonial Power in British India* (Cambridge: Cambridge University Press, 2017); Anupama Rao, 'Problems of Violence, States of Terror: Torture in Colonial India', *Interventions: International*

Journal of Postcolonial Studies 3, no. 2 (2001): 186–205; Kim Wagner, *The Skull of Alam Bheg: The Life and Death of a Rebel of 1857* (London: C. Hurst and Co. Publishers Ltd, 2017); Kim A. Wagner, *The Amritsar Massacre: An Empire of Fear and the Making of Massacre* (New Haven and London: Yale University Press, 2019).

2. David Graeber, *The Utopia of Rules: On Technology, Stupidity and the Secret Joys of Bureaucracy* (New York and London: Melville House Printing, 2015).

3. Max Weber, *Economy and Society* (Berkeley: University of California Press, 2002 [1922]); Max Weber, 'Bureaucracy', in *From Max Weber: Essays in Sociology*, ed. H.H. Gerth and C. Wright Mills, pp. 196–244 (Oxford: Oxford University Press, 1946).

4. Akhil Gupta, Red Tape: Bureaucracy, Structural Violence, and Poverty in India (Durham, NC: Duke University Press, 2012); Matthew Hull, *Government of Paper: The Materiality of Bureaucracy in Urban Pakistan* (Berkeley: University of California Press, 2012); Nayanika Mathur, *Paper Tiger: Law, Bureaucracy, and the Developmental State in Himalayan India* (Cambridge: Cambridge University Press, 2016); Taylor C. Sherman, William Gould and Sarah Ansari, *From Subjects to Citizens: Society and the Everyday State in India and Pakistan, 1947–1970* (Cambridge: Cambridge University Press, 2014).

5. Veena Das, 'The Signature of the State: The Paradox of Illegibility', in *Anthropology in the Margins of the State*, ed. V. Das and D. Poole, pp. 225–252 (New Delhi: Oxford University Press, 2004); A. Gupta, 'Blurred Boundaries: The Discourse of Corruption, the Culture of Politics, and the Imagined State', *American Ethnologist* 22, no. 2 (1995): 375–402; Michael Taussig, *The Magic of the State* (New York, NY: Routledge, 1997).

6. T. Mitchell, 'Society, Economy, and the State Effect', in *State/Culture: State Formation after the Cultural Turn*, ed. G. Steinmetz, pp. 76–97 (Ithaca: Cornell University Press, 1999); James. C. Scott, *Seeing like a State: How Certain Schemes to Improve Human Condition Have Failed* (New Haven, CT; London: Yale University Press, 1998).

7. Franz Kafka and D. Wyllie, *The Trial*, Dover Thrift Editions (Mineola; New York: Dover Publications, 2012); Franz Kafka, *The Great Wall of China: Stories and Reflections*, trans. Willa Muir and Edwin Muir (New York, NY: Schocken Books, 1948); Franz Kafka, 'Before the Law', in *Franz Kafka: Collected Stories*, pp. 173–175 (New York, NY: Everyman's Library, 1998); Franz Kafka, *The Castle*, trans. Mark Harman (New York, NY: Schocken Books, 1998).

8. Hannah Arendt, *Eichmann in Jerusalem: A Report on the Banality of Evil* (New York: Penguin Classics, 2006).

9. Bernard Cohen, *Colonialism and Its Forms of Knowledge: The British in India* (Princeton, NJ: Princeton University Press, 1996).

10. Eric Stokes, *The English Utilitarians and India* (Delhi: Oxford University Press, 1990), p. 372.

11. J.H. Burns and H.L.A. Hart, eds., *An Introduction to the Principles of Morals and Legislation* (London: Athlone Press, 1970. The Utilitarian philosopher Jeremy Bentham formulated a framework for calculating the amount of pleasure or pain that a specific action is likely to cause. The calculation included several variables (intensity, duration, certainty, propinquity, fecundity, purity and extent), which Bentham referred to as 'circumstances'. Early colonial liberal thought (for example, Macaulay) was guided by such a Benthamian philosophy and argued that the East India Company needed to create new, better and modern laws for Indians. Such laws were supposed to be better than the traditional practices of adjudication (despotism).

12. Jonathan Saha, 'Colonization, Criminalization and Complicity: Policing Gambling in Burma c. 1880–1920', *South East Asia Research* 21, no. 4, Special Issue: Colonial Histories in South East Asia–Papers in Honour of Ian Brown (December 2013): 655–672; also see William Gould, 'Subjects to Citizens? Rationing, Refugees and the Publicity of Corruption over Independence in UP', *Modern Asian Studies* 45, no. 1 (January 2011): 33–56.

13. Lloyd I. Rudolph and Rudolph Susanne Hoeber. 'Barristers and Brahmans in India: Legal Cultures and Social Change', *Comparative Studies in Society and History* 8, no. 1 (October 1965): 24–49.

14. Hull, *Government of Paper*.

15. Ben Kafka, *The Demon of Writing: Powers and Failures of Paperwork* (Cambridge, MA: Zone Books, 2012), p. 16

16. Ibid., p. 11.

17. Ibid., pp. 81–82.

18. Matthew S. Hull, 'Documents and Bureaucracy', *Annual Review of Anthropology* 41, no. 1 (2012): 251–267.

19. Elizabeth Kolsky, *Colonial Justice in British India: White Violence and the Rule of Law* (New Delhi: Cambridge University Press, 2010), p. 252; Radhika Singha, *A Despotism of Law: Crime and Justice in Early Colonial India* (New Delhi: Oxford University Press, 1998), pp. xxix and 342.

20. Talal Asad, 'Where Are the Margins of the State?' in *Anthropology in the Margins of the State*, ed. Veena Das and Deborah Poole (Santa Fe: SAR Press), p. 287.

21. See 'Inquiry about the detention of Mr. Peter Budge about a year without produced before court', File No. 814/48, Home Department (Criminal), Uttar Pradesh State Archives (UPSA), Lucknow.

22. This is an observation made in the enquiry report submitted by Justice Desai. The author had access to the English translation of the documents

related to the case. These documents were part of File No. 814/48, Home Department (Criminal), UPSA, Lucknow.

23.   Taylor C. Sherman, William Gould and Sarah Ansari, 'From Subjects to Citizens: Society and the Everyday State in India and Pakistan, 1947–1970' (Special Issue), *Modern Asian Studies* 45, no. 1, (2011): 2.

24.   For example, Vazira Fazila-Yacoobali Zamindar, *The Long Partition and the Making of Modern South Asia: Refugees, Boundaries, Histories* (New York: Columbia University Press, 2007); Ritu Menon and Kamala Bhasin, *Borders and Boundaries: Women in India's Partition* (Delhi: Kali for Women, 1998). Other more recent analysis of it can be found in Ian Talbot, 'Punjabi Refugees' Rehabilitation and the Indian State Discourses, Denials and Dissonances', *Modern Asia Studies* 45, no. 1 (2011): 109–130.

25.   Sherman, Gould and Ansari, 'From Subjects to Citizens', p. 3.

26.   Ibid.

27.   K.G. Kannabiran, *The Wages of Impunity: Power, Justice and Human Rights* (New Delhi: Orient Longman, 2004), pp. 30–31.

28.   A.K. Gopalan, *In the Cause of the People: Autobiographical Reminiscences* (Madras: Sangam Books, 1976), p. 168.

29.   See concurring opinion of Justice Shah in *State of Gujarat vs. Vora Fiddali Badruddin Mithibarwala* (1964) 6 SCR 461, p. 136; For a detailed discussion see Gautam Bhatia, *The Transformative Constitution: A Radical Biography in Nine Acts* (Noida: Harper Collins India, 2019), pp. xvii–xxiii.

30.   'Release after Nearly a Years' Jail as Undertrial', *The Pioneer*, 11 May 1948.

31.   Veena Das and Deborah Poole, eds., *Anthropology in the Margins of the State* (Santa Fe: SAR Press, 2004).

32.   Nasser Hussain, *The Jurisprudence of Emergency: Colonialism and the Rule of Law* (University of Michigan Press, 2003), pp. 35–68.

33.   Austin Sarat and Conor Clarke, 'Beyond Discretion: Prosecution, the Logic of Sovereignty, and the Limits of Law'. *Law and Social Inquiry* 33, no. 2 (Spring 2008): 389.

34.   Andrew B. Lowenstein, 'Judicial Review and the Limits of Prosecutorial Discretion', *American Criminal Law Review* 38 (2001): 357.

35.   Amie N. Ely, 'Prosecutorial Discretion as an Ethical Necessity: The Ashcroft Memorandum's Curtailment of the Prosecutor's Duty to "Seek Justice"', *Cornell Law Review* 90 (2004): 237.

36.   Laurie L. Levenson, 'Working Outside the Rules: The Undefined Responsibilities of Federal Prosecutors', *Fordham Urban Law Journal* 26 (1999): 557.

37.   Angela J. Davis, 'The American Prosecutor: Independence, Power, and the Threat of Tyranny', *Iowa Law Review* 86 (2001): 393–465.

38. James Vorenberg, 'Decent Restraint of Prosecutorial Power', *Harvard Law Review* 94 (1981): 1521–1574.
39. Hussain, *The Jurisprudence of Emergency*, pp. 4–5.
40. Ibid., p. 5.
41. Ibid., p. 6.
42. For a larger overview of Uttar Pradesh, see 'Uttar Pradesh: History, Economy, People and Politics' in Paul Brass, *Factional Politics in an Indian State: The Congress Party in Uttar Pradesh* (Berkley and Los Angeles: University of California Press, 1965), pp. 5–33.
43. See Shail Mayaram, *Resisting Regimes: Myth, Memory and the Shaping of Muslim Identity* (Delhi: Oxford University Press, 1997), p. 298.
44. 'Unlicensed Firearms in UP', *The Leader*, 21 May 1947, p. 5.
45. Ibid.
46. Ibid.
47. 'Deterrent Punishment for Rioters, Ordinance Promulgated in U.P.', *Hindustan Times*, 26 May 1947.
48. Ibid.
49. Ibid.
50. See National Archives of India, File No. 38/37/47-Public (A).
51. Walter Benjamin and P. Demetz, *Reflections: Essays, Aphorisms, Autobiographical Writings* (New York: Schoken Books, 1986), p. 287.
52. Ibid.
53. Ibid., p. 280.
54. Ibid.
55. Ibid., p. 281.
56. See Note (Page 5) (Judicial enquiry report) by District Magistrate, Lucknow, A.D. Pandit, dated 15 May 1948, part of File 814/48, Home Department (Criminal), UPSA, Lucknow.
57. See Appendix 2, containing roman transliteration of 'Naqalrapat number 22 roznamcha-am muwarakha, June 2, 1947, 11 ¼ bajey, Thana Allambagh, Lucknow', part of File no. 814/48, Home Department (Criminal), UPSA, Lucknow.
58. See Judicial Enquiry Report, and the draft of the report by the District Magistrate, p. 20, part of File no. 814/48, Home Department (Criminal), UPSA, Lucknow.
59. Michael Lipsky, *Street-Level Bureaucracy: Dilemmas of the Individual in Public Services* (New York: Russell Sage Foundation, 1980).
60. Paul Ricoeur, *Freud and Philosophy: An Essay on Interpretation*, trans. Denis Savage (New Haven: Yale University Press, 1970), p. 8; also see Paul Ricoeur, 'The Model of the Text: Meaningful Action Considered as a Text', *Social Research* 38 (Fall 1971): 529–526.

61. Paul Ricoeur, 'The Hermeneutical Function of Distantiation', *Philosophy Today* 17 (Summer 1973): 129–141.

62. Ranajit Guha, ed., 'Chandra's Death', in *Subaltern Studies*, vol. 5, *Writing on South Asian History and Society*, pp. 135–166 (Delhi: Oxford University Press, 1987).

63. Asad, 'Where Are the Margins of the State?' p. 28.

64. Ibid.

65. Section 152 CrPC deals with 'Assaulting or obstructing public servant when suppressing riot, etc.'

66. Section 188 IPC deals with 'Disobedience to order duly promulgated by public servant'. What is significant about this section is that it is not necessary that the 'offender' should intend to produce harm or contemplate his or her disobedience as likely to produce harm. It is sufficient that he or she knows of the order that he or she disobeys, and that hi or /her disobedience produces, or is likely to produce, harm.

67. See Note (p. 5) (Judicial Inquiry Report) by District Magistrate, Lucknow, A.D. Pandit, dated 15 May 1948, part of File 814/48, Home Department (Criminal), UPSA, Lucknow.

68. See 'Release after Nearly a Years' Jail'.

69. Ann Laura Stoler, *Along the Archival Grain: Epistemic Anxieties and Colonial Common Sense* (Princeton: Princeton University Press, 2009), pp. 141–178.

70. Michel Misse, 'O papel do inquéritopolicial no processo de incriminação no Brasil: algumas reflexões a partir de umapesquisa', *Revista Sociedade e Estado* 26, no. 1 (2011): 15–27; also see Paula Chagas Lessa Vidal, '*Osdonos do carimbo': investigaçãopolicialcomoprocedimentoescrito* (Rio de Janeiro: Lumen Juris, 2013).

71. Misse, 'O papel', p. 19.

72. See File No. 462/1948, Home Department (Police) V, 'Criminal Law Amendment Act, Question of Issue of Orders under Section 144', p. 1, part of File 814/48, UPSA, Lucknow.

73. See File No. 462/1948, Home Department (Police) B, 'Criminal Law Amendment Act, Question of Issue of Orders under Section 144', p. 1, part of File 814/48, UPSA, Lucknow.

74. See File No. 462/1948, Home Department (Police) B, 'Criminal Law Amendment Act, Question of Issue of Orders under Section 144', p. 3, part of File 814/48, UPSA, Lucknow.

75. Ibid.

76. Ibid.

77. Ibid.

78. Ibid.

79. *Ahalmad* is also a junior clerk in courts, responsible for maintaining the judicial record of the cases pending in a court. He or she is also responsible

for maintaining case files according to dates of adjournment and to issue notices in the case.

80. See File No. 462/1948, Home Department (Police) B, 'Criminal Law Amendment Act, Question of Issue of Orders under Section 144', p. 4, part of File 814/48, UPSA, Lucknow.

81. Ibid.

82. Ibid.

83. See File No. 462/1948, Home Department (Police) B, 'Criminal Law Amendment Act, Question of Issue of Orders under Section 144', p. 5, part of File 814/48, UPSA, Lucknow.

84. Ibid.

85. Meaning a letter delivered by hand rather than post.

86. *Chalanbahi* is the book (record) of reciepts and acknowledgements of documents sent or received.

87. See File No. 462/1948, Home Department (Police) B, 'Criminal Law Amendment Act, Question of Issue of Orders under Section 144', p. 5, part of File 814/48, UPSA, Lucknow.

88. See File No. 462/1948, Home Department (Police) B, 'Criminal Law Amendment Act, Question of Issue of Orders under Section 144', p. 10, part of File 814/48, UPSA, Lucknow.

89. See File No. 462/1948, Home Department (Police) B, 'Criminal Law Amendment Act, Question of Issue of Orders under Section 144', p. 9, part of File 814/48, UPSA, Lucknow.

90. Ibid.

91. See section 249 of the CrPC.

92. Ibid.

93. See File No. 462/1948, Home Department (Police) B, 'Criminal Law Amendment Act, Question of Issue of Orders under Section 144', p. 9, part of File 814/48, UPSA, Lucknow.

94. Gupta, *Red Tape*; Das and Poole, 'The Signature of the State: The Paradox of Illegibility', in Veena Das, *Life and Words: Violence and the Descent into the Ordinary* (Berkeley: University of California Press), pp.162–183; Veena Das and Deborah Poole, 'State and Its Margins: Comparative Ethnographies', in *Anthropology in the Margins of the State*, ed. Veena Das and Deborah Poole, pp. 3–33 (Santa Fe: SAR Press, 2004).

95. Hull, *Government of Paper*.

96. Ibid., p. 1.

97. A cognisable offence is an offence where a police offer can arrest without a warrant.

98. A non-cognisable offence is an offence where a police officer can arrest only with a warrant.

99. This section laid down that a police officer knowing of a design to commit any cognisable offence may arrest, without orders from a magistrate and without a warrant, the person so designing, if it appears to such officer that the commission of the offence cannot be otherwise prevented.

100. See File No. 462/1948, Home Department (Police) B, 'Criminal Law Amendment Act, Question of Issue of Orders under Section 144', p. 2, part of File 814/48, UPSA, Lucknow.

101. Ibid.

102. See Note (p. 3) (Judicial Enquiry Report) by District Magistrate, Lucknow, A.D. Pandit, dated 15 May 1948, part of File 814/48, Home Department (Criminal), UPSA, Lucknow.

103. These two lists were sent to the inspector general of prisons.

104. This list contains undertrial prisoners in sessions court who have been in jail for more than six months from the date of committal and those in magistrate's court who have been in custody for more than three months. The district magistrate gets from the jail a list of undertrials over one month old.

105. See Note (p. 3) (Judicial Enquiry Report) by District Magistrate, Lucknow, A.D. Pandit, dated 15 May 1948, part of File 814/48, Home Department (Criminal), UPSA, Lucknow.

106. See Note (pp. 4–5) (Judicial Enquiry Report) by District Magistrate, Lucknow, A.D. Pandit, dated 15 May 1948, part of File 814/48, Home Department (Criminal), UPSA, Lucknow.

107. Hull, *Government of Paper.*

108. See Note (p. 3) (Judicial Enquiry Report) by District Magistrate, Lucknow, A.D. Pandit, dated 15 May 1948, part of File 814/48, Home Department (Criminal), UPSA, Lucknow.

109. Sherman, Gould and Ansari, *From Subjects to Citizens*, pp. 33–56.

4

Lineages of a Postcolonial State

The Disposition of State-Sponsored Vigilantism in
the United Provinces, 1948

With the advent of the Second World War, politics in colonial India created diverse priorities and new contradictions amongst political groups. The Congress party demanded the creation of a central Indian national government in lieu of providing support for war efforts and sought political guarantees of freedom from the colonial state after the war concluded. In contrast, the Muslim League and the communists supported British war efforts against Germany and its allies. The tussle between the Congress and the colonial state had escalated prior to this due to Viceroy Lord Linlithgow declaring India at war in the Second World War in September 1939 without consulting the elected provincial governments or political stakeholders in India. As a protest, all Congress ministries resigned in October 1939. Within the United Provinces (UP), the campaign for releasing revolutionaries and other political prisoners had already created an antagonistic relationship between the colonial state and the provincial government during this short period. The Cripps Mission struggled to secure Indian support for the British war effort. The situation only intensified with Gandhi launching the Quit India movement in August 1942, resulting in the arrest of almost the entire Congress leadership. The war became a moment of uncertainty for both the colonial state and the nationalists due to rising mutual mistrust and antagonism.

After the Second World War, the colonial state initiated negotiations with different political stakeholders in India to explore the possibilities of independence. Extensive deliberations with the Congress, the Muslim League and Sikh leaders resulted in Lord Mountbatten drawing a plan in June 1947 for creating two new independent dominions of India and Pakistan. Soon, the British Parliament passed the 1947 Indian Independence Act, which received royal assent on 18 July 1947, and Pakistan and India attained independence in August 1947. The partition of British India into India and Pakistan did not establish peace. Instead, it unleashed spectacular cycles of violence and migration, which various scholars have amply investigated. Administrations across the regions put in place strict preventive and prohibitory measures to control the situation. For example, in UP, the Communal Disturbances Act of 1947, the Indian Arms Act, curfews and the promulgation of section 144 were the instant response of the provincial government. Partition was not a singular moment but a long process that occurred over many years. Its aftermath has become an example of one of the biggest mass killings in South Asia. The fragility of the social in such a situation is undeniable. The UP government did not waste time introducing new measures to establish its power and authority in the postcolonial context.

Previous chapters have shown that intelligence-gathering, the prevention of crime and disorder, reading and classifying populations and identifying problem characters were some of the main activities of the colonial administration in India. The previous chapters have shown that there was little or no separation between the executive and the judiciary during public-order crises. The duplication of functions of some offices highlights the blurry legal and institutional nature of colonial governance. While Peter Budge's story has pointed out the gaps in the functioning of the colonial bureaucracy, the following chapters will show the administrative thinking of the postcolonial system and its efforts to establish power and gain authority amongst the citizens. Examining a system through various policing strategies and contrasting it to a fragment to delineate its everyday practices complement the broader understanding of the postcolonial state and its operations. The office of the district magistrate was important in this regard because it was responsible for managing the bureaucracy of a district. A district magistrate could also serve as a first-class magistrate invoking extraordinary legislation whenever required or deemed necessary by him. These were discretionary powers, as amply discussed in the previous chapters. The colonial bureaucracy thrived on portraying all administrative work as non-political, but there existed contradictions within the broader tactics of its governance, which continued to haunt the postcolonial administration in India.[1]

This chapter discusses three crucial administrative policies of the UP government from 1948 to make sense of the newly found independence in India. These policies were the discussions in January 1948 regarding issuing of guns to villages and the formation of Village Defence Societies (VDS) to fight dacoits in UP, followed by the passing of the Rakshak Dal Act, 1948, in April 1948 and, finally, the passing of the UP Prevention of Crime (Special Powers) Bill, 1948, by the end of the year. These discussions were initiated within the first six months of India attaining its independence. The official communication regarding these policies will bring to our attention various vulnerabilities of the postcolonial state and highlight how the provincial government and the law and order bureaucracy perceived its citizens. The chapter will argue that, on the one hand, the administration in UP distrusted the population due to the ongoing communal tensions and consistently occupied itself with identifying problem categories because it enabled the administration to claim power over the citizens. Therefore, it tried to sustain a distinction between the governing and the governed. On the other hand, its new policies increasingly blurred the assumed boundaries between society and the state, revealing its lack of resources and efforts to gain authority amongst the population. The instances from earlier chapters have already highlighted some of these issues. This chapter takes the discussion forward by emphasising the formative years of postcolonial India and will identify some of the initial challenges it faced. It will lay bare at least three issues that rest at the heart of public-order administration, that is, its politics, processes and power.

Scholars have shown that the postcolonial state is an arena of both political and cultural struggle. They have shown that the local and the global constantly challenged the state's authority and that growing demands for widening the ambit of rights and recognition have revealed the myth of the state as a constant source of social order and embodiment of popular sovereignty.[2] Other recent works have investigated police authority and its relationship to social order, democratic politics and conceptions of security. Such works have highlighted the paradoxical demands made on the Indian police, for example, expecting them to extend their authority into several official and unofficial tasks. Such works have argued that police authority in India is 'provisional' at three levels.[3] First, it is shifting across place and time; second, it is subject to availability and movement of resources;

and third, this authority is further dependent on shared moral codes and relentless instrumental demands placed on policemen. Such studies have concluded that a provisional police authority should not be seen as the violence of the law but as a contingent social resource in a postcolonial democracy like India. However, what is equally important is to investigate moments and discussions when administrative policies were drafted and later implemented on the ground. Such policies grant authority to policemen on the ground and result in 'vulgar manifestations of raw power'. Excessive violence, corruption and criminalisation of individuals through creating problem categories result from various administrative policies and repressive laws. As the chapter will show, official documentation highlights that the excess of control in the form of various administrative policies revealed the vulnerability of the state and the flimsy basis on which it proposed such policies.

For example, the figure of the *daku* (dacoit or bandit) or the goonda was not something entirely new. The colonial state had already innovated such categories to control and punish individuals who created administrative challenges to its power and authority.[4] In the emergent postcolonial environment, the administration, a colonial remnant, was unsure of its authority. The only response it knew was the demonstration of power through repressive techniques. The trope of repression through which this space of articulation and action became available under the 'sign of the state' drowned the voices of the ordinary and recognised their political aspiration as relevant only for the sustenance of state sovereignty.[5]

Other studies – especially on postcolonial states – suggest that law and order remained one of the main preoccupations of the modern state and argued that while postcolonies live in states of endemic disorder, many of them fetishize the law, its way and its means.[6] In this light, maintaining peace and tranquillity is one of the important stated aims of all postcolonial administrations. However, it achieves this tranquillity through a tactical deployment of control mechanisms. The northern state of UP – renamed Uttar Pradesh from 1950 onwards – was no different in this regard. In India, section 144 of the Code of Criminal Procedure (CrPC) and curfews remained an essential part of such control mechanisms. In the post-independence political and social fervour, it was an expectation that many aspects of Indian social and political life would change. However, a cursory look at the administrative files of the UP government suggests otherwise. A police department and the judiciary inherited from the erstwhile colonial administration did not allow space for a significantly different trajectory. It, in turn, created confusion, anxiety and much discussion within the UP government, exposing the attitudes of the government and its officials towards the ideas of democratic local governance.

The partition of India and the transfer of power emerge as the great dividing line of South Asian history. It is important to emphasise at the outset of this chapter that the colonial project did not die with independence; instead, it inspired the foundations of the postcolonial state. Undoubtedly, colonialism was over physically after independence, but its philosophy and structural legacy continued to thrive. Retaining the Indian Penal Code (IPC), the CrPC and the organisation of the police based on colonial policies and bureaucratic structures continued the colonial project, even if in a more indirect form. William Gould has pointed out that there was considerable confusion over what freedom from colonial rule meant.[7] In a situation of uncertainty and flux, this chapter will demonstrate, legality often occupies the moral-political vacuum. While partition could be a life-changing experience for the people – particularly in areas most directly affected by violence and migration – it became the context for a case of 'emergency' for the state. Also, the assassination of Mohandas Karamchand Gandhi in January 1948 added to the political crisis that India had to face soon after the transfer of power in August 1947. Some clarifications regarding constitutional emergency and its roots in the colonial set-up are necessary here.

Granville Austin, amongst others, has argued that there were many anxieties among Indian leaders during the constitution-making process that followed the achievement of independence in 1947.[8] Many Indian leaders were highly conscious that the compartmentalised nature of Indian society along the lines of caste, class, religion, region and language was a powerful obstacle to national integration, which remained their highest priority and determined how they envisioned the codification of the state (province)–centre relations. Distressed by the recent experience of partition, the constitution of independent India was to ensure that the centre could overrule the state(s) when it came to matters of national integrity. Austin called it 'the Union's long arm', which had a direct and immediate impact on 'Emergency Provisions' at the state or province level.

The United Provinces was renamed Uttar Pradesh in 1950. The ongoing impact of partition was visible in the province.[9] Therefore, it made a case for the urgent need to maintain public order and enacted a range of extraordinary legislation. Almost immediately after independence came the United Provinces Maintenance of Public Order (Temporary) Act, 1947, and the United Provinces Communal Disturbances Prevention Bill, 1947. Ironically, these pieces of legislation were enacted under sections 88 and 89 of the Government of India Act, 1935, respectively, because free India had no constitution yet. It highlights how colonial principles continued post-1947. We notice the strength of the colonial foundations of this new order in terms of its legal logic and their transition into the law and order administration of a postcolonial state like India.

The United Provinces Maintenance of Public Order Ordinance, 1947, could prohibit the entry into the province of any document or newspaper and impose collective responsibility on the inhabitants of specified areas to perform or abstain from performing specific duties or acts. The second amendment added section 10A to this Act, empowering the provincial government to seek civil assistance to perform administrative duties for 'securing public safety', the 'maintenance of public order' or 'to maintain essential services to the life of community'. This law made it mandatory for the population of UP to act as extended organs of the state in maintaining public order. It included an obligation to provide knowledge of any information on activities that could lead to disorder. The provincial government could impose collective fines on the inhabitants of a particular area for any contravention of such orders. In case of failure to pay such a fine, a person would be punishable with imprisonment for up to a year, even though the ordinance stated that while fining individual persons for contravention of such orders, the court should consider the amount of collective fine apportioned on the accused. This law (second amendment) came into existence on 9 October 1947.[10] This extraordinary law was amended and extended on 22 December 1947. The new amendment empowered the provincial government to confiscate or seal 'property of persons engaged in activities detrimental to public peace and to impose collective responsibility for the protection of property and the furnishing of information'.[11]

The United Provinces Communal Disturbance Prevention Bill, 1947, aimed at dealing with the threat to 'public peace and order' from communal strife and 'empower[ed] the authorities' to take special measures to prevent or extend such disharmony.[12] In Chapter III of this law, under 'offences and punishments', section (13) stated:

Notwithstanding anything contained in section 188 of the Indian Penal Code,[13] whoever wilfully disobeys in any communally disturbed area any order lawfully promulgated under section 144 of the Code of Criminal Procedure, 1898, passed in connexion with the prevention of any communal activity or communal disturbance, shall be liable to a sentence of imprisonment for a term of not less than two years and not more than five years and with fine in the discretion of the court.[14]

Section 144 CrPC, which dealt with unlawful assemblies and potentially riotous mobs, was utilised simultaneously with the above-mentioned laws. But whereas earlier section 144 restricted unlawful assembly, the new prevention of communal violence and maintenance of public order ordinances expanded the state's reach and aimed to activate ordinary citizens as its machinery. As the following sections will demonstrate, the content of these legislations points to the fact that UP broadly turned into a constitutional edifice where boundaries between the state and society were no longer meaningful – the state–society relationship was expected to differ from the colonial context after the transfer of power in 1947 continued.

Most importantly, the provincial government in the newly independent India remained obsessed with extraordinary measures and resorted to such laws to conduct everyday governance in the aftermath of partition because it lacked clarity and confidence in its capacity and purpose. As a result, the UP government resorted to using extraordinary measures to achieve everyday peace and order in more and more districts and towns of the province. This chapter will broadly highlight two aspects of the UP administration: First, the postcolonial UP administration maintained everyday public order by following a two-pronged strategy. On the one hand, it argued for the cultivation of responsible citizenship by militarising society and, on the other hand, it resorted to special powers and extraordinary legislation to inculcate the fear of police in the minds of the masses. Second, such cultivation created a discourse revolving around the binary between what the government defined as 'reliable villagers' and 'social pests'.[15]

Finding 'Reliable Villagers': Dacoity and the Proposal of Issuing a Gun to Every Village in UP, 1948

Eric Hobsbawm offered a compelling account of popular outlaw figures, which he termed 'social bandits'. For Hobsbawm, these are proto-revolutionary peasants who defy an oppressive and illegitimate state or system and draw popular support from their local communities.[16] He proposed that 'social bandits' emerged in times of famines and political crisis when the state failed to provide for the people and when an unstable government weakened the state's police power.[17] Hobsbawm noted that the social bandits were mostly peasant outlaws whom the establishment regarded as criminals but were considered heroes, champions, avengers and fighters for justice and admired and supported by their communities.[18] Such outlaws thrived on a retributive and deterrent approach, sometimes combined with an element of redistribution. Hobsbawm's reliance on mostly folklore characters to propose the figure of a noble bandit has been amply criticised by scholars such as Anton Black, Pat O'Malley, Boon Kheng Cheah, Richard White, Donald Crummey, Stephen Wilson and Phil Billingsley.[19] However, this section of the chapter deals with outlaws/ bandits of fact rather than mere outlaws/bandits of folklore.

Scholars have extensively studied the raiding communities of early colonial India and the politics in which they thrived. Such studies have investigated systematic plunder deployed by actors ranging from petty marauders to tribal chiefs and Rajput and Maratha rulers.[20] They have noted that such plunder served diverse purposes ranging from extracting revenue, rebelling against superiors, intimidating rivals, conquering new territories and sometimes even establishing new states. The continued use of robber communities in contemporary Indian rural politics has further highlighted the sustained significance of studying such communities and the various challenges to governance posed by them.[21] For example, the uneasy alliance between the Congress Socialist Party's Azad Dastas (Band of Free Brothers) and the dacoits in the first half of the 1940s is well documented by Vinita Damodaran.[22] Damodaran has highlighted the complexity of organising underground political movement in the face of the Quit India movement and the arrest of the Congress leadership. Such covert mobilisation by Azad Dastas against state repression sustained itself in collaboration with various popular bandits in Bihar and, for our purpose, lays bare a nexus between administrative practices and socio-economic conditions in the rural areas. This political alliance was motivated by 'a conscious desire to protest against social injustice and political oppression'.[23] This period witnessed an increase in the prices of grains, especially wheat and rice. *Bania*s (a trading caste), *beopari*s (traders) and wholesale merchants thrived in such seasons of crisis and resorted to extracting exorbitant profits. As a result, the general population was suffering from acute inflation and a shortage of food grains, at least in UP and Bihar.

The narrative of dacoity is quite similar in Bihar and UP in the 1940s. The bandits or dacoits were known as *daku*s in the vernacular. Markus Daechsel has highlighted that 'the daku bore a clear imprint of the colonial system'.[24] According to Daechsel, the term *daku* was given a precise legal definition as a robber operating in a gang by the Bengal Police Code and later adopted in other provinces. Colonial discourse through Police Administration Reports and the related press releases sketched the *daku* as the most notorious criminal of the region.

Notably, dacoities or robberies by such *daku*s were few compared to other crimes in the provinces, but it came to be referred to as the 'barometer of crime' by the colonial police. However, after the 1920s, with an increase in revolutionary activities, dacoity gained a revolutionary status and represented armed resistance to the colonial state. The revolutionary activities of figures in UP such as Ram Prasad Bismil and Chandra Shekhar Azad highlight that dacoity was a subversive act against the colonial state.[25] As Damodaran has highlighted, the figure of the dacoit or bandit belonged mainly to the low castes and attacked both state and private property. Bandits were sustained and supported by village communities.

Campaigns of mass criminalisation of such castes by the administration failed to catch the dacoits.[26] However, there existed a distinction between popular famine looting and organized armed activities of professional dacoits, as Vinita Damodaran and David Arnold noted.[27] When the district officials talked of an increase in dacoities in Bihar in 1942–1943, 'they tended to mean only the depredations of organised dacoit gangs'.[28] The organised and professional dacoits were a more significant threat to the colonial administration because they were seen as a threat to the 'security and property of the rural propertied class' and the state's 'authority and capacity to exercise effective control in the countryside'.[29] In UP and Bihar, there emerged a convergence between social crime and political crime in the early 1940s. As a repressive regime paying little attention to the welfare of its rural subjects, the colonial state was seen as distant and alien. As a result, the popularity of many bandits during the period and even later highlights community claims to justice through outlaws bypassing state institutions. The discussion on Azad Dastas in Bihar appears closer to Hobsbawm's argument that local communities often preferred their local bandits to foreign occupiers, and the connection to the revered pioneers is clear.[30] These (social) bandits also provided lawmakers or the state and the general population with a counter-perspective about their evaluation of the legitimacy of specific laws or the status quo in general.

The challenge of social bandits exposed an imaginative deficit on the part of the state and the public. The bandits or dacoits demonstrated the results of an alternative system that challenged the dominant perspective of the state. While the general Congress mobilisation on the ground during the Quit India movement resulted in episodes of wilful civil disobedience by civilians, it was the bandits in rural areas who demonstrated defiance and counter-authority. If dacoity had a revolutionary character and was earlier seen as a subversive act against the colonial state, the postcolonial state strove to establish an order that sought to delegitimise challenges to the nationalist hegemony and postcolonial sovereignty. In such a context, the defiance and counter-authority of bandits could not be but a threat to public order. As a result, the state required an image rehabilitation as against the dacoit or outlaw or bandit. The productive role of dacoits is evident in such efforts of image rehabilitation.

In 1948, the Police Reorganisation Committee (PRC) in UP resolved to introduce a policy to arm 'reliable' citizens across villages to counter the threat of dacoits. The policy was implemented on a trial basis in a few districts initially. However, it was extended to all districts of UP within a short period. During implementation, as the following discussion will show, the policy created numerous challenges for the administration though. This section will make three arguments while discussing the implementation of this policy. First, the policy exposed the administration's distrust of ordinary villagers. Second, it laid bare the state's incapability to establish order. And most importantly, it tried to shift state responsibility onto private citizens. This section argues that the policy of issuing guns to reliable villagers outsourced sovereign violence to private individuals and led to the establishment of state-sponsored vigilantism in UP.

When the PRC was set up in 1948, the administration was already struggling on various fronts – be it the influx of refugees due to partition and the communal disturbances that followed or other issues like creating the sense of 'citizenship' among the population of UP in the post-independence scenario.[31] Scholars have studied, for instance, anti-corruption drives in post-independence UP, which often rested on vague notions of duty and belonging.[32] Along with the strained relations between the landed and the landless labour class, for the administration dacoits constituted a significant threat to everyday law and order in certain regions of UP. Landholding classes in the province supported the Congress and the Muslim League during the anti-colonial struggle. The colonial model of governance and the anti-colonial movement had a fair share of upper-class support at various levels. As a result, such people, especially the *zamindar*s who often acted as community leaders in their respective villages, continued to hold extraordinary influence, control and power.[33] On many occasions, such landholders or wealthy persons in the villages became the targets of dacoities. Dacoits posed a great challenge to the provincial administration's law and order. The instances of dacoity were higher in some districts than others. Official communication of district magistrates, to be discussed in detail in the following sections, points out that Girand(ar) Singh, Birey and Bashira were some of the notorious dacoits operating across various districts in UP.[34]

The making of public order in a modern nation-state is closely tied to the issue of sovereignty. More precisely, as Klem Bart and Bert Suykens have recently argued, it must be understood as linked to the question of de facto sovereignty.[35] The entire apparatus of legal bureaucracy participates in the maintenance of such an order. De facto sovereignty, however, is most specifically tied to the idea of social control. Michel Foucault has extensively engaged with the question of mechanisms of social control. In the context of the newly acquired independence in 1947, various provinces in India were struggling to establish control over the population. The existing institutions and resources were perceived to be insufficient to maintain public order. For example, in UP, the provincial administration often lamented that bad characters, dacoits and other unruly citizens created administrative challenges for the provincial administration.

In January 1948, the district collector of Bareilly, L.C. Jain, in a top-secret letter to the divisional commissioner of Rohilkhand, N.B. Bonarjee, requested permission to try out an experiment in his district.[36] As a measure against dacoities, he proposed to provide every village with a gun each. Conscious that selecting the 'right type of men' to be issued these guns was necessary, the district collector proposed Aonla tehsil of Bareilly for the experiment. According to the collector, it was near Budaun and Rampur and in close proximity to the Moradabad border. It was geographically located in the western part of UP, where dacoity was a particular problem. At the same time, this region was deficient in road accessibility from Bareilly due to the absence of a bridge on the Ramganga river, which made centrally organised police operations more difficult. The idea of the district collector was to select 'one man of approved character and standing' in every village under his guidance.[37] The district collector believed that if such men were chosen with sufficient care, it might give villages considerable self-confidence against bad characters. Also, under this scheme, it would be the duty and responsibility of the gun licensee to go to the rescue of a neighbouring village on 'information of trouble'.[38] The district collector further proposed that if the policy was unsuccessful after a fair trial for six months, such gun licences could be recalled.

On receiving the proposal, the home secretary to the UP government, R. Dayal, forwarded it to the inspector general of police (UP), B.N. Lahiri, for comments. The latter agreed that 'it is certainly worth a trial'.[39] However, he added that it might be advantageous to constitute village defence societies/committees in particular villages with gun licensees as their leaders. He also reiterated the Bareilly district magistrate's point that such selection had to be made with 'due care'.[40] The government agreed with the proposal of issuing at least one gun licence to every village as a measure to prevent dacoities, initially as a temporary measure lasting for a period of six months. The UP government also wanted to experiment with lending suitable muzzle-loading and breech-loading guns from the *malkhana* (storehouse in the police station). Muzzle-loading guns with a rifled barrel involved a complicated process where the bullet and gunpowder were inserted from the front, while breech-loading guns were modern and used ready-made cartridges and could be quickly loaded and fired. Once the dacoity situation was under control, the government wanted those guns withdrawn, but the temporary licence of such villagers who would do 'exceptionally good work' could be permanent. Recommendations for the trial of this scheme in Etah and Mainpuri districts of the Agra Division of UP were made because of the activities of a notorious dacoit, Girend(ar) Singh.[41]

The UP government also allowed the divisional commissioner of Rohilkhand to follow the example of Bareilly and to provide selected villagers with at least one gun licence in every village as a 'preventive measure against dacoity'. The government directed the district magistrate of Bareilly to try out the experiment in the areas of his district where he was keen and deemed necessary to implement this scheme. The measure aimed to create village-level committees that would serve as vigilantes fighting dacoity. The administration was willing to make arrangements for the gun licences but did not want to incorporate them into the official policing structure. Such a quasi-official move argued to kinder the spirit of vigilantism in the villagers against the 'menace' of dacoits.

Scholars in the past have argued that 'all social problems turn out ultimately to be problems of social control'.[42] However, their focus remained very elementary, given the narrow attention paid to the study of social control that involved public opinion and the institutional forms of social control. More recently, Michel Foucault extensively delineated the modalities and implications of social control.[43] Foucault's analysis offered a simple yet potent framework that emphasised that the deviant figure, the abnormal, is served as a template of threat, or the undesired, to society. The discourse of governance rests on the binary of the 'normal' and the 'abnormal' or the deviant. Such discourse also thrives by sustaining a binary between the legitimate and the illegitimate. And what is not legitimate is, for the state, necessarily criminal. Crime remains the preoccupation of legal bureaucracy and is often highlighted as the major challenge to peace and order in a society. While some might attribute the existence or increase of crime to a lack of effective state intervention, insufficient attention has been paid to the character of the intervention itself.

Thakur Phool Singh, a member of the UP legislative assembly from the Meerut constituency, also expressed his concern about dacoities. He wrote to the premier, G.B. Pant, that 'dacoities are becoming common because people have smuggled arms during last disturbances'.[44] He added that the government had only two alternatives: to comb the districts for these arms, which, according to him, was very difficult owing to the large population, or arm the people. Emphasizing his suggestion that there should be at least one firearm in each village, there should be no restriction on the possession of sharp-edged weapons, which would necessitate the repeal of the Arms Act. This suggestion was contradictory and reflected the conflicted nature of state–society relations at the time. On the one hand, he suggested combing villages for arms and, on the other, he suggested arming ordinary citizens in UP – the population was alternatively seen as a potential problem category for the state to control and as an extension of the state apparatus itself.

The government sought data from district administrations across UP regarding the prevalence of dacoity and the villages most vulnerable to dacoits. Meanwhile, the collector of Bareilly, L.C. Jain, apprised the divisional commissioner of Rohilkhand about the status of the 'Anti-Dacoity Scheme'. According to him, by August 1948, after scrutiny of applications, 60 licences were sanctioned in his district.[45] Out of these, only 43 were actually issued; the remaining 17 awardees had failed to deposit the necessary fee for the licence. Out of the 43 licences issued, only 11 could secure weapons, while guns did not cover the remaining 32 licences yet. Out of the 11 licensees who secured guns, 5 were holding licences earlier, but their licences were cancelled. Hence, only 6 new guns were purchased in villages with no guns. The main reason for such poor results was the cost of guns and the difficulty of finding 'one reliable man' in each village to invest in a gun. He added that the number of confiscated arms was small, and it was challenging to provide arms to the villagers under this scheme. As for the idea of issuing arms from the *malkhana*, the district magistrate of Bareilly added, it held only unserviceable or damaged arms. The district magistrate also stated that after consultation with his superintendent of police (SP), he found that no dacoity occurred in villages where a licensed gun was available. He contended that it could serve as a strong argument in favour of the continuance of the experiment.

The district collector of Etah, Ram Kinker Singh, reported that the dacoity-combating scheme was introduced in 13 out of 15 *thana*s (police stations) of the district. The scheme was active in 1,322 inhabited villages of the police circles.[46] Out of these 1,322 villages, 846 villages now had VDS. However, the SP was only able to recommend 30 applicants who were subsequently granted licences. The SP experienced considerable difficulty in recommending applications because most people who could afford firearms did not want to work under the VDS. Those willing to work under the VDS scheme could not afford to buy firearms. Also, people did not want to purchase muzzle-loading guns and preferred breech-loading guns for defence against dacoits. Such guns were not available in the *malkhana*s. The few muzzle-loading guns available in the *malkhana*s were unserviceable and needed repairs for which there were no funds. Moreover, according to the district magistrate, there were special circumstances in some of the police circles, most notably in Aliganj, Patiali, Jaithra, Ganjdundwara and Sahawar, where the gang of a notorious dacoit, Girand(ar) Singh, operated. A large number of people in these police circles, it was reported, were sympathisers and supporters of Girand(ar) Singh. Therefore, the administration was anxious to recommend firearms in such villages as they might fall into the hands of dacoits.

Police circle Sirhpura granted 18 licences for breech-loading guns and 2 for muzzle-loading guns. No dacoity occurred in this police circle since the issuing of gun licences. The district magistrate expressed that it might take some months for the complete implementation of the scheme and the granting of licences in the 846 villages where VDSs were organised.

The district collector of Mainpuri also expressed his opinion on the operation of this scheme.[47] He stated that the scheme had been a success to some extent. According to him, there were 27 dacoities in Mainpuri district from October 1947 to February 1948. However, since the implementation of the scheme, there occurred only 10 dacoities. There were a few cases where armed villages offered resistance to the dacoits. Hence, the increasing number of arms licences in villages had a salutary effect in keeping the dacoits away. The district collector of Mainpuri stated that the success of the scheme was somewhat limited because of the insufficient number of breech-loading guns available.

On behalf of the deputy inspector general of the police headquarters of UP, the SP sent a list of districts where no firearms were available.[48] According to the letter containing the list, these villages also recorded higher cases of dacoity and were recommended for the provision of one gun to 'reliable residents' in each of these villages. The list included villages from the districts of Agra, Ballia, Budaun, Deoria, Sitapur, Etawah, Bareilly, Jhansi, Farrukhabad, Etah, Saharanpur, Hardoi, Meerut, Bulandshahr, Mainpuri, Moradabad, Muzaffarnagar, Jalaun and Aligarh. These districts, according to the list of the police headquarters, were notorious for the prevalence of dacoity. Some districts had more villages nominated to the list than others, for example, Etawah, Jhansi, Aligarh and a few others. These lists alarmed the government, resulting in making the case urgent. The UP government sent a letter to the district magistrates of the districts mentioned earlier, directing them to go ahead with the scheme at a faster pace.[49] The letter instructed that since guns were not readily available in the market and prices were too high, the district magistrates should sell guns in a serviceable condition out of the quota of 10 per cent forfeited and confiscated firearms in the *malkhanas* to selected villagers in dacoity-prevalent areas. It explained that a case might arise where the number of villagers chosen in a district would exceed the number of guns available; in that case, the government was willing to consider the district magistrates' proposals for the sale of guns out of the district reserve forfeited arms. Also, district magistrates could fix the price of the guns at their discretion. However, the government re-emphasised the careful selection of 'reliable and public-spirited' villagers who actually resided in villages. More than one gun could be issued to a village in compelling cases. The government was willing to sell weapons to villagers at a special concession on the promise that they would assist the administration in preventing dacoity. Authorities would cancel their licences if it appeared that they were not providing any assistance to the state.

While the colonial state was fearful of insurrections, the postcolonial state was more concerned about the counter-conduct of its citizens. Such counter-conducts aimed to be partially mitigated by subcontracting law enforcement to 'reliable' citizens. Such citizens were always men belonging to the landed upper castes. The postcolonial state, despite all sophistications, operated in the ambit of a Hobbesian conception of a security state – a security state where the representing sovereign disapproved of the 'natural state of man'. One point of analysis could be that the postcolonial state did not expect social opposition to the new order, given that most socio-political contradictions were supposed to have been resolved with partition. The dacoits challenged an expectation of a hegemonic postcolonial state. The lack of a different register of politics and the force of circumstances made the administration devise strategies different from the erstwhile colonial state. In other words, the law-and-order administration protested the destruction of life and property by the dangerous others. It required a law-and-order administration where policing apparatus ruled people for the sake of the sovereign. A deficit in state power is plugged by subcontracting the citizenry for law enforcement. The legitimisation of domination thus took place through measures that attempted to safeguard 'precarious' citizens from the 'dangerous' others. It succeeded in creating a juridico-political split in the citizenry. Such policies increasingly resulted in blurring the dividing line between society and the state. It created a spill-over effect by transferring state responsibility onto a selection of individuals. The official communication from the district-level bureaucrats highlighted a narrative of suspicion that emphasised the unreliability of villagers. There was often a contradiction in the broader moral politics of non-violence that the Congress preached, and the seduction of extra-legal measures exposed the state's incapability to establish order. It points out that there was a trust deficit in the administration too. It was not only the masses who did not know what independence entailed, but the administration also did not know what to expect. Such moments erased the differentiation of state sovereignty and popular sovereignty in some ways because the popular was burdened with the moral responsibility to assist the state in purging undesired elements. Pertinently, the discourse of reliable villagers suggests that the UP administration did not see the larger population as trustworthy.

Various districts took up this scheme actively hereon. By the end of 1950, in the 18 districts with a high prevalence of dacoity, approximately 1,118 guns were issued to various 'reliable and public-spirited villagers' willing to help the administration fight against dacoits.[50] By the end of February 1951, the Uttar Pradesh government gave orders to all district magistrates to freely issue 'licenses for firearms to reliable members of Village Defence Societies' found qualified for the purpose.[51] It was hoped that they would help the state government in 'combating dacoity menace and lawlessness' prevalent in the villages. Notably, a government scheme that was supposed to be experimental in the first place quickly escalated into a full-fledged policy. At a certain level, such a policy further aimed to reduce the gap between the state and the society by granting almost a commissioned sovereignty to such 'reliable villagers' who could act as protectors of villagers against dacoities and possessed the authority to kill the dacoits.

The discussion here has shown that whereas the UP government was hesitant to issue guns earlier, it gave them freely later. Furthermore, in some cases, villagers were sympathetic to dacoits. The issue of guns to villagers, on the one hand, and legislators also arguing for allowing the possession of a sharp-edged weapon, on the other hand, appears confusing and misguided given that these were the times of intense communal conflict due to the unfolding process of partition and the migration waves that followed. A gap in thinking between the administrators and the politicians becomes prominent here. On the one hand, the UP administration wanted to maintain public order and communal harmony by banning unlawful assemblies and, on the other hand, it officially issued weapons to 'reliable' villagers and formed VDS to fight dacoits. When such organisations had a greater chance of being utilised by their leaders for communal violence, their creation and existence are questionable. Notably, promulgating extraordinary laws and putting restrictions alone was not sufficient; the government needed to issue guns for a state-sponsored vigilante to act on behalf of the community and, in hindsight, the state. As the discussion earlier has highlighted, such a step expanded the state's vision of a disciplined and militarised society prepared to challenge all kinds of enemies. However, it is uncanny of a provincial government first to lament the uncooperative behaviour of its citizens and then arm 'reliable villagers' from amongst the same population. Once again, such administrative moves highlight the provincial government's efforts to increase its legitimacy among the people by incorporating them into quasi-policing structures.

This chapter contends that the policy to issue a gun to every village in UP falls somewhere between social control and crime control. It has emphasised that extra-legal activity endorsed by the state enables social control while also accomplishing the objective of controlling crime. Conspicuously, less attention is given to state-sponsored extra-legal activity. Incredibly, very little attention is paid to extra-legal activity in the form of such manufactured vigilantism, which has historically so profoundly made its mark upon Indian social life and Indian institutions. What is noteworthy is the acceptance that extra-legal activity comes to be enjoyed by various sections of the population and is later endowed with the tradition and dignity of an accepted institution. A vast amount of literature that focuses on extra-legal activity has primarily focused on mob violence culminating in a lynching. Such literature tends to club laws, crime and vigilante formations into one group. This chapter has taken state-supported vigilantism in early postcolonial India as its main point of departure and has endeavoured to discuss its implications on social control, which would entail achieving more than one objective.

As promulgating extraordinary laws and issuing guns were not yet sufficient, the UP government proceeded to form a civilian defence force known as the Prantiya Rakshak Dal (PRD).

Rakshak Dal Act and the Logic of Defence and Policing in UP

Scholars such as Markus Daechsel[52] and William Gould[53] have pointed out that physical culture comprised a significant part of various nationalist organisations. Fitness and bodily control were subjects of interest and concern for a range of nationalist ideologies. For instance, in UP, Congress leaders such as P.D. Tandon, who generally would take sides with the Gandhian idea of non-violence, took initiatives to militarise society by making a case for Hindu defence in the early 1940s.[54] These initiatives not only popularised such organisations but legitimised them too. Tandon's participation in Hindu defence projects centred around his involvement in the organisation of the Hind Rakshak Dal.[55] His speeches of endorsement for this organisation often embarrassed the Congress but demonstrated the widespread support for semi-militaristic organisations.[56] This section will show that the post-1947 Congress government in UP continued with such projects and officially recognised Tandon's Hind Rakshak Dal by legislating the Rakshak Dal Act, 1948.[57] As will be explained in this section, such organisations aimed to inculcate a notion of responsible citizenship by involving larger sections of society in policing activities. On the face of it, it fits well with the Weberian perspective that understands the state as a compulsory association that organises domination.[58] The state's necessity to create organisations like the Rakshak Dal in postcolonial India emphasises a triad of historical contingencies, political exigencies and local conditions against universal institutions, especially when dealing with public-order issues.

While the VDS were created to train villagers to defend themselves against dacoits, the police administration of UP was further interested in developing other organisations to help with local policing in case of urgent emergencies. In the earlier section, we noticed that while issuing a gun to every village was being considered, the inspector general of police, B.N. Lahiri, also suggested the formation of the VDS. The stated aim of these VDS was to instil confidence in villagers in case of an attack by dacoits. The primary purpose of the earlier Hind Rakshak Dal was to protect village communities from possible invasion attacks during the Second World War and to guard the Hindu community in UP in case of any violence by supporters of the Muslim League. The now official PRD would have policing duties sanctioned by the district authorities. The preamble of the U.P. Rakshak Dal Act, 1948, stated that the purpose of the constitution of this force was

> the preservation of public peace, training of men in the use of arms, to inculcate self-help and discipline and the protection of the life of the community and property within the United Provinces.[59]

The British depended on broadly two models of policing, that is, the civilian model originating in the Metropolitan Police of London and the imperial model inspired by the Royal Irish Constabulary.[60] This chapter contends that after independence, the provincial government in UP continued with an existing model that incorporated civilians into policing structures on an ad-hoc basis. The institution of *chowkidari* (village watchmen) and *mukhiyagiri* (village headmen) to be discussed in the following chapter bears testimony to it. The move was an attempt to add supplementary numbers to an already strained formal and regular institution of the police. It equipped the provincial government to maintain a facade of numbers and demonstrate state resources that did not exist in reality.

The UP Police faced numerous challenges immediately after independence. Communal frenzy, refugee mobility and dacoits all necessitated a larger police force.[61] The Rakshak Dal, which had its foundations in the Second World War, became an important inspiration in such circumstances. Therefore, the government of UP after 1947 not only accelerated its plans for the reorganisation of the police but also became active regarding the incorporation of the civilian population into what had conventionally been police concerns. It was an attempt to establish authority amongst postcolonial subjects through a framework of state–society cooperation for the development of the nation. It aimed to create a hegemonic dynamic of subservience towards the state from a diverse set of citizens who had not yet fully comprehended the developmental thrust and future objectives of the postcolonial state.

In addition to the various changes made to the structure and functioning of the police in UP, the PRD was officially created by the United Provinces Rakshak Dal Act, 1948. It received the assent of the governor of UP on 4 December 1948 and got published in the *U.P. Government Gazette* on 11 December 1948. The organisation was voluntary and set up across the entire province, but teams operated at the district level. The philosophy of rural development guided its scope.[62] The main idea behind the setting up of the PRD in April 1948 was to mobilise a voluntary force in the village that, in cooperation with police and other organisations, could bring about a sense of security and discipline among the villagers and channel their efforts into development schemes for the betterment of their living conditions. It also rendered social service to the local administration to maintain order during fairs and other public events.[63] However, enrolment in the organisation imposed various obligations on the member too. The Act stated that a volunteer had to 'declare and affirm' that they understood the 'responsibilities and duties' that the organisation's membership imposed upon them. They would sign a declaration committing to 'honestly and faithfully serve' for any period or place prescribed by the authorities and would always be ready to protect even at the cost of their life 'the honour, integrity, the constitution' and 'flag' of India.[64] The membership statement made amply clear that the scope of the Rakshak Dal was more than an ordinary civilian voluntary organisation. It imposed a military commitment on the persons taking up its membership. The urgency takes into account the potential of war-like situations. It was also when independent India and Pakistan were recently created, and a mass exodus of Muslims was taking place from India, including UP. The recent formation of Pakistan created an urgent emergency for the government of UP. Also, the government would now use the Rakshak Dal force to deal with policing mass gatherings, fairs, religious fairs and pilgrimages to important sites in UP and to serve as local committees to deal with dacoits and robbers. Above all, it provided the government with an ever-ready pool of state-enrolled vigilantes trained in weapon handling and combat and to be put to any use by the state. It was a calculated governmental move that productively incorporated civilians into policing activity at a mass level while being economically efficient by avoiding the need to employ a permanent police force. According to the Act, persons joining this force will be relieved by their employer when called to duty. The employers could not dismiss, remove, suspend or take any action against employees because they had joined the Rakshak Dal. However, the state government promised to pay the compensation and allowances of the job to the members for the period they would be assigned a duty. Members had to join their original place of employment as soon as the duty assigned by the Rakshak Dal was over.

Broadly, four conditions would make a person ineligible for membership of the Rakshak Dal. A person was ineligible if he had not attained 18 years or was over 45 years of age. A person who failed the medical test and was considered unfit to perform the duties required, or was convicted of an offence involving 'moral ineptitude' was ineligible for membership. Ineligibility clauses also included persons under police surveillance or restraint under any provision of law for the time being.

As opposed to a centralised approach, the Rakshak Dal followed a devolution approach. Given that various places in each district might have different policing requirements at various moments, the Rakshak Dal added to the multitude of policing strategies available to the provincial government. Scholars have lucidly argued that a better way of applying a typology of police structures would be to broaden it beyond 'the institutional confines of accountability, organisation and finance to incorporate legal, cultural, functional and intellectual structures and influences'.[65] In this light, it is important to identify patterns of modification between the late colonial and the postcolonial police structures and the reasons for such modifications. The structure of the Rakshak Dal was very similar to that of a police force. It aimed to foster a new state–citizen relationship at the local level. The Rakshak Dal was largely conveyed as community service and a contribution to the nation's development, and hence *rakshaks* (protectors or defenders) were meant to be doing service in a social spirit rather than law enforcement. However, these *rakshaks* were assigned to enforce state-imposed tasks and reported to their commandants, who were actual police officers.

A form of mutual commitment on the part of the state and the *rakshaks* was considered an obvious expectation here. The headquarters of the UP Rakshak Dal was situated in Lucknow, with five regional headquarters. In each district, the organisation consisted of one or more battalions, and each battalion could not exceed four companies based on one company per *tehsil*. If a district had more than four *tehsils*, the number of companies for such districts could be raised. Also, four platoons comprised each company.

The chain of command was very similar to that of a police force, but at a higher level, it had commandants, thus making it more military in nature. The degree of discipline expected from a *rakshak*, at least on paper, was no less than was expected from a soldier. At the head of the PRD organisation was the administrative commandant, usually an officer of the Indian Police Service (IPS). Three assistant commandants assisted him, one each for training, physical culture and youth welfare.[66] Though here we are concerned with the PRD immediately after independence, it is worth mentioning that an important development in the history of the PRD was the creation of a police wing in the districts of Lucknow, Agra and Varanasi later in September 1957. The necessity for such a police wing resulted from the enormous increase in police work, given that both the central and the UP governments had passed several legislative enactments against social disorders. It was, therefore, decided to call upon certain PRD personnel under the UP Rakshak Dal Act, 1948, and post them under the administrative control of the senior superintendent of police (SSP) of the districts mentioned earlier. They were further utilised to maintain order at fairs and social functions, assist in traffic control and conduct night vigils, among other tasks. The structure of the Rakshak Dal maintained a facade of an autonomous organisation where the state was willing to partially concede a part of its power to maintain public order. Such organisations cannot be understood merely in technical terms – there is a political nature to such policies aimed at crime prevention and maintenance of public order.

Referring to Max Weber's famous maxim concerning the state having a monopoly over the legitimate use of physical violence, Beatrice Jauregui has noted that it is crucial to distinguish between the legal and the legitimate. For Jauregui, 'Legality relates to rational procedural law or legal formalism; legitimacy refers to the likelihood that people will obey a command because they believe that it emerges from a source of moral power and right.'[67] Organisations such as the VDS and the PRD underline the careful co-option of society into the structures of the state not very long after independence. While armed VDS were created to defend villages against dacoits, the PRD was created to help police in its operations and train the VDS. The most significant element of such organisations was their ability to instil a sense of security and responsibility in the minds of citizens when it came to maintaining law and order. It surreptitiously aimed to legitimise a certain acceptance of participation in violence and surveillance on behalf of the state by creating quasi-policing and state-sponsored vigilante organisations. The Raskhak Dal in UP filled a gap left by a limited and strained state bureaucracy. The work of the *rakshak*s depended on the state summoning them for various community assignments and only expanded the police state. It served as an economical way of preserving state authority. The Rakshak Dal served the regulatory needs of a modern postcolonial nation – an attempt to extend the presence of the state as one capable of maintaining security and order in the hinterlands and during moments of public gatherings, such as regulating people and traffic at fairs and gatherings.

The provincial government in UP did not stop with issuing guns and creating a quasi-police organisation like the Rakshak Dal; it aimed to secure extraordinary powers that could bypass ordinary procedures while dealing with criminals. To further fortify its authority, the UP government had dealt its trump card by the end of 1948 in the form of the UP Prevention of Crime (Special Powers) Act, 1948.

Fighting 'Bad Characters' and 'Social Pests': The UP Prevention of Crime (Special Powers) Act, 1948

Building upon the momentum of its strategies of social control, the Congress government in UP was keen on dealing with all kinds of public disorder swiftly. It contemplated introducing a new extraordinary law called 'The UP Prevention of Crime (Special Powers) (Temporary) Bill, 1948'. Its main premise was that it would not automatically apply to the whole of the province but only to the designated area(s) and for a specific period as notified by the government in the gazette. It was directed against a specific list of potential offenders. Therefore, the government deemed it useful that all the district magistrates would prepare lists of the persons who could be potentially prosecuted under this law. The government emphasised that the lists of such persons 'should be checked and rechecked' and every effort made to eliminate undue hardship or harassment to any person. Also, 'complete secrecy' was to be maintained in the preparation and maintenance of such lists.[68] Secrecy appears to be a constituent of the state–citizen relationship, as a means and sign of power that both sides derive from this relationship. State secrecy is considered rational owing to the 'reasons of the state' that range from symbolic to material to relational objectives; secrecy amongst citizens becomes the subject of suspicion and is considered questionable. The state considers it a given affirmation that the citizen would behave consciously and reflectively when it comes to law. The intention of the law, however, is seldom questioned.

Michel Foucault's genealogy of the modern state, where he traces two ideal and different power arrangements, namely 'sovereign power' and 'governmentality', could help us understand the legislative urge of the modern (postcolonial) state.[69] Since sovereign power and governmentality aim for different ends, their constantly changing permeation at the level of the state is always imbalanced. The operation of governmentality according to the law must be backed by juridical frameworks devised by the sovereign power itself; however, juridical frameworks often prove inadequate to contain the diverse operations and implementations of governmentality. As a result, as Foucault has rightly identified, governmentality as power is intertwined with the state in such a way that it cannot be juridically contained by it. The state cannot appropriately regulate 'governmentality as a form of power' through its legal regulations. Hence, governmentality constitutes an excess vis-à-vis the legal regulations.[70] Despite the availability of various punitive sections in criminal law (section 110 CrPC) quite capable of dealing with various criminals, the UP government could not resist the seduction of the excess of law. The colonial Goonda Act that the new legislation replaced was already considered too notorious because it provided sweeping powers to the police.[71]

Based on a police report or otherwise, a magistrate could act against persons if he was satisfied that the necessary preconditions under this Act were met. The main reason for such a magisterial action would have to justify that the person was by repute a bad character. This legislation described a 'bad character' as a person who habitually committed or attempted to commit or abetted the commission of offences involving a breach of peace. Furthermore, according to this law, a bad character was a person who was so dangerous that his being at large outside the knowledge of security organisations (police) was hazardous to the community.[72] Four kinds of activities would testify to the bad character of a person according to this law. First, if a person was a habitual offender; second, if the person habitually manufactured, imported or sold any intoxicant in contravention of the United Provinces Excise Act, 1910; third, if a person was a keeper of a 'gambling den'; and fourth, if a person had committed or was about to commit a non-bailable offence contained in Chapter XVI or XVII of the Indian Penal Code.[73] Vague suspicions became the basis for discretionary punitive administrative action.

As per the proposed new law, once a notice was issued to a 'bad character' by the magistrate, he had to appear before the magistrate in person and submit a personal bond of two sureties not exceeding 1,000 rupees each. This law made punitive action possible even before proving the accusations. This bond was a security deposit 'for the good behaviour' or keeping 'the peace' or both until the case was disposed of in accordance with the law. A person failing to appear before the court and refusing to submit the bond would entail arrest until the security bond was deposited. Such a security bond served as a licence for such 'criminals' to exist in society as against being detained in prison. It was an efficient arrangement since prison remains an expensive arrangement for the state and might not be as effective. Security bonds served as an administrative warning to such designated 'criminals' and gave them an official opportunity to own their freedom.

Generally, filing a case against a person, producing witnesses and gathering evidence was the supposed duty of the administration. This law also allowed the accused or blamed to explain and produce evidence supporting his representation. Without trial, a person was declared guilty unless proven innocent, in a way very similar to the terrorism trials of contemporary times. This opportunity could also be curtailed or denied if the judge considered any evidence unnecessary for disposing of the case.

Based on the judicial discretion of another order, it could allow arbitrary decisions of judges and could obstruct the process of presenting evidence. However, the judge could also disallow any evidence that in his opinion was unnecessary for disposing of the case. If jurors adjudicating such a case were unanimous in their opinion, but the judge disagreed with their opinion, after recording his own opinion and the reasons for the disagreement, the judge would have to submit the entire record of the case to the chief justice of the High Court of Judicature at Allahabad and send information thereof to the concerned magistrate. On the other hand, if the jurors were divided in their opinion, the judge could pass such order as might appear to him to be just and proper. This legislation repealed 'The United Provinces Goondas Act 1932', a colonial law notorious for its operation outside standard legal procedures. Georg Rusche and Otto Kirchheimer have famously argued that '[p]unishment as such does not exist; only concrete systems of punishment and specific criminal practices exist' and emphasised that punishment in its specific manifestations must be investigated.[74] The manifestation of the modified Goonda Act becomes apparent in the 'Statement of Objects and Reasons' signed by the then minister for police for UP, Lal Bahadur Shastri. It read:

> The United Provinces Goonda Act (No. I of 1932) was enacted to deal with the problem of habitual bad characters. But in the light of the changed conditions, it is considered antiquated. It is proposed to repeal that Act and replace it by a more suitable enactment. The object of the present Bill is to enact a short and speedy procedure to be applicable in dealing with habitual bad characters and social pests whose criminal and anti-social activities may require speedy preventive action. This new enactment will be in force for a limited period of twelve months unless the Legislature extends it further. It will be applicable only to specified areas which may be notified from time to time by the Provincial Government.[75]

Under the new law, the precise and well-defined colonial problem category of a 'goonda' now extended to potentially the whole population, although supposedly aimed at the prevention of crime broadly and particularly aimed at 'bad characters' and 'social pests'.

The stated motives behind the new law were efforts towards crime prevention. Crime prevention has been a key subject of study in the field of criminology. Scholarship in criminology suggests that a great deal of attention is given by the state to what is known as crime prevention.

Though the term 'crime prevention' has only begun to be used recently, historical analysis suggests that the phenomenon has historical roots and has been discussed as a concern since at least the eighteenth century. Charles Reith, for example, has pointed out that the principal object of the police since their establishment as a permanent force in England in 1829 has been the prevention of crime.[76] The contemporary use of the term 'crime prevention' is sometimes used complementarily and at other times in opposition to traditional institutional responses such as the police, prisons and probations.

'Crime' itself is not a precise term; it remains too vague and broad to fit into a straightforward definition. It involves not only the practices of the entire criminal justice system but also social and public policies and private citizens and private enterprises as well. The term 'prevention' would entail that anything that has to be prevented needs prediction first; only then could an intervention be possible. However, prediction itself is not an easy and straightforward task. Among other questions, one significant question that cannot be ignored is: Who is predicting what? Furthermore, what needs to be considered is whether the prediction is at the level of an individual or a population. The task of prediction cannot be anything but a multidisciplinary project. A broader survey of the scholarship in criminology has pointed out that there are three main constitutive elements of crime prevention, that is, prediction, intervention and implementation. The very human process of implementing is where the politics of policymaking emerges.[77] It tells us that crime prevention relies on ideology as much as on statistics and science.

There is always a demand for crime prevention no matter how effective the ongoing practices or legislations are. Scholars in criminology have attributed this demand to what they refer to as 'preventionism'.[78] Preventionism consists of the belief that social problems can be prevented rather than solved.[79] Hence, it emerges within the political arena. It lends itself to interventionist expansionism, increasing the encroachment of public agencies into areas of life that would otherwise be considered private. The political utility of preventionism cannot be ignored and has two main beneficiaries: those who have the knowledge and expertise to intervene to prevent, and the executive arm of the state, which uses the prevention of social problems as a source of its legitimacy. Freeman has rightly noted that preventionism is essentially a strategy of governance.[80] While tracing the genealogy of what he called governmentality, Foucault traced a paradigmatic shift from a Machiavellian understanding that aimed to preserve sovereignty to a modern utilitarian maxim which aimed at the well-being of the entire nation.[81] The significance of granting special powers to the local law-and-order administration in UP rests on such a utilitarian maxim. It conveniently ignored the existing laws that could deal with the challenges and felt completely justified in granting more extraordinary powers to the local administration. The sacrifice of due process and the inconvenience to the few rested on the premise that it was done for the security of the general population.

A letter by the order of the home secretary of UP was sent to all the district magistrates of the province. It categorically stated that 'before taking any further action under this Act, Govt. wish to make it clear that in dealing with crime they would like that action should, as far as possible, be taken under ordinary law'.[82] Action under the new law should only be recommended to the government 'if the law is not found to prove effective in dealing with notorious criminals'.[83] In this light, the UP government asked for revised lists of persons to be booked under the new law. These lists had to specify, first, the 'reasons why the ordinary law does not prove effective and why the use of this Act has become necessary'; second, 'brief comments on the general crime situation in the District and the nature of the problems faced'. The lists had to mention the total number of persons against whom the action under the new law was proposed, divided into the categories for the offences for which they were to be booked.[84]

The inspector general of police of UP, B.N. Lahiri, was rather keen for this legislation to swing into action. He did not want to wait until the government made a formal notification enforcing the provisions of this law. He wrote to the home secretary of the UP government, Govind Narain:

> My view is that as lawlessness is on the increase all over the province, there is need to make the Act applicable to the entire province. Will you please let me know if any action is being taken in this connection?[85]

Meanwhile, newspapers were already publishing news regarding the new Act. The media did not criticise the government regarding the new legislation in any way and actively reported on the administrative progress made in the matter. The media reiterated the provincial government's position that only 'habitual offenders' need to fear the new law. For instance, the *National Herald* reported that 'while disclosing to press correspondents', Lal Bahadur Shastri, the police minister of UP, affirmed 'that Government were taking every precaution to guard against any possible misuse of the act'.[86] The *National Herald*, Lucknow, further reported that '[r]eports received from nearly 36 district magistrates at the provincial headquarters' indicated 'a general desire for a speedy enforcement of the act in their areas'.[87] The life of this Act was reported to be for two years and was to be enforced in the major cities of the province, among other towns and districts. The press did not question the necessity that required such extraordinary legislation to deal with ordinary crimes.

Soon, most of the district magistrates provided statistics to the provincial government regarding the scope of the new law in their districts, along with their opinion on the scope of this law. In their response letter to the UP government, most of the district magistrates vociferously justified the urgent necessity of such a strict and extraordinary law to be extended to their respective districts. Only a few remained hesitant. However, they too in a couple of months would begin to see the administrative benefits of extraordinary legislation and would request the government to extend the new law to their districts as well. The following figures provide an estimate of the scale at which the new law was planned to be used in some of the districts. The number of persons proposed to be booked under the new law was 52 in Bara Banki, 217 in Aligarh, 80 in Mathura, 10 in Etah, 348 in Bijnor, 237 in Unnao, 12 in Nainital, 10 in Pilibhit, none in Garhwal and Jaunpur, 123 in Ballia, 49 in Sultanpur, 10 in Fatehpur, 43 in Gonda, 36 in Meerut, 73 in Deoria, 79 in Shahjahanpur and 358 in Kanpur. The following sections will look at perspectives that resulted in the generation of these numbers by the respective district administration.

Scholarship in the revisionist history of criminology has revealed two major traditions: the governmental project and the science of causes project.[88] The governmental project referred to the series of empirical enquiries since the eighteenth century to enhance the efficient and equitable administration of justice. Such a project charted two sets of inquiries. One, the patterns of crime and, two, monitoring the practice of police and prisons. David Garland has argued that western governments have increasingly used fact-gathering techniques like censuses and other social statistics to describe 'essential features' of a range of 'problem categories'. When combined with scientific and statistical surveillance, statistics established a system of expert administration to regulate human behaviour. Data collection began to be designed in such a way as to guide governments and the police in deploying police resources, working with certain typologies and identifying potential criminals and areas in cities with higher crime rates, and so on. No matter what, the availability of numbers did not justify special powers in UP, especially in a country that had recently achieved its independence from a brutal and expropriating colonial relationship.

For example, the district magistrate of Bara Banki, M.G. Kaul, responded[89] by stating that it was 'very necessary' for the Act to be made applicable to Bara Banki district. According to him, Bara Banki was an 'extremely dangerous district', and crimes like dacoity and murder were widespread. The onus here is on the geography and its inhabitants without explaining as to what happened to the recently implemented policies like the issuing of guns, the constitution of the VDS and having the Rakshak Dal at the disposal of the local police. Admitting the 'considerable lawlessness' in most of Bara Banki district, the district magistrate lamented that the 'hardened criminals and bullies' were in the habit of terrorising people. Therefore, 'ordinary law' did not 'prove effective in dealing with these desperate criminals'. He failed to mention any possible failures of the criminal justice system anywhere in his lament. The main reason he provided was that it was very difficult for the police to get local people to come to the courts to give evidence against such criminals. The reason for this was partly the fear of reprisals and partly because he believed witnesses in Bara Banki district were 'extremely unreliable and easily bought over'. The magistrate did not hold the local population in very high regard. For him, the witnesses often turned hostile in court and went contrary to the statement made before investigating officers. Recent scholarship has amply pointed out the complicated relations between the police and the general population in the colonial period, where it was the use of bribes, threats and sometimes torture that brought witnesses to the courts in the first place rather than the spirit of cooperation with the police.[90]

For M.G. Kaul, socialists were another element that had been 'infusing spirit of lawlessness among the general masses'. This only points out that the socialists remained a challenge to the Congress provincial governments even after independence. They surely disagreed with the Nehruvian paradigm of governance and development. The district magistrate of Bara Banki highlighted that it was common knowledge that zamindars and taluqdars, who were locally influential, kept bad characters as servants to maintain their hold and influence over their tenants. Hence, such bad characters got protection from zamindars and taluqdars, and the police found it 'very difficult to get at them through the normal process of law'. The magistrate was concerned that 'notorious badmashes' had become bolder because 'changed conditions' had 'decreased the fear which was once inspired by the police'. The most critical point that Magistrate Kaul's report brings to our attention is that evidence collection was a cumbersome process, and prosecution of these 'badmashes' needed proof according to the ordinary law. There is active advocacy for scuttling the due process already established and available in law. The magistrates had conveniently forgotten their law lessons from the university, where the basic maxim of 'law must serve the last man' was argued to be the central purpose of the justice system. According to the district magistrate of Bara Banki, in addition to the lack of public cooperation in such cases, the standards of investigation had deteriorated mainly because experienced officers had either been promoted or retired. The lack of experienced police officers added to the woes of the administration. Therefore, M.G. Kaul recommended that it was 'absolutely essential' to extend this Act to Bara Banki district.

Others had had enough of the independence and transfer of power. The SP in Bahraich, for example, felt that 'with the advent of freedom the public at large had developed peculiar psychology confusing liberty with license'.[91] He believed that a public that did not 'consider police as their friends' would not render necessary cooperation. Therefore, the new Act would ensure that the 'bad characters' were nabbed despite the lack of public cooperation and cumbersome rules of evidence gathering. Rather than gaining the public's confidence, the SP suggested the tried and tested colonial approach of threats and fear tactics. A colonial approach to maintaining law and order through pre-emptive emergency legislation was by no means dead – neither institutionally nor in terms of administrative doctrine. The a priori profiling of 'bad characters' in UP reminds us directly of the anti-Thuggee campaign in early nineteenth-century colonial India. Orders were issued that, as per Rule 31 (b) of the UP Prevention of Crime Act, 1948, '[t]he Magistrate shall have fingerprints of the person proceeded against taken by a Police proficient and shall further have his photograph taken under the supervision of a responsible police officer'.[92] Colonial biopolitics began to be normalised in the postcolonial state. The creation of new classificatory information, including signatures, thumb impressions and photographs, would create a file on the 'criminal' to be kept at the administration's disposal.

If laws to deal with Thugs in early colonial India underlined the despotism of (colonial) law, the repackaging of colonial laws to fight crime in UP (and elsewhere) highlighted the despotism of the postcolonial state.[93] The district magistrate of Aligarh further emphasised the difficulty of operating within the ordinary laws. He lamented how the earlier provision of section 110 CrPC was insufficient to book 'habitual offenders' and was 'very lengthy, cumbersome and under the existing conditions very difficult for successful prosecution'.[94] The district magistrate of Mathura also argued that the 'capability and efficiency' of ordinary laws was insufficient and admitted that the influence of the police had declined and burglaries, robberies and dacoities in the district had increased. The district magistrate of Aligarh presented administrative failure in the form of a legal challenge. Notably, the district magistrate of Mathura blamed the situation on the administrative and political challenges that had emerged due to independence and opined that the open support to the police during the colonial regime strengthened it but alienated the public. Such an alienation between the police and the public, according to the district magistrate of Mathura, persisted. Such comments from administrators warrant the urgency of studies in contemporary history that must investigate the extent and ways in which decolonisation of the criminal justice system has taken place in a postcolonial state like India. The public's unwillingness to share the administration's opinion and to refuse participation in government policies highlight at least one great hindrance faced by the provincial government in the maintenance of public order in UP. The post-independence provincial government failed to create a consensus about the future. The political vocabulary that could have worked in the colonial set-up was undeniably unacceptable to the public in the new context. It did not inspire trust and confidence. The gravity of public defiance becomes clearer when the district magistrate of Etah expressed that 'once a criminal is let off, he feels emboldened to carry on his nefarious activities'.[95] He admitted that 'the public does not extend cooperation in the detection and investigation of crimes in sufficient measure'.[96] He added that 'the police does not inspire fear. Ignorant and illiterate people have got erroneous and perverted conceptions of freedom. They have no respect for authority'.[97]

The district magistrate also admitted the existence of dacoits like Girand Singh, Birey and Bashira in Etah district. The main problem for the district administration of Etah was that some criminals committed crimes 'in the expectation that their crimes would be attributed to the gangs of Birey and Bashira'.[98] The district magistrate of Bijnor also acknowledged that 'many of the real dacoits' escaped punishment as the 'public activity helped them and spoilt prosecution evidence'.[99] The popular support for bandits points out that the authority of bandits trumped the authority of the police. The abhorrence of public behaviour by the district magistrate of Etah and the district magistrate of Bijnor noted earlier highlights the confusion in governance that emerged in the aftermath of independence.

On the one hand, the governing – both elected and administrative – did not feel that the population was now worthy of becoming individual citizens and believed they had misplaced conceptions of freedom. On the other hand, the governed – the population – did not completely perceive the government as its own and maintained a distance from its apparatuses. Therefore, it can be deduced that the potential of the new extraordinary law could enable the administration to create a perceived threat for the larger disobeying public through the problem category of a 'habitual offender'. The 'habitual offender' was proposed to be outside of the civilized citizenry, who was clearly defined as not the enemy of the state but society too. Therefore, the new extraordinary law aimed to provide special powers to the state's law-and-order machinery by short-circuiting the existing process of the rule of law. It also created a threat perception amongst the general masses to deter it from supporting such offenders. There is a contestation between two divergent visions of a 'new' public order. The provincial administration appears to be more inclined towards repression rather than making any attempts to ideologically cultivate acceptance amongst the citizens.

In many other districts too, for example, the district magistrates of Lucknow, Ballia, Gonda, Meerut, Deoria, Shahjahanpur, Nainital, Unnao, Pilibhit, and so on, either lamented the inefficiency of the ordinary law, the reluctance of the witnesses to come forward or expressed helplessness due to the rise of crimes like dacoities, robberies and bullying in their respective districts. The majority of the district magistrates requested the extension of the new extraordinary law to their districts too. This craving for an increased dose of the force of law highlights that the local administration, especially the police and the district magistrate, wanted an absolutist authority as against a 'provisional authority'.[100]

In certain districts, the district magistrates reported that crime existed in conjunction with local politics. For example, the district magistrate of

Sultanpur, in a letter, reported that during the nascent and transitional stage of India's independence, leaders of various groups 'try to influence the illiterate people with confusing ideologies and promises, the administration is being denied the requisite cooperation of the public, without whose support and evidence cases cannot be successful'.[101] This is evidence of the onset of criminalisation of politics in postcolonial UP. The Sultanpur district magistrate's observation suggests that only the Congress's politics was to be considered legitimate; all others were either deviants or a threat to public order. Also, in the city of Sultanpur, there was a curious circumstance of two factions of Congress leaders who not only opposed each other in every matter but also made complaints against each other as well as each other's supporters. This led to the formation of two different *seva dals*, each comprising several 'very undesirable persons' as members.[102] The district magistrate's observations became self-contradictory because even the Congress was not out of the purview of being a disturbance to peace. Its members were responsible for discord at the local level.

The district magistrate of Sultanpur also reported two cases that had to be discharged under the ordinary law because socialists and certain members of the PRD sometimes combined to defend the accused. As a result, 'bad characters enrolled in rival Seva Dals' and 'fanned the spirit of defiance'.[103] Such a situation put the district administration of Sultanpur in a difficult position. In Sultanpur district in 1948, about two-thirds of the total 362 cases sent to court under the ordinary law had failed. Such instances highlight that despite the provincial government's drive to create problem categories of habitual offenders as outside the standard understanding of citizenship, local members of the Congress party often complicated it. It also shows executive frustration at the underbelly of postcolonial Congress politics at local levels, where the stakes had shifted from anti-colonial mobilisation to a new phase of power grabbing. Therefore, the district magistrate in a way implored the state government to extend the new Act to Sultanpur, where the new extraordinary Act would resolve not only the issue of the decline in administrative and public confidence in the ordinary process of law but also ensure swift action against the activities of other non-Congress organisations like the communists, Forward Blockists and various communal organisations.[104] The district magistrate of Sultanpur was luring the Congress government with a positive outcome in its favour. In the report, there exists a hidden promise to achieve the suppression of the opposition, which could not be controlled by ordinary politics.

The DM of Sultanpur very categorically stated that the new law would enable the district administration to get rid of such 'dangers'.[105]

Such 'dangers' in Fatehpur district were reported to have an 'immense terrifying influence over the general public'. The SP of Fatehpur attributed 'expert knowledge' and capability of engineering schemes to such dangers, which he referred to as 'the GURU'.[106] These gurus were stated to be the root of the crime and were believed to be the actual masterminds of crimes. A holistic view of this entire discussion points out that the real masterminds were the administrators in UP. The ordinary law, therefore, was stated to be unhelpful by the SP of Fatehpur in the face of a non-cooperative attitude of the public and growing party factions in villages that supported the activities of the criminals by harbouring them against the opposing party. The administration also did not anticipate the realities of a democratic polity in a decolonised context and did not know what freedom entailed. The collector of Kanpur echoed similar observations when he wrote that 'the criminal' worked 'under the cloak of a political label' to 'gain the backing of a political party making his arrest difficult'.[107] While criminals were said to work in the garb of politicians, it was authoritarianism that worked in the garb of civil servants. The deployment of the term 'dangers' to refer to these 'offenders' or problem categories created a sense of urgency and an increased threat perception of the state towards its enemies. As discussed in the earlier sections, the gap between the governing and the governed was so obdurate that neither fully trusted the other. The UP Prevention of Crime (Special Powers) (Temporary) Bill, 1948, proved to be the wish of the district administrations in UP that was granted under the guise of ridding society of its dangerous elements by declaring them and their supporters among the public as 'enemies' and excluding them from the ordinary process of the rule of law.

When the law started becoming operational, there emerged a difference of opinion between the police and the judiciary on the matter of law and punishment. Where the person responsible for invoking action against 'bad characters' was a district magistrate, a judge was to give a verdict on it. Some of the official communication highlights that judges gave simple imprisonment (SI) rather than rigorous imprisonment (RI) to persons booked under this Act. The magistrates (for example, the district magistrate of Ballia, H.A. Siddiqi) were not happy about this.[108] According to some magistrates, the general practice under ordinary law (section 109 and 110 CrPC, both used to book habitual offenders) was that a person was awarded RI. They appealed to the government, expressing their discontent. The judges were of a different view and had reasonable counterarguments. They opined that if a person was booked under the new Act, he was arrested not as a normal accused but under preventive measures. Therefore, SI did the job by putting the criminal away. Since the proposed person was arrested more on recommendation than trial, RI was not necessary or feasible. A judicial paradox is exposed here. In this case, judges tried to argue in favour of due process and reasonable punishment while implementing a law that had nothing to do with due process in the first place. The Home Department of UP replied that if a judge 'directs simple imprisonment for failure to keep the peace, he is perfectly justified'.[109] Also, if a judge 'directs simple imprisonment even in cases of failure to give security for good behaviour, his order cannot be characterised as illegal'. Even the new Act under section 12(2) said that the judge's order was final and conclusive and could not be called into question in any civil or criminal proceedings. This meant that neither a revision nor an appeal could be filed against any such judicial order. Section 18(2) of the new Act also stated that the proceedings in such cases before the judge were judicial proceedings. Therefore, neither the government nor the district magistrate could issue any instruction to the judge, and if they attempted to do so, they would be guilty of contempt of court.

Initially, only a few district magistrates expressed confidence that ordinary law was sufficient to deal with the crime situation in their respective districts. For instance, the district magistrates of Dehradun,[110] Garhwal[111] and Jaunpur declined to implement the provisions of the new extraordinary law to their districts. However, later, some of the district magistrates, for example, in Jaunpur,[112] realised that the extraordinary legislation had the capability of launching swift action against criminals with minimum administrative responsibility and maximum administrative control and requested the state government to extend the extraordinary legislation to their districts too. In total, by the end of the year 1949, a total of 44 out of 49 districts had recommended and received the extension of the new Act. The majority of the response letters from the DMs of the various districts of UP point to a remarkable seduction of the extraordinary legislation. It highlights a peculiar tendency of the provincial administration in India, and particularly in UP, to resort to absolutist legislation like the one discussed in this section. Even though ordinary laws in the CrPC, such as section 110 CrPC, were available to the administration to deal with local criminals, following standard procedures of the rule of law, such as collecting evidence, having witnesses and subsequent arrests and trials, were repeatedly described by the district magistrates as inefficient and cumbersome. Therefore, almost all of them argued for the extension of the new Act to their districts with the promise of taking swift action against the 'criminals' and their 'well-wishers'. It cannot be ignored that some of the district magistrates reported Congress factionalism at the local level and related it to criminals. However, it appears that the UP Congress-led government wished to aim the new law towards its opposition, such as the communists, Forward Blockists and communal and sectarian organisations. The new law helped the government in smashing unruly and disobeying populations as well as non-Congress mobilisations.

Conclusion

The tactic of issuing guns to 'reliable' citizens offers insights into the strategies of the state in UP. Subcontracting the state's monopoly over the use of violence offered a peculiar intimacy with state power; this meant that it allowed for an intimacy with the sovereign. It permitted participation in conducting or facilitating de facto sovereignty. The state apparatus prioritised and promoted a specific discourse that began by offering a binary of the 'law-abiding citizen' and the 'deviant' or the saboteur. It emphasised that the upholding of sovereign authority was the singular legitimate expression of citizenship. All other expressions of citizenship seemed to be secondary. In this spirit, the state deployed the 'vigilant citizen', who was characterised as either willing to or had actively consented to upholding the monopoly of the state over the use of physical violence. Anything outside state structure or state-licensed institutions was considered illegitimate and hence the primary foe of state sovereignty. In the case of UP, two sets of vigilantes emerged: first, the bandits who, as the official communication highlights, enjoyed the favour of the villagers and created anxiety for the administration, and, second, the 'reliable villagers', who were supposed to extend the reach and presence of law against the bandits. In this light, one set of vigilantes, the bandits, took law into their own hands for various reasons, and the other set was granted power and the backing of the law-and-order administration in their hands.

Both existed outside the formal framework of the state. The incapability of the postcolonial state in UP to maintain everyday law and order, and its failure to defend the law, liberty and property of its citizens, exposed the vulnerability of sovereignty itself. In this light, the reliable villager emerged as the approver of the state's legitimacy and monopoly over the use of physical force. It also aimed to rationalise the perspective of the state. Participation in a state-sponsored experience of citizenship granted a licence to the chosen few to control, regulate and even kill. It aimed to transact the participation of villagers to arm themselves against dacoits as testimony to the legitimacy of state authority.

This chapter has shown that even after independence, the UP government remained keen on utilising extraordinary laws to deal with everyday law and order. This chapter has shown that everyday law-and-order problems in UP were often termed as 'public order' issues in the early years after independence. Unclear about the objectives of independence, the UP Congress government utilised the opportunity to invoke public-order laws freely. Specific extraordinary laws, all dealing with public order and peace, were legislated through the creation of a wider narrative of chaos. This narrative of chaos is reflected in the administrative communication expressing suspicion and unreliability of villagers. There was often a contradiction in the broader moral politics of non-violence that the Congress preached and the seduction of extraordinary measures not very different from the attitude and rationality of the colonial predecessor. It was not only the masses who did not know what independence would entail, but the administration too did not know what to expect of it even though many would frequently refer to 'changed times' or 'independent India'. Also, the police and the judiciary did not always agree with the functioning of such laws. There was a difference of opinion between the executive and the judiciary.

The extraordinary laws displayed a general disregard towards normal procedures to deal with crime, bypassing the foundations of modern law, that is, the production of evidence and witnesses, the particularity of a crime, conducting a trial, preparing accusations and, finally, imprisonment or fine. Preventive laws like the ones discussed in this chapter had a warlike element to them. Such measures played an important role in establishing a violent postcolonial state that otherwise would claim to be democratic in character. When the legislative moments of extraordinary laws are analysed, we begin to see the absolutist potentials of a postcolonial state like India. When discussing Clausewitz in the early chapters of *Society Must Be Defended*, Michel Foucault argued that Clausewitz's maxim 'war is politics by other means' is an inverted one and should be 'politics is war by other means'.[113] In the name of 'emergency' and 'public order', the UP government did follow the latter maxim to some extent. Everything that was perceived as a challenge to the disciplinary thrust of the postcolonial state, be it bad characters, dacoits or the littering masses, was treated as enemies of the state and society. Increasingly, such policies blurred the boundary between the state and society, and the state became dominant in multiple zones of social life. Such moments erased the differentiation of state sovereignty and popular sovereignty in some ways because the popular was burdened with the moral responsibility to assist the state in purging undesired elements, or – as referred to in the 'objects and statements' of the Prevention of Crime law by Lal Bahadur Shastri – 'social pests'. The provincial Congress government treated any outside opposition as an enemy now that the country was independent, and development was thought of as a collective effort of the state and society. Most importantly, the Congress also aimed to activate such laws as discussed in the earlier sections to deal with other political organisations like the communists or socialists in UP. The socialist framework that the Congress sustained with great difficulty during the anti-colonial movement was now too ordinary, and any demand in that spirit from outside the Congress was seen as unworthy of positive attention and considered unnecessary.

The Congress government in UP first created a moral necessity to legislate extraordinary laws, apparently to move towards nation-building. Such laws always stressed an inevitability, very similar to the colonial tactic, that is, the inevitability to justify the existence of a criminal and dangerous other. Bandits, uncivilised masses and bad characters and habitual offenders provided an excellent ground for such laws. However, the functioning of extraordinary laws was not always smooth. The Congress's involvement with criminals or criminals involved in Congress politics would often derail the force or spirit of such laws and create administrative dilemmas.

Above all, this chapter has also presented the broader attitude of the UP administration towards its citizens. The bureaucracy did not see the larger population of UP as trustworthy as was the case in the initial stages of issuing guns. The earlier discussion revealed the invocation of colonial governmentality through extraordinary legislation in cases of public order in the aftermath of partition in UP. Most importantly, many other states in India followed UP's lead and enacted similar public-order laws, thus demonstrating that the conditions for the legislation of 'extraordinary laws' was always there; what mattered was the tactical invocation at the right moment. Also, the inclusion of these sweeping powers in the constitution of independent India was remarkable considering the bitter opposition the Congress posed to less similar provisions in the Government of India Act, 1935. Partition and the broader chaos of decolonisation provided a context to the Constituent Assembly and the leaders of the country to realise the necessity, rather, the inevitability, of such emergency powers in a country like India, which was often prone to fissiparous and centrifugal tendencies.

It is the inevitable aspiration of constitutional sovereignty that the idea of sweeping powers made its mark through the Constituent Assembly and its various committees and was finally incorporated into Part XVIII of the constitution as Emergency Provisions, including Articles 352 to 360, supplemented by Article 365. Such provisions had a serious effect on the fundamental nature of the constitution and the conception of the 'extraordinary', anything that had the potential to challenge the authority of the state. While the emergency measures in the constitution of India were the provisions for national emergencies such as war or external aggression or internal disturbance(s), which made the constitution for all practical purposes a unitary one during the pendency of such emergency, the public-order laws legislated by the states had an authoritative effect to create terror or fear in the mind of its people. Above all, while the emergency measures in the constitution aimed for an indestructible Union, the public-order and other extraordinary legislation in the states were aimed at demonstrating the state's ability to threaten and deter.

Despite administrative efforts to criminalise various activities in UP, the popular came to be understood as something that proved non-compliant with regulations and posed a direct challenge to the idea of an independent nation unified under law. Executive discretion and bureaucratic authoritarian attitudes divorced from an understanding of universal rights of citizens continued to constitute the letter and spirit of the law and led to an understanding that promoted state sovereignty as opposed to popular sovereignty.

Notes

1. Arudra Burra, 'The Indian Civil Service and the Nationalist Movement: Neutrality, Politics and Continuity', *Commonwealth and Comparative Politics* 48, no. 4 (2010): 404–432; Rohit De, 'Rebellion, Dacoity, and Equality: The Emergence of the Constitutional Field in Postcolonial India', *Comparative Studies of South Asia, Africa and the Middle East* 34, no. 2 (2014): 260–278.

2. See Thomas Blom Hansen and Finn Stepputat, eds., *States of Imagination: Ethnographic Explorations of the Postcolonial State* (Durham, NC; London: Duke University Press, 2001).

3. See Beatrice Jauregui, *Provisional Authority: Police, Order, and Security in India* (Chicago: The University of Chicago Press, 2016).

4. Markus Daechsel, 'Ẓālim Ḍākū and the Mystery of the Rubber Sea Monster: Urdu Detective Fiction in 1930s Punjab and the Experience of Colonial Modernity', *Journal of Royal Asiatic Society* 13, no. 1 (2002): 21–43; Sugata Nandi, 'Respectable Anxiety, Plebian Criminality: Politics of the Goondas Act (1923) of Colonial Calcutta', *Crime, Histories and Societies* 20, no. 2 (2016): 77–99.

5. For a discussion on the 'sign of the state', see Veena Das, *Life and Words: Violence and the Descent into the Ordinary* (Berkeley: University of California Press, 2007).

6. Jean Comaroff and John L. Comaroff, *Law and Disorder in the Postcolony* (Chicago: The University of Chicago Press, 2007), p. 27.

7. See Taylor C. Sherman, William Gould and Sarah Ansari, *From Subjects to Citizens: Society and Everyday State in India and Pakistan, 1947–1970* (Cambridge: Cambridge University Press, 2014).

8. Granville Austin, *Working a Democratic Constitution: A History of the Indian Experience* (New Delhi: Oxford University Press, 2003), specifically the chapter 'Making and Preserving a Nation'.

9. For a broader discussion around the impact of partition on the Indian subcontinent, see Ashis Nandy 'Coming Home: Religion, Mass Violence, and the Exiled and Secret Selves of a Citizen Killer', *Public Culture* 22, no. 1, Issue 60 (Winter 2010): 127–147; Yasmin Khan, *The Great Partition: The Making of India and Pakistan* (New Delhi: Penguin Books Limited, 2013), p. 250; Joya Chatterjee, *Bengal Divided: Hindu Communalism and Partition, 1932–47* (Cambridge: Cambridge University Press, 2002), p. 324. For a continuation of her discussion on partition, also see Joya Chatterjee, *The Spoils of Partition: Bengal and India, 1947–1967*, Cambridge Studies in Indian History and Society (New York: Cambridge University Press, 2007), p. 360; Urvashi Butalia, *The Other Side of Silence: Voices from the Partition of India* (Durham, NC: Duke University Press, 2000), p. 328; Gyanendra Pandey, *Remembering Partition: Violence, Nationalism and History in India*

(Cambridge; New York: Cambridge University Press, 2001), p. 236; William Gould, *Religion and Conflict in Modern South Asia* (New Delhi: Cambridge University Press, 2012), p. 175, specifically see Chapter 5, 'State Transformation, Democracy and Conflict', p. 193.

10. See National Archives of India, File No. 87/12/47–Public (A), The United Provinces Maintenance of Public Order (Second Amendment) Ordinance, 1947.

11. See National Archives if India, File No. 5/6/48–Judicial, The United Provinces Maintenance of Public Order (Amendment) Bill, 1947.

12. See National Archives of India, File No. 38/37/47–Public (A), The United Provinces Communal Disturbances Prevention Bill, 1947.

13. Section 188 of Indian Penal Code broadly deals with 'disobedience to an order duly promulgated by a public servant'.

14. See National Archives of India, File No. 38/37/47–Public (A), The United Provinces Communal Disturbances Prevention Bill, 1947.

15. Uttar Pradesh State Archives (UPSA), File 85/1948, see Police Reorganisation Committee Report 1948. See top secret D.O. No. 33/S, dated 18 January 1948, from Collector Bareilly, L.C. Jain, to Divisional Commissioner, Rohilkhand Division, N.B. Bonarjee, part of File No. 513 (10)/48, Home Department Police-B. See letter no.7591-Z/VIII dated 9 December 1948 from Under Secretary to UP Government, Govind Narayan, to all District Magistrates, United Provinces, UPSA, File No. 464/1948 Department (Police) B.

16. Eric Hobsbawm, *Bandits* (London: Weidenfield and Nicolson, 1969).

17. Ibid., p. 26.

18. See Eric Hobsbawm, *Primitive Rebels: Studies in Archaic Forms of Social Movement in the 19th and 20th Centuries* (Manchester: Manchester University Press, 1978); Hobsbawm, *Bandits*.

19. See Anton Blok, 'The Peasant and the Brigand: Social Banditry Reconsidered', *Comparative Studies in Society and History* 14, no. 4 (September 1972): 494–503; Pat O'Malley, 'Social Bandits, Modern Capitalism and the Traditional Peasantry: A Critique of Hobsbawm', *Journal of Peasant Studies* 6, no. 4 (July 1979): 489–499; Boon Kheng Cheah, *The Peasant Robbers of Kedah, 1900–1929: Historical and Folk Perceptions* (New York: Oxford University Press, 1988); Richard White, 'Outlaw Gangs of the Middle Border: American Social Bandits', *Western Historical Quarterly* 12, no. 4 (October 1981): 387–408; and Hobsbawm's responses in 'Social Banditry: Reply', *Comparatives Studies in Society and History* 14, no. 4 (September 1972): 503–505; and *Bandits*, pp. 11–15, 138–64; Donald Crummey, ed., *Banditry, Rebellion and Social Protest in Africa* (Portsmouth, NH: Heinemann, 1986); Stephen Wilson,

Feuding, Conflict, and Banditry in Nineteenth-Century Corsica (New York: Cambridge University Press, 1988); Phil Billingsley, *Bandits in Republican China* (Stanford, CA: Stanford University Press, 1988). Some other critics of the Hobsbawm approach include Ralph A. Austen, 'Social Bandits and Other Heroic Criminals: History, Myth, and Early Modernization in Africa and the West', paper presented to the Symposium on Rebellion and Social Protest in Africa, Urbana, IL, 22–24 April 1982; Billy J. Chandler, *King of the Mountain: The Life and Death of Giuliano the Bandit* (DeKalb: Northern Illinois University Press, 1988); John. S. Koliopoulos, *Brigands with a Cause: Brigandage and Irredentism in Modern Greece, 1821–1912* (Oxford: Clarendon Press, 1987); Richard W. Slatta, ed., *Bandidos: The Varieties of Latin American Banditry* (New York: Greenwood, 1987).

20.   For a detailed discussion on the uses of raiding in early colonial Indian politics, see K.A. Wagner, *Thuggee: Banditry and the British in Early Nineteenth-century India* (Basingstoke: Palgrave Macmillan, 2007); R. Singha, '"Providential Circumstances": The Thuggee Campaign of the 1830s and Legal Innovation', *Modern Asian Studies* 27, no. 1 (1993): 83–14; Anastasia Piliavsky, 'The Moghia Menace, or the Watch over Watchmen in British India', *Modern Asian Studies* 47, no. 3 (May 2013): 751–779; Stewart N. Gordon, 'Scarf and Sword: Thugs, Marauders, and State-formation in 18th Century Malwa', *Indian Economic and Social History Review* 6, no. 4 (2016): 403–429; D. Shulman, 'On South Indian Bandits and Kings', *Indian Economic and Social History Review* 17, no. 3 (1980): 283–306; Stewart N. Gordon, *Marathas, Marauders, and State Formation in Eighteenth-century India* (Delhi: Oxford University Press, 1994); S. Mayaram, *Against History, against State: Counterperspectives from the Margins* (New York: Columbia University Press, 2003); D. Vidal, *Violence and Truth: A Rajasthani Kingdom Confronts Colonial Authority* (Delhi: Oxford University Press, 1997); M. Kasturi, *Embattled Identities: Rajput Lineages and the Colonial State in Nineteenth-century North India* (Delhi: Oxford University Press, 2002), especially Chapters 5 and 6; also see S. Guha, *Environment and Ethnicity in India, 1200–1991* (Cambridge: Cambridge University Press, 1999); A. Skaria, *Hybrid Histories: Forests, Frontiers and Wildness in Western India* (Delhi: Oxford University Press, 1999), especially Chapter 9.

21.   See A. Chakravarti, *Contradiction and Change: Emerging Patters of Authority in a Rajasthan Village* (Delhi: Oxford University Press, 1975), p. 73; Anastasia Piliavsky, 'A Secret in the Oxford Sense: Thieves and the Rhetoric of Mystification in Rural India', *Comparative Studies in Society and History* 53, no. 2 (2011): 290–313.

22. Vinita Damodaran, 'Azad Dasta and Dacoit Gangs: The Congress and Underground Activity in Bihar, 1942–44, *Modern Asian Studies* 26, no. 3 (July 1992): 417–450.

23. Vinita Damodaran, 'Azad Dastas and Dacoit Gangs: The Congress and Underground Activity in Bihar, 1942–44', *Modern Asian Studies* 26, no. 3 (1992): 417–450, p. 441, doi:10.1017/S0026749X00009859.

24. Daechsel, 'Ẓālim Ḍākū and the Mystery of the Rubber Sea Monster', p. 28.

25. Damodaran, 'Azad Dastas and Dacoit Gangs'.

26. Ibid.

27. Ibid.; David Arnold, 'Dacoity and Rural Crime in Madras, 1860–1940', *Journal of Peasant Studies* 6, no. 2 (1979): 140–167, doi: 10.1080/03066157908438071.

28. Damodaran, 'Azad Dastas and Dacoit Gangs', p. 427.

29. David Arnold, 'Crime and Crime Control in Madras, 1838–1947', in *Crime and Criminality in British India* (Association for Asian Studies), ed. Anand Yang, pp. 70–74 (Tucson, Arizona: University of Arizona Press, 1985).

30. Ibid., p. 20.

31. See Khan, *The Great Partition*, p. 250.

32. See William Gould, *Bureaucracy, Community and Influence in India: Society and the State 1930s–1960s*, Routledge Studies in South Asian History (London: Routledge, Taylor and Francis, 2010), p. 226.

33. Vinita Damodaran in her work on Azad Dastas in Bihar has noted that the collaboration between the Azad Dastas and dacoits did not go well with the right-wing Congress establishment that was lodged in jail during the Quit India movement. As soon as their imprisonment ended and the Second World War concluded, the right wing of the Congress regained control of the party and immediately marginalised the Congress Socialist Party and the Azad Dastas. All this was guided by the fear of losing the upper caste and landholders' support who were becoming the targets of dacoits.

34. See, Letter No. 829-2/VIII, dated 9 February 1948, from R. Dayal, Home Secretary, Government of United Provinces, to S.S. Khera, Commissioner Meerut-Agra Divisions, part of File No. 513 (10)/48, Home Department Police-B.

35. Bart Klem and Bert Suykens, 'The Politics of Order and Disturbance: Public Authority, Sovereignty, and Violent Contestation in South Asia', *Modern Asian Studies* 52, no. 3 (2018): 754.

36. See top secret D.O. No. 33/S, dated 18 January 1948, from Collector Bareilly, L.C. Jain, to Divisional Commissioner, Rohilkhand Division, N.B. Bonarjee, part of File No. 513 (10)/48, Home Department Police-B.

37. Ibid.

38. Ibid.

39. See D.O. No. 829-Z/VIII, dated 26/28 January 1948, from R. Dayal, Home Secretary to UP Government, to Inspector General of Police, United Provinces, B.N. Lahiri, part of File No. 513 (10)/48, Home Department Police-B.

40. See D.O. No. 0-228/M, dated 29 January 1948, from Inspector General of Police, United Provinces, to Home Secretary to UP Government, R. Dayal, part of File No. 513 (10)/48, Home Department Police-B.

41. See Letter No. 829-2/VIII, dated 9 February 1948, from R. Dayal, Home Secretary, Government of United Provinces, to S.S. Khera, Commissioner Meerut-Agra Divisions, part of File No. 513 (10)/48, Home Department Police-B.

42. Robert S. Park and Ernest W. Burgess, *Introduction to the Science of Sociology* (Chicago: The University of Chicago Press, 1936), p. 785.

43. Michel Foucault, *Discipline and Punish: The Birth of the Prison* (New York: Vintage Books, 1977), p. 333. Michel Foucault has argued that a new form of power was introduced in the eighteenth century, that is, discipline. It was a form of power in which the subject became complicit and was different from the earlier strategy of regulating bodies.

44. A letter dated 17 June 1948, from Th. Phool Singh, MLA, I/C Refugee Relief Work, Meerut to Premier United Provinces, Govind Ballabh Pant. Part of File No. 513 (10)/48, Home Department Police-B.

45. See, D.O. No. 249/S dated 21 August 1948, from District Collector Bareilly, L.C. Jain, to Commissioner, Rohilkhand Division, N.B. Bonarjee, part of File No. 513 (10)/48, Home Department Police-B.

46. See Express D.O. No. 460/Arms, dated 25 August 1948, from District Collector Etah, Ram Kinker Singh, to S.S. Khera, Commissioner Agra-Meerut Division, part of File No. 513 (10)/48, Home Department Police-B.

47. See Express Letter D.O. No. 190/ST, dated 1 September 1948, from Bisheshwar Nath, District Collector Mainpuri, to S.S. Khera, Commissioner Meerut-Agra Division, part of File No. 513 (10)/48, Home Department Police-B.

48. See Enclosures in Letter No. VI-203-48, dated 6 April 1948, from Superintendent of Police, Headquarters, H.K. Kerr, on Behalf of Deputy Inspector General of Police, Headquarters United Provinces, to the Deputy Secretary of Government, Uttar Pradesh, Home Department (Police-B), part of File No. 513 (10)/48, Home Department Police-B.

49. See Letter No. 2952-2/VIII, dated 3/8 August 1950, from G. Mukharji, Joint Secretary to the UP Government, to the District Magistrates, part of File No. 513 (10)/48, Home Department Police-B.

50. See the draft Annexure to G.O. No. 5201-Z/VIII-513 (10)-48, November 1950, part of File No. 513 (10)/48, Home Department Police-B.

51. Ibid.

52. See Markus Daechsel, *The Politics of Self-Expression: The Urdu Middle-Class Milieu in Mid-Twentieth Century in India and Pakistan*, Royal Asiatic Society Books (London and New York: Routledge, Taylor and Francis, 2006), pp. 94–99.

53. See Gould, *Religion and Conflict*, p. 175. Broadly Chapter 5, 'State Transformation, Democracy and Conflict', pp. 163–194.

54. William Gould, 'Congress Radicals and Hindu Militancy: Sampurnanand and Purushottam Das Tandon in the Politics of the United Provinces, 1930–1947', *Modern Asian Studies* 36, no. 3 (July 2002): 619–655.

55. Hind Rakshak Dal was formed by P.D. Tandon in 1939.

56. See Gould, 'Congress Radicals and Hindu Militancy—'.

57. United Provinces Rakshak Dal Act,1948 (U.P. ACT NO. 38 of 1948). For Statutory Orders and Regulations (S.O.R.), see Gaz. Extra., dated 8 October 1948, adapted and modified by the Adaptation of Laws order, 1950. The Act was passed by the UP legislative assembly on 18 October 1948 and by the UP legislative council on 5 November 1948. The Act received the assent of the governor on 4 December 1948, under Section 75 of the Government of India Act, 1935, as adapted by the India (Provisional Constitution) Order, 1947, and published in UP Government Gazette on 11 December 1948.

58. Max Weber, 'Politics as a Vocation', in *From Max Weber: Essays in Sociology*, ed. and trans. Hans Gerth and C. Wright Mills, pp. 82–83 (Oxford: Oxford University, [1918] 1946).

59. United Provinces Rakshak Dal Act,1948 [U.P. ACT NO. 38 of 1948]. For S.O.R., see Gaz. Extra., dated 8 October 1948, adapted and modified by the Adaptation of Laws order, 1950.

60. Clive Emsley, 'Policing the Empire, Policing the Metropole: Some Thoughts on Models and Types', *Crime, History and Societies* 18, no. 2 (2014): 5–25.

61. See Giriraj Shah, *Indian Police: A Retrospect* (New Delhi, Cosmo Publications, 1989), p. 189, but see especially Chapter 8, pp. 173–187.

62. See Mahesh Chand, *Economic Problems in Indian Agriculture*, second edition (Bombay: Vora & Co. Publishers Ltd., 1950), p. 90.

63. See M. Zaheer and Jagdeo Gupta, *The Organization of the Government of Uttar Pradesh: A Study of State Administration* (New Delhi, S. Chand & Co., 1970), pp. 282–283.

64. It is important to note that even though the legislation is asserting the cultivation of such values, many of these expectations had not yet taken a clear shape immediately after independence. Rather, there was only a blueprint available from the recent nationalist and anti-colonial mobilisation.

65. David G. Barrie, 'A Typology of British Police: Locating the Scottish Municipal Police in Its British Contest, 1800–35', *British Journal of Criminology* 50, no, 2 (March 2010): 259–277, https://doi.org/10.1093/bjc/azp079.

66. See Zaheer and Gupta, *The Organization of the Government*, pp. 282–283.

67. Beatrice Jauregui, 'Cultures of Legitimacy and Postcolonial Policing: Guest Editor Introduction', *Law and Social Inquiry* 38, no. 3 (Summer 2013): 547–552.

68. See Letter No. 7591-Z/VIII, dated 9 December 1948, from Under Secretary to UP Government, Govind Narayan, to all District Magistrates, United Provinces, UPSA, File No. 464/1948 Department (Police) B.

69. Michel Foucault, *History of Sexuality*, vol. 1, *An Introduction* (New York: Pantheon Books, 1978).

70. For a more detailed discussion, see Antoon Braeckman, 'Beyond the Confines of the Law: Foucault's Intimations of a Genealogy of the Modern State'. *Philosophy and Social Criticism* 46, no. 6 (2020): 651–675, https://doi.org/10.1177/0191453719860227.

71. See Sugata Nandi, 'Constructing the Criminal: Politics of Social Imaginary of the "Goonda"', *Social Scientist* 38, no. 3/4 (March–April 2010): 37–54; Prashant Kidambi, 'The Ultimate Masters of the City: Police, Public Order and the Poor in Colonial Bombay, c. 1893–1914', *Crime, History and Societies* 8, no. 1 (2004): 27–47; Vivek Dharishwar and R. Shrivatsa, '"Rowdy-sheeters": An Essay on Subalternity and Politics', in *Subaltern Studies No. 9: Writings on South Asian History and Society*, ed. Shahid Amin and Dipesh Chakravarty, pp. 201–231 (Delhi, Oxford University Press, 1996).

72. See United Provinces Prevention of Crime (Special Powers) (Temporary) Bill, 1948, UPSA, Lucknow, Home Department (Police B) File No. 464/1948.

73. In the Indian Penal Code (IPC) 1860, Chapter XVI broadly deals with offences affecting the human body and concerns issues such as offences affecting life, injuries to unborn children and infants, offences of hurt such as wrongful restraint and wrongful confinement, criminal force and assault, abductions and forced labour, sexual offences and unnatural offences. Chapter XVII deals with offences against property and concerns issues such as theft, extortion, robbery and dacoity, criminal breach of trust, receiving stolen property, cheating, fraudulent deeds and dispositions of property, mischief and criminal trespass.

74. See the introduction in Georg Rusche and Otto Kirchheimer, *Punishment and Social Structure* (London and New York: Routledge, 2017).

75. UPSA, File No. 464/1948 (Police B), No. 7591-Z/VIII, dated 9 December 1948.

76. See C. Reith, *A New Study of Police History* (Edinburgh: Oliver and Boyd, 1956).

77. Daniel Gilling, *Crime Prevention: Theory, Policy and Politics* (London: UCL Press, 1997), pp. 1–15.

78. See D. Billis, 'At Risk of Prevention', *Journal of Social Policy* 10, no. 3 (1981): 367–379.

79. Ibid., p. 375.

80. See R. Freeman, 'The Idea of Prevention: A Critical Review', in *Private Risks and Public Dangers*, ed. S. Scott, G. Williams, S. Platt, and H. Thomas, pp. 34–56 (Aldershot: Avebury; Brookfield, VT: Ashgate Pub. Co., 1992).

81. Foucault, *Discipline and Punish*.

82. See UPSA, File No. 464/1948 (Police B), No. 2566-B/VIII, dated 21 May 1949.

83. Ibid.

84. See Letter No. 2566-B/VIII, dated 21 May 1949, from Secretary UP, by order of Home Secretary UP, to all District Magistrates of United Provinces, File No. 464/1948 Department (Police) B.

85. See Letter No. 3340-B/VIII, dated 3 June 1949, from Inspector General of Police, United Provinces, B.N. Lahiri to Home Secretary, UP Govt., Govind Narain, File No. 464/1948 Department (Police) B.

86. See *National Herald*, Lucknow, dated 9 June 1949.

87. Ibid.

88. David Garland, 'Of Crimes and Criminals: The Development of Criminology in Britain', in *The Oxford Handbook of Criminology*, ed. M. Maguire, R. Morgan and R. Reiner, p. 18 (Oxford: Clarendon Press, 1994).

89. See Secret Letter No. 175/ST, dated 14 June 1949, from M.G. Kaul, District Magistrate, Bara Banki, to the Secretary to Government, Home Department (Police C), Part of File No. 464/1948 Department (Police) B.

90. See Ranajit Guha, 'Chandra's Death', in *A Subaltern Studies Reader, 1986–1995*, ed. Ranajit Guha, pp. 34–62 (Minneapolis: University of Minnesota Press, 1998); Christopher Bayly, *Empire and Information: Intelligence Gathering and Social Communication in India, 1780–1870* (Cambridge: Cambridge University Press, 1999); Anupama Rao, 'Death of a Kotwal: The Violence of Recognition', in *The Caste Question: Dalits and the Politics of Modern India* (California: University of California Press, 2009); Vineeta Damodaran, 'Azad Dastas and Dacoit Gangs: The Congress and Underground Activity in Bihar, 1942–44', *Modern Asian Studies* 26, no. 3 (1992): 417–450; Singha, '"Providential" Circumstances', pp. 83–146.

91. See the copy of Confidential Letter D.O. No. G/37, dated 20 July 1949, from the Superintendent of Police Bahraich to the District Magistrate Bahraich, part of File No. 464/1948 Department (Police) B.

92. See Letter No. 3914-PC/VIII-464-1948, dated 9 August 1949, from Govind Narain, Secretary to Government, United Provinces to All District Magistrates, incharge of District, United Provinces, part of File No. 464/1948 Department (Police) B.

93. For a discussion on despotism of law in early colonial India, see Radhika Singha, *A Despotism of Law: Crime and Justice in Early Colonial India* (New Delhi: Oxford University Press, 1998), pp. xxix, 342.

94. See Secret Letter No. 254/ST, dated 3 June 1949, from J.M. Raina, District Magistrate Aligarh, to the Secretary to Government, UP, Home Department (Police C), Lucknow, part of File No. 464/1948 Department (Police) B.

95. See Secret Letter No. 205/ST, dated 10 June 1949, from District Magistrate Etah, Ram Kinker Singh, to the Secretary to Government (Police C), Lucknow, part of File No. 464/1948 Department (Police) B.

96. Ibid.

97. Ibid.

98. Ibid.

99. See Secret Letter No. 2855/XVIII, dated 10 June 1949, from District Magistrate Bijnor, Raghubanshi, to the Secretary to Government (Police-C), Lucknow, part of File No. 464/1948 Department (Police) B.

100. For a discussion of provisional authority, see Jauregui, *Provisional Authority*.

101. See Letter No. 161/ST, dated 3 June 1949, from H.K. Mathur, District Magistrate Sultanpur, to the Secretary to Government, Home (Police-C) Department, UP, Lucknow, part of File No. 464/1948 Department (Police) B.

102. The *seva dal*s were local community organisations of the Congress Party.

103. See Letter No. 161/ST, dated 3 June 1949, from H.K. Mathur, District Magistrate Sultanpur, to the Secretary to Government, Home (Police-C) Department, UP, Lucknow, part of File No. 464/1948 Department (Police) B.

104. Ibid.

105. Ibid.

106. See copy of the letter dated 1 June 1949, from Superintendent of Police, Fatehpur, B.N. Bhalla, to District Magistrate Fathepur, part of File No. 464/1948 Department (Police) B.

107. See Secret Letter No. 703-B/49, dated 18 June 1949, from Collector Kanpur, Krishan Chand, to Home Secretary to UP Government, Govind Narain, part of File No. 464/1948 Department (Police) B.

108. See D.O. No. 71/VIII from Collector Ballia, H.A. Siddiqi to Session Judge Ballia, Ghulam Sabir, part of File No. 464/1948 Home Department (Police) B.

109. See Letter 6238 PC./VIII-464-49, dated 27 December 1949, from S.N. Mehrotra to Collector and Magistrate Ballia, H.A. Siddiqi, part of File No. 464/1948 Home Department (Police) B.

110. See Letter No. 4871, dated 31 May 1949, from District Magistrate Dehradun, A.D. Pandit, to the Secretary to Government, Home Department (Police C), UP, Lucknow, part of File No. 464/1948 Department (Police) B.

111. See Letter No. 249/ST, dated 7 June 1949, from District Magistrate Garhwal, M.A. Quraishi, to the Secretary to Government, Home Department (Police C), UP, Lucknow, part of File No. 464/1948 Department (Police) B.

112. See Letter No. 44/ST, dated 31 October 1949, from District Magistrate Jaunpur, to the Home Secretary, United Provinces, part of File No. 464/1948 Department (Police) B.

113. Michel Foucault, Mauro Bertani, Alessandro Fontana, François Ewald and David Macey, 'Society Must Be Defended': Lectures at the Collège de France, 1975–1976 (New York: Picador, 2003).

5

Mukhiyas and *Chowkidars*

Understanding the 'New' Sense of Public Order in the United Provinces, 1947–1955

Provincial governments in India inherited their bureaucratic apparatus from the British colonial government. In addition to the police and the judiciary, it also retained some auxiliary institutions of local surveillance and statistics collection. While the police and the judiciary were accepted as prominent foundations of state operations, institutions like *mukhiyagiri* and *chowkidari* attracted criticism, and their relevance was debated in the United Provinces (UP). This chapter discusses an administrative tradition inherited from the colonial government and highlights the continuity of a familiar attitude in the UP administration when it came to governing the village. While the Prantiya Rakshak Dal (PRD) and the special powers to deal with 'habitual offenders' were primarily geared towards urban and rural contexts, issuing guns to 'reliable villages', *mukhiyas* and *chowkidars* were important for the colonial state to govern the countryside. Put together, they constituted the broader strategy of the postcolonial state to maintain public order. This chapter will take the discussion forward and focus on the institution of *chowkidari* and *mukhiyagiri* to show that in the face of political volatility that posed a constant challenge to postcolonial authority, the post-1947 UP government, owing to the sovereign anxiety that acted to mark its territory, could not avoid the seductions of the colonial art of governance. It resorted to rebranding old institutions in the face of 'changed times', where the Congress had to actively function as an independent government rather than just a mass-mobilising front opposing colonial power.

The recruitment of village *chowkidars* was connected to the larger politics of colonial recruitment in the nineteenth and twentieth centuries. In the 1880s, suggestions for employing unemployed and reformed ex-criminals were made. They were expected to serve as effective informers on their fellow members of criminal tribes.[1] Many such 'reformed' members of the criminal tribes were employed for surveillance and monitoring of various criminal tribe settlements. For example, in the late nineteenth century, Sanauriahs of the Lalitpur criminal tribe settlement worked as the village, municipal and railway *chowkidars*. About four hundred such *chowkidars* were guarding Beriahs, Haburahs and Natts in the Etah region. They were employed to monitor and control the annual gatherings of wandering groups in the 1880s.

Similarly, Doms were employed as village *chowkidars* and road cess collectors in the Gorakhpur and Champaran criminal tribe settlements.[2] In the late nineteenth and twentieth centuries, the provincial government deployed *chowkidars* for diverse activities such as camel patrolling, border frontier policing, monitoring villages and guarding railway property, canals and even factories.[3] Scholars have noted that the number of village *chowkidars* in colonial UP in 1897, 1911, 1921 and 1931 was 89,345, 78,319, 40,877 and 29,745, respectively.[4] Especially after the First World War, colonial demand for workforce increased further.[5] The United Provinces remained one of the main contributors to meeting such needs. The annual report for the Criminal Tribes Act in 1917 noted a shortage of constables, watchmen and guards in 'criminal tribe settlements' and rural areas.

The institution of *chowkidari* could be better understood by placing it within the triad of power, surveillance and policing. In this triad, governance as a practice thrives by knowing more about all aspects of the lives of its subjects and then policing what it knows. In short, governance is policing. In this quest, the colonial state felt the necessity of having a class of local collaborators and ended up employing from amongst those it suspected. The following sections will clarify that such institutions had more to do with surveillance than governance aimed at the welfare of their subjects.

Modernising the Police and Fighting Corruption: The Police Reorganisation Committee, 1948, and the Institution of *Chowkidari* in UP

After India gained independence from British rule, some local institutions began to be questioned by the new political establishment.

Prominent among them were the institutions of *chowkidar*s and *mukhiya*s. This section will discuss the significance of the institution of *chowkidar*s for local policing and its subsequent abolition and replacement by village constables in UP. The institution of *chowkidar*s, which was considered vital to the police administration in UP right up to independence, began to be considered unsuitable after 1947. The Police Reorganisation Committee, 1948, paid great attention to this institution and proposed its abolishment and replacement on 'modern' lines.[6]

The figure of the *chowkidar* was a crucial link between the village and the colonial state because he belonged to the village community and was aware of the day-to-day situation on the ground. A *chowkidar* in a village was the local access point for the district police. Births and deaths and other vital information on criminal activities in the village were recorded, maintained and relayed to district authorities by the *chowkidar*s. One member of the colonial legislative council noted that in addition to the *tehsildar*, the district officer and the governor-general, the *chowkidar*s also constituted an essential class of officials crucial to the colonial administration.[7] The significance of the *chowkidar*s was not lost on others either, who argued that they were the 'foundation of the police force'.[8] Some scholars have pointed out the local influences that determined the operation of *chowkidar*s' activities within the colonial network of control and have noted that they had an ambiguous role within the colonial criminal administration.[9]

In the early nineteenth century, the figure of the *chowkidar* stood as an anomaly in the colonial criminal administration because he was serving two masters – the police and the local *zamindar* – at the same time. The *chowkidar*s were not recognised as an 'official' of the police but reported to the sub-inspector, and at the local level, they had to work with the *zamindar*, who could easily manipulate or dominate them and disrupt the stream of information from the village to the district police administration. Furthermore, the *chowkidar*s mostly belonged to 'lower caste' communities and did not command respect in the local social fabric.[10] They did not command respect and trust among the colonial administration too. For example, the judge of Cuttack in 1838 and the lieutenant governor of Bengal in 1856 had concluded on different occasions that the *chowkidar*s were linked to thieves and robbers and were possibly part of all robberies in the villages.[11] Similar observations had led to the *Police Committee Report* in 1838 to note that for 'all practical purposes of Police the watchman is useless'.[12] The Act (VI) of 1870 transformed the position of the *chowkidar* into a respectable and trusted agent of the colonial criminal administration. The fundamental goal of the Act was to refresh the image of this administratively important rural agent and make him a visible figure at the local level.[13] The exercise aimed at resolving earlier doubts about the *chowkidars*' respectability and attending to the challenges of syncing his purpose to the colonial state's policy. A regular cash salary replaced the earlier land grants that made the *chowkidars* dependent on local *zamindars*. It was expected that a cash salary would motivate the *chowkidar* to assist the police more enthusiastically. *Panchayat*, the traditional institution of the village, was modified and would now involve local traders and proprietors of land and landholders. They were expected to assist the police and to extract a special tax from the community to pay the salary of the *chowkidar*. Such attempts aimed at streamlining the structures of local governance that were conducive to the colonial administration. Gradually, the 'contribution' of the village community to pay the *chowkidar* became obligatory, or a compulsory tax.

The institution of the *chowkidar* became liminal in the sense that it simultaneously made him a partisan of the state and the community. The earlier traditional remuneration of the *chowkidar* that depended upon the goodwill of the village community had now become an obligatory administrative demand. The village community members soon became uncomfortable with the arrangement and did not see any merit in a service imposed by the colonial administration that they neither sought nor desired.[14] The *zamindar* continued to influence even in the new arrangement because he was made responsible for the village *chowkidar's* nomination, appointment and payment. This modified self-governance model was dependent upon the specific needs and requirements of the colonial state rather than the rural community.[15] The fragile relationship between the village and the colonial administration in the nineteenth century, for example, in Bengal, has been studied by various scholars.[16] Crispin Bates argues that the *panchayat* was a colonial construction that created an 'Orientalist' image of rural India as one frozen in antiquity.[17] John McLane has noted that the local political authority was fragmented and delegated and re-delegated where 'kingship' remained informally influential, resulting in a dependence on particular persons with power.[18] P.J. Musgrave had also noted that the hierarchy of employees managing estates was more or less a loose clump of relationships and controlled by the local landlord.[19] Anand Yang has questioned such emphasis placed on the multi-layered influence at the local level but recognised the significance of the local levels of control, particularly the *zamindar*s who monopolised the production and distribution of local land resources.[20] Attempts towards the devolution of control hindered the state's penetration into the local systems and enabled local authorities to exist and adapt to the changes introduced by the colonial state. Despite having local informers such as the *chowkidar*s to report on persons and events, there remained a gap or lack of authentic connection between the colonial state and its subjects. Guided by political anxiety, the colonial state relied on quasi-official and ad hoc arrangements to make its presence felt. At the same time, it could not have been further away from the everyday lives of its subjects. Even the ordinary figure of the *chowkidar* was seen as the punitive appendage of the colonial state.

Some perceived the Act (VI) of 1870 as having the desired effect.[21] The number of *chowkidar*s under the Act grew from 53 per cent to 93 per cent by 1904. The figure of the *chowkidar* became a vital indirect tool of the criminal justice system. *Chowkidar*s could avoid the legal restrictions that a police officer was bound to. According to the Code of Criminal Procedure (CrPC), a police officer could arrest an accused or let them go until having sufficient evidence. The dilemma remained that such an accused could neither be arrested due to a lack of evidence nor be allowed to escape. The *chowkidar* kept an eye on such an accused and assisted the police in gathering information and confessions about the case, which an investigating officer could later record.

An extensive survey of *chowkidari* is required here to sketch its significance and character and trace its evolution as an institution in the career of the colonial state, thus highlighting its remarkable place in the local administrative arrangement. Scholarship dealing with a diverse set of issues have made varied observations about the institution of *chowkidari* and the figure of the *chowkidar*. It includes discussions on the colonial imposition of the institution on villages, pointing out its failures, highlighting the paradox of the policy, its significance for the surveillance of roads, ports and medicine, and its corruption and participation in local crime. Scholars have, for example, noted that the 1870 Act was one of the critical steps towards the introduction of local government in villages. It constituted a new *panchayat* system by legislating 'the Bengal Village Chowkidari Act'. The purpose of these *panchayat*s was to collect local tax for the maintenance of village *chowkidar*s and did not provide any other services at the local level.[22] Literature discussing the incompetence of the *chowkidar*s have noted that they often failed to report crimes to the police, and the police did not always submit charge sheets.[23] Others have highlighted the paradox of the institution. They note that the British ruled villages from a distance because they established their centres of power in the towns and cities. It rested on an earlier Mughal presumption that villages in India are self-governing. Village institutions such as the *panchayat*, the *chowkidar* and the caste system were despised as symbols of backwardness but vigorously utilised as 'the basis of a system that contributed to maintaining order in the countryside'.[24] Various studies have also noted the significance of *chowkidar*s for broader colonial governance. Illustrating the linear nature of colonial power concerning the management of roads, David Arnold has shown that after the formal set up of colonial police forces in India in 1860, its revisions and its deployment thereafter worked with the assumption that constabulary ought to be deployed in towns, cities and important checkpoints between them. Policing in villages was left to *chowkidar*s – the old village police – because the deployment of poorly paid constables to rural interiors was considered inadvisable.[25] Ian Copland has pointed out that the *chowkidar*s from surrounding villages were often requisitioned to provide backup to the police during Hindu and Muslim religious processions.[26]

Similarly, Clare Anderson has pointed out that at ports, *chowkidar*s accompanied migrants to prevent them from deserting on their embarkation. The journey of the indentured labourer and those sentenced to transportation had a similar pattern. Such a supervisory role blurred the legal status of the convicts and migrants.[27] Others have highlighted that the *chowkidar*s and other government officials also became local nodal contacts for medical governance in colonial India. For example, they were responsible for distributing quinine during malarial outbreaks and countered contraband and adulterated quinine distribution.[28] Such moves were possible because of the *chowkidar*s' locality, the shared language and culture between the villagers and them and, most importantly, their awareness of the rhythms of local daily life.

Another set of scholarship had discussed the liminality of the *chowkidar*. Shail Mayaram, for example, points out that after the passing of the Criminal Tribes Act, 1871, later amended during colonial rule in 1897 and 1911, the *chowkidar*s were drawn from erstwhile criminals and members of militia groups. The *chowkidar*s assisted the local police in roll calls, regulating the ticket leave system and general surveillance of designated criminal tribe members. They also aided the administration in imposing regulatory control on 'criminal tribes' and containing them in enclosures, and implementing the policies of 'reform' geared towards their correction.[29] On the other hand, Andrew Major has shown that *chowkidar*s (along with village headmen and the *thanadar*, or the in-charge of a police station) were an integral part of a corrupt local apparatus because they often took a share of the plunder from burglars and thieves as the price of protection or for not reporting.[30] For example, Moghias became part of a colonial legion of watchmen communities. Anastasia Piliavsky provides intricate details of administrative efforts to deal with the 'Moghia menace'.[31] In Mewar, a Moghi *jemadar* (headman) was responsible for protecting eight to ten villages. He was also responsible for the duties and conduct of the *chowkidar*s employed in these villages. Across regions of Mewar, Moghia *chowkidar*s received rent-free land and a monthly salary. It is a classic example of the colonial administration employing erstwhile plunderers for village protection and surveillance duties.

Piliavsky has noted that the erstwhile plunderers now employed as *chowkidar*s 'knew everything that was going on in the society, and raider-protectors enjoyed a measure of respect in local society'.[32] Soon, they became 'the main source of intelligence, surveillance, protection, intimidation, and mediation'; their role was no less than executive police in such cases.[33] Piliavsky noted the volatility of employment of such *chowkidar*s in detail. She observed that disgruntled or dissatisfied watchmen sometimes turned against their patrons and joined rivals when presented with a better opportunity. When dismissed by their masters, these *chowkidar*s once again resorted to pillaging the countryside.[34]

The formal institution of village *chowkidar*s created by the colonial state under the Village Chowkidar Act, 1870, was considered one of India's oldest indigenous institutions. *Chowkidar*s, traditionally in some regions, were originally called 'Goraits' and worked as village servants.[35] During early colonial times, *chowkidar*s were appointed by the *zamindar*s and landholders to protect or oversee the persons and properties of the tenants. They were also used by the *zamindar*s for their private business and were paid for by grants of land. They mainly served as watchmen and were the only information-gathering agency to inform police work in rural areas. In 1863, when the recent formation of the police organisation in the then North-Western Provinces was re-examined, the 'Rural Beat System' replaced the 'Rural Walk System'.[36] It implied a growing recognition of the village *chowkidar*'s utility as a reporting and patrolling agency. When the colonial state took a more active role in policing the country, the idea of village *chowkidars* underwent some changes. With the formal institutionalising of *chowkidari* with the Village Chowkidar Act in 1870, village policing was overhauled. Preserving 'law and order' and the 'prevention of crime' in the countryside was no more under the prerogative or the responsibility of landholders and *zamindars*. Instead, it now lay with the colonial state. For example, *chowkidars* in the former province of Agra were regularised as a state force with the passing of the Local Rates Act (XVIII of 1871) and in Avadh under the Avadh Laws Act (Act XVIII of 1876). The most important feature of these two Acts was that *chowkidars* had to be paid in cash thereon, not by land grants. However, a payment system by land grants continued until the end of the nineteenth century and was mentioned negatively in the UP Police Committee of 1890. Owing to many complaints, it recommended introducing a good conduct allowance to entice *chowkidars* to perform their duties more enthusiastically. Despite such regulation, the old customs of 'Goraits' continued in UP as late as 1936, for example, in the district of Mirzapur, where they were paid by land grants rather than in cash.

The modernising of the institution of *chowkidari* by the colonial state had much to do with installing informants at the lowest local level.[37] Apart from regular village *chowkidars*, there used to be road *chowkidars* who patrolled the roads and were part of the apparatus to prevent robberies and Thuggee. In 1916, the road *chowkidars* were disbanded in UP and numbered only 3,128 at that time. In 1871, the colonial state in India had suggested that there should be one *chowkidar* for every 1,000 houses. Later, the Indian Police Commission, 1902–1903, recommended that the ratio of village *chowkidars* should be one to every 600 persons of the rural population. The government accepted this proposal, but even in 1911, the ratio was only one *chowkidar* to 482 persons. The Civil Police Committee of 1919 recommended that the total number of *chowkidars*' that existed at that point in time should be divided into five groups. It was proposed that this division be based on the 'criminality and density of the population' of these areas. These ratios started from one *chowkidar* for 600 people to one *chowkidar* for every 1,000 people. It aimed to govern the population by managing crime rates and sustaining a local surveillance apparatus.

The less 'criminal' an area was, the more people a *chowkidar* could have under his responsibility and vice versa.

In the year 1890, the strength of *chowkidars* in UP was 113,979. It reduced to 80,000–88,000 between the years 1900 and 1921. In 1924–1925, the strength of *chowkidars* was 51,929, which reduced to 43,797 by 1931. In 1947, when India gained independence, the number of permanent *chowkidars* in UP was 43,876, plus the 5,127 temporary *chowkidars*. In total, in 1947–1948, UP had 49,003 *chowkidars* at its disposal, incurring an expenditure of 2,121,000 rupees. A *chowkidar* received 3 rupees per mensem from the government.[38] The village *chowkidari* force was separate from the police force as the *chowkidars* were not enlisted in the Police Act as they were not subject to police discipline. In 1948, the duties of the *chowkidars* broadly dealt with the surveillance of bad characters in the village and the reporting of crime and other occurrences to the nearest police station. *Chowkidars* continued to assist in the investigation of a crime, with arresting criminals and in tracing absconders. They also served as watch and ward in the village during fairs and festivals and had to report every birth and death in the village to the local police station. Their duty also included informing the local authorities of the outbreak of any infectious disease.

The post-1948 state administration in UP aimed to underwrite most, if not all, relations of power and authority. The modality of control emerges as a substantive issue here. The relationship between the state and its citizens was set in a paradigm of security, where security was proposed as foundational to justice and governance. Institutions such as *chowkidari* offered the state a chance to mediate quotidian operations of its citizens. It ensured the presence of the state as against a condition of desolation and anarchy that independence could potentially usher. However, in reality, postcolonial sovereignty needed the protection of institutions such as *chowkidari* and aimed to impose a familiar mode of political life through them subtly. The issue here is more of power and obligation than of imperialism or colonialism. The postcolonial UP administration was wary of citizenship granted to the masses without them being adequately disciplined yet. However, the state also felt the necessity to appear to be acting in consonance with the changed political scenario.

The UP Police Reorganisation Committee, 1948, doubted the utility of village *chowkidars* as it moved forward to 'modernise' the police system to make it compatible with the new political reality of independence.[39]

The committee opined that given the multifarious duties and responsibilities carried out by the *chowkidar*s, their efficiency was doubtful. The committee argued that the beat of *chowkidar*s was vast, and it was impractical for them to carry out their duties simultaneously with their private work in the fields or elsewhere. Such an overworked figure, it was argued, was unlikely to be of great use in investigations. Also, there was a concern about whether a *chowkidar* actually reported all crimes or instead concealed crucial information at times. The majority of the village *chowkidar*s were completely illiterate, and their reporting of diseases was also questionable, as they did not know one disease from another. Such scepticism was not entirely unprecedented. The Police Decentralisation Committee of 1923 – still under colonial control – had already floated the abolishing of *chowkidar*s and suggested field trials in selected areas. The colonial government did not accept this recommendation then.

The Police Reorganisation Committee of 1948 held that spending 2,000,000 rupees per annum on an institution whose intelligence was inaccurate was questionable. Also, it suggested that an 'intelligent officer' could do the same information-gathering work by closely questioning the villagers. The committee was conscious of a gap between the police and the public due to the recent colonial experience. In other words, the police were aware that the public distrusted them. The most crucial function that the *chowkidar*s performed during the colonial era was providing a link between the police station and the village for reporting subversive activities in a village. The committee of 1948 held that the public's consciousness was developing; therefore, a purpose serving colonial times might not be useful anymore. Also, the police did not need to maintain an 'imperialistic hold'[40] over the people in an independent India. *Chowkidar*s were to be abolished, and a 'better class of men who will be better paid' was thought to replace them.[41]

Now that the argument for the abolition of *chowkidar*s was made, recommendations for replacing them came flooding in. To deal with the abolition of the *chowkidari* system, the Police Reorganisation Committee, 1948, recommended two alternatives. The first alternative proposed that the strength of the regular police force could increase to provide a few extra constables in every police station to which *chowkidar*s were previously sanctioned. During the discussion, the number of such police stations was about 700 and would require estimated recruitment of 6,000–7,000 new policemen. It was argued in the proposal that the state exchequer could maintain the new force within the same amount of money that the *chowkidari* system had utilised.

The second alternative proposed creating a new class of police constables who would be required to live within their village beats and paid 15 rupees per month. The Police Reorganisation Committee was more inclined towards the second alternative as it wanted to have an agent of the police directly based in a village to report incidents of crime and movements of bad characters. Policemen stationed in the police station could not adequately fulfil the task of such surveillance. The new force was to be called 'village constables'.[42] They were supposed to be literate, with the view that they would be able to send in written reports to the police stations they would be attached to. After calculations, the committee proposed that the strength of the new village constables should be one-fourth of the total available strength of the former village *chowkidars*. The village constables would come under the Police Act and be liable to the same disciplinary rules applicable to other regular policemen. As the village constables were supposed to live in their villages, it was proposed that they be given cultivation rights by the government. The village constable would also undertake 'detective duties' at the village level.[43] Finally, the Police Reorganisation Committee strongly recommended that the institution of the *chowkidars* should not be abolished all at once but gradually phased out over the next five years.

The UP Police Reorganisation Committee, 1948, consisted of 10 members.[44] In the final report, three members of the committee had issues with the recommendations of the committee. Two of them were the Indian National Congress (INC) party MLAs V.N. Tivary and Nafisul Hasan and one inspector of police, M.S. Mathur. They expressed grave doubts over the replacement of *chowkidars* by the new force of village constables on the grounds of efficiency. They conceded that complaints about harassment by *chowkidars* were not infrequent but argued further that when 'half-trained and unseasoned but uniformed policemen' would be placed in rural areas far away from police stations, the likelihood of harassment would be even greater.[45] Also, they emphasised that a reduction in the number of village police could greatly hamper the intelligence-gathering system at the village level. Their comments further emphasised that the matter of pay was not as important as the majority opinion in the committee believed. They argued that it was for 'prestige' and not monetary gain that villagers used to volunteer themselves for the post of a village *chowkidar*. According to an example given in the notes on the discussion, these dissenting members claimed:

> [I]t is the experience of one of us that in one district when the village Chowkidars of a particular circle agitated for an increment of their pay, they were asked to put in their resignations and make room for others who were prepared to come in for the same pay but not one of the agitators tendered their resignation.[46]

The abolition and replacement of *chowkidar*s by fewer village police constables, the three dissenting members further argued, would create difficulties for station officers to find men to guard vulnerable points during emergencies, manage their fairs and festivals, or make arrangements for journeys of high-profile personages passing through these villages. Also, a reduction of village constables to one-fourth of the *chowkidar*s could increase crime. The dissenters opined that the services of the village *chowkidar*s were of the 'greatest value' to the administration in detecting and reporting crimes and surveillance over bad characters. According to them, it was because of such indispensable services that such a 'hoary institution'[47] had survived for so long.

The abolition of the old institution of *chowkidar* was announced in December 1948, and a phased timetable for the next five years was set. The deadline for the complete abolition of the village *chowkidari* system coincided almost precisely with the abolition of another important village institution, *mukhiyagiri* (village headmen), discussed in the following section. The UP press gave substantial coverage to the recommendation of the Police Reorganisation Committee, 1948. The abolition of *chowkidari*, among other modifications in the UP police, received wide press coverage. For example, *Dainik Vishwamitra*, a Hindi daily, wrote that the institution of *chowkidar*s did not have any value as they usually served only the *mukhiya* or the *zamindar*. [48] Therefore, the recent move by the UP Congress government to replace them with village policemen provided a properly official and neutral – rather than tied to landed interest – presence in case of theft, robbery, murder and other crimes. Another Hindi daily, *Jawala*, wrote that it would be better if the government tried to revive the ancient police traditions of India rather than replacing them with western models.[49] For this newspaper, the actual *chowkidari* system before the British modified it was one of such institutions and involved community spirit and policing. Another newspaper, *Sanmarg*, warned that abolishing *chowkidars* would only render thousands of men unemployed.[50] It further argued that *chowkidari* was an essential aspect of ancient village practices of India. Since the *chowkidars* knew a village in and out, they were better suited to detecting crime than the newly recommended village constables.

The press note from the Information Directorate, which announced the abolition of *chowkidari*, is noteworthy for its language and line of argumentation. It asserted that the 'ill-paid village *Chowkidars* have no place in a modern police system, and this age-old institution must now be replaced by a better class of men, who will be better paid'. This statement did not raise issues or problems with the *chowkidari* system but portrayed its abolition simply as the necessity of modern times and the changed scenario of administrative expectations in UP in a new and independent India.

Catching the Mice Is More Important than the Colour of the Cat: *Mukhiyas* and the Politics of Everyday Public Order in UP, 1948–1955

Another remnant of the colonial order in UP was the *mukhiya* and the institution of *mukhiyagiri*. While *chowkidars* were abolished and replaced by village policemen after the recommendations of the UP *Police Reorganisation Committee Report 1948*, the institution of *mukhiyas* attracted considerable discussion within the UP administration.[51] This section will show how the local administration dealt with public-order issues and its subjects, who were now citizens of an independent India, when it came to entrusting them with the responsibility of local governance.

The institution of the *mukhiya* or *mukhiyagiri* was one of the most important local institutions in India's apparatus of colonial governance. The *mukhiya* was the village headman, often a higher caste person and always male, the primary contact with the colonial administration. The head of the traditional caste *panchayats* was also called *mukhiyas*. However, there was an official and particular institution of *mukhiya*, with important duties assigned, available in the CrPC itself.

A year after India's independence, the Congress government in UP was vigorously preoccupied with local governance issues. Files from the UP administration show that the government was concerned with issues of democracy at the local level. A driving concern was not so much the opportunity for creative political thinking amongst the UP Congress leadership but rather the increasing number of complaints against *mukhiya*s that the minister of police, Lal Bahadur Shastri, received from various districts. In May 1949, in a letter to the home secretary of UP, Shastri wrote that he was not aware of the responsibilities and duties of *mukhiya*s and did not know about their recruitment process.[52] However, he still advised that the complaints he received against them might be because these *mukhiya*s were very old and should be replaced with younger and better men. Shastri contended that they should be left to the district magistrate to appoint anyone he considered fit. He was unsure whether to retain these *mukhiya*s once the new *panchayat* system started functioning. He advised that it was not necessary to dispense with all of them by making new appointments. Instead, the district magistrates should look into individual cases whenever complaints were received. Unsurprisingly, the post-independence Congress government in UP perceived this institution as an effective tool of outreach and gaining popularity.

The institution of the *mukhiya* was significant in the operations of local-level village surveillance. The CrPC, 1898, Part III, Chapter IV, section 45, empowered a district magistrate or, in some cases, a sub-divisional magistrate to appoint a village headman. When required, there could be several *mukhiya*s. A response note (dated 16 May 1949) from the home secretary to the minister of police Shastri brings to our attention that the powers that a *mukhiya* held were not ordinary and simple. Broadly, the institution of the *mukhiya* was a primary point of reference for not only the magistrate but also the officer-in-charge of the nearest police station. He was expected to communicate the permanent or temporary residence of any notorious person(s) in his village and the presence or passage of such notorious person(s) whom the headmen knew of or reasonably suspected to be thugg(s), robber(s), habitual offender(s) or even escaped convict(s). Most importantly, he was also responsible for reporting a violation or a possible violation of orders under section 144 of the CrPC. Section 144 dealt with the management of disorderly or riotous mobs and crowds, as we have discussed in earlier chapters. A *mukhiya* was also responsible for reporting all matters likely to affect the maintenance of order, preventing crime or anything hampering the safety of a person or property as per the general or special order made by the district magistrates. Special orders of the district or sub-district magistrates derived their authority through the government authorisation of the magistrates to direct such communication of information.

The response of the home secretary that informed the minister of police about the institution of the *mukhiya* stated that the rules regarding the appointment of headmen were in Chapter II, Volume I of the Manual of Government Orders (MGO).[53] The appointing authority for village headmen or *mukhiya*s was the district magistrate or the sub-divisional magistrate. In appointing a *mukhiya*, a district magistrate had to consider the person's character, position and influence. However, the police appeared to have no connection whatsoever with the appointment of *mukhiya*s and had no direct authority over them. The district magistrate and the sub-divisional magistrate could remove them at any time, and it was not necessary to record any reasons for such removal. Also, it was at the discretion of the district magistrate or the sub-divisional magistrate to add or reduce the number of village headmen appointed to a village. But according to the rules in the CrPC, the first point of providing intelligence input for such *mukhiya*s was, in most cases, the local police station.

Discussion regarding the retention or abolition of the institution of the *mukhiya* started circulating at different levels of the administration in UP when the Congress government began to think about creating a new system of local self-government based on *gram panchayat*s.[54] One of the major concerns was whether it was necessary or administratively feasible to retain *mukhiya*s after implementing the new elected *panchayat* system. The main issue here was that *panchayat*s were to become overtly 'political' bodies now, based on elections and involving party membership of its delegates. *Mukhiya*s, in contrast, had both political and ostensibly non-political functions – chiefly amongst them their role in local intelligence-gathering and crime-prevention work. This conflation of roles had not mattered to the colonial state when all administration was essentially deemed 'non-political'. But under the new reality of independence, such pretence was no longer defensible. The home secretary's response to Shastri captured the dilemma well:

> [P]arty politics is essential feature of any democratic system but we cannot apply that to the functions which should appropriately be performed by public servants. Mukhia is not a paid public servant but he performs those duties, which really come within the province of public servants. He gives valuable information to the officers of the state which he will not be able to do without bias and partiality if he takes active part in politics.[55]

The home secretary's main point was that a *mukhiya* must essentially be a person free from political bias. He further stated that *mukhiya*s faced prejudice from some sections of local society precisely because of their association with the police. The opposition arose from their role as 'information providers' to the local administration, especially the police, and therefore they were likely to make many enemies while performing the duties required of them by law. The expectation of a similar function from an elected member or members of a *panchayat* was unrealistic because, under pressure from political parties, they would find it difficult to execute such judicial and administrative functions.

Most importantly, it was necessary to maintain the popularity of the new *panchayat*s by keeping them away from the duties that a *mukhiya* performed. The main reason stated by the home secretary was that the new *panchayat*s were bound to lead members of the *panchayat* into controversies and party factions. However, the home secretary emphasised that 'times have changed considerably',[56] and it was now necessary to drop those who could not change their attitudes with the times. The home secretary's statement shows that he realised that in a newly independent India, *mukhiya*s would become untenable if they continued to hold attitudes of the former order and a colonial relationship with the administration. He added that it was about time that younger and vigorous *mukhiya*s replaced older men. It duly emphasised the need for the institution of the *mukhiya* to evolve in postcolonial times. It reflects the moral pressure that the UP government faced while dealing with institutions that were remnants of the colonial administrative structure. Most interestingly, the home Secretary gave a wartime (emergency or exceptional) example to make his point. He wrote:

> I remember that when an invasion from Japan was imminent in 1942 it was found necessary to replace the older Mukhias to obtain persons who could be more active in sending information about the serial bombing etc. and the DM's were asked to examine the list of their Mukhias and eliminate persons found old and decrepit and therefore unsuitable. Similar instructions may issue now. The District Magistrates may go through the lists with a view to find out who of these should be replaced. They can do so under the powers in paragraph 1106 of the MGO Volume 1.[57]

But there was also another problem at play. India's new political institutions were still fragile, while expectations of the newly independent government were sky high. It appeared inevitable to retain some of the ideologically questionable but effective colonial institutions for a transitional period. Shastri wrote:

> The Panchayats will take some time before they begin to function. It would be better to ginger up the mukhias, at least during the interval. The activities of the various parties who are trying to encourage lawlessness is on the increase. The chaukidars and mukhias are not keeping the police informed of such activities. Mukhias might be instructed to be vigilant, and those who do not care to perform their duties satisfactorily should be replaced by others.[58]

The scale of expectations and desire for change had become a popular discourse against 'corruption', which also included the institution of *mukhiyagiri*. In December 1949, the Socialist Party of Moradabad district sent a letter to the UP government, submitting a resolution passed at the meeting of the party. Arguing for abolishing the institution of the *mukhiya*, it called them police agents whose removal would help end corruption.[59] In August 1950, the home minister of UP held a meeting with the inspector general of police and all other director inspector generals of police to discuss the law-and-order situation in UP.[60] Among other issues, it again addressed the necessity of *mukhiyas* and the formation of new *panchayats*. The general opinion was that although *mukhiyas* were not as effective as before, they were still helpful to the police and their continuation was necessary. Without *mukhiyas*, there would be considerable dislocation in police work in the villages. It reconsidered the earlier suggestion that the presidents of the *gaon sabhas* (village councils) or *panchayats* may be appointed as *mukhiyas*. The meeting held that while in some villages it might work well, in others it might lead to further difficulties and could generate an estrangement between the *panchayat* and the police. In the end, the meeting concluded that where the district magistrate and the superintendent of police would consider it fit, the presidents or members of the *gaon sabhas* could serve as *mukhiyas*. But these appointments would be liable to removal if they failed in their duties and would not get relaxations in rules applicable to everybody else. It only highlights the tension between the law-and-order establishment of UP and the newly found local democracy of a newly independent India.

By 1951, discussions of the 'future of *Mukhiyagiri* system' were still gathering pace in government circles.[61] The state home secretary issued a letter to all divisional commissioners and selected district magistrates seeking their opinions. Their replies were almost unanimous. The majority of them held that it would be premature to abolish the *mukhiyagiri* system or change the existing system substantially. The main contention was that since the introduction of the new *panchayat*s was only recent, it was desirable to watch their development before attempting to do away with the 'old and well-tried institution' of the *mukhiya*s. The commissioners and magistrates held that despite individual weaknesses, this institution had 'stood the test of time' and was still of 'considerable use' to the local authorities in carrying out their day-to-day administration. There were only two dissenters – the district magistrates of Basti and Lucknow. The former was not dissenting at all. He opined that given that the available source of *mukhiya*s had dried up, it was difficult to secure suitable persons for appointments as *mukhiya*s under the existing system. He recommended that in the future, *sabhapati*s (chairman or head) of *gaon panchayat*s (and not members) should be appointed as *mukhiya*s if found suitable. However, the district magistrate Lucknow, Harpal Singh, was strongly opposed to the institution of *mukhiya*s itself and called for its abolition. He favoured assigning the duties of *mukhiya*s to village *panchayat*s. He argued that the abolition of *mukhiya*s would undoubtedly remove a notorious source of corruption from the village. As the Panchayati Raj Act provided for the formation of sub-committees to deal with various subjects, a sub-committee may easily take up the duties of a *mukhiya*. He suggested that a provision be made in the rules to allow the district magistrate to appoint a chairman of such a sub-committee from the most suitable *panch* (member of a *panchayat*) or *sarpanch* (head of a *panchayat*). As the institution of the *mukhiya* was a subject of the CrPC, the district magistrate Lucknow further suggested that consequential amendments in the CrPC and the MGO would not be difficult. He further suggested amending the rules to enable essential duties for quick intelligence-gathering about serious crimes and other incidents and should be assigned to the proposed sub-committee under the available Panchayati Raj Act. However, the home secretary contended that the majority opinion was sound and that until a sufficiently solid and healthy alternative emerged, it was better to keep the 'pillars' of local administration intact. Therefore, according to the home secretary, the existing system could not be considered superfluous until a new system had replaced it.

The local District Congress Committees were also not very comfortable with the institution of *mukhiya*s. In a letter written in April 1951, the

District Congress Committee of Muzaffarnagar forwarded a resolution to the UP government.[62] It was passed at a meeting of the Jansath Tehsil Congress Committee and recommended the abolition of the *mukhiyagiri* system and suggested entrusting the duties of a *mukhiya* to the president of the *panchayat*. Such ideas did not find favour with the sitting administration, however. The district magistrate of Muzaffarnagar reacted to the resolution in a largely negative way.[63] He gave several reasons for his opposition to the idea of entrusting the duties of a *mukhiya* to the president or member of the *gaon panchayats*. According to him, *mukhiyagiri* was an old and tried system while the *gaon panchayat* was a very new institution and hence entrusting the duties of a *mukhiya* to the *gaon panchayat* in any form was likely to dislocate the village intelligence system. Also, the *gaon sabhas* strictly fell within the purview of the judicial administration, and the *mukhiyas* appointed from the members of the *gaon sabhas* were likely to be less responsive to the executive administration. The residents of the *sabhas* were elected on party lines and consequently, in some cases, were found to command no influence at all, a feature essential for being a *mukhiya*. It highlights the muddled institutional logic that an intelligence gatherer did not need influence. These remarks by the district magistrate of Muzaffarnagar reflected how the local administration viewed the *mukhiya* as 'one of their own' and as sharply distinct from 'party politics' in a newly democratised system.

The district magistrate Muzaffarnagar further argued that given some *gaon sabhas* comprised of more than one village, the *pradhans* or presidents of such *sabhas* when appointed as *mukhiyas* would not be able to perform their duties as a resident *mukhiya* in all the villages simultaneously. The only way to involve popular opinion in the appointment of *mukhiyas* was to amend the rules to make a consultation with *gaon sabhas* compulsory. There was a provision in section 22 of the Panchayati Raj Act where a *gaon panchayat* could recommend the appointment or dismissal of a *mukhiya*; so the district magistrate was merely emphasising a possible administrative tactic already available in the Panchayati Raj Act to deal with the issue at hand.

Faced with the necessity to please both the administration and the local Congress or other parties, the institution of *mukhiyagiri* was bound to become a confused institution that could not last much longer. In February 1953, the senior superintendent of police and the district magistrate of Allahabad raised some fresh concerns. They informed the home secretary that the office of the *mukhiya* had become redundant in the existing set-up since the new *panchayat*s started functioning. The *mukhiya* had begun to work as a 'tout', a peddler of information loyal to none in the new circumstances. With an elected *sabhapati* of the *gram sabha* in practically every village, the raison d'être of the office of the *mukhiya* had disappeared altogether. They further recommended that the government should take steps to give more prestige to the *sabhapati* rather than nourishing a functionary who had now become a 'misfit'. They added that this was why the collection of revenues was no longer entrusted to *lambardars*[64] in the new system. The police officers and district magistrates urged the home secretary and others to invite fresh views on this subject.

In his response, the home secretary only reminded government officials that while discussing the matter a few years ago, the minister for local self-governance had observed:

> I don't think that Gaon President or any other member should be appointed as Mukhiya. The experiment if any, may be tried with any public man of good repute, one who is neither the president nor a member of the panchayat.[65]

A year later, the home secretary was still wary of the idea of tampering with the institution of *mukhiya*s.[66] Given the discussion that the issue had generated, he felt some pressure and conceded that if 'an experiment has to be made, perhaps the Inspector General of Police must be advised to select a few districts of villages for trying other methods in place of the old ones'.[67] He also floated the idea that it might be worthwhile to ask the Village Defence Societies (VDS) to select five or ten persons to replace the *muhkiya*s potentially. As an alternative, after informally consulting the leading members of the VDS, the district magistrate may be asked to select one person for one year to start with. The decision was left to the home minister of UP, while the home secretary of UP expressed that he had no problems with either of these recommendations. A month later, the additional secretary followed up on the issue.[68] He stated that the inspector general of police had suggested that the experiment regarding the appointment of *mukhiya*s from among a panel selected by the VDS, a remnant of the war years, should be first tried in the districts of Meerut, Muzaffarnagar (as there were complaints from the Socialist Party from these districts), Bareilly, Bijnor, Allahabad, Jalaun, Banaras, Deoria, Sitapur and Faizabad. He proposed including the Pratapgarh district in the villages selected for this experiment as 'desired' by the home minister.

The additional secretary noted that, presumably, the experiment would run for a period of one year.

In May 1955, the UP government abolished the institution of the *mukhiya* despite administrative opposition and official discussions that lasted for some years.[69] Despite numerous deliberations, the UP government was convinced that the idea of retaining the institution of the *mukhiya* created further complications and confusion and did not yield any results. So, the UP Congress government abolished it. The institution of the *mukhiya* in UP, originally established for the North-Western Provinces and Oudh by the then lieutenant governor and chief commissioner on 19 January 1895, finally came to an end after a career of 61 years.

The bureaucratic discussions around the local institution of the *mukhiya* offer some critical insights. *Mukhiyagiri*, during its existence, was a significant aspect of the Indian leviathan until 1955. Also, attitudes of suspicion were inherent in not only the colonial administration but also in the post-independence Congress government and the bureaucracy of UP. Official discussions around the institution of the *mukhiya* demonstrate that the provincial government was anxious or rather uncomfortable with too much democratisation. It was unsure of its capacity to negotiate or coordinate renewed differences of caste, class and property that emerged with the arrival of independence and the corresponding expectations of social and political transformation. Though the institution of the *mukhiya* was supposed to be for local governance, it was primarily a central aspect of local surveillance and security. The administrative communication discussed earlier points to the exceptional and indispensable character of the institution of the *mukhiya* for the UP administration. The province of UP had to deal with an unignorable conundrum. On the one hand, post-independence communal and sectarian violence, Rashtriya Swayamsevak Sangh (RSS) activities, dacoits, robbers, and so on, compelled the state to maintain this institution. On the other hand, the legacy of Gandhi's *gram sabhas* or *panchayats*, the ideology of social welfare of the Congress and a new political scenario that demanded the inclusion of Indians in the decision-making process urged the Congress government to do away with it.

Therefore, the institution of the *mukhiya* was supposed to be the eyes and ears of the administration in every village. Emphasis on local modes of government since the days of the colonial company-state is brought to our attention by recent works of scholars such as James Jaffe. Jaffe's study allows us to appreciate the trajectory of local governance institutions in India, from *panchayat*s as judiciary forums to *panchayat*s imagined as an institution of village and municipal governance. We know that these 'local governance' *panchayat*s in the second half of the nineteenth century were not representative because they were mainly comprised of 'respectable' Indians who often belonged to the upper castes. Local British officers appointed these 'respectable' Indians, educating them in the art of western-style government.

During the Royal Commission of Decentralisation in 1908, both the British and Indians lauded the institution of the *panchayat* as the potential site for the growth of civil society in India. Application of imported British ideas of liberalism in India was often confused with suspicion towards the local population. The British administration did not trust the uneducated Indian masses and primarily relied on either western-educated men of distinction or the propertied caste and class. It appears that during the late colonial period, a time of high nationalism, the colonial state used such a civil society with the aim of nation-building – in other words, to neutralise anti-colonial state attitudes by making the local population understand the virtues of the British administration and concern through such men of 'distinction' and 'repute'. Jaffe urges us to understand the nature of such a civil society as opposed to the existing understandings. Such a civil society neither fell into the very recent theoretical accounts of civil society nor the one proposed by scholars such as Partha Chatterjee, who further suggests the notion of a political society as distinct from the western ideas of civil society. Rather, it should be understood in its historical context as indicating a specific set of conservative institutions based not only upon an idea of progress but, more specifically, upon the rule of law, the right to private property and the importance of elite participation in governance.[70] Different leaders had different opinions on the potential of these local bodies. For example, both Gandhi and Ambedkar had strong views on the institution of the *panchayat*. Whilst Gandhi saw it as a unique way of democracy operating through these micro-republics called *panchayat*s, Ambedkar saw it as a tool of caste oppression and, therefore, undemocratic and anti-liberal.

Conclusion

Information-gathering about life, people, issues and events in the countryside was an essential exercise in maintaining quotidian public order in UP. The basic structure of the government in post-independence UP was not starkly different from the recent colonial set-up. Given that the bureaucratic system was carried over from the colonial period, it too followed an administrative ambition based on maintaining a world of knowers and the known. Information-gathering at local levels through *mukhiyas* and *chowkidars* was a vital arrangement in this regard. This chapter has pointed out that *mukhiyas* and *chowkidars* did maintain routine surveillance at the village level. While the *mukhiyas* did not fit into the political calculations of the new government, *chowkidars* became an unnecessary, uneconomic and inefficient burden on the government. Such institutions were prominently perceived as the remnants of the colonial order and were invaluable for the administration but needed repackaging and further indigenisation to meet the demands of the 'new' emerging postcolonial public order. At face value, these changes could be seen as the necessary labour pains for the birth of a postcolonial order that could unsuspectingly utilise the same set of colonial institutions but with an invigorated legitimacy. However, in reality, the postcolonial masters were perpetually unsure of their power, and hence compulsively driven to mask the expressions of their authority in pursuits such as the disciplining and control of citizens. The creation of repackaged colonial institutions, based on presumptuous knowledge, was an unpredictable collision between ambitions and necessities. The ambitions of the postcolonial order were not immediately transparent to itself, which legally weaponised the new-found freedom against its citizens. Control became the priority of the postcolonial state in a conception of sovereignty that operated by regulating potential threats to the new order.

The new *panchayats* that saw the abolition of *mukhiyas* were calibrated to undoubtedly serve the provincial government in normalising its governmental discourse and decisions among the rural population. The new village constables replaced the underpaid, illiterate, overburdened and unreliable *chowkidars*. In both cases, the arrival of the postcolonial state was declared by making certain administrative facelifts, thus highlighting the powerful and uncomfortable continuities between the colonial and postcolonial state. These initial administrative decisions by the UP government were as crucial as the initial moves of a chess game. It would facilitate the underlying complicity between the colonial and the postcolonial order. The new government aspired to become the dominant protagonist in determining political and administrative possibilities, and it required some course of action to deal with them.

A narrative of sovereign anxiety is reflected in the administrative communication on the *chowkidar*s and *mukhiya*s. There was often a contradiction in the broader anti-colonial politics of the Congress that preached *swaraj* and freedom and the realities of governance on the ground, which were complicated. The seduction of surveillance and policing of the village continued the attitude and rationality of the colonial predecessor. The citizens did not trust the police, but the administration also faced challenges in establishing a democratic relationship with them. As noted in this chapter, many would frequently refer to 'changed times' or 'independent India', but none had any idea how to decolonise administrative power and authority. The provincial government, officers of the police, and magistrates did not always agree on the relevance of such local institutions.

Local policing institutions and figures of authority strengthened and supported the colonial state and boosted its confidence by assuring that it could know and therefore control and regulate everything. In the postcolonial scenario, new political obligations led to administrative confusion over such institutions. Official efforts to discuss these institutions highlight the postcolonial anxiety that arose partially from the incomprehension of their precise utility and partially from a political suspicion of them. However, the quick 'abolition' and rebranding of the same institutions point out that the postcolonial state lacked a mature democratic imagination and did not know any better. The rebranding of these two institutions replenished governmental power that could not do away with the surveillance and policing of its citizens in the countryside.

Notes

1. See File No. 380/1887, Box No. 52, List No. 28a, Police Block, Uttar Pradesh State Archives (UPSA); also see Kaushik Roy, *War, Culture and Society in Early Modern South Asia, 1740–1849* (London and New York: Routledge, 2011), p. 67.

2. See File No. 380/1887, Box No. 52, List no. 28a, Police Block, UPSA; File No. 84. Box 74, List 2, Dept. XIII, Varanasi Regional Archive (VRA).

3. Aparajita Mukhopadhyay, 'Wheels of Change Impact of Railways on Colonial North Indian Society 1855–1920' (PhD thesis, University of London, 2013), p. 97.

4. See J.B. Thomson, *Report on the Administration of the Police of the North-Western Provinces and Oudh for the Year ending 31st Dec 1897* (Allahabad: NWP and Oudh Government Press, 1898), pp. 34a–40a; also see A.C. Turner,

Census of India, 1931: United Provinces of Agra and Oudh. vol. XVIII, Pt. 1, Report (Allahabad: The Government Press, 1933), pp. 403, 436.

5. Kaushik Roy, 'Race and Recruitment in the Indian Army: 1880–1918', *Modern Asian Studies* 47, no. 4 (2013): 1341, 1343.

6. UPSA, File 85/1948, *Police Reorganisation Committee Report UP, 1948.*

7. George Henry Mildmay Ricketts, *Extracts from the Diary of a Bengal Civilian in 1857–59: And Further Notes of Service and Experiences from 1849 to 1879 in Bengal, Punjab and the United Provinces* (1913), p. 109.

8. L.M. Morshead, *Police Administration Report for the Lower Provinces of Bengal for the Year 1909* (Calcutta: Bengal Secretariat Press, 1909).

9. Rajwinder Kaur Dhillon, 'Colonial Legal Institutions and Their Impact upon Indigenous Practices in Bengal, 1860–1914' (PhD thesis, Edinburg University, 2012); David A. Campion, 'Watchmen of the Raj: The United Provinces Police and the Dilemmas of Colonial Policing in British India' (PhD dissertation, University of Virginia, 2002); Michael Silvestri, 'The Dirty Work of Empire: Policing, Political Violence and Public Order in Colonial Bengal, 1905–1947' (PhD dissertation, Columbia University, 1998).

10. *Police (Bird) Committee Report* (Calcutta: Bengal Government Press, 1838), p. 17.

11. Anonymous, 'The Village Watch in Bengal: Or a Century of Abortive Reform', *Calcutta Review* (1885): 109.

12. *Police (Bird) Committee Report* (1838), p. 14

13. 'Statement of Object and Reasons for Acts Passed in 1870' in L/PJ/5/105; also see A Chaukidari Manual with the Village Chaukidari Act, 1870 (Bengal Act VI of 1870) and the Bengal Village Chaukidari Act, 1871 (Bengal Act I of 1871): as modified up to the 1 January 1916, compiled by the Honourable Mr H. Wheeler.

14. See Judicial No. 13D, dated 14 September 1826, 'Establishment of a Subsidiary Police' in Bengal Judicial Letters, p. 11; 'The Origins & Causes of the Disturbances which occurred in the Town of Bareilly in 1816 in Consequence of the Introduction of the Chowkeedarry System', Bengal Judicial Consultations, dated 25 October 1816, p. 448.

15. Dhillon, 'Colonial Legal Institutions', p. 75.

16. Basudeb Chattopadhyay, *Crime and Control in Early Colonial Bengal 1770–1860* (Calcutta: KP Bagchi & Company, 2002); Ranjan Chakrabarti, *Terror, Crime and Punishment: Order and Disorder in Early Colonial Bengal 1800–1860* (Calcutta: Reader's Service, 2009); Chittabrata Palit, *Tensions in Bengal Rural Society: Landlords, Lanters and Colonial Rule 1830–1860* (Calcutta: Progressive Publishers, 1975); Anand Yang, *The Limited Raj: Agrarian Relations in Colonial India, Saran District, 1793–1920* (California: University of California Press, 1989).

17.   Crispin Bates, 'The Development of Panchayati Raj in India', in *Rethinking Indian Political Institutions*, ed. Crispin Bates and Subho Basu, pp. 169–184 (London: Anthem South Asian Studies, 2005).

18.   John McLane, *Land and Local Kingship in Eighteenth Century Bengal* (Cambridge: Cambridge University Press, 1993), p. 307.

19.   P.J. Musgrave, 'Landlords and Lords of the Land: Estate Management and Social Control in Uttar Pradesh 1860–1920', *Modern Asian Studies* 6, no. 3 (1972): 272.

20.   Yang, *The Limited Raj*, p. 230.

21.   See reports about the Rajshayee Division where the new Act was extended in more than 3,000 villages. Also see *Reports on the Administration of Police in the Lower Provinces of Bengal* for the Year 1873, 1877, 1878, 1879.

22.   D. Bandopadhyay, Saila K. Ghosh and Buddhadeb Ghosh, 'Dependency versus Autonomy: Identity Crisis of India's Panchayats', *Economic and Political Weekly* 38, no. 38 (20–26 September 2003): 3984.

23.   See Arun Mukherjee, *Crime and Public Disorder in Colonial Bengal* (Calcutta: K.P. Bagchi and Company, 1995).

24.   Julia Wardhaugh, 'The Jungle and the Village: Discourses on Crime and Deviance in Rural North India', *South Asia Research* 25, no. 2 (2005): 135.

25.   David Arnold, 'On the Road: A Social Itineration of India', *Contemporary South Asia* 22, no. 1 (2014): 15.

26.   Ian Copland, *The British Raj and the Indian Princes: 1857–1930* (Bombay: Orient Longman, 1982).

27.   Clare Anderson, 'Convicts and Coolies: Rethinking Indentured Labour in the Nineteenth Century', *Slavery and Abolition: A Journal of Slave and Post-Slave Studies* 30, no. 1 (2009): 96–97.

28.   Rohan Deb Roy, 'Quinine, Mosquitos, and Empire: Reassembling Malaria in British India, 1890–1910', *South Asian History and Culture* 4, no. 1 (2013): 68.

29.   Shail Mayaram, 'Criminality or Community? Alternative Constructions of the Mev Narrative of Darya Khan', *Contributions to Indian Sociology* 25, no. 1 (1991): 61.

30.   Andrew J. Major, 'State and Criminal Tribes in Colonial Punjab: Surveillance, Control and Reclamation of the "Dangerous Classes"', *Modern Asian Studies* 33, no. 3 (1999): 661

31.   Anastasia Piliavsky, 'The Moghia Menace, or the Watch over Watchmen in British India', *Modern Asian Studies* 47, no. 3 (2013): 751–779.

32.   Ibid., p. 758.

33.   Ibid., p. 757; also see Chapter 1 in David Arnold, *Police Power and Colonial Rule, Madras 1859–1947* (Delhi: Oxford University Press, 1986).

34.   Piliavsky, 'The Moghia Menace', p. 759.

35. See Gyan Prakash, *Bonded Histories: Genealogies of Labor Servitude in Colonial India* (Cambridge: Cambridge University Press, 1990), p. 57.

36. Earlier, the responsible policeman for a particular village was sent on patrol or walks around a village or villages to assess the law-and-order situation. However, after the Rural Beat system came into existence, the policeman in charge of a village (which was his beat) was held officially responsible for any matter of public order in the respective village.

37. For a broader background discussion see, C.A. Bayly, *Empire and Information: Intelligence Gathering and Social Communication in India, 1780–1870* (New York: Cambridge University Press, 1996).

38. UPSA, File 85/1948, see *Police Reorganisation Committee Report 1948*.

39. Ibid.

40. UPSA, File 85/1948, p. 94, see Chapter X, 'Chaukidars and Village Policing' of the *Police Reorganisation Committee Report 1948*.

41. UPSA, File 85/1948, see *Police Reorganisation Committee Report 1948*.

42. UPSA, File 85/1948, p. 95, see Chapter X, 'Chaukidars and Village Policing' of the *Police Reorganisation Committee Report 1948*.

43. UPSA, File 85/1948, p. 96, see Chapter X, 'Chaukidars and Village Policing' of the *Police Reorganisation Committee Report 1948*.

44. The Police Reorganisation Committee (UP) 1948 when appointed consisted of Dr Sita Ram (chairman), Venkatesh Narayan Tivary (MLA), Nafisul Hasan (MLA), Ziauddin Ahmad (retired district and sessions judge), Vinayanand Pathak (IP), B.N. Jha (ICS), Rajeshwar Dayal (ICS), H.C. Mitchell (IP), and D.P. Kohli (IP and also acted as the secretary of the committee). Subsequently A.D. Pandit (ICS) was included in the committee on the retirement of Vinayanand Pathak and M.S. Mathur (IP) replaced H.C. Mitchell who was proceeding on long leave.

45. UPSA, File 85/1948, see Note by Messrs. M.S. Mathur, V.N. Tivary and Nafisul Hasan regarding village *chaukidars*, p. 99.

46. Ibid., p. 100.

47. Ibid., p. 101.

48. See *Dainik Vishwamitra* issue of 22 December 1948.

49. See *Jawala* issue of 24 December 1948.

50. See *Sanmarg* issue of 31 December 1948.

51. UPSA, Home (Criminal) File no. 749/49. Particularly see a letter dated May 1949 from Lal Bahadur Shastri, Minister Police to Home Secretary.

52. UPSA, Lucknow, Home (Criminal), File No. 749/49, Complaint against Mukhias and subsequent abolition of Mukhiagiri.

53. UPSA, Home (Criminal) File No. 749/49. Specifically see a Note from Home Secretary dated 16 May 1949.

54. For a broader discussion, see Crispin Bates and Subho Basu, *Rethinking Indian Political Institutions* (London: Anthem Press, 2005), especially Chapter 9 by Crispin Bates, 'The Development of Panchayati Raj in India', pp. 167–182.

55. UPSA, Home (Criminal) File No. 749/49. Specifically see a Note from Home Secretary dated 16 May 1949.

56. Ibid.

57. Ibid.

58. UPSA, Home (Criminal) File No. 749/49. Specifically see a Note from Lal Bahadur Shastri dated 7 June 1949.

59. Letter to UP government from Socialist Party, Moradabad, dated 9 December 1949.

60. An extract note in the file from Home Police, File No. 260/50 regarding DIGs conference held by Home Minister Police, dated 24 August 1950. The meeting took place on 22 August 1950.

61. UPSA, Home (Criminal) File No. 749/49. Specifically see a Note by Home Secretary dated 2 March 1951 titled 'Future of the Mukhiagiri System'.

62. See Main File 749/9, Serial Number 43, extract from letter from District Congress Committee Muzaffarnagar no. 603 dated 25 April 1951.

63. See Main File 749/9, Serial Number 44, reply of DM Muzaffarnagar to the Demi official letter dated 12 April 1951 at Slip Z.

64. A *lambardar* was the headman of a village or a village officer, a very important link between the collector and the village community to recover land revenue, cess and taxes.

65. A note from Home Secretary UP dated 28 July 1953.

66. A note from Home Secretary UP dated 27 July 1954.

67. Ibid.

68. A note from Additional Secretary UP dated 24 August 1954.

69. The institution of *mukhiyas*/*mukhiyagiri* was abolished vide a Government Order No. 1114/VI-749/1949 dated 2 May 1955.

70. James Jaffe, *The Ironies of Colonial Governance* (Cambridge: Cambridge University Press, 2015), p. 9.

Conclusion

The management of public order thrives on a two-pronged approach of the state. One sustains the narrative of its necessity, and the second involves strategies and tactics that maintain it. These strategies involve violence of various kinds and range from the spectacular to the quotidian. Across scholarship on colonial India, emphasis is laid on the spectacular. The book began with a discussion on a similar premise, and as it progressed, it began to move away from it and showed that the state of exception in colonial India established itself in an order. It was first institutionalised and then normalised in the everyday discourse of the colonial state. To make sense of colonial violence, its form must be understood. The colonial state did resort to exemplary and spectacular violence, as shown in the discussion on Ghadar, Jallianwala Bagh, the Defence of India Act and the Rowlatt Bills in the first chapter. Another set of examples from the United Provinces (UP) followed in the second chapter, where the provincial government, after 1937, frequently invoked section 144 of the Code of Criminal Procedure (CrPC), instituted curfews, and defended *lathi* charges and police firing on protestors. The understanding is complicated with the arrival of provincial ministries, where Indians became politically responsible for governing many aspects of their lives. The career of public-order laws like section 144 CrPC, curfews and police firing saw not only growth but a renewed force that became increasingly intolerant to political opposition. Opportunities for the decolonisation of the colonial order ended in reifying it. This is evident in the second chapter, where a discussion on the Kanpur labour strikes and the Madh-e-Sahaba controversy took place.

In UP, the Congress ministries felt it necessary to resort to police repression of its citizens. Provincial ministries could not escape the tropes of violence deployed by the colonial administration. Chapter 2 is instructive in understanding the perception of law and order amongst nationalist stalwarts such as Jawaharlal Nehru and G.B. Pant. Public-order laws at once became convenient for the provincial government to regulate political opposition. Three forms of violence of law can be noted in the career of the state in the early twentieth century.

Peter Budge's story exposed that state violence does not have to be spectacular all the time. The state's institutions and officials conduct the 'other' violence of law on its citizens with little regard either for the correct procedure or the liberty of the citizens. The facade of ordered functioning of state institutions (law and order) was marred by overwork and a lack of interest, proper information sharing and proper training of its officials. A general attitude of carelessness guided the legal bureaucracy. The force of law was utilised more as a tool of repression than to provide justice and was weakened by the chaotic order within these institutions. While the state argued that there was chaos on the street and invoked public-order laws to control it, its functioning did not exhibit order. Its vulnerabilities, inefficiency and ineffectiveness are laid bare in the fourth and the fifth chapters, where non-state individuals wielded more authority than the state. To wrest authority back for itself, the state resorted to extraordinary policies, going as far as sub-contracting sovereign violence to vigilantes. Issuing of guns to 'reliable villagers' and the abolishing of *chowkidari* and *mukhiyagiri* only to replace them with similar local policing institutions outline the strategies of the emerging postcolonial state to maintain order. The discussion across chapters identifies three forms of violence: the spectacular, the quotidian and the ones guided by the state's overt and covert policing strategies. The state felt vulnerable and was chaotic in its approach. Close attention to the working of the law-and-order administration outlines a narrative of chaos to deflect attention from sovereign vulnerabilities.

The book investigated how law was used as a tool of governance in late colonial and early postcolonial India, with particular reference to the invocation of states of exception or simply extraordinary laws. The question is closely related to another issue, the creation of specific 'problem categories' to whom the normal process of law did not apply and represented a legalised and permanent state of exception. With regard to both questions, the book has examined events and incidents that saw the invocation of key public-order laws and found consistency in perspectives across the colonial–postcolonial divide. Chapters 4 and 5 have shown that bureaucrats in independent India were just as obsessed with maintaining public order or 'peace and tranquillity' as the colonial administration was. The events and incidents discussed in this book were diverse in terms of the political context and the analytical angle involved. However, a certain overall pattern emerged, highlighting an important but subtle difference between the kind of situations that lead to the invocation of extraordinary legislation and the nature of the 'exceptional categories' of people or problem categories. To what extent the former (exceptional laws) could sustain itself without the latter's existence (problem categories) is another question that requires answers.

With the advent of the First World War and the Ghadar mutiny plot, as Chapter 1 has shown, the necessity for the invocation and promulgation of extraordinary laws like the Defence of India Rules and the Rowlatt Bills became acute. The introduction of wartime measures like the Defence of India Rules ushered in an era of legal exceptionalism in a colonial situation. It set a precedent for making the Rowlatt Bills possible. While the war was an international affair, the colonial government took the opportunity to lump two enemy categories together to expand the scope of the problem categories to which the normal operations of the law could no longer apply. The enemies of the Raj outside, like the Germans, and the enemies of the Raj at home, such as the Bengali revolutionaries and the Ghadar Party, were in collusion with each other and posed an existential threat to internal peace. They were no longer simply a criminal or even a law-and-order problem but 'enemies' of the sovereign government in Carl Schmitt's totalising sense. The Ghadar Party's avowal to be the 'enemy of the British Raj in India' added weight to such totalising claims of the colonial administration. The Rowlatt Act highlighted the awareness of the colonial administration that revolutionary organisations and the growing anti-colonial nationalist movement in India could only be suppressed by ignoring the usual protocols of the due process of justice. In principle, it made a clear distinction between its enemies and friends. In reality, this distinction was not so clear. The Rowlatt Bills had the potential to book anti-colonial agitators, whether they were part of a revolutionary organisation or not. At this moment, the specificity of an enemy category was given up, and the general population was declared as, at least potentially, a hotbed of revolutionaries. It legitimised the colonial strategy of emphasising legal distinctions between its friends and its enemies. Eventually, the Raj declared that the much-trumpeted rule of law – which was so central to its self-justification – applied only to friends, while when dealing with enemies, the administration did not have to necessarily follow the rule of law.

In consequence, during the First World War and its immediate aftermath, the colonial administration normalised legal exceptionalism by making extraordinary laws permanent. Maintaining order, peace and tranquillity, preventing civil war, and dealing with revolutionary violence were some of the justifications cited by the colonial administration for such decisions. The Jallianwala Bagh massacre proved that even peaceful gatherings of otherwise unspecified groups of people could be declared as standing outside the law. It also highlighted colonial rage and the growing impatience against the difficult-to-discipline Indians.

The colonial administration continuously operated by identifying specific problem categories and then pushed such groups beyond the purview of ordinary law(s). Thuggee serves as an excellent early example and offers a paradigmatic case for the workings of colonial legality in this regard. Later, 'revolutionaries', '*satyagrahis*', 'habitual offenders', 'bad characters', 'the illiterate masses' and trade unionists populated an ever-increasing list of problem categories. Such administrative moves were always aimed at maintaining dominance over the population. By the use of extraordinary legislation, the late colonial state in India managed to distance itself from an active responsibility towards its subjects. It managed to set a clear boundary for what was allowed in terms of political protest and what was not.

Law-and-order situations were an administrative question for colonialism and a challenge of crisis management. Leaving aside the ability to use a declaration of a state of exception as a reaffirmation of sovereign power, a whole range of tactical moves could be observed. The interwar period witnessed excessive and frequent use of pre-emptive laws like section 144 CrPC. Preventive detentions and curfews became routine. The broader strategy adopted by the colonial law-and-order machinery and its repeated resort to extraordinary legislation had more to do with instituting a rule of fear than the proper application of the law. Such governmentality highlights the vulnerability and fragility of the colonial order. Although it was not necessarily intended as such at the time, the passing of the Government of India Act, 1919, marked the beginning of the long process of decolonisation with the introduction of 'diarchy'. The process continued with the passing of the Government of India Act, 1935, devolving more powers to provinces and invigorating the Indian political scene with elections and the possibility of representation. It offered an opportunity to its subjects to share limited sovereignty by encouraging and strengthening provincial politics and promised an extension of liberal constitutional legality. However, ground realities were often different. In the late 1930s, extraordinary legislation was frequently used as a tool to depoliticise dissent. Indigenous political parties, including the Congress, by no means always rejected such colonial manoeuvres. It sometimes contested political dissent and sometimes affirmed it. The language of legality was involved in such choices. The discourse of public order emphasised human rights and notions of legal citizenship that were sustained through other special categories when the law was pre-emptively used. Extraordinary legislation got normalised whilst also getting reintegrated into the rule-of-law myth. Draconian preventive measures like banning people from public places or police firing often remained embedded in a nominally 'normal' legal framework, typically tied to 'ordinary' laws like section 144 CrPC. The discursive link between legality and legal exceptionalism enabled the colonial administration to maximise its might and derive a certain moral legitimacy for itself.

Confrontational situations provided justification to the colonial government to invoke public-order laws and impose curfews or resort to police firing to enhance its administrative calculations. However, it defeated its principle of maintaining state impartiality over competing political groups on numerous occasions and facilitated administrative intervention in community lives. It played out in different ways in the incidents discussed in Chapter 2. For example, the issue of the Mazdoor Sabha and the mill strikes of Kanpur in the 1930s and the Madh-e-Sahaba issue in Lucknow had to face the invocation of section 144 CrPC, curfews and police firing. In these cases, the justification for police violence progressed from a situation of disorder that 'necessitated' state violence in achieving the ideal of justice as law's end, that is, violence begets violence. Both the colonial government and the dominant Congress ministry in UP responded to challenges of public order by imposing a violent legal culture upon all the indirect stakeholders in the conflicts in Kanpur and Lucknow.

The provincial Congress ministry rejected the social consensus that criticised police violence and the imposition of extraordinary laws like section 144 CrPC and curfews. The logic of 'maintaining public peace and tranquillity' for the Congress government in UP – and supported by prominent nationalist leaders such as Jawaharlal Nehru, Mohandas Gandhi and Govind Ballabh Pant, although from different perspectives – during acute situations of anti-government mass mobilisations further safeguarded the self-sufficiency of these laws.

The discussion in Chapter 2 highlighted that the Congress ministries in the provinces where anti-colonial mobilisation was spearheaded by 'nationalists' of the ruling party itself also justified pre-emptive public-order legislation. Right from the moment they were involved in provincial self-governance, the nationalist elite-in-waiting normalised and prescribed to populations the 'correct' way of behaving by invoking extraordinary legislation. Its invocation unified legal norms and political facts. The late colonial state, working in tandem with Congress nationalists, fine-tuned the argument over the use of extraordinary legislation, frequently arguing that 'facts on the ground' made it impossible to maintain order through the use of ordinary laws. Though the colonial administration emphasised its impartial role in the justice system, it and the Congress ministries in the 1930s criminalised mass politics in the name of a political rationality, where 'public order' came to be thought of as a priori to any political discussion.

Across chapters, the book has highlighted the use of laws like section 144 CrPC in cases of intense political confrontation. The story of Peter Budge in Chapter 3 highlighted the careless attitude of the late colonial and early postcolonial governments towards the civil liberties of ordinary individuals. It posed questions on the fictitious nature of the colonial bureaucracy, which relied heavily on paperwork. Individuals like Budge and possibly many others could figuratively be brushed under the carpet if they did not have any political value. It raised some questions regarding the nature of paperwork that sustained the colonial bureaucracy. Low-level officials not entirely at home with switching between English, Hindi and Urdu often made mistakes that led to blunders and miscarriage of justice. Right until the end of colonialism in India, administrative practice defended itself with claims of a de-politicised bureaucracy, impartial judiciary, rule-bound norms and very dutiful police. Ironically, all these claims become questionable by how Budge was arrested and then made to suffer a lengthy ordeal of incarceration. Significantly, Budge's case was entirely run and managed by

Indians, right from the invocation of extraordinary legislation and arresting the accused to the transfer of his case between various offices, his detention in jail and his subsequent presentation (or non-presentation) before a court. The judges appointed to hear the case were all Indians. In addition to the police, as Budge's case revealed, even judges were careless in following the rules. Such moments dismantle the usual separation between the coloniser and the colonised. The binary does not offer much analysis or a nuanced understanding of Indians' participation in the structures of governance in general and legal governmentality in particular, even when the process of decolonisation was well underway.

The most striking conclusions about the decolonisation of public order in India come to the fore with the postcolonial initiatives activated right after independence. Expectations of independence and freedom from colonialism and imperialism put tremendous pressure on the successors of the colonial administrators. Despite best intentions, these initiatives to bring administrative practice in line with the new reality of independence did not achieve much – as demonstrated throughout Chapter 5. The basic formula of managing populations and the art of colonial legal governmentality was challenging to do away with. Postcolonial law-and-order management retained the framework as well as the catalogue of colonial policies of control. When reconsidering old colonial institutions like *chowkidari* and *mukhiyagiri*, the administration and the political elite became entangled between the rhetoric of independence based on the promise of better times to come and the usefulness of a colonial apparatus for continuing the dominance of the state in the lives of its citizens. At places, administrators had to acknowledge the effectiveness of the colonial way of managing disorder. Discussions around new laws to deal with 'habitual offenders' or 'bad characters', who could not be dealt with under the ordinary sections of the CrPC, serve as the best example.

State suspicion towards the citizens of a new India was revealed when the issuing of guns to every village to protect them against dacoits was under consideration. Ordinary villagers were deemed unreliable to be issued a gun. The focus on 'dacoits' served as a significant reminder of how much the new administrative thinking was still preoccupied with identifying specific legal problem categories in advance to subject them to extra-legal measures. The dacoits of the 1950s emerged as a familiar challenge that resembled the Thugs of the 1830s in this regard. In addition to issuing guns to 'reliable villagers', society was further militarised with the creation of quasi-military organisations like the PRD. Its scope and composition blurred the boundaries between the state and society.

After deliberations, the nascent postcolonial state realised that it had to move away from maintaining public order to managing chaos. The Congress was at the helm in various provinces or states and was often involved with criminal elements at the local level. A significant shift back to normality occurred when the new (and old) problem categories listed by the postcolonial state in India – 'social pests' like bandits, goondas, habitual offenders, bad characters and illiterate masses – were once again made the subjects of extraordinary law and were regarded as the enemies of the state. The attitude was not altogether dissimilar to that of the colonial state, but the tone was reformative. Hence, as outlined in this book, the bureaucratic apparatus in postcolonial India continued colonial instructions and preserved the potential for state repression in the times to come.

The study of the process of the decolonisation of public order in India has a bearing on contemporary debates about the continuing practice of the Indian state to declare states of exception and to use extraordinary colonial-era laws to deny citizens their rights in the twenty-first century. Such a repressive vision of legal governmentality in India is reflected in various laws dealing with terrorism, sedition and tribal and secessionist insurgency. Recent debates around the question of repressive police action and the administrative response that followed the cases of land acquisition by the state governments for corporates, urban protests that took place regarding the issue of women's safety and rape in India, nationwide protests in India in the wake of everyday atrocities against Dalits and 'fake' encounters have once again brought to our attention the colonial character of the law in India. Furthermore, the narrative that normalises state violence in the mind of most Indian citizens when it comes to maintaining public order, peace and tranquillity in 'disturbed areas' of the 'Red Corridor', the North-Eastern states of India and in the state of Jammu and Kashmir demands careful attention. The idea of citizenship that has emerged in contemporary India appears to be more in agreement with the repressive colonial tactics of dealing firmly with 'problem categories' of all classes, especially when it comes to maintaining the sovereignty of the Indian state, rather than citizens in a democratic self-determined nation. There is a continued significance of understanding colonial legal governmentality to make sense of politics in contemporary postcolonial societies like India.

Bibliography

Primary Sources

National Archives India, Delhi
Transfer lists no. 7, 8, 19, 20, 69, 71, 103, 106.

Uttar Pradesh State Archives, Lucknow
List no. 80, 81A, 82A, 83A, 83B, 84B, 86A, 78, 91B, 92A, 97A, 99, 100A.

British Library, India Office Records, London
File Series L/PJ/5, L/PJ/ 6, L/PJ/7, IOR/R/3/1, IOR/R/3/2, IOR/V/8, IOR/V11, IOR/V22, IOR/V24, IOR/V26, IOR/E4, MssEur E293.
Microfilms: SM15, SM48, SM179, SM209, SM104, SM77, SM52, SM45, SM60, SM94, SM147, SM164.

Books and Articles

Agamben, Giorgio. *Infancy and History: The Destruction of Experience*. London; New York: Verso, 1993.
———. *The Coming Community*. Minneapolis: University of Minnesota Press, 1993.
———. *Homo Sacer: Sovereign Power and Bare Life*. Stanford University Press, 1998.
———. *The Man without Content*. Meridian. Stanford, Calif: Stanford University Press, 1999.

———. *Means Without End: Notes on Politics*. Theory out of Bounds. University of Minnesota Press, 2000.

———. *The Open: Man and Animal*. Meridian. Stanford, Calif.: Stanford University Press, 2004.

———. *What Is an Apparatus? And Other Essays*. Meridian. Stanford University Press, 2009.

Agamben, G., and A. Kotsko. *The Use of Bodies*. Meridian. Stanford, CA: Stanford University Press, 2016.

Agamben, G., and K. Attell. *State of Exception*. Chicago; London: The University of Chicago Press, 2008.

Agamben, G., L. Chiesa and M. Mandarini. *The Kingdom and the Glory: For a Theological Genealogy of Economy and Government*. Meridian: Crossing Aesthetics. Stanford, CA: Stanford University Press, 2011.

Agamben, Giorgio, and Daniel Heller-Roazen. *Potentialities: Collected Essays in Philosophy*. Stanford, CA: Stanford University Press, 1999.

Ahmad, A. *In Theory: Classes, Nations, Literatures*. Cultural Studies. London: Verso, 1994.

Alam, M. *The Languages of Political Islam: India, 1200–1800*. London: Hurst & Company, 2004.

Alam, M., and S. Subrahmanyam. *The Mughal State, 1526–1750*. Oxford in India Readings: Themes in Indian History. New Delhi; Oxford: Oxford University Press, 2000.

Alavi, Hamza. 'India and the Colonial Mode of Production'. *Economic and Political Weekly* 10, no. 33/35 (1975): 1235–1262.

Ali, M.A. *Mughal India: Studies in Polity, Ideas, Society and Culture*. New Delhi: Oxford University Press, 2008.

Amin, S. *Event, Metaphor, Memory: Chauri Chaura*. New Delhi: Penguin Group, 2006.

———. *Conquest and Community: The Afterlife of Warrior Saint Ghazi Miyan*. New Delhi: Orient BlackSwan, 2015.

Ali, Amir. 'Evolution of Public Sphere in India'. *Economic and Political Weekly* 36, no. 26 (2001): 2419–2425.

An Account of the Ghadr Conspiracy, 1913–1915. Compiled by F.C. Isemonger and J. Slattery, Indian Police, Punjab. Lahore, Punjab: Printed by the Superintendent, Government Printing, 1919.

Anderson, Clare. *The Indian Uprising of 1857–8: Prisons, Prisoners and Rebellion*. London; New York; Delhi: Anthem Press, 2007.

Anderson, Michael. 'Islamic Law and the Colonial Encounter in British India'. *Reproductive Health Matters* 4, no. 8 (1996): 154–154.

Arendt, Hannah. *On Violence*. Boston, MA: Houghton Mifflin Harcourt, 1970.

———. *The Origins of Totalitarianism*. Harvest Book. New York: Houghton Mifflin Harcourt, 1973.

———. *Eichmann in Jerusalem: A Report on the Banality of Evil*. New York: Penguin Classics, 2006.

Arnold, D. 'The Police and Colonial Control in South India'. *Social Scientist* 4, no. 12 (1976): 3–16. doi:10.2307/3516332.

———. 'Labour Relations in a South Indian Sugar Factory 1937–1939'. *Social Scientist* 6, no. 5 (1977): 16–33. doi:10.2307/3520086.

———. 'The Armed Police and Colonial Rule in South India, 1914–1947'. *Modern Asian Studies* 11, no. 1 (1977): 101–125.

———. 'Looting, Grain Riots and Government Policy in South India 1918'. *Past and Present* 84, no. 1 (1979): 111–145. https://doi.org/10.1093/past/84.1.111.

———. 'Industrial Violence in Colonial India'. *Comparative Studies in Society and History* 22, no. 2 (1980): 234–255.

———. 'Sitarama Raju's Rebellion: A Response'. *Social Scientist* 13, no. 4 (1985): 44–49. doi:10.2307/3517517.

———. 'Cholera and Colonialism in British India'. *Past and Present*, no. 113 (1986): 118–151.

———. 'Disease, Rumor, and Panic in India's Plague and Influenza Epidemics, 1896–1919'. In *Empires of Panic*, 1st ed., edited by R. Peckham, pp. 111–30. Epidemics and Colonial Anxieties. Hong Kong: Hong Kong University Press, 2015.

———. *Toxic Histories: Poison and Pollution in Modern India*. Science in History. Cambridge: Cambridge University Press, 2016.

Asad, T. *Anthropology and the Colonial Encounter*. London: Ithaca Press, 1973.

Ashar, Meera. 'Decolonising What? Categories, Concepts and the Enduring "Not Yet"'. *Cultural Dynamics* 27, no. 2 (1 July 2015): 253–265. doi:10.1177/0921374015585231.

Attell, Kevin, 'Sovereignty, Law and Violence'. In *Giorgio Agamben: Beyond the Threshold of Deconstruction*, edited by Kevin Attell, pp. 125–166. New York: Fordham University Press, 2015.

Austin, G. *Working a Democratic Constitution: A History of the Indian Experience*. Oxford India Paperbacks. New Delhi; New York: Oxford University Press, 2003.

Āzād, A. *India Wins Freedom*. New York; London; Toronto: Longmans Green and Co., 1960.

Bagchi, J., and S. Dasgupta. *The Trauma and the Triumph: Gender and Partition in Eastern India.* The Trauma and the Triumph: Gender and Partition in Eastern India. Kolkata: Stree, 2003.

Bahadur, L. *The Muslim League: Its History, Activities and Achievements.* Lahore: Book Traders, 1979.

Bajpai, R. *Debating Difference: Group Rights and Liberal Democracy in India.* New Delhi: Oxford University Press, 2015.

Bamford, P.C. *Histories of the Non-Cooperation and Khilafat Movements.* Delhi: Deep Publications, 1974.

Banerjee, Abhijit, and Lakshmi Iyer. 'History, Institutions, and Economic Performance: The Legacy of Colonial Land Tenure Systems in India'. *American Economic Review* 95, no. 4 (2005): 1190–1213.

Banerjee Sumanta. 'Mediating between Violence and Non-Violence in the Discourse of Protest'. *Economic and Political Weekly* 45, no. 11 (2010): 35–40.

Bapu, Prabhu. *Hindu Mahasabha in Colonial North India, 1915–1930: Constructing Nation and History.* London; New York: Routledge, 2013.

Basu, A., and S. Roy. *Violence and Democracy in India.* Kolkata: Seagull Books, 2007.

Bataille, G., and R. Hurley. *The Accursed Share: An Essay on General Economy.* New York: Zone Books, 1993.

Baxi, U. *The Crisis of the Indian Legal System.* Alternatives in Development: Law. New Delhi: Vikas, 1982.

———. 'Kar Seva of the Indian Constitution? Reflections on Proposals for Review of the Constitution'. *Economic and Political Weekly* 35, no. 11 (2000): 891–895.

Baxi, U., and B.C. Parekh. *Crisis and Change in Contemporary India.* New Delhi: Sage Publications in association with the Book Review Literary Trust, 1995.

Bayly, C.A. *Rulers, Townsmen and Bazaars: North Indian Society in the Age of British Expansion, 1770–1870.* Cambridge: Cambridge University Press Archive, 1988.

———. *Indian Society and the Making of the British Empire.* Cambridge: Cambridge University Press, 1990.

———, ed. *The Raj: India and the British, 1600–1947.* London: National Portrait Gallery Publications, 1990.

———. *Empire and Information: Intelligence Gathering and Social Communication in India, 1780–1870.* Cambridge Studies in Indian History and Society. Cambridge: Cambridge University Press, 1999.

———. *Recovering Liberties: Indian Thought in the Age of Liberalism and Empire*. Cambridge; New York: Cambridge University Press, 2011.

Bender, J.C. *The 1857 Indian Uprising and the British Empire*. Cambridge: Cambridge University Press, 2016.

Bendersky, Joseph W. *Carl Schmitt: Theorist for the Reich*. Princeton, NJ: Princeton University Press, 1983.

Benjamin, Walter. *Walter Benjamin: Selected Writings: Volume 2, Part 1, 1927–1930*. Edited by Michael W. Jennings, Howard Eiland and Gary Smith. Cambridge, MA; London: The Belknap Press of Harvard University Press, 2005.

———. *Illuminations*. London: Random House, 2011.

Benjamin, W., and P. Demetz. *Reflections: Essays, Aphorisms, Autobiographical Writing*. New York: Schocken Books, 1986.

Benton, Lauren. 'Colonial Law and Cultural Difference: Jurisdictional Politics and the Formation of the Colonial State'. *Comparative Studies in Society and History* 41, no. 3 (1999): 563–588.

Bernstein, J. *Dawning of the Raj: The Life and Trials of Warren Hastings*. Chicago: Ivan R. Dee, 2000.

Bobbio, Tommaso. *Urbanisation, Citizenship and Conflict in India: Ahmedabad 1900–2000*. London; New York: Routledge, 2015.

Boehmer, E. *Empire, the National, and the Postcolonial, 1890–1920: Resistance in Interaction*. Oxford: Oxford University Press, 2005.

Booker, M.K. *Colonial Power, Colonial Texts: India in the Modern British Novel*. Ann Arbor, MI: University of Michigan Press, 1997.

Brass, P.R. *Factional Politics in an Indian State: The Congress Party in Uttar Pradesh*. Berkeley, CA; Los Angeles: University of California Press, 1965.

———. *Theft of an Idol: Text and Context in the Representation of Collective Violence*. Princeton Studies in Culture/Power/History. Princeton, NJ: Princeton University Press, 1997.

———. *The Production of Hindu–Muslim Violence in Contemporary India*. Jackson School Publications in International Studies. Seattle; London: University of Washington Press, 2005.

Breckenridge, C.A., and P. van der Veer. *Orientalism and the Postcolonial Predicament: Perspectives on South Asia*. New Cultural Studies. Philadelphia: University of Pennsylvania Press, 1993.

Bredekamp, Horst, Melissa Thorson Hause, and Jackson Bond. 'From Walter Benjamin to Carl Schmitt, via Thomas Hobbes'. *Critical Inquiry* 25, no. 2 (1999): 247–266.

Bridge, C. *Holding India to the Empire: The British Conservative Party and the 1935 Constitution*. South Asian Publications Series. New Delhi: Sterling Publishers, 1986.

Broomfield, J.H. *Elite Conflict in a Plural Society: Twentieth-Century Bengal*. Berkeley, CA; Los Angeles: University of California Press, 1968.

Brown, J.M. *Gandhi's Rise to Power: Indian Politics 1915–1922*. Cambridge South Asian Studies. London: Cambridge University Press, 1974.

Brown, Mark. 'Crime, Governance and the Company Raj: The Discovery of Thuggee'. *British Journal of Criminology* 42, no. 1 (2002): 77–95.

Butalia, Urvashi. *The Other Side of Silence: Voices from the Partition of India*. Durham, NC: Duke University Press, 2000.

Calarco, Matthew, and Steven DeCaroli. *Giorgio Agamben: Sovereignty and Life*. Stanford, CA: Stanford University Press, 2007.

Carroll, Lucy. 'Colonial Perceptions of Indian Society and the Emergence of Caste(s) Associations'. *Journal of Asian Studies* 37, no. 2 (1978): 233–250. doi:10.2307/2054164.

Chakrabarty, B. *The Partition of Bengal and Assam, 1932–1947: Contour of Freedom*. London: Taylor & Francis, 2004.

———. *Social and Political Thought of Mahatma Gandhi*. Routledge Studies in Social and Political Thought. London: Routledge, 2006.

Chakrabarty, D. *Rethinking Working-Class History: Bengal, 1890–1940*. Princeton Paperbacks. Princeton, NJ; Delhi: Princeton University Press, 2000.

———. *Habitations of Modernity: Essays in the Wake of Subaltern Studies*. Chicago: The University of Chicago Press, 2002.

———. *Provincializing Europe: Postcolonial Thought and Historical Difference*. Princeton Studies in Culture/Power/History. Princeton, NJ: Princeton University Press, 2009.

Chakrabarty, D., R. Majumdar and A. Sartori. *From the Colonial to the Postcolonial: India and Pakistan in Transition*. New Delhi: Oxford University Press, 2007.

Chakravarty, G. *The Indian Mutiny and the British Imagination*. Cambridge Studies in Nineteenth-Century Literature and Culture. Cambridge; New York: Cambridge University Press, 2005.

Chand, M. *Economic Problems in Indian Agriculture*. Bombay: Vora, 1950.

Chandavarkar, R. *Imperial Power and Popular Politics: Class, Resistance and the State in India, 1850–1950*. Cambridge Studies in Indian History and Society. Cambridge: Cambridge University Press, 1998.

———. *The Origins of Industrial Capitalism in India: Business Strategies and the Working Classes in Bombay, 1900–1940*. Cambridge: Cambridge University Press, 2002.

———. 'Customs of Governance: Colonialism and Democracy in Twentieth Century India'. *Modern Asian Studies* 41, no. 3 (2007): 441–470.

———. *History, Culture and the Indian City*. New York: Cambridge University Press, 2009.

Chandra, Bipan. 'Colonial India: British versus Indian Views of Development'. *Review (Fernand Braudel Center)* 14, no. 1 (1991): 81–167.

Chatterjee, P. *Nationalist Thought and the Colonial World: A Derivative Discourse*. ACLS Humanities E-Book. Minneapolis: University of Minnesota Press, 1986.

———. *The Politics of the Governed: Reflections on Popular Politics in Most of the World*. Leonard Hastings Schoff Lectures. New York: Columbia University Press, 2004.

———. *Lineages of Political Society: Studies in Postcolonial Democracy*. Cultures of History. New York: Columbia University Press, 2011.

Chatterji, J. *Bengal Divided: Hindu Communalism and Partition, 1932–1947*. Cambridge South Asian Studies. Cambridge: Cambridge University Press, 2002.

———. *The Spoils of Partition: Bengal and India, 1947–1967*. Cambridge Studies in Indian History and Society. New York: Cambridge University Press, 2007.

Christopher, A.J. 'Patterns of British Overseas Investment in Land, 1885–1913'. *Transactions of the Institute of British Geographers* 10, no. 4 (1985): 452–466. doi:10.2307/621891.

Comaroff, J., and J.L. Comaroff. *Law and Disorder in the Postcolony*. Chicago: The University of Chicago Press, 2007.

Copland, I., I. Mabbett, A. Roy, K. Brittlebank, and A. Bowles. *A History of State and Religion in India*. Routledge Studies in South Asian History. London: Routledge, Taylor & Francis, 2013.

Daechsel, M. 'Ẓālim Ḍākū and the Mystery of the Rubber Sea Monster: Urdu Detective Fiction in 1930s Punjab and the Experience of Colonial Modernity'. *Journal of the Royal Asiatic Society* 13, no. 1 (2003): 21–43.

———. *The Politics of Self-Expression: The Urdu Middleclass Milieu in Mid-Twentieth Century India and Pakistan*. Royal Asiatic Society Books. London; New York: Routledge, Taylor & Francis, 2006.

———. *Islamabad and the Politics of International Development in Pakistan*. Studies in International Planning History. Cambridge; New York: Cambridge University Press, 2015.

Dalton, D. *Mahatma Gandhi: Nonviolent Power in Action*. New York: Columbia University Press, 2012.

Darian-Smith, Eve, and Peter Fitzpatrick. *Laws of the Postcolonial*. Ann Arbor, MI: University of Michigan Press, 1999.

Das, Veena. *Life and Words: Violence and the Descent into the Ordinary*. Berkeley, CA: University of California Press, 2007.

Datta, U. *The Great Rebellion, 1857*. Calcutta: Seagull Books, 1986.

Davidson, A.I., G. Burchell, and M. Foucault. *On the Punitive Society: Lectures at the Collège de France, 1972–1973*. Michel Foucault, Lectures at the Collège de France. Basingstoke; New York: Palgrave Macmillan, 2015.

Derrida, J., and G. Anidjar. *Acts of Religion*. New York; London: Routledge, 2002.

Derrida, J., and G. Bennington. *The Beast and the Sovereign*. The Seminars of Jacques Derrida. Chicago; London: The University of Chicago Press, 2011.

Devji, Faisal. *The Impossible Indian: Gandhi and the Temptation of Violence*. London: Hurst Publishers, 2012.

Duara, P. *Decolonization: Perspectives from Now and Then*. Rewriting Histories. London; New York: Routledge, Taylor & Francis, 2004.

Dube, S. *Stitches on Time: Colonial Textures and Postcolonial Tangles*. E-Duke Books Scholarly Collection. Duke University Press, 2004.

'Endless Curfew-Raj?' *Economic and Political Weekly* 25, no. 2 (1990): 64–65.

Engineer, A. *Communal Riots in Post-Independence India*. Hyderabad: Sangam Books, 1991.

Engineer, A.A. *They Too Fought for India's Freedom: The Role of Minorities*. Sources of History Series. Gurgaon: Hope India Publications, 2006.

Epstein, J. *Scandal of Colonial Rule: Power and Subversion in the British Atlantic During the Age of Revolution*. Critical Perspectives on Empire. Cambridge: Cambridge University Press, 2012.

Fanon, F. *Studies in a Dying Colonialism*. Development Studies. London: Earthscan, 1965.

———. *Black Skin, White Masks*. Get Political. New York: Grove Press, 2008.

———. *Decolonizing Madness: The Psychiatric Writings of Frantz Fanon*, ed. Nigel Gibson. London: Palgrave Macmillan, 2014.

Fanon, F., and H. Chevalier. *A Dying Colonialism*. An Evergreen Book. New York: Grove Press, 1994.

Fanon, F., R. Philcox, H. Bhabha, and J.P. Sartre. *The Wretched of the Earth*. New York: Grove/Atlantic, 2007.

Farwell, B. *Armies of the Raj: From the Mutiny to Independence, 1858–1947*. New York: Norton, 1989.

Fazal, T. *Minority Nationalisms in South Asia*. Routledge South Asian History and Culture Series. London: Routledge, Taylor & Francis, 2013.

———. 'Nation-State' and Minority Rights in India: Comparative Perspectives on Muslim and Sikh Identities. Routledge Contemporary South Asia Series. London: Routledge, Taylor & Francis, 2014.

Fhlathuin, Maire ni. "'That Solitary Englishman": W.H. Sleeman and the Biography of British India'. Victorian Review 27, no. 1 (2001): 69–85.

Fischer-Tiné, Harald, and Michael Mann. Colonialism as Civilising Mission: Cultural Ideology in British India. London: Anthem Press, 2004.

———. Counterflows to Colonialism: Indian Travellers and Settlers in Britain, 1600–1857. Delhi: Permanent Black, 2006.

Fitzpatrick, Peter. Modernism and the Grounds of Law. Cambridge: Cambridge University Press, 2001.

———. The Mythology of Modern Law. Sociology of Law and Crime. London; New York: Routledge, Taylor & Francis, 2002.

———. Law as Resistance: Modernism, Imperialism, Legalism. Collected Essays in Law. Burlington, VT: Ashgate, 2008.

Foucault, Michel. Discipline and Punish: The Birth of the Prison. Peregrine Books. New York: Vintage Books, 1977.

———. The Birth of Biopolitics: Lectures at the Collège de France, 1978–1979. New York: Picador, 2010.

———. The History of Sexuality: An Introduction. Westminster: Knopf Doubleday Publishing Group, 2012.

———. The History of Sexuality, vol. 2: The Use of Pleasure. Westminster: Knopf Doubleday Publishing Group, 2012.

———. The Order of Things: An Archaeology of Human Sciences. New York: Vintage Books, 1994.

Foucault, M., A.I. Davidson, and G. Burchell. Security, Territory, Population: Lectures at the College De France, 1977–78. Michel Foucault, Lectures at the Collège de France. London: Palgrave Macmillan, 2007.

Foucault, M., and P. Rabinow. The Foucault Reader. Penguin Social Sciences. London: Penguin Books, 1991.

Foucault, M., P. Rabinow, and N.S. Rose. The Essential Foucault: Selections from Essential Works of Foucault, 1954–1984. Essential Works of Michel Foucault, 1954–1984. New York: The New Press, 2003.

Foucault, Michel, Mauro Bertani, Alessandro Fontana, François Ewald and David Macey. 'Society Must Be Defended': Lectures at the Collège de France, 1975–1976. New York: Picador, 2003.

Foucault, M., V. Marchetti, A. Salomoni and G. Burchell. Abnormal: Lectures at the Collège de France 1974–1975. London; New York: Verso, 2003.

Frank, Andre Gunder. 'Emergence of Permanent Emergency in India'. *Economic and Political Weekly* 12, no. 11 (1977): 463–475.

Fraser, B., S.S. Gupta, S. Chaudhuri, S.D. Gupta and J. Gupta. *Bengal Partition Stories: An Unclosed Chapter*. Anthem South Asian Studies. London; New York; Delhi: Anthem Press, 2008.

Freitag, Peter J. 'The Authoritarian Society'. *High School Journal* 68, no. 3 (1985): 103–108.

Freitag, Sandria B. 'Sacred Symbol as Mobilizing Ideology: The North Indian Search for a "Hindu" Community'. *Comparative Studies in Society and History* 22, no. 4 (1980): 597–625.

———. 'Crime in the Social Order of Colonial North India'. *Modern Asian Studies* 25, no. 2 (1991): 227–261.

Fremont-Barnes, G. *The Indian Mutiny 1857–58*. London: Bloomsbury Publishing, 2014.

Frese, Glenn C. 'The Riot Curfew'. *California Law Review* 57, no. 2 (1969): 450–489. doi:10.2307/3479513.

Fuller, Chris. 'Legal Anthropology: Legal Pluralism and Legal Thought'. *Anthropology Today* 10, no. 3 (1994): 9–12. doi:10.2307/2783478.

Gallagher, J., G. Johnson, and A. Seal. *Locality, Province and Nation: Essays on Indian Politics 1870 to 1940*. London: Cambridge University Press, 1973.

Gandhi, R. *Gandhi: The Man, His People, and the Empire*. Berkeley, CA: University of California Press, 2006.

Gearey, Adam. 'Pierre Legendre and the Possibility of Critique: Myth, Law and Shelley's "Prometheus Unbound"'. *Cardozo Studies in Law and Literature* 11, no. 2 (1999): 135–159. doi:10.2307/743441.

Ghose, A. *The Doctrine of Passive Resistance*. Pondicherry: Sri Aurobindo Ashram, 1966.

———. *The Moments of Bengal Partition: Selections from the Amrita Bazar Patrika, 1947–48*. Bakhrahat: Seribaan, 2010.

Ghosh, B.B., and B. Ghosh. *British Policy Towards the Pathans and the Pindaris in Central India, 1805–1818*. Calcutta: Punthi Pustak, 1966.

Gilmartin, D. *Empire and Islam: Punjab and the Making of Pakistan*. Comparative Studies on Muslim Societies. Berkeley, CA; Los Angeles; London: University of California Press, 1988.

Gilroy, P. *There Ain't No Black in the Union Jack*. Routledge Classics. London: Routledge, Taylor & Francis, 2013.

Godlewska, A., and N. Smith. *Geography and Empire*. Blackwell Readers. Oxford: Blackwell, 1994.

Golder, Ben, and Peter Fitzpatrick. *Foucault's Law*. New York: Routledge, 2009.

Good, M.J.D.V., S.T. Hyde, S. Pinto and B.J. Good. *Postcolonial Disorders. Ethnographic Studies in Subjectivity*. Berkeley, CA: University of California Press, 2008.

Goodrich, P., L. Barshack and A. Schutz. *Law, Text, Terror*. London: Routledge, Taylor & Francis, 2013.

Goodrich, P., and P. Legendre. *Law and the Unconscious: A Legendre Reader*. Language, Discourse, Society. London: Palgrave Macmillan, 1997.

Goodyear, S.S. *The Rhetoric of English India*. Chicago: The University of Chicago Press, 2013.

Gooptu, N. *The Politics of the Urban Poor in Early Twentieth-Century India*. Cambridge Studies in Indian History and Society. Cambridge: Cambridge University Press, 2001.

Gottlob, M. *History and Politics in Post-Colonial India*. New Delhi: Oxford University Press, 2011.

Gould, William. 'Congress Radicals and Hindu Militancy: Sampurnanand and Purushottam Das Tandon in the Politics of the United Provinces, 1930–1947'. *Modern Asian Studies* 36, no. 3 (2002): 619–655.

———. *Hindu Nationalism and the Language of Politics in Late Colonial India*. Cambridge; New York: Cambridge University Press, 2004.

———. 'The U.P. Congress and "Hindu Unity": Untouchables and the Minority Question in the 1930s'. *Modern Asian Studies* 39, no. 4 (2005): 845–860.

———. *Bureaucracy, Community and Influence in India: Society and the State, 1930s–1960s*. Routledge Studies in South Asian History. London: Routledge, Taylor & Francis, 2010.

———. *Religion and Conflict in Modern South Asia*. New Delhi: Cambridge University Press, 2011.

Gramsci, A. *Prison Notebooks*. London: Lawrence and Wishart Limited, 1998.

Green, J. *Gandhi and the Quit India Movement*. Days of Decision. London: Capstone Global Library Limited, 2014.

Grewal, J.S. *The Sikhs of the Punjab*. Cambridge: Cambridge University Press, 1998.

Gross, O., and F.N. Aoláin. *Law in Times of Crisis: Emergency Powers in Theory and Practice*. Cambridge Studies in International and Comparative Law. Cambridge: Cambridge University Press, 2006.

Guha, R. *Dominance Without Hegemony: History and Power in Colonial India*. Convergences. Cambridge, MA: Harvard University Press, 1997.

———. *Elementary Aspects of Peasant Insurgency in Colonial India*. Oxford India Collection. Delhi: Oxford University Press, 2005.

Gupta, Charu. 'Articulating Hindu Masculinity and Femininity: "Shuddhi" and "Sangathan" Movements in United Provinces in the 1920s'. *Economic and Political Weekly* 33, no. 13 (1998): 727–735.

Haldar, Piyel. *Law, Orientalism and Postcolonialism: The Jurisdiction of the Lotus-Eaters*. London; New York: Routledge, 2007.

Halliday, P.D. *Habeas Corpus: From England to Empire*. Cambridge, MA: The Belknap Press of Harvard University Press, 2010.

Hansen, Thomas Blom, and Finn Stepputat. 'Sovereignty Revisited'. *Annual Review of Anthropology* 35 (2006): 295–315.

Hardiman, D. *The Coming of the Devi: Adivasi Assertion in Western India*. Oxford India Paperbacks. Delhi: Oxford University Press, 1987.

———. *Feeding the Baniya: Peasants and Usurers in Western India*. New York: Oxford University Press, 1996.

Harris, Cole. 'How Did Colonialism Dispossess? Comments from an Edge of Empire'. *Annals of the Association of American Geographers* 94, no. 1 (2004): 165–182.

Harris, J. *The Indian Mutiny*. Military History Series. Ware, Hertfordshire: Wordsworth Editions, 2001.

Hasan, F. *State and Locality in Mughal India: Power Relations in Western India, c. 1572–1730*. University of Cambridge Oriental Publications. Cambridge: Cambridge University Press, 2004.

Hobsbawm, Eric. *Bandits*. London: Weidenfield and Nicolson, 1969.

———. *Primitive Rebels: Studies in Archaic Forms of Social Movement in the 19th and 20th Centuries*. Manchester: Manchester University Press, 1978.

Holmes, T.R. *A History of the Indian Mutiny and of the Disturbances Which Accompanied It among the Civil Population*. London: Macmillan and Company Limited, 1904.

Hull, M.S. *Government of Paper: The Materiality of Bureaucracy in Urban Pakistan*. Berkeley, CA: University of California Press, 2012.

Husain, S.M. *Bahadur Shah Zafar and the War of 1857 in Delhi*. New Delhi: Aakar Books, 2006.

Hussain, N. *The Jurisprudence of Emergency: Colonialism and the Rule of Law*. Law, Meaning, And Violence. Ann Arbor, MI: University of Michigan Press, 2009.

Jacob, T.G. *National Question in India: CPI Documents, 1942–47*. New Delhi: Odyssey Press, 1988.

Jaffe, James. *Ironies of Colonial Governance*. Cambridge: Cambridge University Press, 2015.

Jalal, A. *The Sole Spokesman: Jinnah, the Muslim League and the Demand for Pakistan*. Cambridge South Asian Studies. Cambridge: Cambridge University Press, 1994.

Jayal, N.G. *Citizenship and Its Discontents: An Indian History*. Cambridge, MA: Harvard University Press, 2013.

Johnston, H.J.M. *The Voyage of the Komagata Maru: The Sikh Challenge to Canada's Colour Bar*. Vancouver: University of British Columbia Press, 2014.

Joshi, C. *Lost Worlds: Indian Labour and Its Forgotten Histories*. Anthem South Asian Studies. London: Anthem Press, 2005.

Joshi, S. *Struggle for Hegemony in India, 1920–47: The Colonial State, the Left and the National Movement*. Struggle for Hegemony. New Delhi: Sage Publications, 1992.

Juan, E.S. *Hegemony and Strategies of Transgression: Essays in Cultural Studies and Comparative Literature*. SUNY Series in Postmodern Culture. Albany, NY: State University of New York Press, 1995.

———. *History and Form: Selected Essays*. Quezon City: Ateneo de Manila University Press, 1996.

———. *Beyond Postcolonial Theory*. New York: Palgrave Macmillan, 2000.

'Judicial Control of the Riot Curfew'. *Yale Law Journal* 77, no. 8 (1968): 1560–1573. doi:10.2307/794836.

Just, Peter. 'History, Power, Ideology, and Culture: Current Directions in the Anthropology of Law'. *Law and Society Review* 26, no. 2 (1992): 373–411. doi:10.2307/3053902.

Kafka, Ben. *The Demon of Writing: Powers and Failures of Paperwork*. Cambridge, MA: Zone Books, 2012.

Kafka, F., and A. Bell. *The Castle*. Oxford World's Classics. Oxford: Oxford University Press, 2009.

Kafka, F., and D. Wyllie. *The Trial*. Dover Thrift Editions. Mineola, NY; New York: Dover Publications, 2012.

Kafka, Franz, Stanley Corngold and Jack Greenberg. *Franz Kafka: The Office Writings*. Princeton, NJ: Princeton University Press, 2009.

Kakar, S. *The Colors of Violence: Cultural Identities, Religion, and Conflict*. Chicago: The University of Chicago Press, 1996.

Keedy, Edwin R. 'Ignorance and Mistake in the Criminal Law'. *Harvard Law Review* 22, no. 2 (1908): 75–96. doi:10.2307/1324143.

Khalidi, Omar. 'Hinduising India: Secularism in Practice'. *Third World Quarterly* 29, no. 8 (2008): 1545–1562.

Khan, Yasmin. 'The Independence of India and Pakistan: Sixtieth Anniversary Reflections, University of Southampton, 17–20 July 2007'. *History Workshop Journal* 65, no. 1 (2008): 276–277. https://doi.org/10.1093/hwj/dbn017.

———. *The Great Partition: The Making of India and Pakistan*. New Delhi: Penguin Books Limited, 2013.

———. *The Raj at War: A People's History of India's Second World War*. Gurgaon: Penguin Random House India, 2015.

Killingray, David. 'The Maintenance of Law and Order in British Colonial Africa'. *African Affairs* 85, no. 340 (1986): 411–437.

King, Christopher. 'The Hindu–Urdu Controversy of the North-Western Provinces and Oudh and Communal Consciousness'. *Journal of South Asian Literature* 13, no. 1/4 (1977): 111–120.

Kinnvall, C., and T. Svensson. *Governing Borders and Security: The Politics of Connectivity and Dispersal*. PRIO New Security Studies. Hoboken: Taylor & Francis, 2014.

Klarman, Michael J. 'The Racial Origins of Modern Criminal Procedure'. *Michigan Law Review* 99, no. 1 (2000): 48–97. doi:10.2307/1290325.

Kolsky, Elizabeth. 'A Note on the Study of Indian Legal History'. *Law and History Review* 23, no. 3 (2005): 703–706.

———. *Colonial Justice in British India: White Violence and the Rule of Law*. Cambridge Studies in Indian History and Society. Cambridge: Cambridge University Press, 2009.

———. 'The Rule of Colonial Indifference: Rape on Trial in Early Colonial India, 1805–57'. *Journal of Asian Studies* 69, no. 4 (2010): 1093–1117.

Krishna, S. *Postcolonial Insecurities: India, Sri Lanka, and the Question of Nationhood*. Minneapolis: University of Minnesota Press, 1999.

Kumar, Mukul. 'Relationship of Caste and Crime in Colonial India: A Discourse Analysis'. *Economic and Political Weekly* 39, no. 10 (2004): 1078–1087.

Kumarasingham, H. *A Political Legacy of the British Empire: Power and the Westminster System in Post-Colonial India and Sri Lanka*. International Library of Twentieth Century History. London: I.B. Tauris, 2013.

Lapping, B. *End of Empire*. London: Paladin, 1989.

Levine, Philippa. 'Venereal Disease, Prostitution, and the Politics of Empire: The Case of British India'. *Journal of the History of Sexuality* 4, no. 4 (1994): 579–602.

Lévi-Strauss, C. *The Savage Mind*. Nature of Human Society. The University of Chicago Press, 1966.

———. *Myth and Meaning*. Routledge Classics. Taylor & Francis, 2003.

Levy, J.T., T. Alfred, D. Chakabarty, E. Dussel, E. Eze, V. Hsueh, M. Kohn, P.B. Mehta, S. Muthu and B. Parekh. *Colonialism and Its Legacies*. Plymouth: Lexington Books, 2011.

Limaye, M. *Mahatma Gandhi and Jawaharlal Nehru: A Historic Partnership*. Delhi: B.R. Publishing Corporation, 1990.

Lipsky, Michael. 'Protest as a Political Resource'. *American Political Science Review* 62, no. 4 (1968): 1144–1158. doi:10.2307/1953909.

Llewellyn-Jones, R. *The Great Uprising in India, 1857–58: Untold Stories, Indian and British*. Worlds of the East India Company. Woodbridge: Boydell Press, 2007.

Low, D.A. *Eclipse of Empire*. Cambridge: Cambridge University Press, 1993.

Lowe, T. *Central India During the Rebellion of 1857 and 1858....* London: Longman, Green, Longman, and Roberts, 1860.

Macaulay, T.B. *Essays on Lord Clive and Warren Hastings*. Whitefish, MT: Kessinger Publishing, 2010.

Major, A. *Sovereignty and Social Reform in India: British Colonialism and the Campaign Against Sati, 1830–1860*. Routledge/Edinburgh South Asian Studies Series. Abingdon: Routledge, Taylor & Francis, 2010.

Major, A., and C. Bates. *Mutiny at the Margins: New Perspectives on the Indian Uprising of 1857*, vol. II., *Britain and the Indian Uprising*. Mutiny at the Margins. New Delhi: SAGE Publications, 2013.

Malik, N.S., and Izhar Research Institute of Pakistan. *The Formative Years of All India Muslim League, 1906–1919*. Lahore: Izharsons, 2007.

Mallampalli, Chandra. *Race, Religion and Law in Colonial India: Trials of an Interracial Family*. Cambridge: Cambridge University Press, 2011.

Mantena, K. *Alibis of Empire: Henry Maine and the Ends of Liberal Imperialism*. Princeton, NJ; Oxford: Princeton University Press, 2010.

Marshall, P.J. *The Eighteenth Century in Indian History: Evolution or Revolution?* Oxford India Paperbacks. New Delhi: Oxford University Press, 2005.

———. *Bengal: The British Bridgehead: Eastern India 1740–1828*, vol. 2. Cambridge: Cambridge University Press, 2006.

Marston, D. *The Indian Army and the End of the Raj*. Cambridge Studies in Indian History and Society. Cambridge: Cambridge University Press, 2014.

Marzia Casolari. 'Role of Benares in Constructing Political Hindu Identity'. *Economic and Political Weekly* 37, no. 15 (2002): 1413–1420.

Mayaram, S. *Against History, against State*. New Delhi: Permanent Black, 2006.

Mayaram, S., M.S.S. Pandian, and A. Skaria. *Muslims, Dalits, and the Fabrications of History*. Subaltern Studies. New Delhi: Permanent Black and Ravi Dayal Publisher, 2005.

Mbembe, Achille. 'Provisional Notes on the Postcolony'. *Africa: Journal of the International African Institute* 62, no. 1 (1992): 3–37.

———. *On the Postcolony*. Studies on the History of Society and Culture. Berkeley, CA: University of California Press, 2001.

McLachlan, Campbell. 'The Recognition of Aboriginal Customary Law: Pluralism beyond the Colonial Paradigm: A Review Article'. *The International and Comparative Law Quarterly* 37, no. 2 (1988): 368–386.

Mcveigh, Shaun. *Jurisprudence of Jurisdiction*. Abingdon: Routledge, 2007.

Mehta, U.S. *Liberalism and Empire: A Study in Nineteenth-Century British Liberal Thought*. Chicago; London: The University of Chicago Press, 1999.

Menon, Nivedita. 'Democracy and the Violence of the State'. In *Empire and Nation*, edited by Partha Chatterjee, pp. 181–202. Selected Essays. New York: Columbia University Press, 2010.

Menon, V. *From Movement to Government: The Congress in the United Provinces, 1937–42*. SAGE Series in Modern Indian History. New Delhi; Thousand Oaks; London: SAGE Publications, 2003.

Menon, V.P. *Transfer of Power in India*. Princeton Legacy Library. Princeton, NJ: Princeton University Press, 2015.

Merry, Sally Engle. 'Anthropology, Law, and Transnational Processes'. *Annual Review of Anthropology* 21 (1992): 357–379.

Misra, B.B. *The Congress Party and Government: Policy and Performance*. New Delhi: Concept Publishing Company, 1988.

Mitchell, W.J.T.. *Landscape and Power*, Second Edition. Cultural Studies: Art History. Chicago: The University of Chicago Press, 2002.

Moir, M., D.M. Peers and L. Zastoupil. *J.S. Mill's Encounter with India*. Toronto: University of Toronto Press, 1999.

Moon, P. *Divide and Quit*. Berkeley, CA: University of California Press, 1962.

Moore, Sally Falk. 'Law and Anthropology'. *Biennial Review of Anthropology* 6 (1969): 252–300.

Motha, S., and H. van Rijswijk. *Law, Memory, Violence: Uncovering the Counter-Archive*. Abingdon; New York: Routledge, Taylor & Francis, 2016.

Mukherjee, Aditya. 'The Return of the Colonial in Indian Economic History: The Last Phase of Colonialism in India'. *Social Scientist* 36, no. 3/4 (2008): 3–44.

Mukherjee, M. *Peasants in India's Non-Violent Revolution: Practice and Theory*. SAGE Series in Modern Indian History. New Delhi: SAGE Publications, 2004.

Mukherjee, R. *Awadh in Revolt, 1857–1858: A Study of Popular Resistance.* New Delhi: Permanent Black, 2002.

Mukherji, M. *India in the Shadows of Empire: A Legal and Political History (1774–1950).* Oxford India Paperbacks. New Delhi: Oxford University Press, 2011.

Mukta, Parita. 'The "Civilizing Mission": The Regulation and Control of Mourning in Colonial India'. *Feminist Review* 63, no. 1 (1999): 25–47.

Muldoon, A. *Empire, Politics and the Creation of the 1935 India Act: Last Act of the Raj.* Farnham: Ashgate Publishing Limited, 2013.

Mussawir, E. *Jurisdiction in Deleuze: The Expression and Representation of Law.* Abingdon: Taylor & Francis, 2011.

Nandi, Sugata. 'Respectable Anxiety, Plebian Criminality: Politics of the Goondas Act (1923) of Colonial Calcutta'. *Crime, Histories and Societies* 20, no. 2 (2016): 77–99.

National Documentation Centre (Pakistan). *Disturbances in the Punjab, 1947: A Compilation of Official Documents.* Islamabad: Government of Pakistan, Cabinet Division, National Documentation Centre, 1995.

Neal, Andrew W. 'Cutting Off the King's Head: Foucault's Society Must Be Defended and the Problem of Sovereignty'. *Alternatives: Global, Local, Political* 29, no. 4 (2004): 373–398.

Newbigin, Eleanor. *The Hindu Family and the Emergence of Modern India: Law, Citizenship and Community.* Cambridge: Cambridge University Press, 2013.

Nijhar, P. *Law and Imperialism: Criminality and Constitution in Colonial India and Victorian England.* Empires in Perspective. London: Taylor & Francis, 2015.

Noorani, A.G. 'Repressive Laws in Punjab'. *Economic and Political Weekly* 22, no. 36/37 (1987): 1521–1521.

Nussbaum, M. *The Clash Within: Democracy, Religious Violence, and India's Future.* Cambridge, MA: Harvard University Press, 2009.

O'Hanlon, Rosalind, and David Washbrook. 'Histories in Transition: Approaches to the Study of Colonialism and Culture in India'. *History Workshop* 32, no. 1 (1991): 110–127.

O'Neill, D. *Edmund Burke and the Conservative Logic of Empire.* Berkeley Series in British Studies. Oakland, CA: University of California Press, 2016.

Pandey, G. *Remembering Partition: Violence, Nationalism and History in India.* Contemporary South Asia. Cambridge; New York: Cambridge University Press, 2001.

———. *The Ascendancy of the Congress in Uttar Pradesh: Class, Community and Nation in Northern India, 1920–1940.* Anthem South Asian Studies. London: Anthem Press, 2002.

————. *Routine Violence: Nations, Fragments, Histories*. Cultural Memory in the Present. Stanford, CA: Stanford University Press, 2006.

————. *The Construction of Communalism in Colonial North India*. Oxford India Paperbacks. New Delhi; New York: Oxford University Press, 2006.

Pandian, Anand. 'Pastoral Power in the Postcolony: On the Biopolitics of the Criminal Animal in South India'. *Cultural Anthropology* 23, no. 1 (2008): 85–117.

Parel, A. *Gandhi, Freedom, and Self-Rule*. G-Reference, Information and Interdisciplinary Subjects Series. Lanham, MD: Lexington Books, 2000.

Pati, B. *The Great Rebellion of 1857 in India: Exploring Transgressions, Contests and Diversities*. Routledge Studies in South Asian History. London; New York: Routledge, Taylor & Francis, 2010.

Peers, D.M. *India under Colonial Rule: 1700–1885*. Seminar Studies in History. London: Routledge, 2013.

Peers, D.M., and N. Gooptu. *India and the British Empire*. Oxford History of the British Empire Companion Series. Oxford: Oxford University Press, 2012.

Pettigrew, Joyce. 'The Indian State, Its Sikh Citizens, and Terror'. In *Terror and Violence: Imagination and the Unimaginable*, edited by Andrew Strathern, Pamela J. Stewart and Neil L. Whitehead, pp. 89–116. London: Pluto Books, 2006.

Philips, C.H., and M.D. Wainwright. *The Partition of India: Policies and Perspectives, 1935–1947*. Cambridge, MA: MIT Press, 1970.

Pirbhai, M. Reza. 'British Indian Reform and Pre-colonial Trends in Islamic Jurisprudence'. *Journal of Asian History* 42, no. 1 (2008): 36–63.

Pound, Roscoe. 'The Administration of Justice in the Modern City'. *Harvard Law Review* 26, no. 4 (1913): 302–328. doi:10.2307/1326317.

Prior, Katherine. 'Making History: The State's Intervention in Urban Religious Disputes in the North-Western Provinces in the Early Nineteenth Century'. *Modern Asian Studies* 27, no. 1 (1993): 179–203.

Raheja, Gloria Goodwin. 'Caste, Colonialism, and the Speech of the Colonised: Entextualization and Disciplinary Control in India'. *American Ethnologist* 23, no. 3 (1996): 494–513.

Raman, B. *Document Raj: Writing and Scribes in Early Colonial South India*. South Asia Across the Disciplines. Chicago: The University of Chicago Press, 2012.

Ramnath, Maia. *Haj to Utopia: How the Ghadar Movement Charted Global Radicalism and Attempted to Overthrow the British Empire*. Berkeley, CA: University of California Press, 2011.

Rao, Anupama. 'Problems of Violence, States of Terror: Torture in Colonial India'. *Economic and Political Weekly* 36, no. 43 (2001): 4125–4133.

Richards, T. *The Imperial Archive: Knowledge and the Fantasy of Empire.* London: Verso, 1993.

Robinson, Francis. 'Varieties of South Asian Islam'. Research Papers in Ethnic Relations. Centre for Research in Ethnic Relations, University of Warwick, 1988.

———. *Islam and Muslim History in South Asia.* Oxford India Collection. Delhi: Oxford University Press, 2003.

———. *Separatism among Indian Muslims: The Politics of the United Provinces' Muslims, 1860–1923.* Cambridge: Cambridge University Press, 2007.

Rose, Nikolas, and Peter Miller. 'Political Power beyond the State: Problematics of Government'. *British Journal of Sociology* 43, no. 2 (1992): 173–205. doi:10.2307/591464.

Roy, M.N., and E. Roy. *One Year of Non-Cooperation: From Ahmedabad to Gaya.* Calcutta: Communist Party of India, 1923.

Roy, T. *The Politics of a Popular Uprising: Bundelkhand in 1857.* New York: Oxford University Press, 1994.

Rudolph, L.I., and S.H. Rudolph. *Postmodern Gandhi and Other Essays: Gandhi in the World and at Home.* Chicago; London: The University of Chicago Press, 2010.

Sadullah, Mian Muhammad. *The Partition of Punjab, 1947: A Compilation of Official Documents*, vol. 1. Lahore: Sang-e-Meel Publications, 1993.

Samaddar, R. *The Materiality of Politics: Subject Positions in Politics.* Anthem Politics and IR. London: Anthem Press, 2007.

———. *Ideas and Frameworks of Governing India.* Abingdon: Routledge, Taylor & Francis, 2016.

Sarat, A. *The Blackwell Companion to Law and Society.* Wiley Blackwell Companions to Sociology. Malden, MA; Oxford; Carlton: Wiley, 2008.

Sardar, Z. *Orientalism.* Concepts in the Social Sciences. Buckingham: Open University Press, 1999.

Sartre, J.P. *Being and Nothingness.* New York: Philosophical Library/Open Road, 2012.

Schmitt, C. *Theory of the Partisan: Intermediate Commentary on the Concept of the Political.* New York: Telos Press Pub., 2007.

———. *Dictatorship.* Cambridge; Malden, MA: Polity Press, 2014.

Schmitt, C., G. Schwab and T.B. Strong. *Political Theology: Four Chapters on the Concept of Sovereignty.* Chicago: The University of Chicago Press, 2010.

Schmitt, C., G. Schwab, T.B. Strong and L. Strauss. *The Concept of the Political: Expanded Edition*. NONE Series. Chicago: The University of Chicago Press, 2008.

Schwarz, Henry. *Constructing the Criminal Tribe in Colonial India: Acting Like a Thief*. Malden, MA; Oxford: John Wiley & Sons, 2010.

Scott, David. 'Colonial Governmentality'. *Social Text* 43, no. 1 (1995): 191–220. doi:10.2307/466631.

Scott, James C. *Seeing Like a State: How Certain Schemes to Improve the Human Condition Have Failed*. New Haven, CT; London: Yale University Press, 1998.

———. *The Art of Not Being Governed: An Anarchist History of Upland Southeast Asia*. New Haven, CT: Yale University Press, 2014.

Sen, S. *Disciplined Natives: Race, Freedom and Confinement in Colonial India*. Delhi: Primus Books, 2012.

Sengupta, J. *At the Margins: Discourses of Development, Democracy, and Regionalism in Orissa*. New Delhi: Oxford University Press, 2014.

Shakoor, A. *Congress–Muslim League Tussle: 1937–40: A Critical Analyses*. Delhi: Aakar Books, 2003.

Sharafi, M. *Law and Identity in Colonial South Asia: Parsi Legal Culture, 1772–1947*. Studies in Legal History. New York: Cambridge University Press, 2014.

Sherman, Taylor C. 'From Hell to Paradise? Voluntary Transfer of Convicts to the Andaman Islands, 1921–1940'. *Modern Asian Studies* 43, no. 2 (2009): 367–388.

———. *State Violence and Punishment in India*. Abingdon: Routledge, 2010.

———. *Muslim Belonging in Secular India: Negotiating Citizenship in Postcolonial Hyderabad*. New York: Cambridge University Press, 2015.

Sherman, Taylor C., William Gould and Sarah Ansari. *From Subjects to Citizens*. Delhi; New York: Cambridge University Press, 2014.

Shore, Z. *A Sense of the Enemy: The High Stakes History of Reading Your Rival's Mind*. New York: Oxford University Press, 2014.

Shromaṇī Guraduārā Prabandhaka Kameṭī, G.S. Talib and G.S. Talib. *Muslim League Attack on Sikhs and Hindus in the Punjab, 1947*. Amritsar: Shiromani Gurdwara Parbandhak Committee, 1950.

Singh, Birinder Pal. 'Ex-Criminal Tribes of Punjab'. *Economic and Political Weekly* 43, no. 51 (2008): 58–65.

Singh, Gajendra. *The Testimonies of Indian Soldiers and the Two World Wars: Between Self and Sepoy*. London; New Delhi; New York; Sydney: Bloomsbury, 2014.

Singh, Pritam. 'Hindu Bias in India's "Secular" Constitution: Probing Flaws in the Instruments of Governance'. *Third World Quarterly* 26, no. 6 (2005): 909–926.

Singh, Ujjwal Kumar. *Political Prisoners in India*. New Delhi: Oxford University Press, 2001.

———. *The State, Democracy and Anti-Terror Laws in India*. New Delhi: SAGE Publications India, 2007.

Singha, K. *Select Documents on Partition of Punjab-1947: India and Pakistan: Punjab, Haryana, and Himachal-India and Punjab-Pakistan*. Delhi: National Book Shop, 1991.

Singha, Radhika. '"Providential" Circumstances: The Thuggee Campaign of the 1830s and Legal Innovation'. *Modern Asian Studies* 27, no. 1 (1993): 83–146.

———. *A Despotism of Law: Crime and Justice in Early Colonial India*. Oxford India Paperbacks. Delhi: Oxford University Press, 2000.

———. 'Punished by Surveillance: Policing "Dangerousness" in Colonial India, 1872–1918'. *Modern Asian Studies* 49, no. 2 (September 2015): 241–269. doi:10.1017/S0026749X13000462.

Skuy, David. 'Macaulay and the Indian Penal Code of 1862: The Myth of the Inherent Superiority and Modernity of the English Legal System Compared to India's Legal System in the Nineteenth Century'. *Modern Asian Studies* 32, no. 3 (1998): 513–557.

Somers, Margaret R. 'Citizenship and the Place of the Public Sphere: Law, Community, and Political Culture in the Transition to Democracy'. *American Sociological Review* 58, no. 5 (1993): 587–620. doi:10.2307/2096277.

Spear, Thomas. 'Neo-Traditionalism and the Limits of Invention in British Colonial Africa'. *Journal of African History* 44, no. 1 (2003): 3–27.

Spivak, G.C. *A Critique of Postcolonial Reason*. Cambridge, MA: Harvard University Press, 1999.

Stepputat, Finn. 'State/Violence and "Fragmented Sovereignties"'. *Etnofoor* 24, no. 1 (2012): 117–121.

Stokes, Eric. 'The First Century of British Colonial Rule in India: Social Revolution or Social Stagnation?' *Past and Present* 58, no. 1 (1973): 136–160.

———. *The Peasant and the Raj: Studies in Agrarian Society and Peasant Rebellion in Colonial India*. Cambridge South Asian Studies. Cambridge: Cambridge University Press, 1980.

Stokes, E., and C.A. Bayly. *The Peasant Armed: The Indian Revolt of 1857*. Oxford: Clarendon Press, 1986.

Stoler, Ann Laura. 'Colonial Archives and the Arts of Governance'. In *Archives, Documentation, and Institutions of Social Memory: Essays from the Sawyer Seminar*, pp. 267–79. Ann Arbor, MI: University of Michigan Press, 2006.

Strachan, H. *The First World War*, vol. I: *To Arms*. Oxford: Oxford University Press, 2003.

Streusand, D.E. *The Formation of the Mughal Empire*. Oxford India Paperbacks. Delhi: Oxford University Press, 1999.

Svirsky, M., and S. Bignall. *Agamben and Colonialism*. Critical Connections. Edinburgh: Edinburgh University Press, 2012.

Szasz, Thomas S. 'Psychiatry, Ethics, and the Criminal Law'. *Columbia Law Review* 58, no. 2 (1958): 183–98. doi:10.2307/1119827.

Tagore, R. *Nationalism*. Publication (Book Club of California). London: Macmillan, 1917.

Tagore, R., and S. Bhattacharya. *The Mahatma and the Poet: Letters and Debates between Gandhi and Tagore, 1915–1941*. New Delhi: National Book Trust, India, 1997.

Talbot, Cynthia. 'Inscribing the Other, Inscribing the Self: Hindu–Muslim Identities in Pre-Colonial India'. *Comparative Studies in Society and History* 37, no. 4 (1995): 692–722.

Talbot, I. *Provincial Politics and the Pakistan Movement: The Growth of Muslim League in North-West and North-East India, 1937–1947*. Karachi: Oxford University Press, 1988.

Tarling, N. *The Cambridge History of Southeast Asia*, vol.2: *The Nineteenth and Twentieth Centuries*. Cambridge Histories Online. Cambridge: Cambridge University Press, 1992.

Tejani, S. *Indian Secularism: A Social and Intellectual History, 1890–1950*. Bloomington, IN: Indiana University Press, 2008.

Tendulkar, D.G. *Mahatma; Life of Mohandas Karamchand Gandhi: Illus. Collected and Arranged by Vithalbhai K. Jhaveri; Foreword by Jawaharlal Nehru*. Bombay: The Times of India Press, 1951.

Tilak, B.G., and B.A. Ghose. *Bal Gangadhar Tilak: His Writings and Speeches*. Madras: Ganesh, 1919.

Tomlinson, B.R. 'Colonial Firms and the Decline of Colonialism in Eastern India 1914–47'. *Modern Asian Studies* 15, no. 3 (1981): 455–486.

Torpey, J. *The Invention of the Passport: Surveillance, Citizenship and the State*. Cambridge Studies in Law and Society. Cambridge; New York: Cambridge University Press, 2000.

Vanaik, A. *The Painful Transition: Bourgeois Democracy in India*. London: Verso, 1990.

Varouxakis, G. *Utilitarianism and Empire*. G-Reference, Information and Interdisciplinary Subjects Series. Oxford: Lexington Books, 2005.

Varshney, Ashutosh. *Ethnic Conflict and Civic Life: Hindus and Muslims in India*. New Haven, CT: Yale University Press, 2008.

———. 'Contested Meanings: India's National Identity, Hindu Nationalism, and the Politics of Anxiety'. *Daedalus* 122, no. 3 (1993): 227–261.

Villa, Dana R. 'Beyond Good and Evil: Arendt, Nietzsche, and the Aestheticization of Political Action'. *Political Theory* 20, no. 2 (1992): 274–308.

Vismann, C., and G. Winthrop-Young. *Files: Law and Media Technology*. Meridian: Crossing Aesthetics. Stanford, CA: Stanford University Press, 2008.

Viswanathan, G. *Masks of Conquest: Literary Study and British Rule in India*. Oxford India Paperbacks. New York: Columbia University Press, 2014.

Wagner, Kim A. 'The Deconstructed Stranglers: A Reassessment of Thuggee'. *Modern Asian Studies* 38, no. 4 (2004): 931–963.

Weber, Max. *The Protestant Ethic and the Spirit of Capitalism*. Mineola, NY; New York: Dover Publications, 2012.

———. *The Protestant Ethic and the Spirit of Capitalism*. Edited by Talcott Parsons. London; New York: Routledge, 2003.

Weber, Samuel. 'Taking Exception to Decision: Walter Benjamin and Carl Schmitt'. *Diacritics* 22, no. 3/4 (1992): 5–18. doi:10.2307/465262.

Weiner, Myron. 'Political Development in the Indian States'. In *State Politics in India*, edited by Myron Weiner, pp. 3–58. Princeton, NJ: Princeton University Press, 1968.

Werbner, R.P. *Memory and the Postcolony: African Anthropology and the Critique of Power*. Postcolonial Encounters. London: Zed Books, 1998.

Whitaker, R., G.S. Kealey and A. Parnaby. *Secret Service: Political Policing in Canada: From the Fenians to Fortress America*. Toronto: University of Toronto Press, 2012.

Wilson, W., A. Shaw, and United States President (1913–1921: Wilson). *The Messages and Papers of Woodrow Wilson: With Editorial Notes*. New York: Review of Reviews Corporation, 1924.

Woddis, J. *An Introduction to Neo-Colonialism*. Little New World Paperbacks. New York: International Publishers, 1972.

Wood, C. *The Moplah Rebellion and Its Genesis*. New Delhi: People's Publishing House, 1987.

Yang, A.A. *The Limited Raj: Agrarian Relations in Colonial India, Saran District, 1793–1920*. Berkeley, CA: University of California Press, 1989.

———. *Bazaar India: Markets, Society, and the Colonial State in Bihar*. Berkeley, CA: University of California Press, 1999.

Yegenoglu, M. *Colonial Fantasies: Towards a Feminist Reading of Orientalism.* Cambridge Cultural Social Studies. Cambridge: Cambridge University Press, 1998.

Young, R. *White Mythologies: Writing History and the West*. London; New York: Routledge, 2004.

Yousaf, N. *Pakistan's Freedom and Allama Mashriqi: Statements, Letters, Chronology of Khaksar Tehrik (Movement) Period: Mashriqi's Birth to 1947.* New York: AMZ Publications, 2004.

Zartaloudis, T. *Agamben and Law*. Philosophers and Law. London: Routledge, 2015.

Index